JENNISON'S JAYHAWKERS

COLONEL CHARLES RAINSFORD JENNISON

JENNISON'S JAYHAWKERS

A Civil War Cavalry Regiment and Its Commander

STEPHEN Z. STARR

Louisiana State University Press
BATON ROUGE AND LONDON

Copyright © 1973 by Louisiana State University Press
All rights reserved
Manufactured in the United States of America
Designed by Dwight Agner
ISBN 0-8071-1883-4 (paper)
Library of Congress Catalog Card Number 72-94152

The paper in this book meets the guidelines for permanence and durability of the
Committee on Production Guidelines for Book Longevity of the Council on Library
Resources. ∞

Louisiana Paperback Edition, 1993
02 01 00 99 98 97 96 95 94 93   5 4 3 2 1

To

The Misses Klara Bader Starr
Elizabeth Hines Starr
and Anna Edmondson Starr

and to

Messrs. Elisha Starr Cooper,
James Tremaine Cooper, and
Stephen Zoltan Starr II

Privatim et seriatim

With amazement, and much love.

THE STORY of the Seventh Kansas will never be written—can never be written. The story of a few battles—not a tenth part told; a sketch of many skirmishes—but briefly related, are mere suggestions of four years of energetic action, of hardship and suffering, and of gratification that strength had been given to endure it all. I have not told the story of marches under a midday sun that . . . seemed to shrivel up the brain as you gasp for breath in the dust beaten up by the horses' feet; of marches through mud and never-ceasing rain that soaked you, saturated you . . . of marches through winter storms of sleet and driving snow, without hope of shelter or rest; of struggles against almost irresistible drowsiness when sleep had been denied you for days and to sleep now would be death; of weeks of tossing in the fever ward of a field hospital where the oblivion of stupor came to you as a blessing; . . . this part of the story has not been told. The thrill and excitement of battle were wanting in all this; it was only plain, monotonous duty, made endurable by the grim humor that jeered at suffering and made a joke at the prospect of death. . . . A cavalry regiment does not usually suffer a heavy loss in any one engagement; it is one here, two or three there—a constant attrition that is ever wearing away the substance; it is the aggregate that tells the story. The dead are scattered here and there, buried by the wayside where they fell. Few have been gathered into the national cemeteries, but they rest as well, and the same glory is with them, wherever they may sleep.

First Lieutenant and Regimental Adjutant Simeon M. Fox, Seventh Kansas Volunteer Cavalry, "The Early History of the Seventh Kansas Cavalry."

Contents

Preface
xi

Acknowledgments
xv

I
Bleeding Kansas
3

II
Three Officers
15

III
"Prepare, Prepare the Iron Helm of War"
43

IV
The Regiment
65

V
Marching as to War
80

VI
The Scourge of War
96

VII
Exit the Colonel
119

VIII
The Politics of Command
145

IX
Exit Anthony
166

X
A Season in Mississippi
191

XI
A Road South
219

XII
The Home Front in Kansas
245

XIII
The Veteran Seventh
267

XIV
Return to Battle
292

XV
The Border in Peace and War
317

XVI
The Last Post
340

XVII
The Way Home
370

Bibliography
387

Index
393

Preface

THE AMERICAN Civil War inspired the writing and publication of the histories of about eight hundred of the some two thousand regiments of infantry and cavalry and batteries of artillery that fought for the Union.

With only two or three exceptions, regimental histories were written by members of the regiment, by colonels, chaplains, surgeons, officers of all grades, and enlisted men of every rank or none, either alone or as members of a committee. Produced by ex-soldiers for comrades and their widows, descendants, and relatives, regimental histories were inevitably works of piety. A minority were outspoken enough, but the conscious intent of the great majority was to erect a memorial to the glory and military virtues of the regiment and of all who belonged to it. Any blemishes on their respective records were to be minimized, explained away, or ignored altogether.

Not until most of the Boys in Blue were in their graves, and their unedited (and unbowdlerized) letters and diaries became available in historical societies, libraries, and in print, did it become apparent that the Civil War had not been the glamorous, high-spirited affair that regimental histories had generally represented it to be; that, far from being a large-scale Boy Scout excursion with only a few, wholly incidental infelicities in the way of hardships, disease, wounds, and death, it was as grim as any other war, and as destructive. It became apparent also that not all who "drew their swords" in defense of the Union were heroes, and even fewer were saints. There were, indeed, surprisingly many of both, but they were the exception, not the rule.

The Seventh Kansas Volunteer Cavalry was raised and organized by its first and most memorable commander, Charles Rainsford Jennison. It was a tough, seasoned, and effective cavalry regiment long before the Federal Cavalry as a whole ceased to be the butt and the joke of both armies. Its credentials as a fighting regiment were excellent; but the Jayhawkers did not publish a regimental history. This may have been due to chance, or, perhaps, those veterans who had the skill and willingness to write a history of the regiment did not have the leisure to do so. On the other hand, the reason may have been quite different. No other regiment in the Union army had so bad a reputation as the Seventh Kansas or had worked so diligently to deserve it; and its veterans, advancing in age and respectability in the postwar years, may have been content to sacrifice the pleasure of seeing in print the tale of their military glories and virtues in order to make sure that the story of their misdeeds remained in oblivion.

This book attempts to provide the Seventh Kansas with an account, which it failed to provide for itself, of its genesis, organization, activities, and corporate character. The emphasis is necessarily on the deeds and personality of Charles Jennison. He led (the word should properly be in quotation marks, for much of his leadership was exercised *in absentia*) the Seventh for only eight months; but to an important degree, the impress of his discordant personality remained upon the regiment all its days. He was himself a product of the Bleeding Kansas era, and many of his pre-Civil War cronies and marauding companions enlisted in the Seventh, attracted by the prospect that, under his leadership, they would be allowed, and indeed encouraged, to continue the war against Missouri that had begun in 1854. Jennison did not disappoint them. He believed that in a civil war, anyone who was not an active ally was an enemy, whose will to fight had to be destroyed by robbing him of his means of livelihood and by turning his country into a desert. But the robbery and destruction were excusable when committed in the service of great causes: to free the slave, smash the Slave Power, and preserve the Union.

The Seventh Kansas was Jennison's creation, but he could not have molded it in his own image if its spirit had not been the product of seven years of bloody conflict on the Kansas-Missouri border. The regiment was a cosmopolitan unit, with many troopers from Illinois, Ohio, and Missouri in its ranks. Nevertheless, it was a *Kansas* regiment, and that is the key to its corporate personality. It was an abolitionist regiment from the beginning, long before the administration and the North as a whole were ready to face the fact that the war concerned the status of the Negro as much as it did the fate of the Union.

There were exceptions, of course, but man for man, the troopers of the Seventh were no different—no better and no worse—than the men of any other regiment in the Union army. But as a regiment, they killed civilians and prisoners, they pillaged the loyal and disloyal alike, and they burned homes and barns wherever they went. They justified these misdeeds on the ground that they were not fighting an open, uniformed enemy, but the "cowardly, skulking" bushwhacker and guerilla, and a population without whose active support it would have been impossible for the bushwhacker and guerilla to operate. The present writer does not ignore, try to explain away, or excuse the atrocities committed by the Seventh Kansas. It is a fact that equally grave atrocities were committed by the other side. And inevitably, each side claimed, and perhaps believed, that its atrocities were merely reprisals for the atrocities committed by the other. One can only deplore this kind of "war"; but it would be absurd to declare one side wholly culpable and the other wholly free from blame.

But there is much more to the story of the Seventh Kansas and its relations to the world around it than the chronicle of its misdeeds. It is proper to repeat that the young men and boys who made up the regiment were not different in any essential way from those of any similar unit of the armies of their own time, or of more recent times. Let this account of their history show to their credit that they were volunteers to a man, unashamedly patriotic, and devoted to their duty, to their regiment, and to the cause in which they believed and for which they fought.

Acknowledgments

THIS HISTORY of the Jayhawkers owes more than a conventional acknowledgment can express to the unstinted help of Joseph W. Snell of the Kansas State Historical Society, Topeka, Kansas, and to my friends, Alan T. Nolan, Esq., Indianapolis, Indiana, William H. Wright (sworn enemy of the adjective "very"), Los Angeles, California, and Professor T. Harry Williams, Baton Rouge, Louisiana.

In common with all Civil War scholars, I am deeply indebted to the staff of the Army and Navy Branch, National Archives and Records Service, Washington, D.C.

I acknowledge with gratitude the prompt and unfailingly courteous assistance, in answering my many inquiries, of the staffs of the Public Library of Cincinnati and Hamilton County, the Illinois State Historical Library, the Chicago Historical Society, The State Historical Society of Missouri, The Western Reserve Historical Society, the University Library of the University of Kansas, the Historical Society of Quincy and Adams County (Illinois), the Ashtabula County Historical Society (Ohio), the Ohio Historical Society, The State Historical Society of Wisconsin, the Massachusetts Historical Society, and the Jackson County Historical Society (Missouri). My special thanks are due to the Kansas State Historical Society, the Chicago Historical Society, and The State

Historical Society of Wisconsin for making available, and permitting me to quote from, manuscript materials in their collections.

I have been deeply conscious, while writing this history of the Seventh Kansas Volunteer Cavalry, of the obligation implied by the words of a great and wise historian, Pieter Geyl: "We are always trying to state past reality in terms of certainty, but all that we are able to do is to render our own impression of it."

The errors and wrongheadedness in this book are entirely my own; whatever merit it possesses, and the pleasure I have derived from working on it, we, the book and I, owe to my dear wife.

Stephen Z. Starr

Cincinnati, Ohio
September 27, 1972

JENNISON'S JAYHAWKERS

CHAPTER I

Bleeding
Kansas

THE PASSAGE by Congress in 1854 of Senator Stephen Douglas' Kansas-Nebraska Bill made Kansas the focal point of the irrepressible and insoluble conflict between North and South over the containment or expansion of slave territory. More than thirty years before, the Missouri Compromise had "forever prohibited" slavery in that portion of the vast area comprising the Louisiana Purchase which lay north of the line 36° 30', but the issue was reopened by the subsequent acquisition of new territory, first the annexation of Texas and then the conquest of the northern provinces of Mexico. The problem was once more "settled forever" by the Compromise of 1850. Four years later, the Kansas-Nebraska Bill reopened the question for the last time and in such terms as to make impossible any solution short of the utter defeat of one side or the other; for the debates over the bill in Congress and in the country at large released a tidal wave of unreason and passion that no rational agency could thereafter dam.[1] And yet, strictly speaking, the Kansas-Nebraska Bill dealt with a matter of intrinsically minor importance—the organization of the territories of Kansas and Nebraska as a first step toward

1. Allan Nevins, *Ordeal of the Union* (New York, 1947), II, 122 *et passim*. "Fountains of the Deep," the words of Genesis chosen by Nevins as the title of the chapter in which he describes the impact of the Kansas-Nebraska Bill upon the nation, are eminently appropriate, for indeed the fountains of the deep were opened by the bill, not to close until Appomattox, eleven years later.

eventual statehood. To the question, shall the new states, when formed, be slave or free, Douglas offered an ostensibly reasonable and democratic solution. The people of the territories were themselves to decide, said Douglas, and not the members of Congress in a feverish atmosphere of sectional and partisan prejudice. This was the doctrine of popular sovereignty; and had the Kansas-Nebraska issue arisen thirty or forty years earlier, Douglas' formula might well have served as the basis for a temperate, amicable settlement, largely predetermined in any case by the dominant facts of soil and climate. But 1854 was too late for the temperate or amicable settlement of any question involving, however remotely, the inflamed issue of slavery. In the case of Kansas, slavery was the central issue. A settlement based on reason having become impossible, a solution was eventually reached in a welter of unreason, chicanery, pillage, arson, and murder, not unmixed, however, with heroism and dedication to principle.

The slave state of Missouri was bounded on two sides by the free states of Illinois and Iowa. If Kansas were settled by "slave-stealers," as Missourians called them, and became a free state, Missouri would be bounded on yet a third side by a state to which her slaves could escape, and from which, Missourians believed, would flow a ceaseless stream of abolitionist propaganda to destroy slavery in their state. In 1854, Missouri had a slave population of 100,000, valued at more than $35,000,000, and at least two thirds of all the slaves were held in the hemp- and tobacco-growing counties near the Kansas border.[2] The economic importance of slavery was not, however, the sole determinant in fixing the attitude of Missouri toward the Kansas question; by 1854, although slavery was still discussed mainly in political, constitutional, and economic terms, it had become primarily an emotional issue. Missouri could not alter the status of Illinois and Iowa; they were already in the Union as free states. Kansas, however, might enter the Union as either a free or a slave state, and proslavery Missourians were resolved that it should be the latter. Missourians as Missourians could not accomplish this by any legal and

2. John McElroy, *The Struggle for Missouri* (Washington, 1913), 6. By 1860 the slave population of Missouri had grown to 115,000, of whom 77,000 were held in the thirty-one counties north and west of St. Louis, and mainly in the fertile belt on both banks of the Missouri. See Allan Nevins, *The War for the Union: The Improvised War, 1861–1862* (New York, 1959), 332.

constitutional means. That made no difference; illegal and unconstitutional means would have to serve. Led by fire-eating Senator David Atchison, a truculent champion of slavery, a meeting of Missouri slave-owners had resolved, as early as 1853, that "if the Territory shall be opened for settlement, we pledge ourselves to each other to extend the institutions of Missouri over the Territory at whatever sacrifice of blood and treasure."[3] Initially, Missouri sacrificed only the democratic process and respect for law; the sacrifices of blood and treasure were exacted from it when the day of retribution came, for the "Border Ruffians" of Missouri laid up in Kansas a reservoir of hatred which within a decade turned the richest part of their state into a blood-soaked, ruined, deserted wilderness.[4]

The determination of proslavery Missourians to make Kansas a slave state was matched by northern determination to preserve it for freedom. But the means used by the North to achieve its goal differed markedly from those used by Missourians. At first, antislavery northerners confined their efforts to the encouragement of emigration of free settlers— farmers, artisans, and mechanics—to the newly opened territory. Emigrant aid societies were formed to provide information and guidance for the journey West to groups of settlers. The first party thus sponsored left Boston in July, 1854, fortified by a hymn written for the occasion by John Greenleaf Whittier:

> We cross the prairies as of old,
> The pilgrims crossed the sea,
> To make the West, as they the East,
> The homestead of the free.
>
> Upbearing like the Ark of old,
> The Bible in our van,
> We go to test the truth of God
> Against the fraud of man.

On the morning of August 1, the twenty-nine members of the pioneer party pitched their tents where the city of Lawrence, named for the wealthy Massachusetts industrialist and philanthropist Amos Lawrence,

---

3. Quoted in Nevins, *Ordeal of the Union*, II, 93.
4. It is said that the term "Border Ruffian" was first used by Horace Greeley. See Lloyd Lewis, "Propaganda and the Kansas-Missouri War," *Missouri Historical Review*, XXXIV (1939), 14.

now stands.[5] One of the twenty-nine was Daniel Read Anthony, who was to play a major role in the careers of the Seventh Kansas Cavalry and Colonel Jennison. It is worthy of mention, for the light it sheds on later events, that the total number of so-called "abolitionists" whose settlement in Kansas was in some measure aided by the emigrant aid societies, was no more than 750 in 1854 and 900 in 1855.[6] Of the population of Kansas in 1860, only 16 percent had come from the northern tier of states. Following the trend that prevailed throughout the period of westward migration, by far the greater number of emigrants had been led by the parallels of latitude from New Jersey, Pennsylvania, Ohio, Indiana, Illinois, and other middle and border states.[7]

Nothing is so clear in the confused history of Kansas from 1854 to 1861 than that the abolitionists properly so called, those, that is, who were willing to go to any length to destroy slavery wherever it existed, were a small minority in the territory, as they were throughout the North; the great majority of Kansans were free-state men, unalterably opposed to the introduction of slavery into the territory, but content not to interfere with it in Missouri or wherever else it had a legal existence. Moreover, the newcomers, whatever their convictions may have been on the slavery issue, were for the most part drawn to Kansas by the availability there of cheap and fertile farmland, or because it was a virgin field in which to practice a trade or profession, or because it offered the chance for quick profits in land speculation. Daniel Anthony was typical of the "settlers" of the third class. A fervent abolitionist, and a speculator as well, he wrote his father from Leavenworth in 1857: "Everybody is a land agent—and most everybody owns land. . . . If I had invested $1,000 here six months ago it would have been worth $10,000 now."[8]

Five sons of John Brown were among those who tried their luck in the new territory. Their father was a footloose native of Connecticut,

5. W. W. Admire, "An Early Kansas Pioneer," *Magazine of Western History*, X (1899), 691. *Cf.* Edgar Langsdorf and R. W. Richmond (eds.), "Letters of Daniel R. Anthony, 1857–1862," *Kansas Historical Quarterly*, XXIV (1958), 7.

6. Nevins, *Ordeal of the Union*, II, 382. Five "companies" sponsored by the Emigrant Aid Society were sent out in the summer and fall of 1854 and five additional companies were sent out between the early spring and July of 1855. See Leverett W. Spring, *Kansas: The Prelude to the War for the Union* (Boston, 1899), 32.

7. James C. Malin, *John Brown and the Legend of Fifty-Six* (Philadelphia, 1942), 515.

8. Anthony to his father, June 10, 1857, in Langsdorf and Richmond (eds.), "Anthony," 9.

with more than a hint of insanity in his heredity. The sire of twenty children, a feckless optimist and an invariably unsuccessful entrepreneur, in the thirty-five years preceding his involvement in the affairs of Kansas, Brown had engaged in at least twenty different business ventures, all ending in failure, usually amid claims of sharp practice, charges of dishonesty, and lawsuits. A caricature of the pushful, not overly scrupulous, get-ahead-at-any-cost spirit of his time, Brown was also different. He was set apart by a monomaniacal hatred of slavery. In an age of philanthropic enthusiasm, he was a fanatic of fanatics. His children grew up in an eerie atmosphere compounded of economic disaster and obsessive abolitionism. Still, it was not their hereditary hatred of slavery that drew the five Brown brothers to Kansas, but the mover's perennial magnet of rich virgin lands to be had for a song. Kansas, the literature of the Ohio emigrant aid societies declared, was a magnificent country in which to start all over again, if free-soil men could keep it from the grasp of the South. [9]

Meanwhile, Missouri gave the world a demonstration of its own special interpretation of the meaning of "popular sovereignty." Even before Kansas Territory was officially opened for settlement, Missourians drifted across the line to take up lands. Some were bona fide settlers; others merely staked out land claims without actually settling on them. In March, 1855, when the Kansas emigration from the East and Middle West was as yet only a trickle, elections were to be held for the territorial legislature. This was a vitally important election; for the new legislature, by the laws it enacted or failed to enact, could materially affect the outcome of the contest over slavery in the territory. Proslavery Missourians therefore conceived it to be their duty to make sure that a proslavery legislature was elected. A Federal census taken in February showed a tally of 2,905 qualified voters in the territory. Probably most of these early immigrants had crossed into Kansas from Missouri and could therefore be expected to vote for proslavery candidates. But the outcome of the election could not be left to mere probability. Hence western Missouri was mobilized. A state of high excitement prevailed; "there were recruitings, organization of companies, drills, armings, as if some

9. Stephen B. Oates, *To Purge This Land With Blood: A Biography of John Brown* (New York, 1970), 84.

great military expedition was afoot"; and on March 30, election day, Kansas was invaded by a mob of five thousand Missourians "with guns on their shoulders, revolvers stuffing their belts, bowie knives protruding from their boot-tops, and generous rations of whiskey in their wagons."[10] The 2,905 legal voters—or as many of them as were not frightened away from the polls by the gangs of Border Ruffians—cast the astonishing total of 6,307 votes. More than half of the votes cast were of course those of the invading army of Missourians, who had no right, other than what their numbers and arms gave them, to vote in the election. The outcome, naturally, was the election of an overwhelmingly proslavery legislature, which proceeded forthwith to enact a stringent slave code. One of the provisions of the code was to make the crime of aiding a slave to escape punishable by death; to kidnap a free Negro and sell him into slavery was punishable by imprisonment for two years.

The invasion of Kansas in March, 1855, was the first of a series of flagrant illegalities committed by organized mobs of Missourians.[11] Later in the spring, when the Missouri River opened for navigation, armed gangs of Border Ruffians halted westbound steamers and subjected emigrants to Kansas to a searching interrogation; those judged to be "unsound" on the slavery issue were arrested and sent back down the river. Merchandise consigned to Kansans of known or suspected antislavery views was seized. A short time later, Indian Agent G. W. Clarke, at the head of a gang of Border Ruffians, "cleaned up" Linn and Miami counties in Kansas; they threw down the fences of antislavery settlers, destroyed their crops, killed or drove off their livestock, and burned their cabins.

Clarke's raid was only one incident in a continuous campaign of terrorism and harassment. The reaction was predictable and was not long in coming. Free-soil settlers began to organize to protect themselves and sent appeals for arms to their eastern friends. In response to these appeals, the famous Sharp's rifles made their appearance in Kansas, and the free-soilers began to fight back.

10. Spring, *Kansas*, 44.

11. Actually, the first such invasion of Kansas Territory had taken place on November 9, 1854, to make certain of the election of the proslavery candidate, John W. Whitfield, as territorial delegate to Congress. But this invasion was on a minor scale.

Contrary to the proslavery propaganda of the day, the common run of free-state immigrants who had come to Kansas before 1856 were primarily settlers; they and their families came to the new territory to make a living. There were crusaders among them, but the majority did not hasten to Kansas to fight and die for their free-soil convictions. Again contrary to proslavery reports, they had not come West armed to the teeth, ready to do battle with slaveowners. The five Brown brothers, for example, had brought with them two rifles, one revolver, one pocket pistol, and a bowie knife, no more than the store of weapons that could have been found in nearly any western farmhouse in 1855.[12]

The rape of the March 30 election was for many Kansans the alarm bell in the night. The Browns and their free-soil neighbors in Miami County organized a militia company which they named the Pottawatomie Rifles. They had decided that force had to be met by force and the powers of evil opposed head on. Still, most free-state men in Miami County wanted nothing better than to be left in peace. The master spirit holding them together was John Brown, Jr., a root-and-branch abolitionist. The force of his convictions and the power of his eloquence, reinforced by the persuasive effect of continuing Border Ruffian lawlessness, turned even his least combative neighbors into zealots for freedom.

In May, 1856, a group of Missourians decided to strike a major blow for popular sovereignty as they interpreted it. Neither the forcible eviction of individual settlers nor the destruction of their scanty means of livelihood were proving sufficiently effective, and the "abolitionist mongrels" were even beginning to fight back. A more drastic method of persuasion appeared to be needed, one that would serve as a lasting deterrent and make enough of a stir to frighten off the whole tribe of free-soilers. Lawrence was the center and fountainhead of free-soil sentiment; let Lawrence therefore suffer the consequences. On May 21 the town was invaded by a Border Ruffian army. The first order of business was to wreck the printing offices; the offending presses were destroyed, and the type, capable of recording obnoxious opinions, was dumped into the streets. Then the Free-State Hotel was burned down, and the stores and homes of the more prominent citizens were looted.

12. Malin, *John Brown*, 8.

Word that the Border Ruffians were headed for Lawrence, and appeals for help, were carried by couriers to the outlying settlements. The Pottawatomie Rifles, fifty or sixty strong, mustered at once and, led by John Brown, Jr., began a forced night march to Lawrence. In their ranks was the elder John Brown, who had come to Kansas in the previous autumn, to find his sons "shivering over their little fires, all exposed to the dreadfully cutting winds, morning and evening."[13] On May 22, near the crossing of the Marais des Cygnes River, the Rifles got word that Lawrence had been destroyed and the Border Ruffians were gone. John Brown, Jr., advised his men to return to their homes; but as for himself, he said "he was going to be in the saddle. . . . The war had now commenced in Kansas and the only way to get out of trouble was to fight . . . to conquer or be conquered . . . and no more compromise could be endured."[14] On the following day, the elder Brown, his five sons, and two other men separated from the rest of the party, and on the night of May 24, near a ford over Pottawatomie Creek called "Dutch Henry's Crossing," they called Allen Wilkinson, William Sherman, William Doyle, and Doyle's two sons out of their cabins and shot and hacked them to death in revenge for Lawrence. None of the five slaughtered "pro-slavery men" owned slaves, and two of them were boys in their teens.

The Missouri attack on Lawrence and John Brown's gruesome reprisal were the beginning of a period of lawlessness worse than anything that had preceded it. Shootings, hangings, robbery, and arson became commonplace. Kansas Territory became Bleeding Kansas. And yet, in spite of, and to some extent because of, these widely publicized troubles, free-state immigrants continued to arrive all through the late 1850s, although for a time, when the troubles were at their worst, the eastward flow of discouraged erstwhile settlers nearly balanced the westward flow of new immigrants.[15] It was said then that Kansas would never become either a free state or a slave state unless "all the rest of the world . . . [became] over-peopled, for nobody that has the strength to walk, or money to pay for conveyance, will stay there long."[16] But

13. Quoted in Spring, *Kansas*, 138.   14. Malin, *John Brown*, 565–66.
15. Albert Castel, *A Frontier State at War: Kansas, 1861–1865* (Ithaca, 1958), 13.
16. Spring, *Kansas*, 270–71.

thousands did stay, and when it became known in the East that the Missouri River route was unsafe for free-state emigrants, they took the much longer and more laborious overland route west across Iowa and south through eastern Nebraska to Topeka. They kept coming, partly at least because the struggle in Kansas involved the magic word "freedom," and partly because of the enormous influence in the North and Middle West of the New England literary school, whose members made the fight for a free Kansas a staple of their writings. [17]

Two efforts were made prior to 1861 to have Kansas admitted as a state. The first was under the free-state "Topeka Constitution," adopted by a "People's Convention" from which proslavery settlers were absent, and the second under the notorious Lecompton Constitution, adopted in an election boycotted by the free-staters. When the Topeka Constitution was presented to Congress in April, 1856, it was discovered that the signatures on the document of all the members of the convention that had adopted the constitution were in the same handwriting, that of James Henry Lane; as a result, the Senate declined to admit Kansas to statehood. The Lecompton Constitution was not submitted to the people of Kansas for outright acceptance or rejection; they were given the choice of accepting it "with slavery" or "without slavery." In the ensuing referendum, 569 votes were cast for the constitution without slavery and 6,226 for the constitution with slavery; but of the latter, 2,720 votes were found to be fraudulent. Senator Douglas recognized the Lecompton Constitution for what it was, a mockery of the idea of popular sovereignty, and his determined opposition caused it to be rejected by the House of Representatives. Eventually, on January 29, 1861, after six of the Cotton States had seceded and their representatives had withdrawn from Congress, Kansas was admitted to the Union as a free state.

The history of Kansas in the eleven years from 1855 to 1866 cannot be told or understood without constant reference to James Henry "Jim" Lane. Indeed, to an important degree the history of the state is an extension of the biography of Lane. The positions assumed by other Kansas politicians on the questions of the day and toward each other, and their actions, were generally governed by their relationship of the moment with Lane, sometimes as allies and sometimes as opponents.

17. Lewis, "Kansas-Missouri War," 12.

Depending on the political needs of the moment, Lane claimed that he had been born in a slave state or a free state, on the Kentucky or the Indiana side of the Ohio River, a short distance below Cincinnati. It is a fact that he was born in 1814, and grew up in Lawrenceburg, Indiana, and practiced law there until, on the outbreak of the Mexican War, he organized a company of infantry of which he was elected captain. He was subsequently elected colonel of the Third Indiana Infantry, of which his company formed a part. The Third Indiana shared with the Mississippi Rifles, led by Colonel Jefferson Davis, the credit for the spectacular American victory at Buena Vista. This success gave Lane a great reputation in Indiana and led to his election as lieutenant governor in 1849. Three years later he was elected to Congress as a Douglas Democrat. As such, he voted for the Kansas-Nebraska Bill, to the great displeasure of his constituents. Suspecting that his vote for the bill made his reelection impossible, and, like any American of his day, seeing wider opportunities in the West, he removed to Kansas in 1855—one of the ten thousand Hoosiers to do so in a decade—and built his family a log cabin on the outskirts of Lawrence.[18] Apparently he intended to organize a Democratic party in the territory as a springboard to high office when Kansas became a state. After the Border Ruffian invasion of Kansas on March 30, 1855, the prospects of building up a Democratic organization in Kansas became worse than zero. Lane was not one to carry party loyalty to unreasonable lengths, and he had his living to make, so he became a Republican. At a meeting of free-state settlers at Big Springs, on October 5, 1855, the objective of which was to work out a common course of action in the face of open aggression from Missouri and the hostility of the Democratic administration in Washington, the virtually unknown newcomer Lane succeeded in harmonizing the wide diversity of opinions represented at the meeting into a Free-State Party, united on a radical, but constructive, platform. Two weeks later he was elected chairman of the unofficial "Executive Committee of Kansas Territory."

18. Lane's wife was a granddaughter of General Arthur St. Clair, first governor of the Northwest Territory. One explanation of Lane's emigration to Kansas is that he went there in the hope of getting from the territorial legislature a divorce from his wife. Edward Channing, *A History of the United States* (New York, 1925), VI, 169. After a brief exposure to the crudities of frontier life, Mrs. Lane returned to the East and the Lanes were divorced, but they later remarried. Lane's infidelities were so notorious that they are frequently referred to in contemporary letters, notwithstanding the customary reticence of the time on such matters.

The ascendancy in Kansas politics that Lane achieved at the Big Springs Convention was to be challenged frequently but never successfully, and he retained it until his death by his own hand in 1866. He possessed all the tools for building a political career in a frontier community that lacked traditions of its own and in which personal and group relationships were fluid and unformed. He had unlimited self-confidence and a frenetic energy. It is said that he once proposed in all seriousness that the issue of slavery in Kansas be settled by a pitched battle between a hundred slaveowners led by Senator Atchison of Missouri and the same number of free-state Kansans led by himself, with twelve members each of the United States Senate and House of Representatives to act as umpires.[19] A cynical, unscrupulous demagogue, Lane used without the least hesitation any and every kind of chicanery and skullduggery to gain his political and personal ends. His enemies declared that he never paid a debt, or told a truth save by accident or under compulsion, that he had no principle he would not sell, made no promise he would not break, and had no friend he would not betray. His appearance was unforgettable. He was well over six feet tall, thin as a lath, with an unusually long, narrow, hollow-cheeked face, lips perpetually set in a "Mephistophelian leer," and eyes that were described by some as dark and restless, burning with the intensity of a charcoal fire, and by others as the "sad, dim eyes of a harlot." His head was topped by wild, uncombed black hair. His costume, which he was in the habit of shedding piece by piece as he warmed up to his oratorical climaxes, was unconventional, even by the lax sartorial standards of the frontier: jeans trousers or overalls, a calfskin vest, and a bearskin overcoat which he wore, winter and summer.

The chief weapon in Lane's political armory was his oratory, described thus by a contemporary:

No night was too dark, no storm too wild, no heat or cold too excessive, no distance too great, to delay his meteoric pilgrimages, with dilapidated garb and equipage, from convention to convention. His oratory was voluble and incessant, without logic, learning, rhetoric or grace. . . . His voice is a series of transitions from the broken screams of a maniac to the hoarse, rasping gutturals of a Dutch butcher in the last gasp of inebriation; the construction of his sentences is loose and disjointed; his diction is a pudding of slang, profanity

19. John J. Ingalls, "Kansas, 1541–1891," *Harper's Magazine*, LXXXVI (1893), 701.

and solecism; and yet the electric shock of his extraordinary eloquence thrills like the blast of a trumpet.[20]

Another Kansan described Lane's oratory more succinctly as a "Niagara torrent of invective, profanity and bad grammar."[21]

A Lane harangue, perfectly suited to the taste and temper of his audience, and delivered as only he could deliver a speech, throwing his bony arms upward and yelling "in the frenzied tones of a Comanche Indian, 'Missourians are wolves, snakes, devils, and damn their souls, I want to see them cast into a burning hell!'" was an experience with a lasting effect.[22] No one could so rouse an audience with the ferocity of his invective; his enemies were never less than outlaws, bloodhounds, villains, devils, rascals, recreants, scoundrels, usurpers, murderers, and thieves, and their criticisms of the speaker were atrocious, disgraceful, hellish, and damnable; nor could anyone else so electrify an audience by pointing a long, bony forefinger at them and shrieking "Great God!!!" as Lane was in the habit of doing when he wanted to emphasize a point.

As soon as word reached Kansas that it had been admitted to the Union, Lane opened his campaign for election to the United States Senate. He borrowed twenty dollars and hitched a ride from Lawrence to Topeka, where, in a scene of utmost confusion and amid charges of a corrupt bargain and bribery, he and Samuel C. Pomeroy were elected to the Senate by the Kansas legislature. Lane then borrowed enough on his life insurance for a decent suit of clothes and travel expenses and departed for Washington and the national stage.

A Kansas tornado of a man was Jim Lane, unpredictable, fierce, destructive. Behind him were all the radical elements of Kansas, Charles Jennison prominent among them.

---

20. John J. Ingalls, quoted in William E. Connelley, "The Lane Family," *Collections of the Kansas State Historical Society, 1923–1925*, XVI, 35–36. It is said that on a typical campaigning day Lane rode ten miles to address a meeting at 8 A.M., then rode thirty miles to speak at a midafternoon meeting, and then rode another twenty miles to make a third speech in the evening.

21. Albert R. Greene, "What I Saw of the Quantrill Raid," *Collections of the Kansas State Historical Society, 1913–1914*, XIII, 447.

22. *Ibid.*

CHAPTER II

Three Officers

CAPTAIN JOHN BROWN, JR.

THE YOUNGER John Brown was not with his father and brothers when the insane Pottawatomie Massacre was committed. But he knew, and acquiesced in, his father's resolve to exact revenge at Dutch Henry's Crossing for the attack on Lawrence. For was it not written in the Bible that "without the shedding of blood there is no remission of sins"?[1] John Brown, Jr., helped to sharpen the double-edged artillery cutlasses with which the Doyles, Wilkinson, and Sherman were butchered. A short time later, when suspicion fell on the Browns as the perpetrators of the massacre, John, Jr., and his brother Jason were arrested. Even before his arrest, John's mind had been unhinged by brooding over the senseless deed committed by his father and brothers, and the mistreatment he suffered while under arrest further aggravated his condition. He was marched twenty-five miles in chains under a burning sun to a prison camp near Lecompton. On June 20 he was bound over to the Grand Jury on a charge of levying war on the peace and security of the United States and its citizens, technically a charge of treason. Not until September was he released on bail, and then only because the prosecution was not ready to present the evidence against him. A year later, in August, 1857, the case against

---

1. John Brown's Biblical quotation is usually given as it appears in the text, but the actual words of Hebrews 9:22 are, "and without shedding of blood is no remission."

him was dismissed. In the meantime, he had left Kansas and made his home in Ashtabula County, in the northeastern corner of Ohio. He realized that his mental breakdown had been precipitated by the turmoil in the Territory and that he could not hope to recover in the midst of the guerilla warfare and atrocities on both sides that the raid on Lawrence and his father's bloody deed had precipitated.

If there was one section of the United States that outdid even New England and northern New York in the fervor of its abolitionism, that area was Ashtabula County, Ohio. The local antislavery society had been founded in 1832, within a year after William Lloyd Garrison printed the first issue of *The Liberator*. In meeting assembled, the men of Ashtabula County had solemnly declared that the Fugitive Slave Law, a part of the Compromise of 1850, was a "law to strip us of our humanity, to divest us of all claims of Christianity and self-respect, and herd us with bloodhounds and men stealers. . . . Cursed be said law!"[2] Ashtabula Harbor served as the gateway to Canada and freedom for the underground railroad that led north from Wheeling and the western counties of Virginia. The county was the home of Joshua Giddings, who walked out of the 1860 Republican National Convention because of its refusal to include in the party platform the "all men are created equal" language of the Declaration of Independence. It was the home also of "Bluff Ben" Wade, who was to become one of the leaders of the Radical Republican group in the United States Senate in the 1860s. Wade hated slavery as intensely as did Giddings, and he fought it with every weapon in his formidable arsenal: a powerful intellect, absolute fearlessness, great political skill, and a deadly gift of repartee. When in the course of the debate on the Kansas-Nebraska Bill, Senator Badger of North Carolina plaintively asked, "You mean that when I go to settle in Nebraska, I can't take my old black mammy with me?" Wade retorted, "We haven't the slightest objection to your taking your old black mammy to Nebraska. What we object to is selling her when you get her there."[3]

In 1859 the elder John Brown made West Andover, in Ashtabula County, his headquarters before departing on his Harper's Ferry raid. After the raid, John Brown, Jr., was summoned to appear before the

2. Henry Howe, *Historical Collections of Ohio* (Cincinnati, 1908), I, 280.
3. Quoted in Burton J. Hendrick, *Lincoln's War Cabinet* (Boston, 1946), 272.

United States Senate to give evidence about it. Upon his refusal to obey, the sergeant-at-arms of the Senate was ordered to arrest him. News of the order caused Brown's neighbors to organize a secret society, the "Independent Sons of Liberty," to protect him, with their lives if need be. The group became known as the "Black Strings" from the badge worn by the members, a black string tied to the buttonhole of their shirt collars. When it became evident that no move would be made to arrest Brown, the Black Strings became an oath-bound political organization; lodges were formed in neighboring counties, dedicated to the overthrow of the hated institution of slavery, by revolutionary methods if legal means failed.

There was little danger that in such an atmosphere John Brown's hereditary abolitionism would either become, or would be allowed to become, lukewarm, especially after the hanging of his father on December 2, 1859. Nor was Brown at all unwilling to discharge the obligations that his status of eldest son of the preeminent martyr of freedom carried with it.

Soon after the outbreak of the Civil War, Brown set about the enrollment of a volunteer company to fight the slave power where he had seen and experienced it at its worst, on the Kansas-Missouri border. Finding like-minded recruits in Ashtabula County presented no difficulties. To them, as to Brown, the war was a holy crusade against Satan and all his works. As one of his volunteers wrote about his fellows, "With them the idea of Union and country is synonymous with the free institutions under which they were born and reared. . . . And they realize that slavery is . . . the animating idea of their enemies." [4] As soon as Brown had forty men enrolled, he sent them west. They became the nucleus of Company K of the Seventh Kansas. [5] In early January, 1862, he followed with the rest of his recruits and assumed the post of captain of Company K.

Simeon Fox, who was to become adjutant of the Seventh Kansas, has left an unforgettable picture of Company K in its early days:

Company K was made up of abolitionists of the intense sort. I believe that it was this company that brought the John Brown song to Kansas. . . . For a

4. A. T. Reeve to Brown, June 26, 1862, copy in Kansas State Historical Society, Topeka.

5. The *Report of the Adjutant General of the State of Kansas for the Year 1864* (Leavenworth, 1865) shows that of the original roster of eighty-four men in Company K, sixty-five were Ohioans and five were Kansans. No information is given about the domicile of the remaining fourteen.

while after the company joined the regiment the men would assemble near the captain's tent in the dusk after "retreat" and listen to the deep utterances of some impassioned orator; the voice was always low and did not reach far beyond the immediate circle of the company, who stood with head bent, drinking in every word. The speaker always closed with "Do you swear to avenge the death of John Brown?" and the answer always came back loud and deep, "We will, we will"; then would follow the John Brown hymn, sung in the same repressed manner, but after the last verse of the original song was sung it would be followed by a verse in accelerated time, beginning with "Then three cheers for John Brown, jr."[6]

At first these quasi-religious ceremonies had the entire regiment for a silent and respectful audience; but by the late winter of 1861–1862, Company K was too busy avenging their captain's father to have time or energy for their nightly ritual. And avenge him they did, with a somber, Covenanter harshness. Brown, fundamentally a kindly man, much loved by his men, was nevertheless proud of their thoroughness in depriving Missouri rebels—a term neither he nor his men were inclined to apply in a narrowly judicial spirit—of every means of sustaining the war against the Union, and he boasted of the despatch with which "'professors' of union sentiment who would take the oath of allegiance in the forenoon and in the afternoon shoot you from behind a thicket . . . were, when caught, generally furnished with a detail to ferry them over the river Styx by the shortest route."[7] This dedication to the war against the sons of darkness was not a mere oratorical pose. In a regiment in which desertions averaged twenty-five per company—Captain Marshall Cleveland's Company H, to be described later, led all others with fifty-eight—Company K had the fewest, a mere seven in a four-year span of service. And in no other company were relations between officers and men, and among the men, so intimate and friendly, inspired as they all were by a common ideal, a common dedication to the cause of human freedom.[8]

Brown himself was in poor health and was frequently absent from duty because of illness. Eventually, after being incapacitated by rheuma-

6. Simeon M. Fox, "The Story of the Seventh Kansas," *Transactions of the Kansas State Historical Society, 1903–1904*, VIII, 26.

7. Brown to Parker Pillsbury, July 18, 1862, copy in Kansas State Historical Society, Topeka.

8. Of the seven deserters, two (one from Memphis, Tennessee, and the other from Leavenworth, Kansas) were men who enlisted in Company K in 1864, long after Brown's resignation. See *Report of the Adjutant General of the State of Kansas* (Leavenworth, 1867), I, 645. This work is not to be confused with the similarly titled report cited in n. 5, above.

tism for two months, he was forced to resign his commission, to the sincere and lasting regret of his men. His resignation was accepted on May 27, 1862, and he returned to his home in Ashtabula County, taking with him a handsome sword, belt, and revolver, a parting gift from the officers and men of Company K. Through the letters of his devoted troopers, Brown kept in touch with the Seventh Kansas until the regiment was mustered out in October, 1865, and he remained proud, to the end, of its abolitionist reputation.

CAPTAIN MARSHALL CLEVELAND

Simeon Fox, a native of Tompkins County, New York, and a graduate of Genessee College, emigrated to Kansas in the summer of 1861. On a September day, shortly after he had enlisted as a trooper in Company C, Seventh Kansas Volunteer Cavalry, he went for a leisurely stroll in company with a fellow recruit to view the sights of Leavenworth, where their regiment was then in the process of formation.[9] The two young men had just paused on Shawnee Street to read a freshly hung poster offering a handsome reward for the apprehension of one Marshall Cleveland, dead or alive, when they saw a striking figure riding toward them. The horseman, tall, handsome, erect, and wonderfully at ease in the saddle, was a figure to arrest the eye. Thin visaged, his complexion was sallow and olive-tinted, eyes black and piercing, hair and beard dark and neatly trimmed. He was dressed with conspicuous elegance in a drab suit, trousers tucked into soft riding boots of a glossy polish, a felt hat cocked gracefully over one eye. As he passed the two sightseers, he revealed on either side of the skirts of his well-brushed frock coat the bulges that made it evident that, in the fashion of the day, he was equipped with the means

9. When first organized and for about five months thereafter, the regiment was known as the First Kansas Volunteer Cavalry. Its numerical designation was changed to "Seventh" at some time in the spring of 1862. The last communication sent to or by the regiment in which it is named the First Kansas Cavalry is dated March 20, 1862. The first communication referring to it as the Seventh Kansas Cavalry is dated April 15, 1862. See Seventh Kansas Volunteer Cavalry, Regimental Letter and Order Book, National Archives, Washington. However, General Orders No. 3, Headquarters, Troops in Kansas, December 31, 1861, *ibid.*, quotes a communication dated December 28, 1861, from Governor Robinson of Kansas, in which the name of the regiment appears as "Seventh Regiment, Colonel Jennison's." Since the regiment was carried on the rolls of the War Department, and was known for nearly its entire existence, as the *Seventh* Kansas Volunteer Cavalry, it will be referred to as such throughout the text.

of defense and attack. The horse he rode was a splendid animal, obviously a thoroughbred. As the two young men turned to resume their walk, Fox remarked to his companion, "That's a mighty fine horse," and the other replied, "It ought to be; he has the pick of Missouri. That's Marshall Cleveland."

If Cleveland was aware of the "Wanted—Dead or Alive" poster, it did not appear to ruffle his composure; nor, clearly enough, did anyone on the streets of the bustling Missouri River town he graced with his presence make any move to arrest him.[10] Neither in 1861 nor for some years afterwards were the people of Leavenworth noted for an excessive devotion to the cause of law and order. Only three years before, a recent emigrant from Massachusetts had written his father: "Since Christmas, a week yesterday, there have been five murders in the city limits all of the worst description in the worst places."[11] The citizens of Leavenworth were content to stand aside while Cleveland and the law settled their differences, whatever they may have been.

When Fox next saw Cleveland, the latter had metamorphosed into Captain Marshall Cleveland, commanding officer of Company H, Seventh Kansas Volunteer Cavalry.

Cleveland was mustered into the United States service on October 14, 1861.[12] Seldom if ever has a commission clothed with the official status of officer and gentleman anyone with a past quite like his. He was a native of New York State, and his real name was Charles Metz. For a time he drove a stagecoach in Ohio. Then he drifted west. Having assumed the name of Moore, he had his first major brush with the law in Missouri and was sentenced to imprisonment in the state penitentiary, from which he escaped. Displeased with the overly well-organized machinery for the protection of life and property in Missouri, he crossed the border to Kansas in the spring of 1861 and, perhaps as an echo of his life in Ohio, assumed the name of Cleveland.[13]

10. Simeon M. Fox, "The Early History of the Seventh Kansas Cavalry," *Collections of the Kansas State Historical Society, 1909–1910*, XI, 244–45.

11. John J. Ingalls to his father, January 2, 1859, in William E. Connelley (ed.), "Some Ingalls Letters," *Collections of the Kansas State Historical Society, 1915–1918*, XIV, 109.

12. *Report of the Adjutant General of the State of Kansas*, I, 612.

13. John J. Ingalls, "The Last of the Jayhawkers," *Kansas Magazine*, I (1872), 360. *Cf.* Fox, "Story," 23.

The coincidence between the outbreak of the Civil War and the arrival of Cleveland in Kansas was, from his point of view, providential. The man and the moment had met. He was presented with a magnificent opportunity to pursue, in the mantle of patriotism, his chosen career of living at the expense of society. Kansas, true to its short but violent past, was fiercely opposed to secession and slavery, whereas a large minority, and perhaps a majority, of Missourians favored slavery and, because of their southern heritage, were believed to be prosecession as well. Moreover, Kansas had a long score of quite legitimate grievances to settle with the Border Ruffians of Missouri. Cleveland, a Kansan of recent vintage, had not suffered in person or property during the Kansas-Missouri border troubles; nor did he, so far as one can learn, have any ideological quarrel with the slaveowning, secessionist elements across the border. But he had other motives for aggression against Missouri which served him equally well. The memory of his recent sojourn in the penitentiary was one of them. Far more important was the fact that Missourians owned blooded horses, mules, cattle, and other chattels for which there was a ready market in Kansas. Hence in the summer of 1861, heeding the call of civic duty, Cleveland joined a band of like-minded patriots, already notorious as the "Jayhawkers," who, under the leadership of Dr. Charles Jennison, made frequent sorties from Mound City, Kansas, across the border into Missouri to spoil the Egyptians.[14] On one such raid in July, 1861, Jennison and Cleveland, at the head of forty-five jayhawkers and several hundred Missouri unionists, captured the hamlet of Morristown and came away with booty to the value of $2,000, which was distributed among the raiders the following day. One of the lesser members of the band proudly informed the readers of the Leavenworth *Conservative* that his share of the loot was writing paper, two hats, a necktie, drawers, a bridle bit, soap, blank books, and an assortment of drugs and medicines.[15] Cleveland, as one of the leaders, undoubtedly fared better, especially since he had distinguished himself on this expedition by shooting a Missourian named White, who had shot and killed Frederick Brown, one of John Brown's

14. William Lyman, "Origin of the Name 'Jayhawker,'" *Collections of the Kansas State Historical Society, 1915–1918*, XIV, 206.

15. Unsigned letter datelined Camp Prince, July 23, 1861, in Leavenworth *Conservative*, July 27, 1861.

sons, in the course of the border troubles of 1856. It appears, however, that in shooting White, Cleveland was not actuated by a desire to avenge the blood of martyrs; White was shot because he owned a mule Cleveland wanted and objected to having the animal taken without payment.[16]

During the summer of 1861, Jennison's band had the status of a Kansas state militia company. Calling themselves the Mound City Sharp's Rifle Guards, they carried on an irregular, raid-and-run partisan warfare in Missouri, sometimes in loose cooperation with the forces of Senator James Lane, sometimes in association with other similar bands of prehensile patriots. Taking small pains to distinguish between the loyal and disloyal, they plundered and burned their way through as much of western Missouri as they could reach. Their activities endangered the exiguous hold of the Federal government on the loyalty of Missouri and became an intolerable nuisance.[17] The army authorities at Fort Leavenworth tried in vain to restrain Jennison's marauding.[18] At last Governor Charles Robinson of Kansas, fearful that these activities, if allowed to continue, would produce a retaliatory invasion of his state by Missourians, and hoping perhaps that a regularization of Jennison's status would impose some restraint upon him, sent him to the department commander, General John Charles Fremont, with the request that he be given authority to raise a volunteer cavalry regiment for the United States service.[19] Fremont agreed and Jennison set about raising the regiment which he was to command and which became the Seventh Kansas Volunteer Cavalry. The Mound City Sharp's Rifle Guards decided to join the new regiment and became the nucleus of its Company H. Since Jennison became colonel of the regiment, the men of Company H elected Cleveland as their captain and were then mustered into the United States service.

But not for long did Captain Cleveland wear the double silver bars of his rank. On October 17 Company H was singled out by the ladies of Leavenworth for the honor of receiving a flag they themselves had sewn.

16. *Ibid.*

17. *The War of the Rebellion: A Compilation of the Official Records of the Union and Confederate Armies* (Washington, 1880–1901), Series I, VIII, 449, hereinafter cited as *Official Records*. Unless otherwise indicated, all citations are to Series I.

18. Captain W. E. Prince to James H. Lane, September 9, 1861, *ibid.*, 482.

19. Charles Robinson, *The Kansas Conflict* (New York, 1892), 434–35.

Only two weeks later, with the regiment still at Leavenworth, the men were marched out for dismounted dress parade. In Colonel Jennison's absence, Lieutenant Colonel Daniel Read Anthony, who had already made a name for himself in the regiment for irascibility, short temper, and a hectoring disposition, was to take the salute. The regiment having been formed in line, with the captains stationed in front of their companies, Anthony noticed that Captain Cleveland was in conspicuously improper garb; he wore his soft felt slouch hat and a regulation jacket over light drab trousers tucked into his boot tops. In a voice that carried from one end of the line to the other, Colonel Anthony delivered himself of some scathing remarks on the subject of Captain Cleveland and his irregular costume and concluded his discourse by ordering that gentleman to return to his quarters forthwith and not reappear until he had changed into correct uniform. Thereupon, says Simeon Fox, who witnessed the incident, "the restive Jayhawker proceeded to advance to the front and center without waiting for orders. There was language, profane and incisive, while each man looked the other directly in the eye. The amenities being passed, they glared at each other a moment, then Cleveland, with a parting compliment which has passed down into history, strode away to his horse . . . and a moment later was galloping toward Leavenworth City." [20] On November 1 Cleveland submitted his formal resignation, which as a volunteer officer he had the right to do, and thereby severed his connection with the Seventh Kansas.

Not so his connection with jayhawking. He let it be known that he was prepared to continue his efforts to sustain the national government and punish its foes, untrammeled by army red tape and regulations, and invited the cooperation of all like-minded patriots. With the reputation he had acquired during the summer, he had no difficulty in attracting a following, described, perhaps uncharitably, as a "score or two of dissolute and dirty desperadoes . . . degraded ruffians of the worst type." [21] Leavenworth and St. Joseph were too strongly garrisoned to be a suitable base for the kind of operations Cleveland had in mind, so he established his headquarters at Renner's saloon, in Atchison. The town was not only free from military busybodies, but it had the further advantage of being located at the apex of a triangle within which lay the richest lands of

20. Fox, "Early History," 244. 21. Ingalls, "Last of the Jayhawkers," 360.

northwestern Missouri, an area abounding in "horses and herds, hogs and cattle. . . . Granary, bin and larder were overflowing. Spacious mansions . . . barns, sheds and outbuildings, reposed in the tranquil seclusion of pastured lawns." [22] With so productive a field for jayhawking only the width of the Missouri River away, Cleveland proclaimed himself "Marshal of Kansas," took possession of Atchison, and defied the municipal authorities to evict him.

Crossing the Missouri presented no problems for Cleveland's gang of cutthroats, especially after the river froze over. Their raids into Missouri became increasingly frequent and damaging. Usually these incursions were preceded by visits of exploration by Cleveland in disguise, to spy out the land of Canaan. He did not bother to confine his attentions to actual or suspected secessionists. The possession of moveable wealth was taken as sufficient proof of a secessionist disposition. Moreover, if "a man had an enemy in any part of the country . . . he reported him to Cleveland as a rebel, and the next night he was robbed of all he possessed and considered himself fortunate if he escaped without personal violence." [23] When a cavalry detachment, sent up from Leavenworth to arrest the gang, appeared before Renner's saloon, Cleveland faced them single-handed, disarmed them, took their horses and equipment, and sent them to trudge back to the fort on foot. One of his incidental exploits was to rob two banks in Kansas City. The banks, however, had anticipated his visit and their cash was securely hidden, so that his total haul in the two robberies was a trifling $3,850. [24]

Cleveland's feats and adventures earned him the inevitable popular accolade of the successful highwayman: he became a hero of romance. Thousands of Kansans believed in all sincerity that he was a man of honor, actuated by the purest of patriotic motives. Strange tales were told of his ability to disguise himself, of his uncanny prowess and good fortune. He was credited with the possession of superhuman courage and endurance, and it was whispered that he led a charmed life. Well before the ice broke up on the Missouri in the spring of 1862, Cleveland had become a legendary figure, the "Phantom Horseman of the Prairie." [25]

22. Ibid., 359.   23. Ibid., 361.
24. Hildegarde Rose Herklotz, "Jayhawkers in Missouri, 1858–1863," Missouri Historical Review, XVIII (1923), 87.
25. Leavenworth Conservative, May 14, 1862.

Major General David Hunter, who had assumed command of the Department of Kansas on November 1, 1861, was not among those who thought that robbery, mayhem, and arson became laudable by being called jayhawking, or excusable when committed ostensibly in the name of patriotism. Immune to the glamor of Cleveland's reputation, he was resolved to put an end to the marauding that had turned the Kansas-Missouri border into a jungle of ferocity and terror. On February 8, 1862, he issued the following order:

The civil authorities of Kansas being manifestly unable to preserve the peace and give due security to life and property . . . and the crime of armed depredations or jayhawking having reached a height dangerous to the peace and property of the whole State and seriously compromising the Union cause in the border counties of Missouri . . . martial law is declared throughout the State of Kansas and will be enforced with vigor. . . . It is the resolve of the general commanding that the crime of jayhawking shall be put down with a strong hand and summary process.[26]

For three months longer Cleveland pursued his occupation, notwithstanding its steadily increasing hazards. But the excesses of his gang, which were not by any means confined to the Missouri side of the river, at last frightened the people of Atchison into a state of belligerency; they rose in wrath, captured most of the band in a well-laid ambush, and drove the rest out of town. [27] His base of operations and most of his gang gone, Cleveland was forced to move to a safer area. He established his headquarters in Osawatomie, south of Leavenworth. Harried by United States troops, he gave up even the pretense of waging war only on the disloyal and became a highwayman pure and simple, a western outlaw whose traditional image he was instrumental in establishing and fixing in the popular mind.

The army tried several times to lay Cleveland by the heels. After a number of attempts to do so by direct methods had failed, craft was resorted to. Lieutenant Anson J. Walker, Sixth Kansas Cavalry, went to Osawatomie in civilian clothes and under an assumed name. Striking up a friendship with Cleveland, he was able to supply his commanding officer, Captain H. S. Greeno, with information about the highwayman's habits,

26. *Official Records*, VIII, 547–48.
27. Ingalls, "Last of the Jayhawkers," 361. The captured desperadoes were taken to Weston, Missouri, and given the choice of serving a term in the Missouri penitentiary or enlisting in the United States Army. Needless to say, they chose the latter.

companions, and plans. On May 10, 1862, Walker got word to Greeno that Cleveland was in Osawatomie. That night, Greeno stationed strong pickets on all the roads leading out of the town and, at daybreak the next day, marched into Osawatomie at the head of fifty men and surrounded the house in which he knew that Cleveland was spending the night. The highwayman was called to the door and invited to surrender. He refused and, in language that lacked neither color nor force, swore to kill anyone who dared lay hands on him. But he thought better of it when Greeno pointed out that the odds against him were fifty to one. He agreed to surrender on condition that he would be permitted to go under guard to a nearby house "to transact some business."[28] The official version of what happened thereafter is that on the way to the house Cleveland suddenly wheeled his horse and tried to escape, firing his revolver at the pursuing guards. His fire was returned and he fell, struck behind the right shoulder by a bullet that pierced his heart and killed him instantly. One may surmise that the actual circumstances of Cleveland's death were somewhat different. "Shot while attempting to escape" is the classic mode of accounting for the death of an inconvenient prisoner. One may doubt that any trooper of the valiant Sixth Kansas was a good enough marksman to score a bull's-eye from the back of a galloping horse; and in any case, if Cleveland was firing at his pursuers when he was shot, he would not have been shot *behind* his right shoulder.

Whatever the facts may have been, Cleveland was undeniably dead. He would have fallen short of the beau ideal of the glamorous highwayman, especially one endowed with his natural advantages, if, in the course of his other activities, he had not provided himself with a wife pro tem, or a "wife by brevet," as such ladies were called during the Civil War. And she it was who loyally saw to it that he was decently buried in the cemetery at St. Joseph, Missouri, and marked his grave with a headstone bearing the epitaph:

> One hero less on earth,
> One angel more in heaven.[29]

28. Report of Captain H. S. Greeno, May 11, 1862, in *Official Records*, XIII, 377–78. Captain Greeno spells Cleveland's name as "Cleavland" throughout his report. *Cf.* Leavenworth *Conservative*, May 14, 1862.

29. Ingalls, "Last of the Jayhawkers," 361.

COLONEL JENNISON

To a degree that manuals of military leadership seldom succeed in producing, the Seventh Kansas was an embodiment of the Jekyll-Hyde personality of its organizer and first colonel, Charles Jennison, who combined in his own person the unprincipled amorality of Cleveland the brigand and the single-minded devotion to principle of Brown the zealot of freedom. In most men, so strange an amalgam would produce a confusion of purposes, indecision, and futility, but not in Jennison. In him, the result was a superabundance of energy, free of any outward sign of an inner conflict. In his slight body, the thief and the apostle lived as amicable neighbors in a completely harmonious unity. With equal zest and conviction, Jennison the robber and Jennison the armed evangelist of freedom pursued their apparently irreconcilable courses in friendly collaboration.

The epithets applied to Jennison by his many enemies, and the terms of praise in which numerous friends and admirers referred to him, make a wildly contradictory catalogue of qualities. In the eyes of hostile critics, Jennison was brutal, cruel, unscrupulous, heartless, vain, ostentatious, and cowardly. He was called a brigand leader, an outlaw, a coward and a murderer, a liar, blackleg and robber, a moral vagabond, a wily free-booter, a moral leper, a thieving wretch, the greatest thief of modern times, and an infamous criminal. His friends, on the other hand, saw him as a paragon of virtue, abounding in kindness, loyalty, generosity, gallantry, amiability, and a rollicking good humor; his military leadership a pattern of boldness, vigilance, and resourcefulness, his personality manly and prepossessing; and above all, his glowing zeal for human freedom worthy of the highest respect and admiration. It was equally easy to love or to hate Jennison, but to be neutral about him was impossible. His virtues and vices were equally melodramatic, and they made him, as was said of him at his death, one of the remarkable trio whose personalities colored the turbulent history of Kansas in the decade of 1855–1865. The other two were Senator Lane and John Brown.[30]

30. "Col. Jennison is the last of the three most conspicuous figures of the Missouri-Kansas Border war . . . John Brown, Lane and Jennison were the remarkable trio of those days, and the last had more qualities than both the others." See Jennison obituary, unidentified clipping, Charles R. Jennison Scrapbook, Kansas State Historical Society, Topeka. This unpaginated scrapbook, with clippings pasted in without regard to chronology, was assembled by Mrs. Jennison, and probably

The early decades of the nineteenth century witnessed strange stir-
rings of the human mind and spirit in the recently formed United States.
These were the years of the Great American Revival, the manifestation
in the religious sphere of an upsurge of restlessly questing energies that
filled the land with clamor. The watchword was overnight reform in
every facet of human life. Nowhere was this ebullience more in evidence
than in the northern and western reaches of New York State. It was in
this region, in Antwerp, Jefferson County, along the eastern shore of
Lake Ontario, that Charles Rainsford Jennison was born on June 6, 1834.
His ancestry was English. His forebears had settled in Vermont, and
several of them fought in the Revolutionary War. His father, an early
pioneer of Jefferson County, boasted the military honorific of "Captain," as common on the frontier as blackberries. The elder Jennison was
a man "of great sternness and force of character, of the strict, sanctimo-
nious, blue-law stripe," the very antithesis of his son.[31] Young Jennison
received an imperfect schooling at Antwerp, reaching a level of semi-
literacy that he never surmounted. In a four line note in his scrapbook,
written some time after 1862, three words are misspelled, five are improperly capitalized, and punctuation is totally absent. In the winter of
1861, while he was in command of the Seventh Kansas, his subordinates
took pains to correct and edit his military reports, a process to which
he submitted with good grace. The labors of his officers succeeded in
the emendation of such orthographical gems as "Shure," "sich," and
"toock" from the colonel's prose. In mid-nineteenth century America,
errors in spelling and grammar frequently went hand-in-hand with a
vigorous, expressive prose style, but this was not true of Jennison. None
of his flamboyant energy is to be found in his drab and formless letters.

In 1846 the Jennison family moved west and settled in Albany, near
Madison, Wisconsin. There, at the age of nineteen, young Jennison took
up the study of medicine. At the age of twenty he married Mary

---

by Jennison himself, and was given to the Kansas State Historical Society in 1907. It contains a large
number of newspaper clippings, pamphlets, documents, and miscellaneous papers (including Confederate currency). The clippings are from a wide range of newspapers, the majority of them unidentified as to source or date. They cover the activities of Jennison, and many of his associates,
allies, and enemies, from the latter part of 1860 to (with the exception of a few later items) 1868.
    31. Undated clipping from the St. Louis *Union, ibid.*

Hopkins.[32] He practiced medicine for a short time in Wisconsin and in Minnesota; then, in 1857, he moved to Kansas. After a brief stay in Osawatomie, in the fall of 1858 he settled in Mound City.

Although the recently founded village of Mound City—the second half of its name represented an aspiration, not reality—already had a medical man in residence, it took Jennison only a short time to establish a flourishing practice, and in addition, he became a leader in the community almost from the day of his arrival. "It made no difference what the moment demanded, whether it was a donation to the preacher, or a collection to pay the fiddler for a dance, or for the relief of some needy person, he made all the boys contribute."[33] In 1859 a dispute arose between Mound City and the equally ambitious hamlet of Paris as to which of them should have the honor and profit of being the seat of Linn County. Paris had that distinction at the moment, but Mound City had won out by a narrow margin in a recently held election intended to settle the issue. Paris declared its resolve to contest the election and to remain the county seat until a new election could be held. Thereupon Jennison led a determined band of Mound City-ans to Paris and, at the point of a loaded howitzer aimed squarely at the hostile courthouse, took possession of the county records, removed them to Mound City, and thus settled the issue once and for all.[34] He gained almost equal credit with an exploit of a different character. The tribes of Creek and Cherokee Indians living on nearby reservations owned large herds of cattle which were decimated in the wintertime by roving packs of hungry wolves. Making use of his knowledge of the pharmacopoeia, Jennison showed the Indians how to use meat poisoned with strychnine to kill wolves; after impressing them with the efficacy of this novel technique, Jennison sold them "at an enormous price" a barrel of flour labeled strychnine.[35]

But Jennison's resourcefulness and leadership qualities came most

32. An undated obituary in an unidentified newspaper gives 1851 as the date of Jennison's marriage. See Jennison Scrapbook. In the absence of documentary evidence, we accept the later date of 1854 as more probable.

33. W. A. Johnson, " The Early Life of Quantrill in Kansas," *Transactions of the Kansas State Historical Society, 1901–1902*, VII, 215.

34. Theodosius Botkin, "Among the Sovereign Squats," *Transactions of the Kansas State Historical Society, 1901–1902*, VII, 431.

35. Letter from an unnamed correspondent, Mound City, Kansas, dated January 1 (or 7), 1861, undated clipping from the Chicago *Democrat*, in Jennison Scrapbook.

prominently to the fore in a different area and in a more ominous fashion. He was an abolitionist by conviction from his earliest days. His Mound City neighbors, hailing from New England, Ohio, and New York in about equal proportions, people of good education for the most part, were "the . . . kind . . . it would have been necessary to kill off before human slavery could have found a home in the territory"; but they were not abolitionists.[36] Because of its location within a few miles of the Missouri border and the known free-state sentiments of its inhabitants, Mound City was quite literally on the firing line. This gave Jennison his opportunity.

Prior to the young doctor's arrival on the scene, the leader of the Mound City and Linn County free-soilers was another abolitionist named James Montgomery. A native of Ashtabula County, Ohio, Montgomery taught school in Kentucky and Missouri for seventeen years before moving to Linn County in 1854. He combined John Brown's hatred of slavery with the cunning of an Indian. After G. W. Clarke's sweep through Linn County in 1856, Montgomery went to Missouri in the guise of an unemployed schoolteacher looking for a post. Having found a job, he taught school long enough to learn the names of twenty of Clarke's accomplices. Thereupon Montgomery the schoolteacher disappeared, to be replaced a few days later by "Colonel" Montgomery at the head of a posse of Linn County neighbors who had been victimized by Clarke and his gang. An old resident recalled many years later the grotesque appearance of Montgomery's little army passing by on its way to Missouri, a heterogeneous collection of infantry, cavalry, and artillery, led by the "colonel" in a ragged simulacrum of an officer's uniform.[37] The twenty Border Ruffians on Montgomery's list were visited in order and thoroughly despoiled of money, weapons, horses, and cattle for the benefit of the Kansans whose livelihood they had destroyed. Through information supplied by spies he planted among the emigrants from Missouri living in the neighborhood of Fort Scott, Montgomery succeeded in heading off many Border Ruffian raids, and those he could not stop he revenged by retaliatory raids into Missouri. One of the numerous explanations of the origin of the word "jayhawker" is that it was first

36. Botkin, "Sovereign Squats," 431.
37. William A. Mitchell, *Linn County, Kansas: A History* (Kansas City, 1928), 94.

applied to Montgomery and his followers, whose sudden and unexpected incursions into Missouri were like the swoop of a hawk pouncing on an unsuspecting and less capably larcenous bluejay.[38] Montgomery took pride in being a "practical abolitionist," which meant that from each of his forays into Missouri, he brought back a few slaves to Kansas and freedom. At the same time, however, he did his best to prevent his followers from indulging in indiscriminate as distinguished from retaliatory plundering. With a sternly puritanical intensity, he pursued a policy of an eye for an eye and a tooth for a tooth; but he was willing to recognize and abide by the limitations imposed by the precept.

Not surprisingly, given his abolitionist convictions and his temperament, Jennison took an active part in these border troubles. He was content for a few months to accept Montgomery's leadership, but grew increasingly dissatisfied with the older man's relatively restrained proceedings against the enemy. Nor did they satisfy the younger, tougher free-soilers, especially after they began to suspect that there might be livelier days ahead under the direction of "Doc" Jennison. In what was in many ways a revolutionary situation, leadership passed by a natural and inevitable process from the comparatively moderate Montgomery to the more radical, more aggressive, more audacious Jennison. Within a year of his arrival in Mound City, the young doctor was a power in the land, with his own enthusiastic following and his own ways of dealing with the enemy.

From its inception, the border war was a no-holds-barred affair. Both sides were in deadly earnest, and one estimate has it that in the thirteen months from November 1, 1855, to December 1, 1856, the toll of lives on the two sides was a staggering two hundred.[39] Jennison's abolitionism was no more uncompromising than Montgomery's; his main contribution to the border troubles was his announced intention to make the war against Missouri "self-sustaining," a term he obviously liked and was to use many times in the next few years. It simply meant that when he led a foray into Missouri, his followers were not only permitted, but encouraged, to pillage to their hearts' content and to destroy what they could not carry away. With as many as four hundred ready to follow

38. Herklotz, "Jayhawkers in Missouri," 271.
39. *Ibid.*, 267.

wherever he led, a Jennison raid became a devastating event. It was said that "if Montgomery and his company forgot, overlooked or omitted anything in the way of retaliatory measures, Jennison and his followers recollected, picked it up, or attended to it."[40] His name became a terror in Vernon and Bates counties in Missouri, and he boasted that Missouri mothers hushed their children to sleep with his name. By a natural and easy process of alliteration, he became Jennison the Jayhawker.

Even after the lapse of many years after these events, Jennison's Linn County neighbors found it difficult to account for his personal ascendancy. He was only twenty-four when he arrived among them, and there was nothing imposing about him, either in manner or in appearance, to compensate for his lack of years. He was small of stature even by the standards of his time. A newspaperman who saw him wearing a pair of high boots reported cheerfully that very little of Jennison was visible above his boot tops.[41] He had a slight figure and a boyish face. He was profane, a hard drinker, and a gambler. Many of his followers were his seniors, men who, apart from their border war activities, were sober and responsible citizens, straightlaced in their own lives, and inclined to be censorious about any falling away from a strict morality on the part of their neighbors. And yet they took to Jennison with enthusiasm. Many were drawn to him by his ardent hatred of anything having to do with slavery. Others were attracted by his own enthusiasm, his high spirits and vitality, his daring and resourcefulness. And without question, his "anything goes" attitude was to the taste of many. As his reputation grew, it too exercised its own allure.

Much of Jennison's success as a leader was because of his flair for the dramatic, for deeds that would be talked about. In the autumn of 1860, the border troubles broke out anew after a few months of an uneasy, suspicion-laden truce. The free-state men claimed, and no doubt believed, that the truce had been broken by the proslavery settlers living in the neighborhood of Fort Scott, who had formed a secret anti-free-state organization called the "Dark Lantern Order."[42] The murder of several free-state men, supposedly by the dark lanternites, was followed

40. Mitchell, *Linn County*, 296.   41. Unidentified clipping, Jennison Scrapbook.
42. William Hutchinson, "Sketches of Kansas Pioneer Experience," *Transactions of the Kansas State Historical Society, 1901–1902*, VII, 401–402.

by retaliation, in which Jennison took the lead. On November 12, 1860, a posse acting under his command rounded up all the proslavery settlers living in the vicinity of the village of Trading Post, a few miles north of Mound City. One of those arrested was a pitiful scoundrel named Russell Hinds, who made a living of sorts kidnapping and taking back to Missouri for a reward of five dollars per head, Negroes who had escaped or been carried off to Kansas. After the Trading Post prisoners had been collected, they were "tried" "according to Vigilance Court order." A "jury" of twelve members of the posse was empaneled and sworn. Evidence bearing on the guilt of the captives was presented. The jury then retired to deliberate and returned the following verdict: "We agree that all the persons, with the exception of Mr. Russell Hinds, shall be discharged from custody, on condition that they leave the Territory within seven days. . . . Further, a clear proof and also his own confession, show that [Hinds] has at different times been engaged in this unhallowed business . . . the said Russell Hinds merits death, and that he shall be hung by the neck until he is dead! dead!! dead!!!"[43] Hinds was then hanged in accordance with the sentence passed upon him by the "jury." Before the crowd dispersed, public notice was given that everyone else engaged in the return of escaped Negroes into slavery would be dealt with as Hinds had been.

Jennison took it upon himself to explain the hanging of Hinds in a statement to the newspapers. He wrote, or more probably someone wrote for him, that "it never was our intention to meddle with any one's political views . . . unless he shall have been engaged in manhunting, or has by the commission of some high crime forfeited the right to live among us"—as clear an exposition of lynch law as one could desire.[44]

James Montgomery's strict moral sense had not been wholly blunted by his border war activities, and he grew to hate Jennison, whom he called in 1862 "an unmitigated *liar*[,] *black-leg* and Robber."[45] But even he saw the hanging of Hinds as an act of justice and cited the sanction of Scripture for it: "He was a drunken border ruffian, worth a great deal to hang but good for nothing else. He had caught a fugitive slave and carried him back to Missouri for the sake of a reward. He was condemned by a jury of twelve men, the law being found in the 16th verse of Exodus XXI."[46]

Within a few days of the hanging of Hinds, Samuel Scott, "a man advanced in years," was arrested by Jennison and his posse and was also given a "trial." Scott confessed "that his course had been one of wickedness, that he had sinned against God and man . . . and could urge no other reason why he should not die, than that he was not prepared for that solemn event." He offered to convey to Jennison all his considerable property and promised to leave Kansas if his life was spared. His pleas for mercy were to no avail. He was "executed publicly upon his premises in broad daylight."[47] Notice of Scott's fate was widely distributed to the newspapers in the area by Jennison's "Editorial Committee," one member of which, John T. Snoddy, was later to be the adjutant and a major of the Seventh Kansas. One Lester D. Moore, also reputed to be a member of the Dark Lantern Order and to have "perpetrated outrages on the free-state men," was visited in the night by a posse led by Jennison. Moore was offered a "trial" if he surrendered; understandably, he preferred to fight, whereupon he was shot and killed.[48]

These lynchings under Jennison's leadership were too flagrant for even Kansas to stomach, and he found himself in serious difficulties. Territorial Governor Samuel Medary offered a reward of one thousand dollars for his arrest. The United States marshals, being powerless to apprehend him, called for military assistance. The army authorities at Fort Scott and Fort Leavenworth, who had tried without much success to maintain a semblance of peace and order in the territory, were eager to help. In early December, 1860, General William S. Harney came down to Fort Scott with a force of infantry, cavalry, and artillery to arrest Jennison and to make a clean sweep of his jayhawking associates. Harney sent two companies of infantry to Mound City under the command of Captain Nathaniel Lyon, soon to become famous as the

---

46. Quoted in Alice Nichols, *Bleeding Kansas* (New York, 1954), 243. The Biblical passage Montgomery referred to reads, "And he that stealeth a man, and selleth him, or if he be found in his hand, he shall surely be put to death."

47. Unidentified clipping, Jennison Scrapbook. The report is captioned "Hung" and is subscribed "J. T. Snoddy, J. F. Broadhead and A. Danford, Editorial Committee."

48. Hutchinson, "Sketches of Kansas," 401.

preserver of Missouri for the Union, with orders to catch Jennison and Montgomery. But when Lyon arrived at his destination, both men had disappeared. It is said that while the soldiers surrounded and searched Jennison's house, he watched the proceedings from the top of a wooded Indian mound behind his house and had a good laugh at the army.[49] In a letter to the newspapers, he justified his evasion of arrest by contending, possibly with justice, that he could not expect fair treatment in a United States court whose judges and marshals, appointed by the Democratic Buchanan administration, would have packed the jury with proslavery men; he promised to submit to arrest if he were assured of a fair trial in his own county "by an impartial, unpacked jury."[50] As he was to demonstrate a number of times in the future, Jennison had most definite ideas as to what constituted fairness and impartiality when his own activities were called into question.

But now the board was swept clean by the outbreak of the Civil War. The fighting of which the Kansas-Missouri border wars of the preceding seven years were at once a foretaste and a contributing cause, became national in scope. The loyalty of Missouri to the Union was in grave doubt. Her avowedly secessionist governor, Claiborne Jackson, answered Lincoln's requisition for troops from Missouri with the defiant message: "Your requisition . . . is illegal, unconstitutional and revolutionary in its objects, inhuman and diabolical, and cannot be complied with." The hereditary sympathies of perhaps three quarters of her white people were with the South; their ownership of slave property to the value of over $35,000,000 exercised its own potent pressure. Politically, they were "Conditional Unionists," with a powerful minority of outright secessionists. But there was no doubt whatever of the loyalty of Kansas, for seven years past a cockpit of the fight between the forces of slavery and freedom. Her people had faced since 1854 an aggressive, ruthless, and utterly unscrupulous slave power. Her energies had been diverted from the urgent task of building a viable commonwealth, to self-defense and political agitation. She had suffered the destruction of much that had been painfully built. Her people believed that they were the victims of the senseless, criminal violence of their proslavery neigh-

49. Lyman, "Origin of the Name Jayhawker," 204.
50. Letter to the editor, [St. Louis?] *Republican*, December 7, 1860, in Jennison Scrapbook.

bors. Kansas was unionist to the core, but unlike the great majority of northerners, for whom the slave power was an abstraction, Kansans saw it as a concrete thing. It was the Border Ruffian whom they had seen with their own eyes, whose handiwork in the form of stolen elections, destroyed farms, and murdered neighbors they had witnessed. By a walk of a few miles across the prairie, by the crossing of an invisible line, they would be in the viper's nest, at the source of everything they had learned to fear and hate since coming to Kansas. To them, it mattered little that, in the event, Missouri remained in the Union, that tens of thousands of Missourians fought loyally and gallantly in the Union armies, that, in fact, in the very counties from which most of the Border Ruffians had come, there were thousands of Missourians as devoted to the Union as any free-state man in Kansas. Missouri was the enemy. Even so clearheaded a moderate as Charles Robinson, the first governor of the state of Kansas, who was bitterly opposed to the radicalism preached by Lane, could write: "There is prospect of stirring times ahead & I do not regret it. Missouri must be taught a lesson & I should be glad of an opportunity to give it."[51]

To Jennison and his followers, with several years' apprenticeship in guerilla warfare, the outbreak of the Civil War was at the same time a vindication and an opportunity. One of the first acts of the legislature after the admission of Kansas to statehood was the passing of a militia law; but Linn and Bourbon counties anticipated the legislative sanction and, on February 14, 1861, joined in the organization of the first militia company in the state, the Mound City Sharp's Rifle Guards, with Jennison as captain. The people of Mound City petitioned Governor Robinson to appoint Jennison second in command of the Southern Division of the state militia, James Montgomery being recommended for the post of commanding officer. The governor, less impressed with Jennison's "military services and talents" than were the Doctor's neighbors, failed to act on the suggestion. He had a change of heart a few months later, however, when Kansas was thought to be in danger of invasion; Robinson urged Secretary of War Cameron to authorize the organization of a Kansas Home Guard and suggested that Jennison be appointed to command it. Robinson's recommendation was heartily

51. Charles Robinson to his wife, June 17, 1861, in Robinson Papers.

endorsed by at least one Kansas newspaper, with the comment that Jennison "is experienced, skillful, and as brave as a lion. He has the confidence of the people, is a terror to the enemy, and is censured only by traitors." [52]

The statement that Jennison was "censured" by some suggests that he was prompt to resume his jayhawking activities when they became in a sense legalized by the outbreak of war. It is quite likely that he did, although for the period from April to June, 1861, there is no documentary evidence of any jayhawking on his part. Governor Robinson, no doubt forgetting his own desire at the time that "Missouri . . . be taught a lesson," wrote many years later that the "tocsin of war was the signal for the resurrection of all the thieves, plunderers and murderers of territorial days." [53] Equally sweeping statements can be found in the works of more recent historians. [54] It was hardly in keeping with Jennison's character and his past, the inclination of his followers, or the presence of Marshall Cleveland and perhaps of others of the same stripe among them, to refrain from invading what to them, if not to the distant national government, was hostile territory; but there is no firm evidence of any warlike or jayhawking operations by the Rifle Guards prior to June, 1861. In fact, the only authentic record of Jennison's activities in the first two months of the war shows him in an entirely non-Jennisonian, idyllic light.

Toward the end of May, the Rifle Guards journeyed from Mound City to Lawrence. When they reached the hamlet of Prairie City, a well-meaning citizen brought out a pail of whiskey to refresh the tired and dusty warriors. The generous offer, we are told, was courteously but firmly declined. Overwhelmed by such unusual, not to say unbelievable abstinence, a "lady of the place" decided to sew a flag for the company as an expression of her admiration and respect. The flag was duly made and presented to the Rifles, whereupon she received the following letter of thanks:

52. Unidentified clipping, Jennison Scrapbook.
53. Robinson, *Kansas Conflict*, 434.
54. *E.g.*, Richard S. Brownlee, *Gray Ghosts of the Confederacy: Guerilla Warfare in the West, 1861–1865* (Baton Rouge, 1958), 40: "In February, 1861, Jennison was made captain of the Mound City guards and in the spring took his command on occupation duties into Missouri." There is not a particle of evidence for Jennison's presence in Missouri in 1861 before June, and he certainly did not perform "occupation duties" there before October, by which time he was no longer captain of the "Mound City guards" but colonel of the Seventh Kansas Volunteer Cavalry.

I am authorized by the "Southern Kansas Jay-Hawkers" to tender to you the unanimously declared thanks of the company, for a beautifully wrought specimen of the American Flag. The members of the company are pleased to learn that your appropriate and timely present, was designed on your part, to approve of, and reward their refusal . . . to partake of intoxicating beverages when the bowl of poison was pressed to their lips. . . . It is but poor courage and worse patriotism, that may be promoted or strengthened by the use of intoxicating drinks; and I am glad to assure you that this is the unanimous conviction of the "Southern Kansas Jay-Hawkers." . . . And Heaven grant, that the banner your fair hands have wrought for us, may never witness in our ranks either cowardice or defeat. Nay, we pledge to you, that it shall not be disgraced—and if need be—shall be defended with our lives. And we further assure you, that the stars and stripes received at your hands, shall when opportunity occurs—and that opportunity is our chief desire—be borne into the thickest of the strife, and *never* fall at the bidding of our country's enemy. It shall be cherished by us as the Banner of Liberty, not qualified or partial, but perfect and universal, from ocean to ocean, and from Key West to the Great Lakes.[55]

Copies of the letter, signed by Jennison, were sent to the newspapers for the edification of patriotic Kansans. Perhaps it is ungracious to express the suspicion, however justified it may be by the normal attitude of Jennison and his men toward the "bowl of poison," that the lady of Prairie City was led to ply her needle on the strength of a grievously inaccurate report of what happened to the pail of whiskey. As to the letter itself, expressing the most exalted sentiments in the sublime diction familiar to students of mid-nineteenth century American culture, it is to be noted that Jennison's company is now called the "Southern Kansas Jay-Hawkers"; more importantly, notice should be taken of the reference to the flag as a symbol of "Liberty . . . perfect and universal." Whatever Jennison's faults may have been, and they were neither few nor slight, a lack of candor about his abolitionist convictions was never one of them. And finally, it is deeply significant that, in the eyes of Jennison and his men, the abolition of slavery in a restored Union is what the CivilWar was all about, from the very beginning.

The first firm evidence of a Jennison-led foray into Missouri in the summer of 1861 comes from an unexpected source, the artist George Caleb Bingham. The outstanding American painter of his generation,

55. Unidentified clipping, Jennison Scrapbook.

Bingham was the first to discover and exploit the possibilities of the western life of his day as a subject for art. A resident of Kansas City, a patriot and an uncompromising unionist, part-time soldier and minor politician, Bingham, in common with his fortunate contemporaries, had not the faintest notion of the nature of a civil war.[56] He was to learn that it meant the use of force, the destruction of life and property, and worst of all, the institutionalized negation of constitutional and legal sanctions that had been the bedrock of civil life in a democratic society. This discovery filled Bingham with horror and rage. And Jennison, the protagonist of unrestrained force and violence, who thumbed his nose at the laws, the Constitution, and morality, came to stand for everything Bingham hated about a war that was turning his familiar world upside down. Bingham wanted the Union preserved, but not by Jennison's methods, and he became the most bitter, most relentless, and most vociferous, of the little Jayhawker's many enemies. From January, 1862, on, through his good friend James S. Rollins, congressman from Missouri, Bingham waged a war of his own against the hated Jennison. His philippics, insofar as they deal in facts, are the principal source of information about the latter's activities in the summer months of 1861.

Bingham is the authority for the fact that in June, not long after the episode of the pail of whiskey, Jennison and the "Jay-Hawkers" were in and about Kansas City, which had been occupied by two companies of infantry and three of cavalry of regulars, commanded by Captain W. E. Prince, First U.S. Infantry. Bingham implies that Jennison and his "Kansas marauders," as he calls them, were attracted to Kansas City by the hope of being able to jayhawk under the protection of Prince's troops; he then asserts that Prince, being "well acquainted with . . . [the] predilection of . . . [Jennison's men] for outrage and pillage, peremptorily ordered them to leave the State."[57]

It is a fact that Jennison was in Kansas City in June. On the nineteenth, prior to Captain Prince's arrival there, he and his followers, numbering

56. Twenty years after the war, General Thomas Ewing, Jr., another of Bingham's aversions and the villain of his painting "General Order No. 11," spoke of the painter as "a man of the highest ideals, but with so little understanding of the necessities of war that before he would commandeer a mule or a load of corn from a farmer in the line of march, he would first have to consult the Constitution to see that he was within the law." See C. B. Rollins (ed.), "Letters of George Caleb Bingham to James S. Rollins," *Missouri Historical Review*, XXXIII (1938), 76, n.

57. Bingham to Rollins, February 12, 1862, *ibid.*, 49–50.

about one hundred, helped the regular army detachment from Leavenworth take possession of the city. The next day, he led his men on a scouting expedition to Independence, having previously created a tremendous sensation and shock among even loyal Missourians by letting them see among his men two Negroes armed with Sharp's rifles. He returned with a prisoner from another scout to a rebel camp at Blue Mill Hills.

In rebuttal of Bingham, Jennison claimed that he had taken his men to Kansas City on Captain Prince's instructions, that while there he operated under Prince's orders, and that he left Kansas City because he was ordered by Governor Robinson to return to Kansas.[58] But Bingham's version is probably not far off the mark. Jennison's explanations, in this and other cases, hardly ever err on the side of a painstaking accuracy. Prince had a conservative regular army officer's dislike of radicalism, irregular military operations, and jayhawking, and it is difficult to believe that he should have invited Jennison to join him in Kansas City. The probability is that Jennison made an unsolicited appearance there; and since he was a captain in the Kansas militia, Prince undoubtedly arranged to have him recalled by Governor Robinson, his official superior. Jennison's explanation of his recall may thus be technically correct, but without invalidating the essence of Bingham's case.

However Jennison's recall may have been managed, he did not remain in Kansas for long. On the morning of July 4 he started out from Mound City with thirteen well-armed and well-mounted followers; and picking up five more men at Fort Scott, he crossed into Missouri the next day. His force grew to eight hundred as Missouri unionists joined him singly and in groups, and for a week he roamed the Missouri countryside "chasing secessionist scouts but never getting sight of the enemy in a body." The expedition was barren of military results, but that it was a success in a jayhawking sense may be deduced from the fact that three of the scouts Jennison sent out "to obtain information" were hanged by the secessionists; their captors no doubt concluded that they had ample justification for hanging the three men, although under the conditions of border warfare then or later, men were executed for no other reason than that they belonged to the opposite camp.

58. Statement of Jennison, May 16, 1862, clipping from an unidentified Washington, D.C. newspaper, in Jennison Scrapbook.

The one official trophy of this expedition was a wagon train belonging to one Myers, which was on its way to Fort Arbuckle, in Indian Territory. The "train" was an insignificant affair, a mere two ox-drawn wagons. It was detained and taken to Mound City because it carried "contraband" consisting of one Sharp's rifle, one shotgun, one saber, one tent, one camp table, and nine camp stools.[59] It turned out subsequently that the train was traveling under a safeguard granted by Major Samuel D. Sturgis of the regular army. Captain Prince learned of the capture of the train and wrote Jennison in terms that typify the problems regular army officers faced in the early months of the war in dealing with the wild and woolly volunteers. Said Prince:

By the Rules and Articles of War, all persons who shall force a safeguard . . . shall suffer death. It is to be presumed that the persons engaged in the capture and detention of this train were actuated by the best motives for the interests of the country and ignorant of the degree of criminality attached to the offense, but . . . these acts [have] the sanction neither of the State or the Federal Government, and when exercised in this arbitrary manner without the color of any law, must be regarded as privateering. . . . You will therefore . . . transfer to Mr. Myers, who is accompanied by an officer of the army, his train intact.

And as to the "contraband" found in the wagons, Price declared: "The private baggage which Colonel Montgomery informs me was examined and seized . . . is the private property of Captain William Steele, formerly of the U.S.A., my personal and warm friend, and it is with the deepest mortification I am informed that this private property has been molested."[60] Such amenities and punctilio between former fellow officers of the regular army were, not surprisingly, beyond the comprehension of volunteers, in whose eyes a rebel was quite simply and without any qualifications an enemy.

Jennison's next expedition to Missouri was an affair of greater consequence. On July 18, Major R. T. Van Horn, with 150 men of the Missouri militia, fought a pitched battle at Harrisonville, Missouri, with a band of about 350 secessionists. Van Horn held his own until nightfall, but being nearly out of ammunition, retreated during the night after des-

59. Letter of July 10, 1861, to the Leavenworth *Conservative, ibid.*
60. Captain W. E. Prince to Jennison, August 5, 1861, in Seventh Kansas, Regimental Letter and Order Book.

patching messengers for help.[61] Among those who responded were a Colonel Nugent, with several hundred Missouri militiamen, and Jennison with forty-five of his jayhawkers. Because of the military reputation Captain Jennison had already acquired, Colonel Nugent and Major Van Horn waived rank and agreed to be commanded by Jennison. Their united forces attacked and drove off a band of guerillas at the village of Morristown and two days later routed the secessionist main body at Harrisonville.[62] Captain Jennison could legitimately claim, and did claim, the credit for the two victories, both of which were followed by wholesale pillaging, in which his men took the lead. It was at Morristown that Marshall Cleveland shot White, whose mule he coveted. At Harrisonville, the stores were emptied, as was the safe of the secessionist sheriff of Cass County. Jennison's own men had been in the van in the attack at Harrisonville and took full advantage of their position at the head of the line when the looting began.

There is no question but that such villainies met with general approval on the Kansas side of the line.[63] Secessionists were simply Border Ruffians under a new name, and as the latter had shown no mercy to Kansans before the war, and were now showing no mercy to Missouri unionists, Kansans would have considered it a mockery of divine justice to show them mercy now, when the tables were happily turned. Hence we find the Wyandotte, Kansas *Gazette* announcing that "in case Secretary Cameron should resign . . . we propose for his successor C. R. Jennison, Captain of the Kansas Jay-Hawkers, and just now the terror and the scourge of the rebels in Southwestern Missouri. We propose Captain Jennison for Secretary of War . . . because we are firmly convinced that his system of warfare has got to be adopted in the end, and the sooner the better."[64]

61. *Official Records*, III, 41–43.

62. Jennison's statement, May 16, 1862, in Jennison Scrapbook. Jennison claimed that Harrisonville was captured after a fight. Bingham, who is far from being one of Jennison's admirers, says that at Harrisonville, "as the Secessionists immediately fled upon [Jennison's] approach, [he] entered the place without having encountered *serious opposition*." See Rollins (ed.), Letters of Bingham," 50 (italics ours). This, in Richard S. Brownlee's version, becomes "Jennison's men were employed as an advance guard . . . against Harrisonville . . . where pro-Southern forces were *supposedly* gathering. The Jayhawkers advanced so rapidly on Harrisonville, *which held not an enemy soldier*, that they had most of the stores broken into and robbed before Van Horn's main body arrived." See Brownlee, *Gray Ghosts*, 43 (italics ours).

63. Numerous unidentified clippings, Jennison Scrapbook.   64. Undated clipping, *ibid.*

CHAPTER III

"Prepare, Prepare the Iron Helm of War"

WHILE JENNISON and Kansas were beginning to fight the Civil War in their own fashion, Senator Lane made his entry on the national stage. Dressed in the shiny new broadcloth uniform of a statesman, he arrived in Washington on the day following the attack on Fort Sumter. The city was alive with wild rumors of an imminent rebel attack aimed at capturing the government buildings and taking the president prisoner. Lane responded to the excitement in a characteristically active way. He devoted the evening of April 13 to some "flaming speech-making." The next day he rounded up all the Kansans he could find and organized them into the "Frontier Guard" under his own command. Four days later, at the special request of General Scott and Secretary Cameron, the Frontier Guard assumed responsibility for protecting the president and, for the next seven nights, stood guard in the White House, "in picturesque bivouac on the brilliantly-patterned velvet carpet" of the East Room. By April 26 enough troops had arrived from the North to protect Washington; the services of the Frontier Guard were no longer needed; and after a ceremonial march to the White House to receive the president's thanks for their patriotic efforts, the Guard disbanded.[1]

1. The entire episode is described in Edgar Langsdorf, "Jim Lane and the Frontier Guard," *Kansas Historical Quarterly*, IX (1940), 13–25. The total membership of the Guard was said to have been 120. The names of fifty-one have been recorded.

The Frontier Guard episode was a performance with comic opera overtones, symptomatic of the first feverish weeks of the Civil War, but it had an important sequel. Lane had already earned the president's political gratitude by his energetic support of the Lincoln–Hamlin ticket in the presidential campaign. But as commander of the Frontier Guard he gained the president's personal regard as well. The impact upon Lincoln of Lane's self-confidence, enthusiasm, and willingness to act without regard for red tape, made the new senator *persona grata* at the White House and lent his requests and recommendations, even those in the military sphere and particularly those concerning the war on the Kansas border, considerable weight. As to Lane's qualifications to offer suggestions on military problems, it must be remembered that in the early months of the war few officers on the Union side had actual fighting experience in responsible command greater than his, and even fewer had his imagination and his urgent passion for action.

Lane lost no time in making use of his influence. He returned from a rapid journey to Kansas with ominous tales of the dangers brewing in the West. Confederate troops were assembling along the southern border of Missouri, plainly intending an invasion of the state. Irregular bands of secessionists were on the move everywhere along the Missouri River and the Kansas border, terrorizing Union men and driving them from their homes. Guerilla warfare and bushwhacking were already a hideous reality. With the exception of St. Louis, firmly in the grip of the same Captain Nathaniel Lyon who a few months before had led the hunt for Jennison, all of Missouri appeared to be in imminent danger of being conquered by the rebels. Were Missouri to fall to the Confederacy, Kansas would be virtually cut off from the Union and would be overrun in its turn. On June 19 Lane proposed to Secretary Cameron that he be given the responsibility of protecting Kansas and the authority to raise two regiments for that purpose. Cameron agreed, subject to the president's approval, which was granted the next day in the most flattering terms: "Since you spoke to me yesterday about General J. H. Lane . . . I have been reflecting on the subject, and have concluded that we need the services of such a man out there at once; that we better appoint him a brigadier-general of volunteers to-day, and send him off with such authority to raise a force . . . as you think will get him into actual work the quickest. Tell him when he starts to put it through. Not be writing or telegraphing back here, but put it through."[2] With this accolade, Lane rushed back to Kansas to raise two regiments for what was to be called the Lane Brigade. Eventually the brigade had three regiments, not two: the Third Kansas, under Colonel James Montgomery, and the Fourth and Fifth Kansas. In addition to its own three regiments, the brigade attracted into a casually loose association a number of small independent units of Kansas militia, the most prominent of which was Jennison's Southern Kansas Jay-Hawkers. But before Lane could take the field, a difficulty arose. Governor Robinson, to whom Lane and all his works were anathema, and who had no intention of losing to him the politically valuable plum of granting commissions to nearly 130 officers, bethought him of Article I, Section 6 of the United States Constitution.[3] He announced that Lane, having accepted a brigadier general's commission, was barred by the Constitution from serving as a senator; he declared that Lane had vacated his seat in the Senate and immediately appointed one of his own supporters to fill the vacancy.

Lane had not worked for six years to gain his seat in the Senate only to allow a constitutional technicality to deprive him of it. He resigned as brigadier general of volunteers, thus foiling Governor Robinson; but then, feeling the need of rank commensurate with the size of the force he was to command, he obtained from his friend, Governor Oliver P. Morton, a brigadier general's commission in the Indiana militia. Having overcome both the constitutional obstacle and Governor Robinson, Lane could now be a brigadier general and a senator simultaneously. It can be said in his behalf that of the many gentlemen elevated to one and two star rank from civilian life in the early months of the war—the names of Banks, Fremont, and Butler come readily to mind—Lane was not by any means the least deserving or the worst qualified.

Lane's fear that Kansas was in imminent danger of a rebel invasion and conquest was not shared by all Kansans. His recruiting was bedeviled by public apathy, the undercover opposition of his political enemies, and

2. *Official Records*, Series III, I, 280–81.
3. "No Senator or Representative shall . . . be appointed to any civil office under the authority of the United States . . . and no person holding any office under the United States shall be a member of either House during his continuance in office."

a shortage of equipment and supplies. Not until mid-August was Lane ready, after a fashion, to take the field, with his regiments below strength, his men lacking uniforms, shoes, blankets, and weapons, and lacking also the smallest trace of training and discipline.[4] Commanding a "ragged, half-armed, diseased, mutinous rabble," as a visitor described the brigade, Lane nevertheless announced that by December he would march to New Orleans, administering on the way as many kicks as possible to the "sore shin" of the Confederacy, namely slavery.[5]

The Lane Brigade, however, was faced with a more urgent and less visionary task than a march to New Orleans. Its commander's fear that Kansas was in danger of invasion was about to appear to be well founded. On August 10 Nathaniel Lyon, now a brigadier general, was defeated and killed at Wilson's Creek by the forces of Generals Sterling Price and Ben McCulloch. The way was wide open for a Confederate invasion of northwestern Missouri and Kansas. Lane, whose brigade was assembling at Leavenworth, was ordered to move by forced marches to Fort Scott, where he would be on the flank of the rebel advance northward, which everyone agreed was now imminent. Price was thought to have twenty thousand men (he actually had about twelve thousand) and Lane had only a little over two thousand, but he did not hesitate. On August 17 his brigade was on the march. Six days later, Montgomery and the Third Kansas were at Fort Scott, and Lane himself with the rest of the brigade was at Fort Lincoln, a dozen miles to the north, where the intrepid senator announced his readiness to "play hell with Missouri" if he were given reinforcements.[6]

Sterling Price was delayed by the same shortages of equipment and supplies that plagued Lane, and he did not make his appearance in west-central Missouri until two weeks after the fight at Wilson's Creek. Preceded by a cloud of guerillas, he moved slowly northward. On August 24 one of his advance parties, five hundred strong, crossed the Kansas line and moved in the direction of Osawatomie and Paola. Lane ordered Jennison to round up whatever local help was available and drive

4. Lane to Fremont, August 16, 1861, in *Official Records*, III, 446. Needless to say, Lane's report to Fremont dealt only with the shortage of uniforms, shoes, blankets, and firearms. It made no mention of the equally woeful lack of training and discipline.

5. Jay Monaghan, *Civil War on the Western Border* (Boston, 1955), 197.

6. Lane to Prince, August 25, 1861, in *Official Records*, III, 454–55.

out the rebels. [7] A week later, Price's main body reached the neighbor-hood of Fort Scott, and one of his scouting parties, venturing within two miles of the fort, brazenly drove off a herd of sixty mules belonging to Colonel Weer's Fourth Kansas. To have livestock jayhawked by Missourians called for prompt revenge; and on September 2 Lane's irregular cavalry, Jennison's men among them, had a brisk skirmish with the enemy at Drywood Creek, twelve miles east of Fort Scott. The fight did not damage the Confederates, nor did it delay their advance, but it did provide Lane with what he took to be an accurate picture of Price's strength and intentions.

Typical of the bitterness of political enmities in Kansas is the letter Governor Robinson wrote to General Fremont at this very time to assure him that Kansas was in no danger of invasion unless Lane got up "a war by going over the line, committing depredations, and then returning into [Kansas]"; and he urged Fremont to "relieve us of the Lane brigade." [8]

The further course of Lane's operations need not be described in detail. Price's objective was the town of Lexington on the Missouri River, some thirty-five miles east of Kansas City. Although urged to harass the Confederate advance, Lane followed at too great a distance to hinder or delay it. Price reached Lexington on September 13 and captured the town on the twentieth, with a large haul of prisoners, weapons, and supplies. Caleb Bingham, then captain of the Kansas City Irish Company, was one of the prisoners. While Price's men were resting after their victory, and General Fremont was assuring Washington that he was concentrating his forces to destroy the enemy, Lane, more than four days' march to the south, took time to sack and burn the town of Osceola. Ordered to march to Kansas City as rapidly as possible, he left Osceola with 350 horses and mules, 400 cattle, and a long train of wagons loaded with flour, sugar, molasses, and miscellaneous plunder, encumbering his progress. The march to Kansas City was marred and delayed

7. *Ibid.*, 455. Price's report on the skirmish, *ibid.*, 163–64.

8. Robinson to Fremont, September 1, 1861, *ibid.*, 469. Rightly or wrongly, Lane himself was convinced that Price intended to invade Kansas. Not until September 4, three days after Robinson wrote his letter to Fremont, did Price state that he had decided not to invade Kansas, which implies that he either had that intention earlier or that he considered an invasion of Kansas as one of the options open to him. In any event, unless one makes the absurd assumption that Price kept Robinson informed from day to day of his plans, it is evident that Robinson could not have *known* on September 1 of a course of action that Price, on his own showing, did not decide on until later.

further by more looting and arson, which turned a long stretch of country into a wilderness. The two hundred Negroes who attached themselves to the brigade at Osceola were joined by dozens more at every crossroad on the way north, confirming Lane in his belief that "slavery would not survive the march of the Union army."[9] He organized the ex-slaves into a brigade under his three regimental chaplains and had the ragged procession march at the rear of the column, followed by a wagon train a mile long carrying their belongings and the children too young to walk. Nearing Kansas City, Lane ordered the brigade of Negroes to turn west, to Kansas. At the border of the free state, the Reverend Hugh Fisher halted the multitude and, standing in his stirrups, his right arm raised in a dramatic gesture, thundered forth: "In the name of the Constitution of the United States, the Declaration of Independence, and the authority of General James H. Lane, I proclaim you forever free!"[10]

It is to be regretted that this solemn scene was not at all typical of the general tenor of Lane's operations. No doubt it was praiseworthy to assist a few hundred Negroes to escape from bondage; but whatever credit the Lane Brigade may have earned by its devotion to human freedom was more than offset by its conduct of the war as a vendetta against Missourians in general. Nor was their lawless conduct confined to Missouri. On September 9 Captain Prince had found it necessary to urge Lane to "adopt early and active measures to crush out this marauding which is being enacted in Captain Jennison's name, as also yours. . . . Captain Wilder will be able to give you details of their conduct at Leavenworth City and doubtless their atrocities in other localities have already been represented to you. Please have a formal examination into the plundering of private and public buildings which has recently taken place, as I am informed, at Fort Scott."[11]

Lane could not help but be aware of the depredations committed by his own men, as well as Jennison's, and he actually tried by fits and starts to control their predatory habits. But his own attitude was ambivalent; he declared on more than one occasion that "everything disloyal, from a Shanghai rooster to a Durham cow, must be cleaned out."[12] It is at any

---

9. *Dictionary of National Biography*, V, 577.
10. Monaghan, *Civil War*, 207.
11. Prince to Lane, September 9, 1861, in *Official Records*, III, 482.
12. William F. Zornow, *Kansas: A History of the Jayhawk State* (Oklahoma City, 1957), 109.

rate quite evident that his undisciplined mob of an army felt under no necessity to heed their commander's occasional antipillaging outbursts. On September 1 he proclaimed in a General Order that "the rights, persons and property of Kansans and loyal citizens of other states must be sacredly observed" and ordered that the property of disloyal persons, when seized for the use of the army, be turned over to the quarter-master.[13] He made no attempt to enforce the order, and it remained a dead letter; but given the state of discipline of his brigade, there is little likelihood that he could have enforced the order even if he had tried to do so. On September 17 he announced to his officers: "The taking and destroying of private property by this army has become an intolerable nuisance; it is demoralizing us and impairing our reputation. It must and shall be checked, and to this end therefore you will be held responsible for the conduct of the men of your command."[14] Two days later Lane used a more direct approach. He assembled his troops and treated them to one of his inimitable harangues. Said he: "You sneaking thieves, what did you think of yourselves when you were invading the premises of that widow in the north part of town, and stealing her nightdress, her skillets and her chickens? Were you acting the part of soldiers then? Did you think we were at war with widows? Did you think we were at war with chickens and skillets? . . . So help me God, if the like occurs again, the guilty party, if found, shall suffer the extreme penalty of the law."[15] No doubt the speech was greatly enjoyed by all who heard it, but its effective-ness may be judged by the fact that the "like" did occur again and in an aggravated form, only three days later at Osceola, and no one suffered "the extreme penalty of the law." The speech might have had a better chance of making a lasting impression if the orator himself had not pre-sided over the sack of Osceola and taken his share of the loot in the form of a fine carriage, a piano, and a quantity of silk dresses, all of which he sent to his home in Lawrence. No doubt Lane would have pleaded in extenuation of his conduct on this occasion that his column was fired on from the brush, as it approached the city, by a force of twenty-five or

13. Wendell H. Stephenson, "The Political Career of General James H. Lane," *Publications of the Kansas State Historical Society*, III (1930), 116, quoting the Leavenworth *Conservative* of September 21, 1861.

14. *Ibid.*, quoting the Leavenworth *Conservative* of October 10, 1861.

15. *Ibid.*, 116–17.

thirty guerillas. But it certainly did not advance the cause of virtue that one of Lane's regimental chaplains openly helped himself to the altar furnishings of Missouri churches to equip his own unfinished House of God in Kansas.

The atrocities committed by unionist and secessionist Missourians against each other were evil enough; and in fact, Missouri unionists, driven from their homes and serving in Kansas regiments, frequently took the lead in despoiling secessionist or merely lukewarm former neighbors; but it was basically Kansas craving for revenge and Kansas craving for loot that set the tone of the war along the Kansas-Missouri border. Nowhere else, with the grim exception of the East Kentucky and East Tennessee mountains, did the Civil War degenerate so completely into a squalid, barbaric, murderous slugging match, as it did in Kansas and Missouri. The Seventh Kansas did not establish the pattern; it merely carried on practices which by the fall of 1861 had already developed the authority of an accepted custom.

Until the early part of August, Jennison hovered on the fringes of the Civil War. As captain of a militia company, and operating on his own or in a loose association with Lane and others, he had little opportunity to display his military talents. To lead hit-and-run raids through sparsely settled country, with nothing more in the way of opposition to be concerned about than hostile bands of guerillas and random home guard units, required ingenuity, endurance, and luck, but little military skill. These raids were a pleasantly exciting and financially rewarding summertime diversion, and nothing more. But at the beginning of August, Jennison was to be given a wider opportunity. Governor Robinson sent him to the department commander, General John Charles Fremont, with a request that he be granted authority to raise a regiment of cavalry for the United States service. It was understood that he would be commissioned colonel of the regiment if he succeeded in raising it.

The governor's reasons for selecting Jennison for this distinction were a puzzle to their contemporaries and are a puzzle to this day. Robinson's explanation is well below the generally low credibility level of official statements intended to explain the inexplicable. As has been mentioned, he claimed many years later that he sent Jennison to Fremont because of his fear that Jennison's jayhawking would precipitate an invasion of Kansas by Missourians bent on revenge, and in the expectation that as colonel of a regiment in the United States service, he would be forced to restrain his jayhawking proclivities.[16] It is difficult to believe that an intelligent and knowledgeable politician, as Robinson undoubtedly was, could be guilty of so gross a misjudgment. He may well have hoped that command of a regiment subject to the orders of the War Department would eventually lead to Jennison's removal from Kansas and the tempting proximity of the houses, barns, stables and slave quarters of Missouri. It is more probable, however, that Robinson was less concerned about Jennison's jayhawking than about his radicalism and his close ties with Lane, whose power was a constant menace and challenge to Robinson's authority as governor of the state. By providing Jennison with a regimental command, the governor could expect to please the radicals, while at the same time he laid the groundwork for the eventual removal from Kansas of one of Lane's most useful supporters. Certainly it is impossible to square Robinson's explanation with the fact that before the end of 1861, he solicited a brigadier general's commission for Jennison and gave him a glowing endorsement:

Kansas is entitled to two brigadier generals. It is but just to our state that they should be selected from our own citizens, especially when we have no lack of good material for such officers.
I would especially recommend for one brigadier from this state Colonel C. R. Jennison. . . .
Colonel Jennison has proved himself a competent and popular officer. . . . He has already acquired a high reputation as a military chieftain and is well qualified for the position in every respect.[17]

The governor's real reasons for recommending Jennison for the command of a regiment, and the latter's reaction to the flattering offer, must alike remain matters for speculation. It is not known whether the offer was volunteered by Robinson, or if it was solicited by Jennison himself or by friends acting in his behalf. At any rate, Jennison accepted the offer without hesitation and as no more than his due. Montgomery was already a colonel; so were other Kansans of much lesser note; and Jennison had more than enough self-confidence to believe that he was more than

16. Robinson, *Kansas Conflict*, 434–35.
17. Robinson to Simon Cameron, December 10, 1861, in Seventh Kansas, Regimental Letter and Order Book.

a match for any of them in military ability. With the governor's letter in his pocket, he traveled to St. Louis to interview General Fremont. On August 10, the day of Lyon's defeat at Wilson's Creek, he received Fremont's written authorization "to raise a regiment of cavalry for service during the war," the regiment to be under his command.[18] To lose no time, he telegraphed ahead to Kansas the news of his success; going well beyond the terms of the authority Fremont had given him, he announced that he had been empowered to raise a Regiment of Independent Mounted Rangers to operate on the Kansas frontier and to be subject to Fremont's orders alone.[19] J. T. Snoddy, who had participated in the hanging of Russell Hinds, was appointed recruiting agent for southern Kansas pending Jennison's return, and Daniel R. Anthony was to act in the same capacity in the northern half of the state.

Anthony had made his first appearance in Kansas as a member of the first party sent to the territory by the Emigrant Aid Society of Boston. He was born in South Adams, Massachusetts, in the Berkshire Hills, in 1824, and was thus exactly ten years older than Jennison. On his father's side, he was a descendant of John Anthony, who came to America from Wales in 1646. His maternal grandfather, Daniel Read, made the terrible march from Maine to Quebec with Benedict Arnold in the early winter of 1775 and fought in the Battle of Bennington. The Anthonys were Quakers, but Daniel Anthony, Daniel Read's father, violated one of the basic rules of the sect by marrying "outside meeting." His wife, Lucy Read, was not only a Universalist and hence by Quaker tenets hardly a Christian, but what was equally deplorable, she had a good voice and was in the habit of singing at her work. Nevertheless, while she never became a Quaker, she was a model wife even by the strict standards of her husband's church, and the two Anthony boys and their five sisters received an orthodox Quaker upbringing.

The elder Daniel Anthony's independence of mind and determination to have his own way, demonstrated by his marriage to a girl who was not of his own faith, were passed on in full measure to two of his

18. Fremont to Jennison, August 10, 1861, in Records of the Adjutant General's Office, Record Group 94, Compiled Service Records of Colonel C. R. Jennison in the Seventh and Fifteenth Kansas Cavalry, National Archives, Washington.

19. Unidentified clipping, Jennison Scrapbook.

children: the eldest son, Daniel Read Anthony, and the second daughter, Susan B. Anthony, the high priestess, with Elizabeth Cady Stanton, of the women's suffrage movement. Until he was ruined in the panic of 1837, Daniel Anthony owned cotton mills, first in Adams, Massachusetts, and later in Battenville, New York; the family lived in comfortable circumstances and the children received an adequate education. Equally as important as their schooling was their exposure to their father's strongly liberal and abolitionist convictions, which at one time led him to try to operate his mills by using only cotton that had not been grown by slave labor. From 1843 on the family lived on a farm near Rochester, New York. They joined the Unitarian congregation of William Henry Channing—the elder Daniel Anthony having been read out of Quaker meeting for wearing, "out of plainness," a camlet coat with a cape and a colored silk scarf; and they entertained at one time or another all the leading lights of abolitionism: William Lloyd Garrison, Theodore Parker, Francis Jackson, Parker Pillsbury, Wendell Phillips, and Frederick Douglass. Young Daniel Anthony clerked in his father's mills, taught school for two years, and then engaged in the insurance business in Rochester until 1854, when he decided to look for greener fields in Kansas.[20]

Anthony's hereditary abolitionism, as well as his lifelong habit of assuming and voicing uncompromising positions on all subjects, were in evidence on July 28 when the emigrant party, having reached the mouth of the Kansas River, and about to enter Kansas territory, held a typical New England town meeting to decide how they should conduct themselves toward the proslavery settlers already in the territory. The concensus was in favor of diplomacy as the better part of valor, and it was resolved that the members of the party should refrain from voicing their sentiments on the subject of slavery when talking to their proslavery neighbors-to-be. Such weak-kneed Laodiceanism was hateful to Anthony, then and later. He declared that he detested slavery and the slave power, and now that he had arrived in the arena in which the contest between slavery and freedom was to be fought out to a finish, he did not

---

20. Admire, "Early Kansas Pioneer," 688 *et seq.*; Frank W. Blackmar (ed.), *Kansas: A Cyclopedia of State History* (Chicago, 1912), I, 79; Rheta Childe Dorr, *Susan B. Anthony* (New York, 1928), 9–20, 77–79.

intend to hold his tongue when the subject of slavery was mentioned.
Having spoken his mind, he formally "withdrew from the meeting."[21]

Anthony had a fluent pen, as well as a fluent tongue, and during the
summer and early fall of 1854 he sent frequent letters to a Rochester
newspaper about his experiences in the new territory. The letters were
widely copied by other newspapers and were one of the main sources of
information that the East received about Kansas affairs. Yet for all his
fiery devotion to freedom, Anthony did not remain in Kansas. His surviving letters do not indicate why he did not stay, but it is clear enough
that, like any Yankee of his generation, he was out to better himself
economically and evidently decided after he got to Kansas that the
opportunities for making money were not as good as he had anticipated,
or that he lacked sufficient capital to speculate in land, the easiest way to
turn a quick profit in a new country. He returned to Rochester and
resumed his insurance business. In July, 1855, he took part in the first
Republican state convention in New York as a delegate from Monroe
County. A devout Republican from the earliest days of the GOP, his
party allegiance was of the most intense stripe; neither in 1855 nor in his
later years could he see any virtue in Democrats, declaring that "God
Almighty has written on their faces . . . the words [sic] Scoundrels."[22]

In the summer of 1857 Anthony disposed of his insurance business in
Rochester and returned to Kansas. He settled in Leavenworth, where he
lived until his death in 1904 at the age of eighty. The letters he wrote
from 1857 to 1861 to his father, his sister Susan, and other members of his
family, give a classic account of what may be called the second stage in
the building of a civilization in the wilderness. Anthony belonged not to
the first wave of land seekers and farmers who came to occupy virgin
land and raise crops, but to the second wave, those who followed close
behind the first, to provide the essential auxiliary services of a settled life
—the merchants, professional men, and every variety of businessman—
all those who came to the new land in the spirit voiced by Anthony in one
of his letters: "I think any man who will come here and adopt the 'go
ahead' system will succeed."[23]

21. Admire, "Early Kansas Pioneer," 691.
22. Anthony to his father, October 1, 1857, in Langsdorf and Richmond (eds.), "Anthony,"
23. Same to same, December 1, 1857, ibid., 29.

In 1857, "here" was Kansas Territory: primitive, crude, turbulent—not the place for the weak, the faint of heart, or the squeamish. At the Planters House in Leavenworth, where Anthony first put up, and which was to be the scene a few years later of a shooting affray between him and Jennison, men slept four and eight to a room and paid two dollars a day for room and board, a high price for those days. When Anthony attended the sale of Delaware Indian lands thirty-five miles west of Leavenworth shortly after his arrival, his residence was a "log shanty with rived shingle roof—cracks all open[,] Hay for flooring—one small box for furniture & Blankets for bedding. . . . Missourians, Border Ruffians, Virginians, Indianans and three New Yorkers are stoping [*sic*] in this hut—We live on crackers, Ham, Tea Sugar Molasses & '*whiskey*' the latter the only staple article of living."[24]

Over and above the normal hardships and hazards of frontier life, immigrants to Kansas had to face the extra jeopardy of a nearly inescapable involvement in the controversy over slavery. In the fall of 1856, the Democratic postmaster of Leavenworth stood on the levee with an axe in his hand and swore that "he would kill any God Damn Yankee who dared land from the Steam Boat."[25] But these were risks that Anthony welcomed. It is said that within a few days after he arrived in Leavenworth, he addressed a Free State meeting in a speech so radical and bitter that he was shot at three times by irate Border Ruffians in the audience before he sat down. A month later, he was chosen a delegate to the Free State Party Convention in Topeka. Three months later, he wrote his sister Susan that "the Pro Slavery Border Ruffian Democracy never attack a man here who says he will defend himself. So I have been compelled to wear a knife and carry a Colts Revolver—and the consequence is no trouble will be made on my account. The hounds never attack a man single handed[;] with very few exceptions they are cowardly dishonorable in all their intercourse with Free State men."[26] Well before the end of his first year in Leavenworth, Anthony had the reputation of being one of the most radical Free State men in Kansas, and was proud of it.

24. Same to same, June 11, 1857, *ibid.*, 12.
25. Same to same, October 1, 1857, *ibid.*, 22.
26. Anthony to his sister Susan, October 20, 1857, *ibid.*, 24.

In January, 1859, Anthony led eight Leavenworth Free Staters in the rescue from custody of a Negro barber named Charley Fisher, who had been arrested by the United States marshal as a fugitive slave. Anthony was indicted for his share in this affair and was released on bail to await trial. He wrote his father that "some of the *Southern Kansas* Boys"—one wonders if Jennison was to be one of them—"will attend our trial to see we have justice done us"; but the help of the "Southern Kansas Boys" was not needed after all, for the indictment was quashed and Anthony went free. [27]

Anthony's political activities went hand in hand with his increasingly successful business operations. He was primarily a fire and marine insurance agent with a shrewd eye for good risks, but he was also a loan broker, lending money on behalf of a New York financier at rates of interest of 4 to 5 percent *per month*; his commission on these loans was "6 percent per annium" plus half of all the interest he could get over and above 20 percent a year. [28] And like everyone else, he speculated in land. All in all, he was a demonstration in his own person of his dictum that "Any business will pay here except doing nothing." [29] He used some of his profits to start a newspaper, the Leavenworth *Conservative*, edited by Daniel W. Wilder. With great good fortune, the first issue of the new paper appeared on January 28, 1861. On the very next day a telegram arrived from Washington with the news that President Buchanan had signed into law the bill admitting Kansas to statehood. Not only did the *Conservative* issue an extra to proclaim the glad tidings, but Anthony himself rode the thirty-five miles to Lawrence, where the territorial legislature was in session, to announce the momentous news to its members.

The editorial stance of the inappropriately named *Conservative* reflected the radical convictions of its pugnacious owner and publisher. His firm Republicanism was rewarded by the new administration with the postmastership of Leavenworth, but it also drew upon him the wrath of rival newspapers of the Democratic persuasion. In the manner of the day he was excoriated in language that lacked neither directness nor vigor. On June 13, 1861, he was given a thorough going-over by the

27. Anthony to his father, April 6, 1860, *ibid.*, 225.
28. Anthony to Aaron McLean, November 26, 1858, *ibid.*, 212.
29. Anthony to his brother Jacob, August 17, 1857, *ibid.*, 20.

Leavenworth *Herald*, being dubbed a liar, among other things. On the following day, he met on the street R. C. Satterlee, the editor of the *Herald*, and demanded a retraction. Satterlee refused to withdraw the offending word and, drawing his pistol, fired at Anthony. His shot missed, but he was mortally wounded by Anthony's return shot and died in a few minutes. Anthony was bound over to the next term of the District Court under exceptionally high bail; but his trial, a five-day affair, resulted in his acquittal.

This was Anthony's career before he undertook to help Jennison recruit troopers for the new regiment of cavalry, whose lieutenant colonel he became. A man with a forceful personality, possessed of a violent temper and a bitter tongue, harsh, rigid, overbearing, insensitive, and impetuous, he either lacked, or was careful not to show, the human qualities that were indispensable to a commander of Civil War volunteers. He was obeyed, but mainly through fear. The men did not like him, and when he resigned his commission and left the regiment in the fall of 1862, there were not many who regretted his departure.

Jennison himself was back in Kansas on August 20, and four days later, the following recruiting poster issued from the printer's hands:

INDEPENDENT

KANSAS

JAY-HAWKERS

Volunteers are wanted for the 1st Regiment of
Kansas Volunteer Cavalry to serve our country
during the War
Horses will be furnished by the Government.
Good horses will be purchased of the owner who
volunteers. Each man will be mounted, and
armed with a Sharp's Rifle, a Navy Revolver,
and a Sabre. The pay will be that of a
regular volunteer.[30]

The poster was a shrewd bit of advertising, but it was considerably more appealing than truthful. The name of the regiment and the emphasis on its independent status were well calculated to reassure those Kansans who might have been reluctant to volunteer for a service in which jayhawking

30. Original poster in Kansas State Historical Society, Topeka.

was frowned upon. They were told, in effect, that the business, under new ownership, would be conducted on the old principles. As further reassurance on that point, the poster was subscribed "C. R. Jennison, Col." No Kansan needed to be told what that meant. But to promise every recruit a Sharp's rifle, a revolver, and a saber, was to promise the moon. Simeon Fox, who was one of those persuaded by the poster to enlist in the new regiment, wrote: "The recruit, in imagination, saw himself bristling with death and desolation, mounted on an Arabian barb, breathing flame as he bore his rider to victory."[31] In actual fact, cavalry arms worthy of the name were nearly unobtainable, especially in the West; Jennison should have taken warning from the carefully noncommittal language of Fremont's instructions to him to "make needful requisition [in St. Louis] for the equipment of [his] regiment. Such articles as are at hand will be furnished at once and the others ordered immediately."[32] Fremont had precious few articles of any kind "at hand"; and an order for more was far from being equivalent to delivery.

Jennison, like a latter-day executive, left the task of assembling and organizing the regiment in the hands of his subordinates, Snoddy and Anthony, while he himself attended to business he considered more important. This was the time, as has been mentioned, when Sterling Price and his army were on the march toward Lexington. To oppose Price, Fremont could call on nothing more than the Lane Brigade, a few scattered regiments of volunteers, and unionist militia. Price was too strong in numbers to be attacked directly with the exiguous Union forces available in northwestern Missouri; and since he was marching through an area half the population of which, more or less, was sympathetic to the South, he was safe from guerilla-style harassment also. But if Price himself was invulnerable, his friends in Missouri were not, and this led to two of the most curious episodes in Jennison's military career: the Independence Corral and the Kansas City Parade.

Independence, Missouri, is today an eastern suburb of Kansas City. In 1861, about ten miles of open country separated the two towns. A wealthy community, the seat of Jackson County, Independence owed its prosperity to the Santa Fe trade. By the modest standards of its place and

31. Fox, "Story," 17–18.
32. Fremont to Jennison, August 10, 1861, in Records of the Adjutant General's Office.

time, it was a city with a history and a tradition. In 1831, the Mormon Prophet Joseph Smith had seen a vision in Kirtland, in the state of Ohio. The Almighty revealed to him that "The land of Missouri is the land which I have appointed and consecrated for the gathering of the Saints. Wherefore this is the land of promise and the place for the city of Zion." Led by the vision, Smith went at once to Independence and was joined in the following year by some 1,500 of his followers. The vision, however, proved to be delusive, and Independence was not destined to be the new Zion, for in 1833 the Saints were driven out of the city by the Gentile inhabitants. And so, five years later, Joseph Smith saw another vision. It was revealed to him that "God's wrath hangs over Jackson County. God's people have been ruthlessly driven from it, and you will see the day when it will be visited by fire and sword. The Lord of Hosts will sweep it with the besom of destruction. The fields and farms and houses will be destroyed, and only the chimneys will be left to mark the desolation."[33] Now, in 1861, Smith's apocalyptic vision was to be fulfilled to the very letter, and through the instrumentality of Charles Jennison.

Price was marching toward Lexington when Jennison returned to Kansas from his interview with Fremont. As mentioned previously, Jennison and his followers, in concert with other bands of irregulars, made futile jabs at the left flank of Price's advance. They claimed that they kept Price out of Kansas, but it is unlikely he intended going there in the first place. Then, for the first three weeks of September, Jennison is lost to sight. He may well have been in Leavenworth, to press forward the organization of his regiment, of which he was formally commisioned colonel on September 4. Then at about the time Price gladdened the hearts of Missouri secessionists by capturing Lexington, the erstwhile medical man of Mound City gave Missourians a demonstration of a new kind of war.

The Civil War, as Jennison saw it, had nothing whatever in common with the glorified militia muster the South looked forward to in the heady aftermath of Fort Sumter. The South had visions of a war fought in bright sunshine by impeccably groomed and barbered gentlemen, a few of whom would regrettably fall in battle and sink gracefully to the ground while voicing sentiments of an exquisite patriotism; a war, too,

33. Bernard DeVoto, *The Year of Decision, 1846* (Boston, 1943), 41.

in which southern noncombatants would continue as a matter of course
to enjoy all the privileges and immunities guaranteed by the United
States Constitution. Jennison was one of the first to drive home the absurdity of such notions and to show the South the face of war as it really is.
He had most definite ideas of the way rebellion should be countered. His
methods were the opposite of romantic. They were destructive, dirty,
ruthless, and (one hesitates to use the word) realistic, but they were brutally effective. In the end, the war was won, as wars are commonly won,
by methods not very different from those he practiced and advocated.

The first large-scale but relatively mild demonstration of the Jenni-
sonian technique of dealing with rebels took place at Independence. The
town itself, and all of Jackson County, were secessionist by a considerable
margin. The "best blood," whatever that may have been, of the county
had enlisted in the Confederate army. Secessionist bands, formed ostensibly to protect the area from unionist raiders from Kansas, exercised the
prerogative of an armed majority by harassing their loyal neighbors. In a
campaign of terrorism that had begun before the election of Lincoln,
several unionists were killed, and the lives of all became insecure.[34] With
Price approaching the Missouri River, the secessionists of Jackson County became even more aggressive, and at length William Miles, city
marshal of Independence, felt it necessary to lead a delegation to Kansas
City to obtain help for the oppressed and persecuted unionists of Jackson
County. Jennison was in Kansas City when Miles arrived; and whether
by accident or design, it was to him that the marshal and his fellow
townsmen addressed themselves.

It may be taken for granted that Miles had little difficulty in enlisting
Jennison's help. The latter had his Southern Kansas Jay-Hawkers with
him, and Lane and his brigade had just arrived, laden with the spoils of
Osceola, so that ample manpower was available to teach the secessionists of Independence a salutary lesson. It could not have been more than
twenty-four or forty-eight hours after Miles's arrival in Kansas City
before Jennison was on the move. With a substantial force, whose exact

34. George Miller, *Missouri's Memorable Decade, 1860–1870* (Columbia, 1898), 90; McElroy,
Struggle for Missouri, 31. *Cf.* the story of the four unionists who were arrested in Independence while
on their way to enlist in General Lyon's army and barely escaped hanging, in an unidentified clipping, Jennison Scrapbook.

size is, however, unknown, he moved out in the night, and by seven o'clock in the morning he had Independence surrounded. With every exit from the town blocked, Jennison's men methodically gathered up all the adult male inhabitants, flushing out some of them from hiding places in barns, attics, and cellars, and marched them to the court house square. While one group conducted the roundup and guarded the prisoners, the rest of Jennison's men collected all the horses, mules, firearms, fine furniture, household goods, jewelry, and other valuables in town. By noon, the court house square was filled with several hundred highly apprehensive prisoners and with large piles of plunder, and it was surrounded by a living corral of Jennison's men on horseback, loaded and cocked rifles and carbines on thigh or revolvers in hand. Jennison now called for silence and read off a list of known Union men. These were permitted to leave the corral. Marshal Miles was then directed to walk through the ranks of the remaining prisoners and pick out all the Union men whose names were not on Jennison's list, under penalty of receiving a saber cut over the head from Jennison himself for every secessionist he picked out, either in error or out of a misplaced sense of compassion. All the Union men having been collected, Jennison tendered them his apologies for the inconvenience he had caused them and then permitted them to leave with their livestock and other belongings.

The righteous sheep having departed rejoicing, the secessionist goats were then made the beneficiaries of a half-hour oration by Jennison on the evils of rebelling against a beneficent government. They were reminded of the wrongs—which were real enough—they had inflicted upon their unionist fellow citizens, for which the loss of property they were about to suffer was an inadequate punishment. They were warned of worse pains and penalties to come if they failed to mend their ways, and they were told specifically that for every Union man killed thereafter, ten of the most prominent secessionists of Jackson County would suffer death.[35] At the conclusion of the speech, the prisoners were permitted to leave. Then the jayhawked horses and mules were hitched to the jayhawked buggies, wagons, and carriages, which were loaded with as

---

35. The story of the Independence Corral is told in Wiley Britton, *The Civil War on the Border* (New York, 1890–99), I, 176–79; also, Bingham to James S. Rollins, February 12, 1862, in Rollins, "Letters of Bingham," 53–54.

much of the jayhawked plunder as the raiders were unable to carry on their persons. This done, Jennison and his men, followed by the inevitable procession of slaves headed for freedom, departed from Independence. They arrived in Kansas City in the best of high spirits and, as an object lesson to the secessionists and lukewarm unionists of that city, marched through the town in a mock parade, the men "dressed in women's clothes, old bonnets and outlandish hats on their heads, spinning wheels and even gravestones lashed to their saddles."[36] By overcoming a considerable degree of scepticism it is possible to accept the spinning wheels; but gravestones, especially in the plural, are too great a strain on one's credulity; the story does indicate, however, the chronicler's high opinion of the thieving capabilities of Jennison's men. It is no ordinary thief who will steal a gravestone, or will even consider a gravestone worth stealing.

Gravestones lashed to saddles is not by any means the only puzzling aspect of this expedition to Independence and the parade through Kansas City. Wiley Britton, the principal contemporary authority, places these events in the month of September, 1861, but states that they were the work of Jennison's "regiment," namely the Seventh Kansas Cavalry.[37] Another contemporary, H. E. Palmer, in a sensational account written forty years after the war, describes the parade through Kansas City without mentioning its date and credits it specifically to the Seventh Kansas.[38] George Caleb Bingham, a third contemporary, describes the Independence "corral" in a long letter written in February, 1862; his account and Britton's are substantially identical, but Bingham's includes a number of dramatic touches and rhetorical flourishes that make its accuracy open to suspicion. Bingham fails to make any mention of the parade, although he was a resident of Kansas City in the fall of 1861; and to add to the confusion, he has the corral take place in November, not in September.[39]

Palmer's story is open to question on a number of counts. It was written many years after the event and, so far as can be determined, without any attempt to test a possibly fallible memory against contemporary evidence. Moreover, Palmer's objective was to prove the thesis expressed

---

36. Henry E. Palmer, "The Black Flag Character of the War on the Border," *Transactions of the Kansas State Historical Society, 1905–1906*, VIII, 460.

37. Britton, *Civil War*, I, 176.   38. Palmer, "Black Flag Character," 460.

39. Rollins, "Letters of Bingham," 53.

by the title of his article, "The Black Flag Character of the War on the Border," and he considered Jennison at least partly responsible for the "Black Flag Character" of the war. He makes his disapproval of Jennison explicit enough by calling him a coward and a murderer. Bingham's account is even more biased than Palmer's. No term of abuse is strong enough to express his detestation and hatred of Jennison, and the long letter in which he describes the latter's activities in Missouri in the summer and fall of 1861 is a prosecuting attorney's harangue from beginning to end.

Simeon M. Fox, who has been cited before and will be cited again, wrote his all too brief account of the early history of the Seventh Kansas, to which he belonged from the beginning, in rebuttal of Palmer's lurid article.[40] He took the trouble to check his own memory of these events with "several . . . old comrades," and he categorically denies that the Seventh Kansas ever paraded through Kansas City as described by Palmer, or that it made the expedition to Independence in September as related by Britton.[41]

The discrepancies and contradictions in these accounts can be resolved satisfactorily. As will appear later, the Seventh Kansas did make an expedition to Independence, but not until November, and it was commanded on that occasion by Lieutenant Colonel Anthony, not by Jennison. Fox's statements to that effect are borne out by the contemporary diary entries and letters of members of the regiment.[42] Was there an earlier expedition to Independence, led by Jennison? Undoubtedly there was, just as Britton described it, his only error being to ascribe the raid to the Seventh Kansas. On September 17 Lane wrote Captain Prince: "I am informed that there are three companies of Jennison's regiment at Fort Leavenworth. . . . They should be armed and sent forward without delay."[43]

40. Fox, "Early History," 239.

41. S. M. Fox to George W. Martin (Secretary, Kansas State Historical Society), December 13, 1908, in Simeon M. Fox Papers, Kansas State Historical Society, Topeka. *Cf.* same to same, December 2, 3, and 10, *ibid.*

42. Webster Moses to Nancy Mowry, December 4, 1861, in [Webster W.] Moses Letters, Kansas State Historical Society, Topeka. *Cf.* Fletcher Pomeroy, "War Diary," typescript, Kansas State Historical Society, Topeka, entry for [?] November, 1861. It should be noted, however, that W. A. Lyman of Company G states that "I distinctly remember that it was Col. Jennison who was in command at the time and ordered the '*corrall*.'" See William A. Lyman, "Reminiscences," typescript, Kansas State Historical Society, Topeka.

43. *Official Records*, III, 499.

In response to Lane's request, five companies of the Seventh, as yet without horses or uniforms, and only partially armed, were hurried to Kansas City on September 26 under the command of Anthony and remained there until mid-October.[44] But this detachment of the Seventh did not make an expedition to Independence during its brief stay in Kansas City. In the light of the available evidence, it appears probable that the Independence raid described by Britton, and the subsequent parade through Kansas City, were performed by a Jennison-led "pickup" force, the nucleus of which may well have been the "Southern Kansas Jay-Hawkers," and that the raid and parade occurred shortly before the arrival on the scene of the five company detachment of the Seventh.[45] The Seventh Kansas Cavalry earned a sufficiently evil reputation by its own well documented acts; it would be a deed of supererogation to saddle it with the odium of a plundering expedition and a clownish parade for which it was not responsible.

44. There is a conflict of evidence on the date of the first visit of the Seventh to Kansas City, as well as on the number of companies in Anthony's detachment. Captain Prince's orders of September 24 directed "The four companies of Jennison's Regt." to leave for Kansas City "at 11 o'clock A.M. tomorrow"—i.e., September 25. See Seventh Kansas Volunteer Cavalry, Regimental Order Book, National Archives, Washington.

45. "These [five] companies made no raids whatever, but did provost duty." See Fox, "Early History," 240. Cf. Fox, "Story," 28–29; Webster Moses to Nancy Mowry, September 28 and October 2, in Moses Letters; and Pomeroy, "War Diary," 11–14. See also Fox to George W. Martin, December 3, 1908, in Fox Papers. It is not impossible that the mock parade through Kansas City actually took place (as Fox suggested) in the course of Jennison's first visit to the city in June, 1861, at the head of his "Southern Kansas Jay-Hawkers."

CHAPTER IV

The
Regiment

WHEN RECRUITING BEGAN for Jennison's regiment, almost ten thousand men, nearly a third of Kansas' male population of military age, had already enlisted. Even Lane had been unsuccessful in filling up the ranks of his regiments; but Jennison started with two important advantages. In August and September, Kansas lay under the threat of being invaded by Price's Confederates. Secondly, Jennison's name was itself a powerful drawing card. Many of his Mound City followers had already enlisted in Montgomery's Third Kansas; but Jennison had enough admirers in Linn County and throughout the state to form a strong nucleus for the new regiment; and in fact the first company—Company A—was mustered into the United States service at Fort Leavenworth on August 27, when the ink was hardly dry on Jennison's recruiting posters.

Company A had been recruited chiefly in Doniphan County, in the northeastern corner of Kansas, by Captain Thomas P. Herrick, destined two years later to become the third colonel of the regiment, and Lieutenant Levi Utt of White Cloud. Utt was the fourth generation of his family to fight for the United States. His great-grandfather served in the Revolutionary War, his grandfather in the War of 1812, and his father in the Mexican War. He himself had already had service in the Civil War, as a three-month volunteer in the First Kansas Infantry. As a result, he knew somewhat more of drill and discipline than the majority of volunteer officers and succeeded in making Company A the best drilled unit in the regiment. Simeon Fox, who, as regimental sergeant major and later adjutant, was in a good position to judge, wrote that it was because of the influence of Utt's personality and the training he had given the company that Company A "became and always remained the most efficient and reliable organization in the regiment. . . . All were good, but Company A was a shade better." [1] The quality of the men of this company was shown in the fight at Coffeeville, Mississippi, in 1862; Private C. Ford was wounded five times in that fight before he could be persuaded to leave the field. Utt himself lost his left foot at Leighton, Alabama, in April, 1863; but as soon as the stump healed, he had himself fitted with a wooden leg and rejoined his company. He was only twenty-four at the time, but his name thereafter was "Old Timber Toes."

The second lieutenant of Company A, Thomas H. Lohnes, was a deserter from the regular army when he joined the Seventh. He quickly established a reputation for cold-blooded bravery, but he also had some less praiseworthy qualities and made a name for himself as a "bilk of the first water." [2] He left the regiment in February, 1862, for, as he put it in his letter of resignation, "good and sufficient reasons." [3] Officially, he resigned, but there is a strong hint that he did so under pressure; that, in fact, he was "kicked out." [4]

The enlisted men of Company A were mostly plainsmen and frontiersmen, which probably accounted for their superb marksmanship. Many of them could consistently hit the bull's-eye offhand at eighty yards with their Sharp's carbines. The company also had in its ranks a number of time-expired veterans of the regular army who had received their discharges at Fort Leavenworth. Henry A. Laverentz of Wolf River, Kansas, generally considered the best soldier not merely in Company A but in the entire regiment, had been a noncommissioned officer

1. Fox, "Story," 18.

2. John H. Utt, "History of the Seventh Kansas Regiment," Kansas State Historical Society, Topeka. This account was compiled by Levi Utt's father from his son's "observations and experiences."

3. Lohnes to Anthony, February 14, 1862, in Seventh Kansas, Regimental Letter and Order Book.

4. Utt, "Seventh Kansas."

in the Prussian army. Another member of Company A was Private James Smith, a native of Armstrong County, Pennsylvania, who had the distinction of being one of seven brothers serving in the Union army; for good measure, their father was also in the service.

Shortly after the arrival of Captain Herrick's company in Leavenworth, a group of about fifty men, recruited in Atchison and Leavenworth counties by Fred Swoyer, joined the regiment. Early in October, these fifty Kansans were joined by a contingent of thirty Chicagoans led by Isaac Gannett and became Company B of the Seventh, with Swoyer as captain and Gannett as first lieutenant. Swoyer was an utterly reckless individual and had an uncontrollable temper besides. One of his exploits was to ride a steeplechase on Delaware Street in Leavenworth one winter day in 1861; seeing a sleigh loaded high with cordwood in his path, he tried to jump his horse over it. The horse took a heavy fall, Swoyer broke his leg, and he was out of action for several months. In August, 1862, he resigned in a huff; but his letter of resignation was returned to him because of its disrespectful language. In the meantime, Swoyer had reconsidered and withdrew his resignation.[5] Later in the same year, a member of another company overheard Swoyer remark to the regimental surgeon that he expected to be killed by his own men.[6] Swoyer's presentiment proved to be correct. In January, 1863, in Somerville, Tennessee, in the course of a disgraceful drunken melee involving nearly the entire personnel of his company, Swoyer was shot through the body by one of his own men and died of his wound the next day. In a spirit of *de mortuis nihil nisi bonum*, the adjutant general of the state of Kansas has recorded for posterity that Captain Fred Swoyer was "killed in action."[7]

Captain William S. Jenkins' Company C was made up predominantly of residents of Leavenworth, with the addition of about twenty-five men hailing from Brown and Doniphan counties. Simeon Fox, whose good humored and sometimes sardonic stories of the Seventh Kansas are a

5. Swoyer to Colonel Albert Lee, August 2, 1862, in Seventh Kansas, Regimental Letter and Order Book.

6. Lyman, "Reminiscences."

7. *Official Records*, XXIV, Pt. 3, 141–43; *Report of the Adjutant General of the State of Kansas*, I, 543. If Simeon Fox's memory is not at fault, Company B had the further distinction of having the only commissioned deserter. This was Lieutenant Charles R. Thompson of Noysville, Illinois, who, however, is shown by the *Report of the Adjutant General of the State of Kansas* as mustered out with the regiment in 1865.

delight to read, started his career in the regiment as a trooper in this company. Company C had the further but questionable distinction of having on its roster the first member of the regiment killed in action—but not action against the enemy; James McNamara was shot and killed by the provost guard at Fort Leavenworth on September 25; the events that led to his death are not noted in the regimental records, and perhaps it is just as well that they should remain in oblivion.

First Sergeant John H. Gilbert, a veteran of the regular army, qualifies as one of the most methodical soldiers of the Civil War on the strength of the manner of his departure from Company C and the Seventh Kansas. Deeply offended by the appointment "of an incompetent, cowardly civilian" to a commission that he believed he had earned, Gilbert decided to desert, and did so in May, 1862; but not until he had arranged in a neat stack in his tent all the government property that had been issued to him and had placed on top of the stack a carefully itemized list of its contents. [8]

Company D must be placed on a special pedestal of honor and gratitude by an historian of the Seventh Kansas Cavalry, for it is mainly in the letters of Webster W. Moses, written in a beautiful Spencerian hand to the girl who was to become his wife, in the diary of Fletcher Pomeroy, in the letters of Daniel B. Holmes to his family, and in the letters of George and Welcome Mowry to their sister, the future Mrs. Webster W. Moses, that the bare chronicle of a Civil War cavalry regiment takes on the color and warmth of life. [9] And Moses, Pomeroy, Holmes, and the Mowry brothers were all members of Company D.

With a few exceptions, the members of Company D hailed from Wyanet, Illinois, a small village, then and now, in Bureau County, about sixty miles due east of Davenport, Iowa. The company was raised in August, 1861, by Clark S. Merriman, railroad station agent at Wyanet. Illinois having already filled its quota under the call for 500,000 volun-

---

8. Fox, "Early History," 250. The reason given by Fox for Gilbert's decision to desert can only refer to the appointment of Jacob M. Anthony, Daniel Anthony's younger brother, as second lieutenant of Company A on April 2, 1862. No other civilian was commissioned in the Seventh within a reasonable time prior to Gilbert's departure. Jacob Anthony proved to be a competent officer and was promoted to captain of Company I in May, 1863. He was neither incompetent nor cowardly.

9. Castel, *Frontier State*, 59, n. 51, is in error in identifying Pomeroy as a member of "John Brown's company." Pomeroy enlisted in Company D, not Company K, and remained a member of it until his promotion to regimental quartermaster sergeant in 1863.

teers that followed the Battle of Bull Run, Captain Merriman and his company decided to go to Kansas, where they could be sure of being accepted into the service. They were to depart on September 1. On that day, the people of Bureau County assembled at Wyanet to bid the company farewell. The patriotic speech of the day was made by Congressman Owen Lovejoy, who presented the company with a fine flag, which was accepted by Captain Merriman with the appropriate sentiments. After partaking of lavish refreshments, the company marched to the railroad station and boarded the cars for Quincy, Illinois, the first stage of their journey to what in the language of 1861 was called "the seat of war."

Except that it was made up almost entirely of residents of another state, Company D could well serve as the statistical average for the entire Seventh Kansas. It contained neither the oldest nor the youngest member of the regiment. Company F had the honor of having the oldest, in the person of a seventy-year-old patriarch, Private Daniel Ellsworth, who, unlike many a younger man, served faithfully with the regiment until the end of his three-year term of enlistment and was mustered out on November 23, 1864. The youngest Jayhawker, George H. T. Springer of Mound City, was claimed by Company G; Springer was fourteen when he enlisted in September, 1861, and he too remained in the regiment until he was honorably discharged on September 29, 1865, a mature veteran of eighteen with four years of army service to his credit.[10]

Company D had its own youngsters—three boys of seventeen—and also its patriarchs—three men in their early forties; but in the age of its men, as in most other respects, Company D stayed close to the statistical mean of the regiment. Of its ninety-one enlisted men, seventy-seven were native-born Americans, twenty-three being natives of Ohio, seventeen of New York, and twelve of Illinois; of the fourteen "foreigners" in the company, seven were of German birth. The percentage of foreign-born in Company D—15.4 percent—was lower than in the three other companies of the Seventh whose vital records are available, the composite figures for Companies D, E, I, and K showing native Americans out-

10. It should be mentioned that the youngest member, as distinguished from the youngest soldier, of the regiment was musician George Corrigan of Company K, who joined up at the age of twelve.

numbering soldiers of foreign birth, 295 to 68. Contrary to one of the southern articles of faith of the war years and later, the native-born in the Union armies outnumbered soldiers of foreign birth by a wide margin, and the Seventh Kansas was a typical regiment in this respect. Of the sixty-eight foreign-born troopers in Companies D, E, I, and K, twenty-four were natives of Germany, twenty-two of Ireland, and twelve of England; one of the troopers of Company E reported himself as having been born "At Sea."[11]

Vital statistics apart, what sort of men made up Company D? Recruited in a farming community, most of them were farm boys, with a farmer's eye for the quality of the land and of the husbandry they saw in their travels through Kansas, Missouri, Kentucky, Tennessee, Mississippi, and Alabama. Some were artisans, some clerks, and a few were college students. Among those who left college to enlist in Company D was Daniel Holmes, a student at Wheaton College and the owner of a "military library" consisting of the Bible, a volume of Shakespeare, a biography of Napoleon, and a book of "Military tactics."[12] On November 3, 1861, Holmes was promoted to first sergeant of Company D. Two months later, almost to the day, he was killed in action.

Company D had in its ranks the only certified poet of the regiment, namely, First Lieutenant Andrew Downing. The pen name of "Curley Q, Esq." under which Downing chose to publish his verses, suggests that the nature and quality of his poetry might best be passed over without comment. Regrettably, Downing at times permitted his poetical avocation to interfere with the proper discharge of his military duties, and there were those among his men who thought that he was "not fit for an officer."[13]

The general educational level of Company D appeared to be somewhat above the regimental standard; and so, certainly, was its moral tone, which, at least in the beginning, was pitched at an unrealistically high level, so much so that one unfortunate was dismissed from the fellowship for becoming intoxicated while the company was on its way

---

11. The statistics in this paragraph have been compiled from the data in *Report of the Adjutant General of the State of Kansas for the Year 1864*, 228–78.

12. Daniel B. Holmes to "Dear Folks," September 8, 1861, in Daniel B. Holmes Collection, Chicago Historical Society.

13. Webster Moses to Nancy Mowry, March 19, 1864, in Moses Letters.

to Kansas. Webster Moses and Fletcher Pomeroy were men of a strict morality, prone to view the backslidings of their fellows with an excessive severity. While recognizing and probably exaggerating the moral lapses of their fellow troopers, they nevertheless make it quite clear that, with a few conspicuous exceptions, Company D was made up of "good steady fellows," moderate in their virtues and vices alike.[14] The company was rather addicted to the signing of ambitious pledges to refrain from the use of alcohol and tobacco, and lived up to them about as well, and for as long, as one might expect.

Notwithstanding the sincere devotion of Company D to a strict code of morality, one can observe among its members the corrosive effect of a war conducted on Jennison's principles. Webster Moses can serve as an example. The same Moses who wrote his "Dear Friend" Nancy Mowry on October 2, 1861, that "Our mess is very steady we go to meeting whenever we can and read a chapter in the bible every evening before going to bed. We have no tobacco or Whiskey users" only a few months later informed her in a perfectly matter-of-fact way that he had "jayhawked some silver cupps and sent them to Illinois. . . . I wish that you would take care of them for me. If I should be killed you can keep one and send the other to Mother. . . . It may seem hard to you to take such things from the secesh but it is no more than they deserve."[15] If the final sentence quoted suggests a residue of doubt in Moses' mind about the morality of jayhawking, his later letters make it evident that as the months passed, he made his own comfortable compromise with corruption. Smoking and drinking were sins to be avoided. Jayhawking, on the other hand, was not only not a sin, but was merely a harmless pastime, an odd but quite natural phase of life in the army in wartime. William Wilson of Company D was the first man taken sick in the regiment. His indisposition was the result of a "fall from the top of a car and over exertion whyle at play." Then, in July, 1862, he deserted, "to escape punishment for thieving," whereupon Moses wrote Nancy that Wilson was a "low lived thief and robber" and that it was a good thing for the

14. Same to same, September 14, 1861, *ibid.* Moses' spelling was far from flawless, his letters abound in grammatical errors, and his punctuation and capitalization are erratic. Nevertheless, his fascinating and delightful letters deserve to be quoted exactly as he wrote them and without an irritating reiteration of "[*sic*]."

15. Same to same, August 16, 1862, and October 2, 1861, *ibid.*

company that he left. [16] Moses' indignation demonstrates that in a manner that is common in such situations, he himself, the men of Company D, and the entire regiment, discovered a broad dividing line between "thieving" and jayhawking and, to their own satisfaction, located the latter on the morally permissible side of the watershed.

Company D had an eventful journey to Kansas. Upon its arrival in Quincy, it learned that guerillas had burned many of the trestles on the line between Quincy and St. Joseph, Missouri, and that train service between the two towns was suspended until the trestles were rebuilt. Train service did not resume until three weeks later. Captain Merriman turned the delay to good account by borrowing Prussian rifles—heavy weapons, with a brutal recoil—for his men and drilled them in infantry tactics for three hours daily. While the Wyanet contingent was waiting for transportation, another company, which became Company E of the Seventh Kansas, arrived in Quincy from Chicago. It too was bound for Kansas because, with the quota of Illinois filled, it could not get into the service as part of an Illinois regiment. The two groups were at last able to leave for St. Joseph on September 19. Since the railroad ran for most of its length through timber and underbrush infested with roving bands of guerillas, some of the men were detailed to ride on the tops of the cars to fight off any attack that might be made on the train. Fortunately, the attacks did not materialize, but the recruits were pleased with this mild taste of danger. The roadbed was in bad repair, and to get the heavily loaded train, which was carrying a large shipment of government horses in addition to the nearly two hundred recruits and their baggage, over the steep grades, the men had to dismount from time to time and push the cars to help the laboring engine. The two hundred-mile journey from West Quincy to St. Joseph took thirty-six (or by another account, fifty-six) hours.

The men from Wyanet and Chicago met Colonel Jennison on the morning after their arrival at Fort Leavenworth. He made them "a nice little speech" and proposed that they join his regiment. He was lavish with promises of Sharp's rifles, Navy revolvers, and sabers, and made much of his own fighting record, boasting of the number of bullets he was carrying in his body as mementoes of the border troubles. The more

16. Same to same, August 16, 1862, *ibid.*

cynical among his hearers suspected that these musket balls were in the colonel's pockets, not in his body.[17] Captain Merriman opposed Jennison's proposal on the ground that more glory was to be won in the infantry than in the cavalry; but to the great majority of the men the mounted arm had an irresistible appeal, and when in fittingly democratic fashion the question was put to a vote, the cavalry won an almost unanimous verdict. The cavalry had a glamor about it in the early months of the war (the glamor was to wear off, with experience) that made it virtually certain that it would win hands down if the men were given a choice. To be armed with carbine, revolver, and saber, instead of the heavy infantry musket, to travel on horseback instead of footslogging through mud, snow, or dust, to have one's belongings carried on a horse's back instead of one's own, to ride down the enemy in a fiery charge instead of walking slowly into a storm of bullets—these allurements were too attractive for any red-blooded young American to resist. Company D, at any rate, never regretted its choice, nor did it ever regret its decision to join the Seventh Kansas; it was proud to belong to a regiment whose fame preceded it wherever it went.

Company E was the second of the three companies of the Seventh Kansas made up almost wholly of men from Illinois. Although organized by Captain George I. Yeager in Quincy, fifty-one of its members, including Yeager himself, were Chicagoans. Not surprisingly, inasmuch as so many of its members came from a large city, Company E had a relatively high proportion of foreign born in its ranks—32 percent, including twelve Irish, seven Germans, and seven English. Captain Yeager forgot, or never learned, the first law of survival of the elected Civil War volunteer officer: to retain his popularity with his men. He became unpopular, and his life was made so uncomfortable that he was glad to resign less than three weeks after his arrival in Kansas.[18] His successor, Captain Charles H. Gregory, was a capable and gallant officer whose

17. Pomeroy, "War Diary," 10. These musket balls, usually eight in number, were a staple of Jennison's wartime speeches. The present author has been unable to find any evidence, apart from Jennison's own claims, to prove or disprove the reality of these wounds. It should be noted, however, that Wiley Britton states, *Civil War*, I, 176, but without citing his source, that "In the contests between the Free-State and Pro-slavery men [Jennison] had been shot and wounded near to death by them in Southern Kansas."

18. Resignation accepted October 8, 1861. See *Report of the Adjutant General of the State of Kansas*, I, 577.

dash and knack of doing the right thing at the right time "produced brilliant results and much of the credit earned by the regiment was due to him." [19] It is a curious fact, not unconnected perhaps with the early command problems of Company E, that of twenty-one of its men who deserted, fifteen, or nearly three quarters, disappeared before the end of 1861, during the first four months of the company's existence; only six more deserted during the following four years.

Company F, recruited by Captain Francis M. Malone, was the third Illinois company in the Kansas regiment. Most of Malone's men came from Christian County, in the center of Illinois, a few miles from Abraham Lincoln's Springfield. Christian County was to earn an unenviable reputation in the last two years of the war as a hotbed of antiwar, Copperhead activity; but when in January, 1864, the Seventh Kansas was asked to reenlist as veterans, the troopers of Company F reenlisted with the rest.

Companies E and F shared a peculiar embarrassment. The rules of the War Department required that boys under eighteen who presented themselves for enlistment were to be accepted only if they had the permission of a parent or guardian to join the army. The rule of course was habitually evaded or disregarded, and boys of fifteen, sixteen, and seventeen, claiming to be eighteen or older, were enthusiastically accepted by officers, or would-be officers, eager to fill up the ranks of their companies. For the most part, once a boy had been mustered in, the parents accepted the situation, but not always. In October, 1861, the parents of Alonzo B. Pennington of Company E, armed with a writ of habeas corpus, snatched him out of the regiment; and in January, 1862, the father of John Allison of Company F did the same. [20]

Company G had a distinguished position in the Seventh Kansas, for, with the exception of a few men from Leavenworth, it was made up entirely of Colonel Jennison's Linn County neighbors and friends, most of them from Mound City. Not surprisingly, therefore, this company shared with John Brown, Jr.'s, Company K and the veteran "Jay-Hawkers" of Company H the reputation of being the most strongly

19. Fox, "Story," 22.

20. Pennington: Special Order No. 7, October 11, 1861, in Seventh Kansas, Regimental Order Book. Allison: Charles Newbold to Jennison, January 27, 1862, and Anthony to Newbold, February 8, 1862, in Seventh Kansas, Regimental Letter and Order Book.

abolitionist group in the regiment. Company G had another distinction as well. In a regiment twenty-four of whose officers resigned, Company G was unique in being led by the same officer from its organization in the late summer of 1861 to its muster-out four years later. This durable gentleman was Captain Edward Thornton of Mound City. Five companies of the Seventh had two captains in succession, three companies had three, and Company H led all the others in having no fewer than five captains at its head in four years. In contrast with the stability of its leadership, however, Company G was second only to Company H in the number of its deserters, forty-six compared to Company H's fifty-eight.

Among the members of Company G was a family group consisting of William N. Hamby and his two sons, James F. and William N., Jr. The three Hambys evidently liked their life in the Seventh Kansas, for in June, 1862, they made a strenuous effort to arrange for the transfer of a third Hamby son, Edom, from the Illinois regiment in which he had enlisted, to their own regiment and company. Their efforts to effect the transfer were unsuccessful.[21]

Captain Marshall Cleveland's Company H was, as has been mentioned, the source from which the Seventh Kansas inherited the name "Jayhawker." Apart from a few Missouri unionists, every member of Company H at the time of its organization was a Kansan, Cleveland himself claiming Leavenworth as his place of residence. Simeon Fox asserted that "Company H was made up of splendid fighting material, but did not have the proper discipline at first."[22] It is entirely unlikely that the company would have been brought under proper discipline by Cleveland even if he had not taken his dramatic departure from the regiment early in the game. But even aside from Cleveland, Company H, which needed firm leadership more than most, was singularly unfortunate in its officers. James L. Rafety, who was promoted to captain in May, 1862, First Lieutenant John Kendall, and Second Lieutenant Joseph H. Nessel were all at different times dismissed from the service in disgrace. Amos Hodgman, who was promoted from first lieutenant of Company E to captain of Company H in July, 1863, was by all accounts

21. Colonel Albert Lee to AAAG, Headquarters, Department of the Mississippi, July 18, 1862, in Seventh Kansas, Regimental Letter and Order Book.
22. Fox, "Story," 25.

an efficient, if somewhat grim, officer. He had command of Company H for only three months before he died of wounds received in action; but in that short time, he made Company H, which contained some of the best and toughest soldiers in the regiment, a solid and fairly well-disciplined fighting organization, a character it retained to the end.

But Company H was never free from disciplinary problems, either before or after the reformation effected by Captain Hodgman. In March, 1862, Alexander Driscoll, whose exploits prior to his enlistment in the company included desertion from the British army during the Crimean War and from General Price's Confederate army at Lexington, Missouri, broke out of the guardhouse in which he was confined for robbing a Union man in Missouri and stabbing a fellow soldier; he escaped on Lieutenant Colonel Anthony's valuable charger; he was recaptured, tried by court-martial for desertion, convicted, and shot. In September, 1864, John Bolton, another member of Company H, was shot by Sergeant James C. Service while resisting arrest for drunkenness, fighting, and disorderly conduct, and died of his wound the next day; it should be said, however, that Bolton had joined the company only three months before.

Company H had a further distinction that must not go unmentioned. In February, 1864, it acquired as a recruit an eighteen-year-old ne'er-do-well who in the course of his still scanty years had already been a pony express rider, a horsethief (an occupation that even he did not try to prettify by calling it jayhawking), and a Leavenworth saloon tough, the companion of "gamblers, drunkards and bad characters generally."[23] The name of this promising lad, who awoke one morning to find himself a soldier in the Seventh Kansas, with no recollection of when or how he had enlisted, was William F. Cody. He was to become internationally famous a few years later as "Buffalo Bill."

Bugler Ira B. Cole of Company H was generally conceded to be the foremost jokester of the regiment. His exploits became legendary. Convicted on one occasion of some minor misdemeanor, he was sentenced to carry a log for a certain length of time. The regimental chaplain happened along while Cole was marching up and down the company street with the log on his shoulder, and the two engaged in a theological discussion.

23. Don Russell, *The Lives and Legends of Buffalo Bill* (Norman, 1960), 60.

To settle the point at issue required reference to the Bible, which Cole offered to get from the chaplain's tent if the latter would hold the log for a moment. The moments succeeded each other and the log grew heavy on the chaplain's shoulder, when one of the officers of Company H appeared on the scene and, after the situation had been explained to him, went to look for Cole, whom he found sleeping peacefully in his tent. When Cole was prodded awake and was asked to justify his conduct, he explained that he understood the purpose of his punishment to be to have the log carried, a function which in his opinion the chaplain could fulfill as well as he could.

Company I, like A, was recruited in Doniphan County; but it also had in its ranks a sizeable contingent of men from St. Joseph, Missouri. Recruited by Albert L. Lee, the first commander of Company I was Captain John L. Merrick of Elwood, Kansas, Lee having been mustered in as a major. Merrick was too stout for a cavalryman—he was described as "somewhat Falstaffian in his proportions"—but he was a steady, reliable officer, characteristics which he was able to inculcate in the men of his company.[24]

It is a great loss to history that in the vast mass of Civil War letters and diaries that has survived the hazards of a century, there should be so little to describe the inner life of what was assuredly one of the most interesting bodies of troops in the Union army, namely Captain John Brown, Jr.'s, Company K of the Seventh Kansas. That it was composed of abolitionists and idealists to a man goes without saying. They accepted the restoration of the Union as the goal and purpose of the war; but to them a Union tolerating the existence of slavery anywhere within its borders was a mockery and a delusion. The real enemy was neither the South nor secession; in a fundamentally moral sense the enemy was slavery. And as the Covenanters in the English civil war of the seventeenth century fought king and priest in the name of the Almighty, so also the men of Company K fought the "nigger drivers" under the banner of the Lord. Did Captain Brown's men, exposed to the hardships, miseries, and boredom of life in the army, eventually lose the fire of their convictions? What little evidence there is indicates that they did not. In June, 1862, they were still proud of the title of "John Brown's boys," and they served

24. Fox, "Story," 25.

in the hope that the "government may soon determine to strike at the heart of the monster."[25]

The resignation of John Brown, Jr., in May, 1862, produced no change in what may be called the spiritual atmosphere of Company K. Brown was succeeded as Captain by Second Lieutenant George H. Hoyt, promoted by election over the head of First Lieutenant Burr H. Bostwick, whom many considered to be a more competent officer. Hoyt was a young lawyer from Atholl, Massachusetts, the son of a Boston publisher and bookseller. He had volunteered his services as defense attorney when the elder John Brown was tried for his life in Charles Town, Virginia, and assumed the leadership of Brown's corps of five defense attorneys. His credentials as an abolitionist were thus as impeccable as those of Captain Brown himself. Hoyt had come to Kansas with the advance group of Company K and was mustered in as second lieutenant on November 11, 1861.[26] From the very first, he was Jennison's devoted shadow and disciple. His character, like that of his newly found hero, was a strange assortment of contradictory qualities. A sincere idealist on the subject of slavery, he was also a braggart, a toady, a shameless liar, and an utterly unscrupulous self-seeker.

This was the Seventh Kansas at the time of its organization in the fall of 1861. The standard establishment of a Civil War cavalry regiment was twelve companies. The Seventh Kansas had only ten, and repeated efforts to obtain permission to add two more companies were unsuccessful.[27] Thus, the Seventh was numerically a small regiment, having a total of only 902 officers and men on its muster rolls on the date when its organization was completed.[28] As the months passed, its numbers

25. A. T. Reeve to John Brown, Jr., June 26, 1862, copy in Kansas State Historical Society, Topeka.

26. The rest of the company, led by Brown, arrived in Leavenworth January 9, 1862.

27. The first such effort was made by Jennison on November 14, 1861, in a telegram to General David Hunter: "My regiment is full. Five more companies are preferred and will join no other command. The case is urgent. Will you give me authority to accept more companies?" Seventh Kansas, Regimental Order Book. Hunter's reply is not in the records, but it was obviously in the negative in spite of the fact that Jennison tried to bring political influence to bear in favor of his request, through Senator Pomeroy.

28. The figure of 902 appears in *Report of the Adjutant General of the State of Kansas for the Year 1864*, 18. On the other hand, the records of the U.S. War Department show that when mustered in on October 28, 1861, the regiment had 882 officers and men. See *Official Records*, Series III, III, 457.

were reduced by 162 deaths, 161 discharges for disability, 248 desertions (most of which occurred during the first few months and the last two or three months of the regiment's existence), 25 dishonorable discharges, and the resignation or dismissal of 27 officers. These losses were only partially made good by the addition from time to time of a total of 356 recruits, enlisted almost without exception through the efforts of the officers and men of the regiment itself.

A modern historian has asserted that "many of the other officers" of the Seventh "were hardly better than Cleveland."[29] Of the thirty-four officers the Seventh had at the start, four at most may, perhaps, be described as hardly better than Cleveland. But a corps of officers that had among its members Albert Lee, Thomas Herrick, Levi Utt, Charles Gregory, Francis Malone, Edward Thornton, Amos Hodgman, John Brown, Jr., and Burr Bostwick, to name only officers commissioned at the time the regiment was mustered in, and all of whom served honorably and in some cases with distinction, hardly deserves being equated with a highwayman.

Through all the changes in its commissioned and enlisted personnel, through all the ups and downs of its fortunes, the Seventh kept an amazingly powerful hold on the affections of its members. When Webster Moses returned to duty in January, 1863, after a long stay in an army hospital in St. Louis, he wrote Nancy Mowry that getting back to the regiment "seemed like getting home."[30] And notwithstanding the seemingly contradictory evidence of the 248 desertions, it can be said also that the Seventh had a superb corporate pride and a high morale.

Few Civil War regiments acquired so evil a reputation as did the Seventh Kansas; but taken individually, the Jayhawkers were neither bearded ruffians nor fierce and ruthless desperadoes. Most of them were young men in their twenties, raised in decent, God-fearing homes. Man for man, they were neither better nor worse than the personnel of almost any other regiment in the Union army. As a regiment, however, they had a reputation handed to them ready-made, through the person of their colonel. And they made the most of it.

29. Castel, *Frontier State*, 58.
30. Webster Moses to Nancy Mowry, January 26, 1863, in Moses Letters.

CHAPTER V

Marching
as
to War

LIKE MANY another Civil War regiment, the Seventh Kansas, or as it was known during the first few months of its existence, the First Kansas Volunteer Cavalry, had no opportunity to go through a leisurely process of organization and training. With the enemy in the person of General Sterling Price in possession of Lexington, and Lane clamoring for help, the first five companies of the Seventh, some of them still short of their full complement of men, were rushed downriver to Kansas City on September 26. Notwithstanding Colonel Jennison's glowing promises, when the men were marched aboard the steamer *Majors* they still wore the nondescript civilian clothing in which they had left their homes, and for weapons they had the scrapings of the barrel from Fort Leavenworth: Belgian muskets, Austrian carbines whose hammers were prone to break when they were fired and for which the only cartridges available were much too small, obsolete dragoon pistols mounted on temporary stocks, and other makeshifts.[1] Nor were any horses or camp equipage to be had as yet. Nevertheless, everything about the business of soldiering was novel and interesting, and the men enjoyed themselves in Kansas City. Lacking tents, they were quartered in churches, schools, and in vacant dwellings, many of which had been abandoned by secessionist owners who fled the city. The Jayhawkers became acquainted with hardtack and

1. *Official Records*, VIII, 654.

made the interesting discovery that this staple of army nourishment, if stored for a sufficient length of time, became both meat and bread, being infested with large, fat grubs.

On October 1, two additional companies of the Seventh arrived in the city. Minus horses, gear, and proper arms, the four hundred Jay-hawkers confined their warlike activities to a schedule of drill prescribed by Anthony: company drills of one and a half hours' duration each in the morning and afternoon, and a half-hour of battalion drill at 4:30 P.M.[2] When not at drill, they patrolled the streets as a warning to the remaining secessionists to behave themselves. Patrolling became more pleasant and more martial in appearance on October 2, when the first instalment of the uniform was issued, namely, cavalry hats ornamented with "ploons."[3]

Colonel Jennison, as was his habit, was absent from the regiment. Daniel Anthony, major until October 30, when he was mustered in as lieutenant colonel, was in command and, by appointment of Brigadier General Samuel D. Sturgis, served as provost marshal of Kansas City. One of his first official acts was to issue an order prohibiting the sale of liquor to any soldier; all stores, eating places, and saloons were ordered to close at 6 P.M., and a 9 P.M. curfew was imposed on all citizens.[4]

For the first seven months of its existence, the Seventh, although universally known as "Jennison's Regiment," saw little of its colonel. Jennison had the rank, the glory, and the acclaim that went with re-gimental command, while the duties of the position were performed mainly by Lieutenant Colonel Anthony. Whenever Jennison did put in an appearance, he invariably wore a tall, brimless fur hat, which added to his scanty inches, whatever it may have lacked in military propriety.

The provost guard duties assigned to the regiment in Kansas City proved to be largely a sinecure. To keep the men occupied and give them experience, Anthony took 150 of them on October 10 to Parkville, a few miles upstream from Kansas City, and returned with a bag of secessionist prisoners. The following week, with Price retreating and Kansas City no

2. Order No. 4, in Seventh Kansas Volunteer Cavalry, Company Order Books, National Archives, Washington.

3. Webster Moses to Nancy Mowry, October 2, 1861, in Moses Letters.

4. Anthony was appointed provost marshal by order dated October 7, 1861. See Seventh Kansas, Regimental Order Book. His curfew order, not dated, is in Seventh Kansas, Company Order Books.

longer in danger of a Confederate attack, Anthony was ordered to take his command back to Fort Leavenworth.[5] The return journey was the occasion of the initiation of the Seventh Kansas into one of the eternal verities of army life. On Tuesday evening the men were directed to prepare for an early reveille, inasmuch as the boat to take them to Leavenworth would be at the levee at four o'clock the next morning. Punctually at 4 A.M., in the predawn darkness of Wednesday morning, the regiment was at the landing. The boat was not. It arrived at noon, eight hours late. Two more hours passed before boarding could begin, and the embarkation took three hours to complete. Not until 5 P.M. did the boat cast off for Leavenworth.

On October 18, the entire regiment, lacking only Captain Brown's Company K, was united for the first time. Complete uniforms were issued the next day, followed a few days later by the issue of horses, which were sorted out according to color before being assigned to the different companies. There was also a partial issue of weapons. Companies A, B, and H were given Sharp's carbines, navy revolvers, and sabers; the rest had to make do with the odd assortment of infantry firearms and antiques they already had, plus revolvers and either bayonets or "saber bayonets," a far cry indeed from the lethal arsenal promised by the colonel's gaudy recruiting poster.

Inadequate, makeshift armament, much of it unsuitable for use by mounted troops, was a fact of life that the Seventh Kansas shared with the entire corps of Federal cavalry. Generally speaking, the eastern regiments fared better than did the western cavalry, and there was a similar geographic cleavage in the West, as between the regiments raised east and west of the Mississippi River; the latter, the Jayhawkers among them, got the dregs of an insufficient store of obsolete infantry weapons, venerable antiques, and the offscourings of European arsenals. In February, 1862, George Hoyt complained to friends in the East that his men were armed with "pistol carbines, a muzzle-loading weapon not well adapted to the kind of warfare [they] were soon to inaugurate."[6] Jennison wrote that "the many diverse patterns of weapons" with which his regiment was

5. Special Orders No. 11, October 15, 1861, in Seventh Kansas, Regimental Order Book.
6. Hoyt to [?—probably George Stearns, Boston], February 12, 1862, in Seventh Kansas, Regimental Letter and Order Book.

armed materially impaired its efficiency.[7] Anthony joined in the chorus with the complaint that seven of his ten companies were armed with "inferior guns — Mississippi rifles, pistol carbines."[8] In June, 1862, when the regiment was already in Tennessee and was expected to fight regular Confederate troops, and not mere guerillas and bushwhackers, Anthony protested to Brigadier General Robert B. Mitchell that the "Prussian rifles which have been furnished this regiment are found to be entirely unfit for service."[9]

None of these complaints and protests had any effect in producing adequate weapons for the Jayhawkers; and as late as December, 1862, Lieutenant Colonel Thomas P. Herrick had to apologize to the Ordnance Office of the Cavalry Bureau for being late with a report on the number, kind, and caliber of the firearms possessed by the regiment, because, he explained, he had been "obliged to alter the form in order to suit the great diversity of arms in [the] regiment. Permit me to call your attention to the remarks appended to the report, showing the unfortunate condition of arms in my command. Cavalry arms cannot be obtained in this department. I have forwarded several requisitions, designed to reach the Ordnance Office in Washington, but have heard nothing from them. If anything can be done by the Cavalry Bureau in a matter of so much importance, it will be fully appreciated by every man in my regiment."[10] Colonel Herrick was no more successful than his predecessors had been in getting proper arms for his troopers. Relief came at last, at the end of 1863, when the regiment had already been on active service for two years; the personal intervention of General William S. Rosecrans produced Colt revolving rifles for the seven companies that had had to make do with weapons that as often as not were more dangerous to the user than to the enemy. Since the Seventh, like most of the western cavalry, did nearly all of its fighting dismounted, and was essentially a regiment of mounted infantry, the Colt rifle met its needs admirably.

However unsatisfactory its weapons may have been, the Seventh was now, in October, 1861, a full-fledged regiment of cavalry, uniformed,

---

7. Jennison to Anthony, March 18, 1862, *ibid.*
8. Anthony to Colonel N. H. McLean, March 18, 1862, *ibid.*
9. Anthony to General R. B. Mitchell, June 15, 1862, *ibid.*
10. Herrick to Captain W. Redwood Price, December 15, 1862, *ibid.*

equipped, and mounted. And on October 28 it became a cavalry regiment *de jure* by being mustered into the United States service. The muster-in ceremony was marred by the ineptitude of Colonel Jennison, who attempted to put the regiment through the manual of arms without having studied his book of tactics with the necessary diligence. After getting himself and the regiment thoroughly "balled up," he rode away, to spend much of his time playing poker at the town of Squiresville (so Simeon Fox tells us), leaving the regiment in Anthony's care.[11]

Friday, November 8, 1861, is the day when the career of the Seventh Kansas as a fighting regiment may be said to have begun. On the morning of that day, five companies—A, B, C, D, and H—led by Anthony, departed from Fort Leavenworth for Kansas City, followed a few days later by Companies E, F, G, and I.[12] This second journey to Kansas City, unlike the first, was not made by boat. The men marched as proper cavalrymen, in all the pride of new uniforms and fresh horses. As was the case with most Federal cavalry regiments in the early months of the war, the Seventh was followed by a baggage train of monumental proportions, no fewer than thirty 6-mule wagons and two 4-mule ambulances, an establishment that would have been considered vastly excessive for a full division of cavalry three years later. In addition to the baggage in the wagons, the men, and of course their steeds, were undoubtedly loaded down also with the mountains of gear and personal belongings that no Civil War cavalryman could live without until, after a few short weeks of campaigning, he learned better. In all probability, the classic description of the trooper of the Fourth Iowa Cavalry, ready for his first march, would have applied equally well to the Jayhawkers as they filed out of Fort Leavenworth on the morning of November 8:

Fully equipped for the field, the green cavalryman was a fearful and wonderful object. Mounted upon his charger, in the midst of all the paraphernalia and adornments of war, a moving arsenal and military depot, he must have struck surprise, if not terror, in the minds of his enemies. . . . When the rider was in the saddle, begirt with all his magazine, it was easy to imagine him protected from any ordinary assault. His properties rose before and behind

---

11. Fox, "Early History," 240.
12. The November 8 date in the text is based on Webster Moses to Nancy Mowry, December 4, 1861, in Moses Letters. The November 11 date in Castel, *Frontier State*, 58, appears to be incorrect.

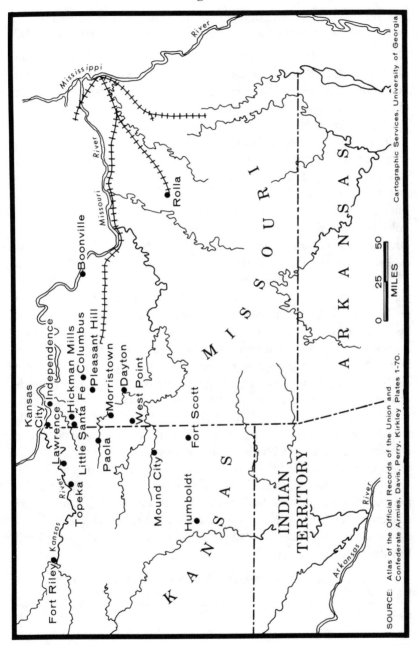

Mississippi River

Mississippi River

Missouri River

Rolla

Boonville

Kansas City
Independence
Hickman Mills
Columbus
Pleasant Hill
Little Santa Fe
Morristown
Dayton
West Point
Lawrence
Topeka
Paola
Mound City
Fort Scott
Humboldt
Fort Riley

Kansas River

Kansas River

M I S S O U R I

A R K A N S A S

K A N S A S

INDIAN
TERRITORY

Arkansas River

MILES
0   25   50

SOURCE: Atlas of the Official Records of the Union and
Confederate Armies. Davis, Perry, Kirkley Plates 1-70.

Cartographic Services, University of Georgia

him like fortifications, and those strung over his shoulders covered well his flanks. To the uninitiated it was a mystery how the rider got into the saddle.[13]

No doubt, too, the Seventh Kansas could have been tracked from Fort Leavenworth all the way to Kansas City by following the line of super-fluities the men discarded as they began the process of stripping down to the amazingly small amount of gear a cavalryman actually needed.

The orders under which the regiment marched to Kansas City and which governed its activities after it got there have not survived, but their purport can be deduced from the movements and operations of the Seventh after its arrival in Missouri. The immediate task assigned to it was to escort a train of five hundred ox-drawn government wagons to Sedalia, Missouri, an escort of a full regiment being needed because the eighty miles between Kansas City and Sedalia were controlled by secessionist guerillas. The broader mission assigned to the Seventh was to deal with the guerillas who had made the counties immediately east and south of Kansas City their happy hunting ground. Jackson County in particular was a cauldron of guerilla activity. As Samuel Ayres, the elderly and ineffectual chaplain of the Seventh Kansas, put it: "Jackson co. Mo. has been represented as conquered by the Union troops 5 times but no sooner are the forces with drawn from their midst than they rise up and com-mence a new their depredations and persecutions of the Union men, confiscating their property, shooting hanging or driving them from the country. . . . I am fully convinced from what I have seen of the move-ments of the secessionists . . . that the only way to subdue them is to take from them all means of subsistence and execute their leaders as fast as they fall into our hands."[14] Neither Jennison nor Anthony was in the least reluctant to follow the first half of Ayres's drastic prescription for dealing with secessionists; but being less bloodthirsty than the nonfighting cler-gyman, they might have hesitated to use the second half. Anthony de-clared on a later occasion that the function of the Seventh was to free all slaves and to confiscate all rebel property. Jennison, on the other hand, had thought up a less severe approach, as ingenious as it was unprece-

13. William Forse Scott, *The Story of a Cavalry Regiment: The Career of the Fourth Iowa Veteran Volunteers* (New York, 1893), 26–27.

14. Samuel Ayres to Liman Langdon, November 15 1861, in Samuel Ayres Collection, Kansas State Historical Society, Topeka.

dented, that he wanted to try first. As the first step in this program, he issued the following proclamation, which deserves to be quoted in full, to the people of Jackson, Lafayette, Cass, Johnson, and Pettis counties:

I have come among you with my command under the authority of the General Government, for the purpose of protecting the Supply Trains, and all other property of the United States Government, and for the purpose of throwing a shield of protection and defense around all men who are Loyal to that Government.

No excesses will be committed by any soldier under my command.

We march to enforce the Laws and sustain the Government. Every loyal citizen is expected to give evidence of his loyalty by active efforts for the protection of the flag. For four months our armies have marched through your country; your professed friendship has been a fraud; your oaths of allegiance have been shams and perjuries. You feed the rebel army, you act as spies while claiming to be true to the Union. We do not care about your past political opinions; no man will be persecuted because he differs from us. But neutrality is ended. If you are patriots you must fight; if you are traitors you will be punished.

The time for fighting has come. Every man who feeds, harbors, protects or in any way gives aid and comfort to the enemies of the Union will be held responsible for his treason with his life and property. While all the property of Union men and all their rights, will be religiously respected, traitors will everywhere be treated as out-laws—enemies of God and man, too base to hold any description of property and having no rights which loyal men are bound to respect. The last [loaf?] and the last slave of rebels will be taken and turned over to the General Government. Playing war is played out, and whenever Union troops are fired upon the answer will boom from cannon and desolation will follow treason. Loyal citizens will be fully remunerated for all property taken from them for the use of the army.

All the land between Fort Leavenworth and the Headquarters of the Army of the West is under the jurisdiction of the United States and we propose to have a regular road over it and safe communication through it, no matter at what cost of rebel treasure and blood.

It is to be hoped that you will see the necessity of abiding by the laws and actively sustaining them. But if you raise an arm against the Government we have sworn to protect, the course I have briefly marked out will be followed to the letter.[15]

15. Copy in Jennison Scrapbook. The proclamation was issued on November 24, 1861. See Herklotz, "Jayhawkers in Missouri," 72.

Having put traitors on notice of the treatment they might expect to receive at his hands, Jennison next proceeded to deal with the real source of guerilla strength, the "peaceful farmer" who tended his fields by day and when Union troops had their eyes on him, and turned guerilla or bushwhacker in the dark of the moon or whenever he could do so in safety. For the actual or potential guerilla, Jennison announced his "Deed of Forfeiture" policy.

The Civil War produced many novelties in tactics, weaponry, logistics, and communications. Jennison's deed of forfeiture policy for dealing with the concealed enemy, the secretly disloyal civilian, is certainly not the least imaginative of the novelties produced by the war. To initiate the policy, Jennison published the following "Propositions," addressed to the armed bands in arms against the government in Jackson, Johnson, Lafayette, Cass, Pettis, and Bates counties in Missouri:

1st. All who are now in arms against the Government of the United States . . . and who will surrender their arms and ammunition to me . . . and shall sign the Deed of Forfeiture . . . and shall hereafter perform their duty as good and loyal citizens, shall not be held responsible for past acts of rebellion, but shall be protected in their lives and property. . . .

3rd. Persons who shall surrender themselves to me, in order to make arrangements for securing peace in their neighborhoods shall be respected in their rights while arranging . . . terms, and shall be allowed to return to their homes, even should we . . . fail to come to any understanding.

4th. All who shall disregard these propositions, and shall continue in armed rebellion against the Government . . . shall be treated as Traitors, and slain wherever found; their property shall be confiscated and their homes burned, and in no case will any be spared, either in person or in property, who refuse to accept these propositions.[16]

Jennison's deed of forfeiture, which ranks as one of the most curious legal documents ever penned in this country, took the form of a conveyance of all the signer's property to the United States Government, the conveyance to be null and void if the signer subsequently gave proof of an active loyalty to the national government.[17] Jennison had a sufficiently

16. Copy in Jennison Scrapbook.
17. The conveyance read as follows:
We whose names are hereunto subscribed, do hereby in consideration and for the purpose of securing the safety of persons and property, and of suppressing, in this State, the rebellion against the Government . . . each for himself, pledges in security for our Loyalty, all and singular our

high opinion of his scheme to have a sizeable supply of the deeds printed, and he actually got a large number of them executed, "some one hundred" in less than a month.[18] The records do not indicate whether this "loyalize or obliterate" policy, as Jennison called it, was his own brainchild. His skill with the pen fell considerably short of the literary quality of the three documents cited; but to think out the main lines of a tough proclamation was not beyond his rhetorical capabilities, and he gave evidence over the years of a sufficiently offbeat imagination to justify the assumption that the whole concept was his invention. It is possible, however, that the idea originated with Hoyt, and it is more than likely that he was responsible for the actual drafting of the documents. It is perhaps unnecessary to state that as a means of putting a stop to guerilla activity in Missouri the deeds of forfeiture were utterly ineffectual. Legally speaking, they were worthless. Nevertheless, it would have made a fascinating addition to American jurisprudence if the government had attempted to enforce one of them through the courts; for one thing, the opinion of the judges on the validity of a conveyance executed "freely and . . . without any compulsion" when presented for signature by a squad of armed Jayhawkers, would make interesting reading.

Curiously enough, the records do not disclose any comment by the military authorities on Jennison's "policy." Perhaps they were unaware of it. But, in any case, one may well ask how a mere colonel of a volunteer cavalry regiment could take it upon himself to initiate a program of his own for dealing with an issue of crucial importance, involving the relations of the national government with a population of deeply divided loyalties in a technically loyal, slaveholding border state. This irrational situation came about partly because of Jennison's overweening self-

---

property, real, personal and mixed . . . and hereby GRANT, BARGAIN, SELL and deliver to the Government of the United States, all and singular our said property. . . . This conveyance is to be void upon the following conditions, to wit:—That we shall each preserve and maintain, at all times, good faith and loyalty towards the said Government . . . and at all times furnish to its officers and agents all information in our possession or knowledge of value to the Government, or of detriment to the rebel enemy, and promptly report to the Government authorities all persons known to be engaged in disseminating treasonable doctrines, making war themselves or encouraging others to make war on the Government of the United States; and further, that we, nor either of us, will not by word or deed, give any advice, information, aid or comfort to the said rebel emissaries . . . known as secessionists.
This conveyance is made by us freely . . . and without any compulsion.
18. Daniel Holmes to "Dear Folks," December 8, 1861, in Holmes Collection.

assertiveness and partly because of the existence of a power vacuum. In the early months of the war a weak national government groped for policies to pursue in the face of the immensely complicated problems created by secession, war, and the infinitely subtle gradations of disloyalty. Its policy-making machinery was absurdly unequal to a task of unprecedented magnitude and complexity, and its power to compel the obedience of its agents, especially those in the volunteer armies, to the policies it did have, was inadequate. Jennison was only one of the numerous colonels and generals who took the direction of the war into their own hands, either by necessity or in the naive arrogance of democracy run riot. The colonel of the Jayhawkers was typical in another respect. Like many another volunteer officer who invaded the policy-making prerogatives of the government, he had the active support of political friends and allies who did their bit for the preservation of the Union by abetting administrative chaos. Thus, Samuel Pomeroy, the junior senator from Kansas, wrote Jennison in mid-November to express his "great faith" in the Seventh Kansas; he invoked the divine blessing on Jennison and entreated the Deity to save the Colonel "from a *conservatism* that would not strike for freedom and the rights of *Man*." [19] Thus encouraged, Jennison declared that by the firm stand he had taken and the policies he had inaugurated, he was "settling fast the difficulties" in western Missouri and announced that, if he were allowed to remain where he was, he would continue the policy he had begun. [20]

With the knowledge he must have had of Jennison's activities in Missouri, Governor Robinson urged his promotion to brigadier general and, in the endorsement previously quoted, pronounced him "a competent and popular officer . . . well qualified for the position . . . in every respect." General David Hunter, who must also have been aware of what Jennison was doing in Missouri, seconded Governor Robinson's recommendation on the ground that Jennison was "one of those men peculiarly fitted for bringing [the] war to a successful termination." [21] The object of all this praise, who had not failed to do a little lobbying in Washington on

19. Pomeroy to Jennison, November 15, 1861, in Seventh Kansas, Regimental Letter and Order Book.

20. Jennison to Major [?] Lee, November 27, 1861, *ibid.*

21. Robinson to Simon Cameron, December 10, 1861, and General David Hunter to the same, December 11, 1861, both *ibid.*

behalf of his own promotion, was assured by Senator Pomeroy that he would "look closely into the matter," and would use to the full "any chances that[could] be turned" in favor of Jennison's promotion.[22]

Meanwhile, the wagon train the Seventh had been sent to Missouri to protect went on its way without any escort and was duly captured by guerillas on November 18; they burned the wagons and stampeded the draft animals.[23] The only explanation of the Jayhawkers' failure to escort the train is a story written thirty-five years later, that some well-meaning people living along the route the train was to follow, afraid that serious trouble would occur if Union troops marched through their area, persuaded the army authorities that the train would not be molested if it was sent through without an escort. The Missourian who is responsible for the story adds that, in the evening after the train left on its slow journey, he met Anthony in Kansas City; Anthony asked him if he thought the train would get through; and when he answered that "no one on earth could tell what would happen," Anthony solemnly raised his hand and said: "Woe to that country if those transports are molested."[24]

Anthony made good on his threat in full measure. But before he could do so, he fought the first battle in the history of the Seventh Kansas, and the costliest in terms of casualties. On the afternoon of November 10, word came to him that Captain Upton Hays, with three to four hundred men raised in and around Westport in Jackson County, "to be taken South for the defense of the Confederacy," was encamped on the Little Blue River, about thirteen miles away.[25] Anthony left Kansas City at once at the head of 150 men of Companies A, B, and H, the only three well-armed companies of his command. The accounts of what happened the next morning, when Anthony reached Hays's camp, are extremely sketchy and fragmentary. Apparently the Jayhawkers succeeded in surprising the Confederates and drove them from their camp. Unlike the usual behavior of untrained men, or of guerillas, in such situations, Hays's

22. Pomeroy to Jennison, December 16, 1861, *ibid.*
23. *Official Records*, III, 367.
24. Miller, *Missouri's Memorable Decade*, 72–73. Richard S. Brownlee is mistaken in stating, *Gray Ghosts*, 44–45, that Jennison was ordered to Missouri "following a guerilla attack on a government train." The attack on the train occurred more than a week after the Seventh had arrived in Missouri. No doubt Brownlee was misled by Bingham's biased account.
25. Albert N. Doerschuk (ed.), "Extracts from War-Time Letters, 1861–1864," *Missouri Historical Review*, XXIII (1928), 108.

men did not scatter and run. They made an orderly retreat to a good
defensive position on high, rocky, wooded ground directly behind their
camp. Anthony might have been able to flank Hays out of his position.
But due to inexperience, or a temperamental inability to do anything but
attack head-on, he ordered thirty-five men of Company A to storm a
strong position held by ten times their own number of straight-shooting
Missourians. The attack failed and Anthony was forced to retreat, with
the loss of nine killed and thirty-two wounded.[26] His assertion that fifteen
Confederates were killed and "a large number" wounded is probably an
exaggeration, as claims of enemy casualties usually are, but he did destroy
Hays's camp and also captured many of his horses.[27]

The Jayhawkers were less pleased with Anthony's handling of the
fight on the Little Blue than was the lieutenant colonel himself. Indicative
of his and Jennison's relative rank in the esteem of their men is the remark
written by one of them to conclude his account of the fight with Hays:
"Tomorrow we expect . . . the Colonel then I reckon we will go down
and clean them out."[28]

Jennison arrived in Kansas City on November 12 with three companies of the regiment; and on the following day, the first half of
Captain Brown's company arrived also. Jennison greeted them with a
speech to delight any Ashtabula County abolitionist. He declared that he
would take all the Negroes he could from the secessionists, arm them,
form companies, battalions, and regiments of ex-slaves, set them to
fighting the rebels and, if the government did not support him, he would
"go on his own hook."[29] He let it be known also that he was having a
flag made for the Seventh in Boston, with a life-size portrait of John
Brown on it.

According to one contemporary source, namely George Caleb

26. For accounts of the fight, see Fox, "Story," 30; Utt, "Seventh Kansas"; and Daniel
Holmes to "Dear Folks," November 11, 1861, in Holmes Collection. The casualty figures given
in the text are from *Report of the Adjutant General of the State of Kansas, 1861–65: Military History
of Kansas Regiments* (Topeka, 1896), 93. Anthony, in a letter to his father dated November 24,
1861, in Langsdorf and Richmond (eds.), "Anthony," 355, gives the number of his wounded as
eight or nine.

27. Anthony to his father, November 24, 1861, in Langsdorf and Richmond (eds.), "Anthony," 355.

28. Daniel Holmes to "Dear Folks," November 11, 1861, in Holmes Collection.

29. *Ibid.*, postscript dated November 15, 1861.

Bingham, Jennison actually proceeded to act on his announced policy of enlisting Negroes to fight secession. Bingham wrote that "in order to impress the minds of our people with a becoming sense of his importance, [Jennison] pompously conducted his Regiment . . . through the Streets of our City. . . . Our population *beheld therein a company composed, exclusively, of negroes, armed, uniformed and mounted as soldiers of the United States and headed by a slave.* . . . This slave shortly afterwards exhibited to me a paper, in which his rank as an officer, was acknowledged over the well known signature of Jennison." [30]

If Bingham's story is true, it would confer on Jennison the distinction of being the first to enlist and use Negroes as soldiers in a regularly mustered Civil War regiment. The chronological context in which Bingham's statement occurs indicates that he is speaking of the arrival of the Jayhawkers in Kansas City on Saturday evening, November 9. It is a matter of record that it was Anthony, not Jennison, who led five companies, and not the entire regiment, into Kansas City that day. Neither Anthony nor any other member of the regiment whose letters or diaries survive, or who wrote about the regiment after the war, makes any mention of Bingham's company of Negroes. Had such a company existed, Anthony at least, writing to his abolitionist family, would surely have boasted of it. [31] Every Union regiment operating in or near slave territory had its retinue of Negro campfollowers, cooks, grooms, and casual hangers-on, and the Seventh Kansas had its share; as Daniel Holmes of Company D wrote: "Negroes are very plenty around our camp every mess has a negro cook and the cry is still they come." [32] The letter in which Bingham speaks of the company of Negroes was written only three months after the event it describes and is therefore essentially a contemporary document. But the company of uniformed and armed Negroes is only one entry in a shrill tale of Jennison's many misdeeds and is a part of a hysterical abuse of the hated jayhawker. It is possible that

30. Bingham to James S. Rollins, February 12, 1862, in Rollins, "Letters of Bingham," 52.

31. Typical of the Anthony family attitude toward Negroes is the following, quoted from a letter Susan B. Anthony wrote her family in 1839: "Since school today I have had the unspeakable satisfaction of visiting four colored people and drinking tea with them." See Dorr, *Susan B. Anthony*, 28.

32. Daniel Holmes to "Dear Folks," November 11, 1861, in Holmes Collection. Holmes wrote that every "mess" of from four to twelve Jayhawkers had its own Negro cook, the standard compensation being rations, clothing, and one dollar per month.

Bingham mistook a group of Negro cooks and grooms, dressed as was usually the case in scraps and bits of uniform and riding jayhawked horses, for a regular company of troopers. It is equally possible—and would have been quite in character—that Jennison deliberately staged a charade for the benefit of unionists like Bingham, by having a number of cooks and grooms dress in parts of the uniform and carry weapons belonging to the troopers, for the occasion of their entry into Kansas City.

The advance detachment of Captain Brown's company received a fast exposure to warfare in the manner of the Kansas-Missouri border; for on the morning after their arrival in Kansas City, they participated in the first raid of the regiment to Independence.[33] In comparison with a number of later forays of the Seventh against the same unfortunate city, this was a milk-and-water affair. There is some question whether Anthony or Jennison was in command on this occasion; it would appear that Anthony was in charge, Jennison being unable to go because of illness. On the way to Independence, the regiment persuaded a number of Missouri farmers to sign deeds of forfeiture. One large grist mill and a number of houses, perhaps a half-dozen, were burned, forty to fifty slaves were liberated, and about fifty horses and mules and a few carriages were jayhawked. Some stores, the number variously reported as two and as "three or four," were plundered.[34] On this visit, or on a second, ten days later, there was a watered-down reenactment of Jennison's "Independence Corral"; the male inhabitants were assembled in the courthouse square, and Anthony made them a speech on the iniquities of slavery, secession, and guerilla warfare. But except for the plundering of a few stores, the Seventh did not on this occasion indulge in the wholesale looting that distinguished or disgraced its operations in

33. This portion of Company K had been mustered in at Fort Leavenworth on November 7. See Fox, "Story," 25.

34. Daniel Holmes to "Dear Folks," November 11, 1861, postscript dated November 15, 1861, in Holmes Collection; also Webster Moses to Nancy Mowry, December 4, 1861, in Moses Letters. Even Bingham does not accuse the Jayhawkers of anything worse than the burning of a mill and five or six houses. See Bingham to James S. Rollins, February 12, 1862, in "Letters of Bingham," 53. An undated slip of paper attached to a letter dated December 9, 1908, from Simeon Fox to George W. Martin, in Fox Papers, states, "Col. Anthony wrote me . . . 'I made this speech to the citizens of Independence while they were coralled in the court house yard. I was in command of the expedition.'"

Missouri in the three months that followed. The men were kept under a tight rein on this occasion at least; the regimental clown, a member of Company A, was beaten by Anthony for marching about wearing a woman's bonnet that he had picked up somewhere.[35] Nevertheless, some of the men, exposed for the first time to the real meaning of jayhawking, were shocked by the experience. Fletcher Pomeroy wrote in his diary:

I will never forget our introduction to the destructiveness of war. Company H was advance guard, marching about one fourth of a mile in advance of the main column. . . . As we marched along, we suddenly discovered a building on fire a short distance in advance. . . . We wondered how it got afire, but we soon learned. We had gone but a little further when a turn in the road brought us in sight of a house. Women and children were fleeing to the woods while members of the advance guard were smashing in the windows and firing the house. Across the street were several stacks of wheat and oats; these were also fired.[36]

Not a pretty picture; it was not in western Missouri that the moonlight and magnolia version of the Civil War was fought. And much worse was to follow. As Pomeroy remarked, "This was but the A. B. C. of what occurred during the next few months."

---

35. Fox, "Early History," 239, n., quoting a letter from E. N. Morrill of Company C.

36. Pomeroy, "War Diary," 15. In Albert Castel's version, *Frontier State*, 58, this becomes, "Company H rode one-fourth mile ahead of the main column as the advance guard. Its movements were marked by the flames of burning houses and wheat *fields*." (italics ours) Any Missouri wheat field still unharvested in *November* is not worth burning, if, indeed, it can be burned at all.

CHAPTER VI

The Scourge of War

BETWEEN THE first visit of the Seventh Kansas to Independence on November 14 and its second visit only ten days later, the character of the regiment underwent a noticeable change for the worse. This change is clearly visible in the actions of the regiment in the next three months; there is a palpable coarsening and deterioration of the moral fiber of its members. Jayhawking ceases to be a pastime to be joked about, a comic sideline of soldiering in enemy country. It becomes undisguised ruffianism and robbery, an accepted way of life, to which soldiering is incidental. And hand in hand with robbery go violence and brutality toward the civilian population.

In January, 1862, Major General Henry W. Halleck, who had succeeded the luckless Fremont in command of what was now called the Department of the Missouri, found it necessary to inform the adjutant general of the army that "Jennison's men . . . do not belong in this department. . . . I have directed General Pope to drive them out, or, if they resist, to disarm them and hold them prisoners. They are no better than a band of robbers; they cross the line, rob, steal, plunder, and burn whatever they can lay their hands upon. They disgrace the name and uniform of American soldiers and are driving good Union men into the ranks of the secession army. . . . If the Government countenances such acts . . . it may resign all hopes of a pacification of Missouri."[1]

General Halleck's censure was not more severe than the behavior of the Seventh warranted. These actions are amply documented. To give an account of the misdeeds the Jayhawkers committed in Missouri presents no problems in documentation, however distasteful the task may be. But to account for such conduct, to explain why and how it began, why and how it grew progressively worse, is very nearly impossible. Was it all the fault of Jennison and Anthony? To a considerable degree it was, for it is impossible to believe that even a newly raised, poorly disciplined regiment would have conducted itself as did the Seventh, in direct opposition to the wishes of its commanding officers. If this is conceded, Anthony must be assigned by far the larger share of the blame attaching to the commander of the regiment; he is condemned by his own statement, written in March, 1862, that "Col Jennison has been col of this regimt six months and *has yet to give the first command* to them—I have always commanded them—Have been with them in all their expeditions into the enemy's country except one time Jennison went to Independence."[2] Anthony's own words are borne out by the statements of Simeon Fox, who has recorded that "Colonel Jennison never for a minute commanded the Seventh Kansas in person on any raid or during any field operation in Missouri. . . . I never knew how or where . . . [he] spent a large portion of his time, or by what authority, other than his own, he was absent from his command. . . . An occasional orderly—his means of communication with the regiment—would sometimes intimate that he was solacing the tedium of existence by . . . draw poker."[3]

Anthony was not one to minimize the importance of his deeds and accomplishments in his letters to his family, and Fox dearly loved a good story; but even if allowance is made for the probable exaggeration in both their statements, it would appear nonetheless that Anthony had a far more direct and constant influence on the actions of the regiment than did Jennison. And Anthony's attitude toward jayhawking was made abundantly clear in a letter to his brother-in-law, Aaron McLean, in

1. *Official Records*, VIII, 507.

2. Anthony to Aaron McLean, March 1, 1862, in Langsdorf and Richmond (eds.), "Anthony," 362.

3. Fox, "Early History," 240.

which he boasted of having taken "a Secesh Stallion worth [$] 1,000 and a Grey horse worth [$] 200," and went on to ask McLean, "dont you want to come out here and speculate in cattle—horses and mules—there is a good chance to buy cheap—and stock a large farm here at little expense."[4] There can be little doubt about the provenance of the cattle, horses, and mules that McLean was to buy cheaply, or about the identity of the sellers.

As to Jennison's attitude toward jayhawking, nothing need be added to what has already been said about that gentleman's opinion of the sanctity of property belonging to rebels. In November and December, 1861, he began to use a phrase that became one of his favorites; the Seventh, he said, was a "Self-Sustaining Regiment," meaning that it took from the "rebels" in Missouri, and turned over to the army quartermasters, food, draft animals, grain, cattle, and other property, worth more than the cost of the regiment to the government.[5] He was to boast that the Seventh had gone into Missouri with six days' supply of army rations, stayed there for three months, living entirely off the country, and "came out with ninety days' rations ahead."[6]

Jennison's and Anthony's orders to the regiment on the subject of jayhawking were certainly unexceptionable. On November 16 it was announced: "If any soldier after this date shall enter a private house and take or steal any property or in any way do violence to any private citizen or make any violent demonstrations towards private citizens without orders, the penalty for such offenses in the Articles of War shall be visited upon the offender and he shall be shot."[7] And a week later this order was reinforced by another which declared that "captains com-

4. Anthony to Aaron McLean, December 3, 1861, in Langsdorf and Richmond (eds.), "Anthony," 356. When Anthony wrote this letter, the government was paying $110–$130 for cavalry mounts.

5. Chaplain Ayres boasted that "As near as I can learn our regiment since it took the field has considerably more than paid its way. According to the Quarter Masters reports we have turned in to government some $1800 more than their expenditures." See Ayres to Liman Langdon, December 29, 1861, in Samuel Ayres Collection. Daniel Holmes wrote that "Our regiment while in Missouri has been self sustaining, we have turned in to the government some twenty thousand dollars worth of property." See Holmes to "Dear Folks at home," December 8, 1861, in Holmes Collection.

6. Unidentified clipping, reporting a speech by Jennison, delivered apparently in the fall of 1862 in Doniphan County, Kansas, in Jennison Scrapbook.

7. General Orders No. 7, in Seventh Kansas, Regimental Order Book.

manding companies . . . will hereafter be held personally responsible for the acts of the soldiers under their separate commands."[8]

These were fair words, but no one in the regiment, knowing as they did Jennison's and Anthony's real feelings towards the rebels and slaveowners of Missouri, was taken in by them for a moment. They knew that these dire threats were for official consumption and not intended to be taken seriously. They acted accordingly, and the process once begun, it was in the nature of things that it should have become steadily worse. A soldier encouraged to steal for the quartermaster will not be stopped from stealing for his own account, certainly not by a lieutenant colonel riding a stolen horse. Also, it may be taken as axiomatic that for every dollar's worth of property turned over to the quartermaster, the men kept two—or more. Only a genius of casuistry could have explained to the troopers of the Seventh the ethical difference between the lawful stealing of food and animals from the "rebels" and the unlawful stealing of such things as photograph albums, furniture, money, and silverware. Moreover, in an area where loyalties were usually uncertain and as often as not open to legitimate suspicion, it was inevitable that the loyal should be plundered no less than the disloyal. And the final, quickly reached stage in this grim process was to resort to force and brutality when mere threats, actual or implied, did not produce loot, or did not produce it fast enough.

Beyond the example and encouragement of their commanding officers, another circumstance may be pleaded in partial extenuation of the conduct of the Jayhawkers toward the civilian population of Missouri. By the winter of 1861, and in fact long before then, atrocities against enemy civilians had become an accepted part of border mores and were condemned only when they were committed against one's own side. Secessionist Missourians committed them against unionist Missourians and vice versa. "For several weeks" prior to July, 1861, months before the Seventh Kansas was organized, Union men from southwestern Missouri sought refuge in Kansas from the "cruel and relentless" persecution that had forced them to leave their homes.[9] Lane's troops

8. General Orders No. 7 [sic], November 23, 1861, ibid.
9. Despatch from Camp Morris, Vernon County, Missouri, July 10, 1861, undated clipping, Leavenworth Conservative, Jennison Scrapbook.

plundered the Missouri countryside through which they passed to such an extent that, in the condemnatory despatches about the "depredations" of Federal troops in northwestern Missouri, the Lane Brigade is usually mentioned in the same breath with Jennison's regiment. General Halleck, for example, wrote that "the conduct of the forces under Lane and Jennison has done more for the enemy in this State than could have been accomplished by 20,000 of his own army. I receive almost daily complaints of the outrages committed by these men in the name of the United States, and the evidence is so conclusive as to leave no doubt of their correctness." [10]

One of the most graphic accounts of jayhawking from the point of view, of those who experienced it, describes incidents that occurred before the arrival of the Seventh in Missouri.[11] The Seventh Kansas did not originate jayhawking; nevertheless, Jennison's own reputation was such, and the words "Jennison's Jayhawkers" rolled so easily and smoothly off the tongue, that the Seventh became the universal villain and was credited with many atrocities committed by others, as well as with all of its own. As Simeon Fox summed up the situation, "internecine strife was continuous with the people themselves, and when the Seventh Kansas first came into Missouri, the desolate monuments that marked the destruction of barns and dwellings were to be seen with pitiful frequency; and yet it is fashionable to charge this desolation to the regiment that became heir to the name of 'Jayhawkers.' What this regiment actually did is sin enough, but it is a very small part when compared to the whole." [12]

A major cause of the atrocities committed by Kansas troops—the Seventh among them—in Missouri in 1861 was without doubt the bitter hostility against all Missourians that had been engendered during the years of border troubles. In a speech to his regiment on Washington's Birthday, 1862, Jennison declared:

I am proud of this regiment, proud of its officers and men. It has passed through the bloody baptism of no great battle, but, nevertheless, it is known, and

10. *Official Records*, VIII, 449.
11. Margaret J. (Mrs. Upton) Hays to her mother, November 12, 1861; Doerschuk (ed.), "Extracts from War-Time Letters," 100–102.
12. Fox, "Early History," 242.

known by its works. It is a regiment which has statistics. Organized in October, it has brought out from bondage a little over seventeen hundred slaves. Its captures of rebel property foot up to large figures in Quartermaster returns. But October was not our birthday. For six long years we have fought as guerillas, what we are now fighting as a regiment. This is a war that dates way back of Fort Sumter. On the cold hillside, in swamps and fens, behind rocks and trees, since '54 we have made the long campaign.[13]

Kansans who participated in the Civil War and commented on this point after the war was over are unanimous in the opinion that along the border the war was a continuation in an aggravated form of the Kansas-Missouri vendetta of the prewar years; one of them wrote after the war: "Men riding solitary were shot down; little companies killed by their camp fires; men fighting on both sides neither asking, giving nor expecting mercy."[14] And even those who in later years came to deplore the atrocities and the remorseless character of this war considered its horrors to be the inevitable result of what had gone before. The old scores left over from the Kansas-Missouri troubles of the fifties called for settlement, and the Seventh Kansas, although only a little more than half its members were Kansans, helped to settle them.

A final, but vital, point needs mention to round out the picture. It is one of the commonplaces of Civil War historiography that among the regularly enlisted troops that fought the war there was no hatred of the enemy. Pathological hatred of the other side, and an equally pathological blood lust, were confined to the mountains of eastern Kentucky and Tennessee, and to the Kansas-Missouri border.[15] The common denominator in these two widely separated areas was the existence in both of widespread guerilla activity. Between the end of the wars of religion in the seventeenth century and the bestialities of World War II, wars between civilized nations were fought with some degree of moderation. Except in the heat of battle, soldiers of opposing armies treated each other humanely, and civilians living in the path of the armies were reasonably safe in person, if not always in property. But guerillas, under whatever

13. Report in the Leavenworth *Conservative*, February 6, 1864, clipping in Jennison Scrapbook.

14. Palmer, "Black Flag Character," 459.

15. Readers with strong stomachs may consult Thomas F. Berry, *Four Years with Morgan and Forrest* (Oklahoma City, 1914), and Thurman Sensing, *Champ Ferguson, Confederate Guerilla* (Nashville, 1942).

name they were known, franc-tireurs, partisans, or bushwhackers, have always been outside the pale. Hated and feared by legitimate soldiers, guerillas have always been the target of the utmost ferocity of every army that has had to deal with them, and with good reason. The civilian inhabitants of areas of guerilla activity, indistinguishable from the guerillas for the very good reason that is what many of them were, have been spared none of the horrors of war because, in enemy eyes, they were either guerillas themselves, or else fed, harbored, and supplied with information those who were.

Under the best of circumstances, the civilian population of western Missouri would have suffered hardships and losses inseparable from the presence of armies among them, but they were themselves partly to blame for the extent to which these hardships and losses exceeded the norm. This was the price they had to pay for the privilege of actively supporting a cause that others considered to be treason. Unquestionably, many of those who suffered were as sincerely unionist in sentiment and as innocent of guerilla activity as were the troopers who drove off their livestock and burned their houses. Among the soldiers, it was an article of faith that all guerillas were demons, that they "supported themselves by robbery, by plundering homes and villages, wrecking and robbing trains, attacking weakly protected supply trains and ambushing soldiers." [16] And to expect soldiers who have just been shot at from ambush by men not wearing uniform to conduct a judicial inquiry to separate the innocent from the guilty and to punish only those proven guilty beyond the shadow of a doubt, is to expect the impossible. This is not the way soldiers with guns in their hands behave, whatever their nationality, and neither the armies that fought the Civil War, nor, specifically, Jennison's regiment, was an exception to the rule.

Before the Seventh is condemned for its behavior in an area in which guerilla activity was endemic, one may well consider how the regiment should have dealt with " 'professors' of union sentiment who would take the oath of allegiance in the forenoon and in the afternoon shoot you from behind a thicket of brush, or in the night saw the timbers of railroad bridges, letting car loads of men, women and children down fearful chasms to instant death, and next day be found at home . . . as good

16. Palmer, "Black Flag Character," 460.

Union men as anybody." [17] In the minds of those to whom bushwhackers were a daily and hourly peril, such words were not mere platitudes or lame excuses for conduct that was felt to require justification. A member of a unionist company organized at Warrensburg, Missouri, writes that while the train carrying his unit was moving through a deep cut, it was ambushed by a band of guerillas. The bushwhackers fired down on the heads of the soldiers, crowded into wooden freight cars, and gravely wounded several of them. When the soldiers moved to the attack, all but three of the guerillas, whose horses broke free before they could mount, escaped on horseback. The three guerillas who were left behind were captured and shot out of hand, and several houses along the right of way were burned. [18]

The following incident, involving two troopers of the Seventh, occurred in January, 1862:

Two of our men who were acting as scouts . . . called at a house just outside of our lines in the early evening. The family, a man and his wife and grown daughter, offered them refreshments. . . . They appeared very friendly, and pressed the boys to stay over night. . . . After a pleasant hour or two the daughter left the room. Some time later the parents excused themselves. . . . Almost immediately shots were fired in through the window. . . . One of the men was killed. The other was badly wounded . . . but succeeded in escaping out into the darkness . . . and came into camp. . . . A company was sent out to the place at once. The dead comrade had been thrown out into the slush and had frozen down, so that the body had to be cut loose with an axe. The house was deserted. [19]

Not surprisingly, the dead Jayhawker's comrades burned down the house before they returned to camp.

When such incidents as these, some not so evil, others far worse, become commonplace, atrocities that are at first committed as legitimate retaliation are in the end perpetrated without any excuse, simply out of

17. John Brown, Jr., to Palmer Pillsbury, July 18, 1862, copy in Kansas State Historical Society, Topeka. Allan Nevins cites the following example: "Secessionist guerillas, after firing into many passenger trains, on September 6 [1861; actually September 3, and the early date of the incident is significant] weakened a 160-foot bridge over the Little Platte so that . . . it collapsed under a train loaded with 80 or 90 men, women and children." See Nevins, *Improvised War*, 332. Richard Brownlee adds that some twenty of the passengers were killed and sixty injured. See *Gray Ghosts*, 24.

18. George S. Grover, "Civil War in Missouri," *Missouri Historical Review*, VIII (1913), 19–20.

19. Pomeroy, "War Diary," entry for January 28, 1862.

habit, and in anticipation of the atrocities the other side will assuredly commit whenever it has the opportunity to do so.[20]

As far as the Seventh is concerned, it began to earn its reputation when word reached Kansas City of the destruction of the government train bound for Sedalia. Two days after Anthony made his threat of vengeance if the train were molested, he and his men put to the torch the area about Pleasant Hill in Cass County, southwest of Kansas City; an eyewitness has written that the day of this burning, a Sunday, was still called Jennison's Day thirty-five years later by those old enough to have seen it.[21] Looting of course went hand in hand with the arson. On this expedition, the eight companies led by Anthony had to run the gauntlet of guerillas, who captured four of the Jayhawkers at a cost to themselves of eleven killed.[22]

This punitive expedition to Pleasant Hill inaugurated a period of violence, much of it senseless. On November 22 the regiment returned to Kansas City. That evening about forty men, most of them belonging to Companies C and H, broke open a store and stole several thousand dollars' worth of goods and money.[23] On the following night, Lieutenant Isaac J. Hughes of Company D, familiarly known as "Shang" Hughes, shot Private James C. Murphy of Company B for disobeying orders; Murphy, it was said, drew his revolver on the lieutenant, and Hughes shot and killed him.[24] The same night, Joseph Raymond of Company C, a Mexican, raped "a common prostitute of the town, who, however, drew the line at Mexicans and resisted his advances"; the

20. An example of retaliation: in a fight at Morristown, Missouri, the Eleventh Kansas, not, be it noted, the Seventh, took prisoner a number of guerillas. Seven of them, chosen at random, were sentenced to death by a drumhead court-martial. Their graves were dug and they were executed by a firing squad. They were shot in retaliation for the killing of seven troopers of the Eleventh Kansas after they had been taken prisoner. Palmer, "Black Flag Character," 456.

21. Miller, *Missouri's Memorable Decade*, 73.

22. Anthony to his father, November 24, 1861, in Langsdorf and Richmond (eds.), "Anthony," 354–55.

23. Webster Moses to Nancy Mowry, December 4, 1861, in Moses Letters.

24. The *Report of the Adjutant General of the State of Kansas* gives November 20 as the date of Murphy's death. Anthony, in a letter to his father, November 24, 1861, in Langsdorf and Richmond (eds.), "Anthony," 355, and Webster Moses, in a letter to Nancy Mowry, December 4, 1861, in Moses Letters, both date it November 23, although Moses erroneously identifies Murphy as a member of Company C. The day after Murphy was shot, Jennison announced that "Henceforth, any person belonging to this regiment, who shall draw a revolver upon his superior officer, will be *courtmartialed and shot*." See General Orders No. 8, November 24, 1861, in Seventh Kansas, Regimental Order Book.

following morning he was tried by court-martial, convicted, sentenced to death, and executed.[25] In letters written for home consumption, members of the regiment reported that Raymond was executed for "stealing and breaking open houses" or for stealing "some property," a curious bit of Victorian squeamishness.[26] The men thought, however, that the death sentence was too severe and the execution unjust—an example of Anthony's tyranny—and they resented it accordingly.

Raymond faced the firing squad at 9 A.M. on November 24. As soon as the formalities of the military execution were over, the regiment marched to Independence. From there, a few days later, a squad of fifteen men, under the command of Lieutenant Francis M. Ray of Company C, was sent north, to an area called Crackers' Neck, with a list of a dozen farmhouses to be burned. An old man—a Union man who had been driven out of the neighborhood—accompanied Lieutenant Ray to identify the houses to be burned. All twelve were put to the torch. Simeon Fox, who, together with E. N. Morrill, a future governor of Kansas, was on this expedition, asserts firmly that Ray maintained strict discipline and permitted no looting, not even of the houses marked for burning. Why were the twelve houses ordered burned? None of the fifteen-man detail knew; they merely obeyed orders.[27]

If Fox's report is accurate, Lieutenant Ray and his men showed much greater self-restraint on their expedition to Crackers' Neck than did their lieutenant colonel back in Independence. A German resident of Lexington, hearing that the regiment was nearby, came to Independence to escape persecution by his secessionist neighbors, to whom all "crop-eared Dutch" were automatically suspect as congenital "nigger-lovers" and abolitionists. The German visited the camp of the regiment and was prevailed upon to enlist in the Seventh. The weather had turned cold, and since the man was insufficiently clothed, some of the soldiers of Company G, which he was to join, "procured" an overcoat for him from a nearby store and, to indicate his status as a recruit, gave him a regulation belt with a large "U.S." buckle on it. Anthony happened to see the

---

25. Simeon Fox to George W. Martin, December 13, 1908, in Fox Papers.

26. "Stealing and breaking open homes," Webster Moses to Nancy Mowry, December 4, 1861, in Moses Letters; stealing "some property," Anthony to his father, November 24, 1861, in Langsdorf and Richmond (eds.), "Anthony," 355.

27. Simeon Fox to George W. Martin, December 8, 1908, in Fox Papers.

man on the street and demanded to know where he had gotten the overcoat and belt. The man tried to explain in his broken English but was unable to make himself understood. Anthony ordered him to take off the overcoat and belt. Instead of obeying at once, the German tried to protest, whereupon Anthony became angry and belabored him unmercifully over the head and shoulders with the flat of his saber. When the unfortunate German started to run to escape the beating, Anthony drew his revolver and threatened to shoot. The trooper of Company G who tells the story adds that this was "but one of several similar exhibitions on the part of Anthony" that he witnessed while the latter had command of the regiment.[28]

By the end of November, Anthony was no longer alone in mistreating those who were unable to defend themselves. On the twenty-eighth, under circumstances that can no longer be established, some members of the regiment killed a secessionist prisoner who may or may not have been a guerilla caught red-handed. The same Webster Moses who a scant two months before had boasted to his sweetheart that there were no tobacco or whiskey users in his "mess" and that they read a chapter of the Bible before "Lights Out" every evening, merely reported: "28th We shot a secesh prisoner."[29] If Bingham is to be believed, this was not the only killing of which the troopers of the Seventh were guilty at this time. They killed a Missourian "in an altercation growing out of his refusal to supply his murderer with liquor." Another unfortunate, who owned three valuable mules and tried to save them from being confiscated by swimming them across the Missouri, "was rudely accosted by a squad of 'Jennison's men.' Justly apprehending personal violence, he began to move out of their way, when one of them advanced upon the harmless, defenseless man and deliberately shot him down."[30] The painter's rhetoric and his lavish use of adjectives inspire an instinctive distrust of his tales, and his bias is apparent; but the essential facts underlying these stories can hardly have been invented. There is little doubt that there

28. Lyman, "Reminiscences."
29. Webster Moses to Nancy Mowry, December 4, 1861, in Moses Letters.
30. Bingham to James S. Rollins, February 12, 1862, in Rollins (ed.), "Letters of Bingham," 55–56. Bingham, a resident of Kansas City, speaks of the two men killed as "our Citizens." Richard S. Brownlee, who cites these stories without giving his source, which is evidently the Bingham letter, states that the killings occurred in Independence, and improves on Bingham by stating that the Seventh killed "at least" two men. See *Gray Ghosts*, 47.

were men in the Seventh who were capable of shooting down a Missourian with much less compunction than they would shoot down a dog.

At the end of November, the rumor spread that General Sterling Price was again marching north through Missouri with a large army, and that he had promised his troops a "wide sweep" into Kansas.[31] The threatened invasion did not materialize, but the baseless rumor that Price was coming produced a marked increase in guerilla activity in the area south of Kansas City. Moreover, a short time before, Price had discharged the three-month units that had joined him in his northward march in August; and the men of these disbanded units, bringing their arms home with them, provided large reinforcements for the guerilla bands already in operation and the manpower for new ones. Colonel Montgomery, then stationed with his regiment at Osawatomie, reported that the countryside for miles around swarmed with guerillas.[32] To deal with this situation, the Seventh, which had returned to Fort Leavenworth on December 4, was ordered to West Point, in Bates County, Missouri, to "protect the frontier of Kansas from incursions of the rebel bands now in that neighborhood."[33]

After its arrival at West Point, the Seventh scouted over a wide area, to Kansas City, Independence, and elsewhere. On one of these scouts, the regimental sergeant major, William A. Pease, was guilty of misconduct that cost him his stripes. On December 28 Anthony preferred charges against him "for disobedience of orders and mutinous and unsoldierly conversations with the men, and unfitness for the position." The charge of disobeying orders grew out of the fact that, on the march from Independence to Kansas City on the previous day, Pease had "deserted the ranks twice after being ordered not to leave the ranks." The charge of using mutinous language sheds a curious and far from creditable light

31. *Official Records*, VIII, 374, 398, and 399.

32. *Ibid.*, 415.

33. On December 4 Jennison was ordered to turn over to Colonel Weir "such stores and other public property as are not absolutely necessary for the use of his troops, and then return with his regiment to Fort Leavenworth." See Special Orders No. 4, December 4, 1861, in Seventh Kansas, Regimental Order Book. The Seventh was ordered to return to Missouri by Special Orders No. 7, December 10, 1861. See *ibid.* and *Official Records*, VIII, 423. The Seventh had left for Missouri several days before December 10, presumably pursuant to verbal orders confirmed on the tenth. Curiously, the December 10 orders were issued by authority of General J. W. Denver, who did not officially assume command of "all the troops within the State of Kansas" until December 21 or 22. *Official Records*, VIII, 456.

on the relations between officers and men in these early days of the regiment. In Independence, on December 26, the men camped in the open. The officers, on the other hand, put up at the local hotel. Pease came to the hotel with the report that the men were saying that "if [the] officers did not come over and camp with them, they would burn their quarters." Pease not only failed to reprimand the men for voicing these threats, but egged them on by saying that officers ought not to have better quarters than the men, and if the hotel were burned down over their heads it would only serve them right.[34]

The Seventh was stationed in the West Point-Morristown area for two months and, with Anthony in command for most of that time, led what Fox called "the strenuous life."[35] Only twice during this period is Jennison's presence with the regiment definitely established. On December 28 he turned up in camp accompanied by his wife; what he did, apart from enjoying (or enduring) a serenade tendered him by the twenty-two buglers of the regiment, does not appear in the records. Nearly a month later, on January 23, he was present at a regimental dress parade. Life was strenuous not only for the regiment, the colonel always excepted, but also for the Missourians who had the ill fortune to have the regiment quartered in their midst. In weather that became progressively worse, with spells of severe cold alternating with snow, sleet, and rain, the men lived in four-man wedge tents and spent much of their time away from camp on lengthy scouts over nearly impassable roads. The troopers suffered, but the Missourians about them suffered even more. On the march to West Point, the regiment liberated 150 slaves and took four hundred horses, mules, and head of cattle. One pro-Missouri historian asks the reader to believe, as an indication of the vast amount of plunder taken by the Seventh on this march, that it was followed to West Point by a train of Negroes, livestock, and wagons loaded with loot, four or five miles long—a patent absurdity.[36] Every house but one along the line

34. Anthony to Jennison, December 28, 1861, in Seventh Kansas, Regimental Order Book.
35. Fox, "Story," 28.
36. Herklotz, "Jayhawkers in Missouri," 73–74. The statement is made without the citation of authority (but probably based on Miller, *Missouri's Memorable Decade*, 75: "One hundred and fifty soldiers of our glorious union . . . carried off a train of stock and richly loaded wagons four to five miles long.") by a historian who in all possible contexts shows a strong pro-Missouri and anti-Jennison bias. Since a six-mule army wagon, allowing for normal intervals, took up forty feet of road, one is tempted to question the tale of a train "four to five miles long."

of march was put to the torch; and as the column moved southward, it could see for miles, off to the left, on the Missouri side of the road, columns of smoke from burning houses and barns set alight by the flankers.

The behavior of the Seventh on this march was so widely publicized in the Kansas newspapers that Brigadier General J. W. Denver, then in command of all troops in Kansas, was forced to take cognizance of it. He had his adjutant write to Jennison:

The General has been informed through the newspapers and from other sources that a part of your command, whilst on their way to West Point, Mo., made an excursion into Missouri, capturing several prisoners and large quantities of stock.

As no report of this expedition has yet been received from the officer in command, the General desires to be furnished, as soon as practicable, with one, together with an inventory of the prisoners and stock captured, and the disposition made of same, and should any of it have been sold, a list of the purchasers and prices obtained for the same.

In the future a like report and inventory will be required at these headquarters of every expedition into the enemy's country made from your command.[37]

The Jayhawkers, with western Missouri at their mercy, were not to be frightened into penitence, much less into a reformation, by threats, implied or expressed, from on high. General Denver's admonition was duly copied into the Regimental Letter and Order Book, but apparently was not even answered. If it had any result other than to provide the adjutant with a few minutes' occupation, there is no indication of it.

A somewhat credulous historian, whose objectivity is something less than impeccable, claims that on this same march to West Point "at least a dozen persons were killed because they were southern sympathizers."[38] No authority is cited for the statement, and it is quoted only to show that any story, however extreme, about the viciousness of the Seventh, was accepted as gospel by its contemporaries and is repeated without further investigation by modern historians as well. If the "dozen persons" were actually killed, was it because of their political sympathies or because they gave a practical expression to these sympathies by doing a little bushwhacking? Not that the Seventh was wholly blameless in such

37. Captain C. Francis Clarke to Jennison, December 28, 1861, in Seventh Kansas, Regimental Letter and Order Book.
38. Herklotz, "Jayhawkers in Missouri," 74.

matters. Chaplain Ayres wrote a friend that "on their march our regiment took a number of prisoners some of whom on investigation were dismissed on their taking the oath of fidelity to our government whilest others have been sent to Kansas city for safekeeping as a general thing we do not calculate to take many prisnors for we have no place for them."[39]

What became of the "prisnors" for whom the Jayhawkers had "no place"? Ayres does not say. If they were bushwhackers or guerillas, their fate is easily guessed. A visitor to the camp of the Seventh wrote with obvious approval: "If there was ever a band of destroying angels in one congregation, I saw them there. They take no prisoners and are not troubled with red tape or sentimentalism in any form."[40] One must remember, not as an excuse for the conduct of the Seventh, but as the frame of reference within which that conduct must be judged, that "with the guerillas and bushwhackers, there was no quarter given or taken."[41]

During December and January the large area extending twenty-five to thirty miles eastward from West Point and Morristown, where the regiment moved on a bitterly cold Christmas Eve, in a blizzard howling down from the north, was thoroughly "sifted" of slaves, livestock, and moveable wealth of all kinds. The detachments sent out to hunt for the small bands of guerillas holed up for shelter in ravines and patches of timber invariably came back to camp loaded with loot. West Point itself, a thriving border town only a few months earlier, was nearly depopulated when the Seventh moved from there to Morristown; and even Chaplain Ayres, whose heart was hardened against secessionists, was moved to exclaim, "O how *desolate.*"[42] Morristown had already been plundered by the Seventh before it moved there, and raids were made thence to Rose Hill, Dayton, Pleasant Hill, and Harrisonburg. It was the same everywhere, a grim tale of arson and looting. At Harrisonburg, where, unaccountably, another unit got in ahead of the Jayhawkers, the depository of the American Bible Society had been looted, before the Seventh arrived, of everything but its stock of Bibles. The Seventh, finding nothing else to take, took the Bibles.

---

39. Ayres to Liman Langdon, in Samuel Ayres Collection.
40. John J. Ingalls to his brother, January 2, 1862, in John Ingalls Papers, Kansas State Historical Society, Topeka.
41. Palmer, "Black Flag Character," 459.
42. Ayres to Liman Langdon, February 17, 1862, in Samuel Ayres Collection.

What became of all the loot? The quartermaster got some, as Jennison claimed, but the government's share could not have been more than a small fraction of the whole. Much of the food and grain taken from the "secesh" went to feed the regiment and its horses. As Daniel Holmes explained to his sister: "We . . . live quite well, not from what we draw from the commissary but what we jayhawked I dont suppose you know the meaning of that word that means when we are traveling through secesh country we come to the home of some leading secesh, or of some man in the secesh army, then we take his horses and property, burn his house, &c, or as we say, clean them out, well, in the operation we generally get a young hog . . . some turkeys, chickens, &c. once in a while a crock of honey, then don't we live." [43] Living off the country when government rations gave out, or merely to vary the monotony of a steady diet of bacon, hardtack, and coffee, was not peculiar to the Seventh; nor, as far as military sins go, was it worse than venial. It is safe to say that there was not a single regiment on either side that did not at some time in its career raid henroosts, pigpens, and beehives, in friendly and enemy territory alike. And habitually ignored or evaded in all armies throughout the war were regimental orders such as those issued by Anthony on December 26, requiring company commanders to "see that no officer or soldier shoots or kills any fowls or stock. Also that no rails are burned or fences torn down. No one allowed without the lines without permission." [44]

The horses and mules taken from Missourians went in part to replace the steady wastage of cavalry mounts and draft animals belonging to the regiment; and in part, and probably in the majority of cases, the Kansas line being conveniently near, they were ridden or driven across the line and either taken home or sold. [45] There can be little question that the men, and the officers up to and including the colonel, did a thriving business in jayhawked livestock; it was not without reason that the pedigree of any handsome Kansas horse was jokingly given as "by Jennison—out of Missouri."

It is said that much of the loot taken in Missouri was subsequently sold

43. Holmes to his sister, December 21, 1861, in Holmes Collection.
44. Special Orders No. 16, December 16, 1861, in Seventh Kansas, Regimental Order Book.
45. Webster Moses to Nancy Mowry, February 9, 1862, in Moses Letters: "The Boys (soldiers) that live in Kansas stole most of the horses we had and took them home or sold them."

by Jennison "at his residence near Squiresville."[46] The historian who makes this statement, as well as Simeon Fox, mentions these sales in words which have sinister connotations. Fox, in fact, writes: "It has been said that Jennison profited by the sale of some of . . . [the jayhawked livestock] but it is understood that his active cooperator, when he resigned and sold his stock, told Jennison to whistle for his share."[47] There is obviously a story behind Fox's ambiguous words, a story he chose to leave untold; nor does he reveal the name of the mysterious "cooperator." Jennison's character, his past, as well as the mores of the Border, fully justify the suspicion that he profited from the sale of chattels jayhawked in Missouri. But to some degree, at least, these sales of plunder could have been of an innocent character, if the word "innocent" may be used at all in such a context; for a letter of Jennison's authorizes and instructs A. B. Squires of Squiresville, *by order of General Hunter,* "to dispose of any stock . . . in [his] possession and belonging to the United States, at private sale, where such disposition will in [his] judgment be more advantageous than a sale at auction."[48] Practically nothing is known of Jennison's finances, but he was clearly quite well to do, both during and after the war. He had apparently ceased practicing his profession some time before 1861, and he drew colonel's pay for something less than two of the four years that the war lasted. Except for an ostensibly legitimate, but highly suspicious, commercial venture in the early part of 1863, Jennison lacked any visible means of support beside his army pay, and it is a legitimate surmise that the homes and farms of Missouri were the principal source of his ample funds.

There was another way in which jayhawked livestock, wagons, agricultural implements, furniture, clothing, and household goods were disposed of. Jennison and Anthony were of the opinion that the owners of slaves owed their human property a debt. What could be more equitable than that they should be made to discharge that debt by being forced to contribute the goods and chattels their Negroes needed to start a new life in free Kansas? Thus, when in the middle of December a portion of the regiment made a circuit from West Point to Kansas City,

46. Herklotz, "Jayhawkers in Missouri," 74.
47. Fox, "Early History," 251.
48. Jennison to A. B. Squires, "by order of Maj. Gen. Hunter," January 8, 1862, in Seventh Kansas, Regimental Order Book.

Independence, Harrisonville, and back to West Point, and liberated 129 Negroes on the way, Anthony, in command of the detachment, "gave the negroes 60 Horses and mules a lot of oxen, 10 waggons & two carriages and all loaded down with Household Furniture—The negroes train into Kansas was over a mile long."[49] This is what it meant to be a "practical abolitionist," and Anthony's generosity with the property of others made it possible for the 129 ex-slaves to enter Leavenworth "in gay procession."[50]

If it is at all legitimate to classify some types of jayhawking as less blameworthy than others, most of the foregoing examples may perhaps qualify for admission to the less reprehensible category. But there cannot be two opinions about Lieutenant "Shang" Hughes's proceedings at Independence; he returned "loaded with jewelry" from the same expedition that produced Anthony's mile-long train of Negroes.[51] In introducing Company D, mention was made of the silver cups jayhawked by Webster Moses and sent to his sweetheart in Wyanet, Illinois. The circumstances in which the cups were taken were these:

When we were at Lone Jack A. Downing and about 10 of us went out jayhawking. We went before breakfast and stopped at a rich secesh and told them we wanted some breakfast while they were getting breakfast we caught their horses and took the best ones when we came to breakfast they did not have dishes enough the negroes sayed that they had them hid we asked the Gentleman where they were and he told us. we found some silver ware among the rest. I got the cupps. two silver Ladles and two sets spoons. they sayed that the spoons belonged to the children and I gave them back. I gave Downing one ladle and the other to Capt Merriman. . . . Some of the boys got in some places about $100.00 worth of silver and some got considerable money.[52]

This was the true face of jayhawking with the glamor and fine words removed. It is worthy of note that the expedition Moses writes about was made for the sole purpose of jayhawking, and it is equally noteworthy that Captain Merriman found it consonant with his status of officer and gentleman to accept a share of the loot. There was little danger that *he* would enforce orders against jayhawking.

49. Anthony to his father, December 22, 1861, in Langsdorf and Richmond (eds.), "Anthony," 356.
50. Daniel Wilder, *The Annals of Kansas* (Topeka, 1886), 274.
51. Webster Moses to Nancy Mowry, December 21, 1861, in Moses Letters.
52. Same to same, February 9, 1862, *ibid*. The incident Moses describes occurred on January 19.

There was an equal lack of glamor about an expedition led by Anthony to Dayton, Missouri, on December 31, or about another, led by Major Thomas P. Herrick to Columbus, Missouri, on January 6.

The scout to Dayton was made as a result of a rumor that a guerilla force of between 150 and 300 men was encamped there. When Anthony arrived at the town at dawn on New Year's Day with two hundred of his Jayhawkers and a twelve-pounder howitzer, no rebels were to be seen; they had scattered to the hills and woods. But they had undoubtedly been at Dayton, and Anthony therefore decided that the town had to be punished since it had "been used voluntarily by its inhabitants as a depot for recruiting and supplying the rebels." He caused all but one of the forty-six homes in the village to be burned, the one exception being the property of a Union man.[53]

The expedition to Columbus was indirectly the result of a plea for help. Three hundred rebels, under the command of a Colonel Elliott, had taken possession of Johnson County, about twenty miles due south of Lexington, and "were committing depredations upon Union men." A dozen of the latter came to Morristown to seek protection and the help of the Seventh to move their families to Kansas and safety. Major Herrick was given the job of dealing with Elliott, and on the morning of January 6, with three inches of snow on the ground, he left for Johnson County at the head of two hundred Jayhawkers.

What occurred at Columbus two days later is of quite minor importance. Nevertheless, it belongs in the history of the Seventh, and beyond that it deserves a prominent place in a work, as yet unwritten, on a fascinating aspect of the Civil War—namely, the fantastically wide gap that frequently exists between the official reports of an event and the informal accounts of the same event in the letters and diaries of participants who wrote about it with no axe to grind. Anthony stated in his official report that Herrick, finding no trace of Elliott on the way to Johnson County, sent Captain Merriman on a scout to Columbus on the morning of the eighth.[54] When he reached the town, Merriman was told by the inhabitants that there were no rebels in the vicinity. He then

---

53. *Official Records*, VIII, 45–46.

54. *Ibid.*, 46–47. Anthony gives the date of the Columbus affair as January 9, but all other accounts agree on January 8 as the date.

turned about to rejoin Herrick. He had gone no more than a half-mile when he was ambushed by Elliott and his men. Merriman was forced to retreat with the loss of five men killed; but now Captain Utt arrived on the scene with fifty men of Company A. Utt and Merriman joined forces and "scoured the brush for miles around" but found no trace of the enemy. They then returned to Columbus; and on the ground that it was "the rendezvous of Colonel Elliott" and that its inhabitants had been instrumental in making possible the ambush of Merriman's detachment, they put the town to the torch.

What actually happened at Columbus was altogether different. Captain Merriman's detachment, consisting of twenty-eight men of his own company and a few each from Companies H and K, arrived at Columbus on the morning of the eighth. Merriman did not know that Utt and his men had arrived there the day before, collected one hundred head of cattle in the neighborhood, and, at nightfall, made camp at the edge of town. While posting his sentries for the night, Utt captured three armed rebels—boys living nearby. During the night, the mother of two of them came to Utt's camp to intercede for her sons' lives. Utt agreed to release the three boys, and, as a return favor, they told him that he was to be attacked in the morning by Colonel Elliott and his two hundred rebels. Thus warned, Utt had his men in the saddle by daylight and, driving his herd of jayhawked cattle, was already several miles from Columbus when Merriman arrived there.

When Merriman's advance guard was a mile from Columbus, it was fired on by a few guerillas who retreated through the town before the cautious advance of the Jayhawkers. Having marched into the town, Merriman gave his men ten minutes to "strip" the single store Columbus possessed. He then decided that nothing was to be gained by chasing the few "secesh" his men had seen and that it was time to return to Morristown. He had hardly begun his retreat when he rode into Elliott's ambush. The Jayhawkers' horses, unused to gunfire, became unmanageable; and the entire detachment, less five men killed and three others thrown by their horses and taken prisoner, set off in a wild stampede. In a short while, they came up with Utt's detachment. Utt proposed to Merriman that they join forces, return to Columbus, and give Elliott a fight, but Merriman refused. This did not discourage the pugnacious Utt; he marched back to Columbus with only his own company, but Elliott was already gone. Utt then took possession of the town, and after burying Merriman's dead and burning and leveling every house with the exception of one inhabited by a poor northern family, he too departed to rejoin Major Herrick.[55]

Company D First Sergeant Daniel Holmes of Princeton, Illinois, was a student at Wheaton College when the war broke out. A somewhat self-consciously sensitive lad, he confessed to a repugnance for "that overexertion of the brain that will undermine one's constitution, destroy his health and happiness besides weakening his mental powers" and expressed a fondness for "communings with nature" in preference to "arduous study."[56] Over the objections of his parents, he left college to enlist in Company D. He made up for his disobedience by sending home frequent and lively letters to his "Dear Folks." He closed a long letter that he wrote to them from Morristown on December 30 with the remark, "I dont know how the report of my being killed could of started. *I believe I am alive.*"[57] Two weeks later, Sergeant Newton, the same Sergeant Newton who had been given the job of burning Columbus, had the task of informing the Holmes family that their son Dan was one of the five men killed when Merriman was ambushed.[58]

The three Jayhawkers taken prisoner by Elliott were released by him the next day on the intercession of the families of the boys whom Utt had released on the night of January 7.

Anthony made his reports on the Dayton and Columbus scouts. On January 20 General David Hunter's adjutant expressed to Anthony the General's surprise that the two towns should have been burned and his opinion that nothing in the reports indicated "a state of facts sufficient to warrant these extreme measures," and Anthony was informed that his reports were "disapproved and held in reserve for further consideration

---

55. The events at Columbus are described in great detail by Sergeant F. E. Newton in a letter of January 15, 1862, to the parents of Daniel Holmes, in Holmes Collection, and in Webster Moses' letter of January 15, 1862, to Nancy Mowry, in Moses Letters. What may be called the Company A version is in Utt, "Seventh Kansas." The number of men Elliott had with him is given by Moses as 150 and by Newton as 300. In the circumstances, neither man could do more than guess, and it is unlikely that they would guess too low.

56. Holmes to "Dear Friend," June 25, 1861, in Holmes Collection.

57. Holmes to "Dear Folks at home," December 30, 1861, *ibid.*

58. F. E. Newton to "Dear Friends," January 15, 1862, *ibid.*

and action."[59] It is not clear what General Hunter expected to accomplish by this tap on the wrist. Had he been really in earnest, he could have taken much sterner measures. Anthony, at any rate, was not to be frightened by mere expressions of official disapproval. He was capable of putting seventeen of his men on "police duty" for what in the Civil War was the trifling offense of leaving camp without permission.[60] He *may* have been able to put a halt to the worst forms of marauding had he been under real pressure to do so. Whether he could have succeeded is another question; by mid-January the contagion of licensed plundering had probably gone too deep to be checked by anyone by any means short of the firing squad.

How deep the contagion had gone was shown on January 17 when Captain Merriman took a squad of twelve men to go jayhawking "for his own benefit"; he returned to camp the next day with two jayhawked wagons filled with furniture, apples, cider, pork, chickens, "&c &c."[61] Merriman did not bother to claim or pretend that this jaunt had a military purpose or objective. Such excuses were no longer deemed necessary, and any expedition, even if there was a military reason for making it, ended as a jayhawking raid. When a 150-man detachment was sent out under Captain Horace Pardee, Cleveland's successor as captain of Company H, to chase a guerilla band led by "a notorious raskal by the name of Quantral," Pardee divided his men into squads of fifteen and turned them loose to jayhawk to their hearts' content.[62] One of these squads came upon some men who were supposedly members of the guerilla band and killed five of them, but Quantrill (to give him his correct *nom de guerre*) himself escaped. Aside from the five dead guerillas, what Pardee had to show for his expedition was "about 150 head of horses and mules and most any amount of Negroes and several carriages," and a good many houses burned.[63]

The full irony of this dismal situation appears in an indignant letter written by Webster Moses in March, after the Seventh had been removed

59. Major Charles G. Halpine to Anthony, January 20, 1862, in *Official Records*, VIII, 508.

60. Anthony to his sister Susan, December 26, 1861, in Langsdorf and Richmond (eds.), "Anthony," 358.

61. Webster Moses to Nancy Mowry, January 18, 1862, in Moses Letters.

62. Same to same, February 9, 1862, *ibid.*

63. *Ibid.*

from Missouri. Joseph Kinnick, a member of Company D, deserted and returned to his home in Wyanet. A short time later the stories Kinnick was telling back home about the doings of the regiment began to filter back to his erstwhile comrades, causing Moses to write: "I have heard that our Rigament has got a hard name there in some places for jayhawking and burning houses. We have been misrepresented by some them deserters have told some outrageous stories about us. I have understood that the reason they give for deserting is because the officers stole so much. . . . Hereafter Joseph Kinnick & Co. will be branded as *thiefs and a traitors* and if they are caught they will be *shot*."[64] A remarkable outburst indeed from the jayhawker of silver cups and ladles.

64. Same to same, March 14, 1862, *ibid.* On August 12, 1862, Kinnick not only returned to duty himself, but also brought his brother with him to enlist in the regiment. He was reinstated without punishment.

CHAPTER VII

Exit
the
Colonel

OF THE MANY crosses President Lincoln had to bear during the war years, Missouri was assuredly one of the heaviest. Of the numberless problems that strained his intellect and tried his patience, the question of how to deal with that troubled state was one of the most intractable. Any course of action pursued by the government, any statement of policy, any appointment, was certain to enlist the passionate support of half of that deeply divided community and arouse the violent resentment of the other half. The government could say or do nothing that half of Missouri did not consider too radical and the other half too conservative, and the opinions of Missourians on the political and military conduct of the war were invariably intense, vehement, and vocal. Missouri could not be dealt with as an enemy state; technically and legally it was as much in the Union as was Massachusetts. But at the same time, Missouri had its star in the Confederate battle flag, and a high percentage of its people were as devoted to the Confederacy as if they had been so many South Carolinians. But the cleavage in Missouri was not merely a straightforward split between unionists and secessionists. The unionists themselves were divided into two camps whose mutual hostility was as virulent as their common hatred of secessionists and, in some respects, even more so. On one side were the radicals, for whom slavery and disunion were merely different names for the same evil, and for whom the destruction of slavery was at least as important as the restoration of the Union; on the other side were the conservatives, whose devotion to the Union embraced an equal devotion to all the institutions sanctioned by the Constitution, slavery included. This radical-conservative fission was not by any means peculiar to Missouri, but nowhere else did the factions harbor so fierce an antagonism toward each other.

When President Lincoln, whose comprehension of the crosscurrents in Missouri went much deeper than that of his subordinates, appointed Major General John M. Schofield to the command of the Department of the Missouri, he admonished Schofield to let his "military measures be strong enough to repel the invader and keep the peace, and not so strong as to unnecessarily harass and persecute the people. It is a difficult role, and so much greater will be the honor if you perform it well. If both factions, or neither, shall abuse you, you will probably be about right. Beware of being assailed by one and praised by the other."[1]

The fortunes of the Seventh Kansas and of Colonel Jennison in the spring of 1862 were to a considerable degree the product of these factional antagonisms in Missouri and of the cautious efforts of the national government to maintain a delicate and always precarious balance between them. The position of the regiment, and the task of the government in dealing with it and with its highly vocal colonel, were further complicated by the fact that whereas the regiment and Kansans generally were of the radical persuasion, the officers of the regular army appointed to high command in the area were mainly conservatives, hostile by instinct and training to Jayhawker radicalism.

There can be little doubt that the activities of the Seventh Kansas in Missouri made it inevitable that the government should eventually intervene. It was all well and good that the movements of the regiment should be "watched with a great deal of pride and interest" by friends of the troopers back home, but not everyone shared these feelings.[2] Stories of the Jayhawkers' misdeeds in Missouri were getting a wide circulation.

1. Lincoln to Schofield, May 27, 1863, quoted in John M. Schofield, *Forty-Six Years in the Army* (New York, 1897), 69.
2. D. Spangler to Daniel B. Holmes, December 27, 1861, in Holmes Collection. Holmes's correspondent goes on to say: "We are glad to know that Col. Jennison's mode of warfare is appreciated in high quarters; proof of which we have in his promotion to an Acting Brig-Gen."

One of the troopers, subscribing himself a lover of his country and of freedom, was impelled to send the Chicago *Tribune* an indignant and far from accurate defense of the good name of the regiment, which, he said, had been "grossly misrepresented and slandered by the friends of slavery all through the North." To contend, as did this lover of country and freedom, that "there has been a strong influence against the regiment. And why? Because *that vile monster slavery has perished in* its *path"* was to oversimplify the issue.[3] It was true up to a point that the Seventh angered the authorities because of the zeal with which it freed the slaves of the disloyal and the loyal alike, although a more accurate statement of the process would probably be that the Seventh willingly acted the part of the vehicle through which slaves made their escape to freedom. In either case, the effect was that slaveholders professing loyalty to the Union saw their valuable Negroes disappearing over the horizon through the instrumentality of soldiers wearing the uniform of the Union army. And they did not like it.

But, for the national government, the resulting clamor cut much deeper than the antagonism of a few dozen or even a few hundred Missouri slaveholders whose loyalty was in any case questionable. The crux of the matter was that each time the Seventh assisted a slave to escape from his master, it raised the one issue the government could not afford to have agitated in 1861–1862, namely, the issue of the survival or extinction of slavery.

General Fremont had raised this issue in August, 1861. Faced with guerilla operations which he did not have the military strength to put down, he proclaimed that all civilians caught in arms in the northern half of Missouri would be tried by court-martial and executed if found guilty of guerilla activity or the destruction of railway track, bridges, or telegraph lines; the real and personal property of Missourians actively aiding

3. Unsigned letter from "Special Correspondent of the Chicago Tribune," April 17, 1862, Jennison Scrapbook. The tenor of this curious letter is well indicated by the statement that Lieutenant Bostwick and Captain Birchard "of our own regiment" were assassinated in Upton Hays's house. The roster of the Seventh does not list any officer named Birchard, or anyone whose name might be mistaken for Birchard, and the "assassinated" Lieutenant Bostwick of Company K was promoted to captain on October 30, 1862, and was mustered out with the regiment in September, 1865. The writer of the letter was probably Private Francis Schilling of Company C, a German immigrant, whom Fox described as a "frequent correspondent of the Chicago Tribune." See "Story," 37. Schilling was killed in the fight at Coffeeville, Mississippi, on December 5, 1862.

secession would be confiscated and their slaves freed. The moral and political impact of Fremont's proclamation far transcended its practical effect within the limits of his military command. It was greeted with great enthusiasm by the powerful radical and abolitionist elements in the North; and their disappointment was correspondingly great when the president, who had to look beyond Fremont's military problems to the uncertain loyalty of the slaveholding border states and had to retain the support for the war of conservative Republicans and unionist Democrats, ordered the proclamation withdrawn.

Jennison's abolitionism did not need the spur of Fremont's proclamation. And given the generally lax discipline in the volunteer armies of the Union, it was unlikely that official disapproval would deter him from acting on his abolitionist convictions. A probably apocryphal story illustrates Jennison's attitude so clearly that it must be told notwithstanding its doubtful authenticity. Jennison, so the story goes, called on President Lincoln not long after he had been forced to withdraw his own military order freeing the slaves of rebels in Cass, Jackson, Lafayette, Johnson, and Pettis counties in Missouri; said Jennison: "Mr. President, I bow gracefully to your will in the matter; but please to remember that when you shall issue your own proclamation of emancipation, as you must before this war is over, I shall claim [a] 'royalty' upon the measure."[4]

Had the Seventh done nothing worse than to free the slaves of secessionist Missourians, the national government would still have been under the imperative necessity of dealing with the regiment and its activities. In the political conditions of 1862, the "practical abolitionism" of the Seventh could neither be ignored nor tolerated. But premature interference with slavery, contrary to the policy the government was forced to pursue at the time, was only one of the Jayhawkers' sins. There was, in addition, their campaign of robbery, arson, and terror, going considerably beyond the limits of what in the relative innocence of 1861–1862 was

4. Mitchell, Linn County, 298. Mitchell claimed to have the story directly from Jennison, which does not necessarily enhance its credibility. Jennison spent three weeks in Washington in May, 1862, and may have called on the much too accessible president, but that is as close as one can get to an authentication of the story. There is nothing in the records to show that Jennison was ordered by the president or by anyone else to rescind the "military order" (presumably his proclamation) referred to.

considered permissible conduct even in avowedly enemy territory. This too had to be halted.

The government did not have to rely on newspaper reports and gossip for its information about the suffering inflicted by the Seventh on Missourians living within reach of its patrols. As early as November, 1861, Hamilton R. Gamble, the loyal governor of the state, had complained to Washington about the "wanton outrages" committed by Jennison's men; and all through December and January, a steady stream of denunciations came from unquestionably loyal Missourians to General Halleck in St. Louis, to members of the Missouri delegation in Congress, and to the secretary of war. Halleck in turn complained repeatedly to the War Department and to General McClellan, and at least some of the complaints found their way to the president's desk.[5]

The volume of complaints from loyal Missourians was such as to make it mandatory upon the government to take steps "to protect the Union men and loyal citizens of Missouri from all illegal force and lawless violence," as Edwin M. Stanton, the new secretary of war, phrased it.[6] The problem was to find a way to accomplish this, and thereby placate the conservative pro (or at least not anti) slavery unionists of Missouri, without arousing the anger of their abolitionist and radical brethren in Missouri itself, as well as in Kansas. The regular army as a corporate body has never been without a useful streak of guile, and the resources of its Machiavellianism were not found wanting when it became necessary to check Jennison and his regiment. At the end of January the Seventh was ordered to move from Morristown to Humboldt, Kansas, about eighty miles south of Lawrence and a little over forty-five miles west of the Missouri border—much too far for quick dashes across the line. Humboldt was located about sixty miles north of the line between the southern border of Kansas and Indian Territory. The town had been attacked twice in the fall of 1861, first by secessionist guerillas aided by Cherokee and Osage Indians, and then by Confederate cavalry, and all but a few of its buildings were in ruins. The orders sending the Seventh to Humboldt

---

5. Governor Gamble's complaint is referred to in his letter of November 21, 1862, to O. G. Gates, in *Official Records*, XVII, Pt. 2, 92. *Cf. ibid.*, VIII, 546.

6. *Ibid.*

have not survived, and it is therefore impossible to determine what the regiment was intended to do there; but it is clear enough that whatever may have been the official reason for its presence in Humboldt was no more than window dressing. One possible reason for stationing it there would have been to protect the town from another Confederate attack. The two raids Humboldt had already undergone would have given this reason a degree of plausibility, but the rebels had left precious little in the town worth protecting. The nearest hostile troops were Confederate Cherokee Indians a hundred miles away, and it was wholly unlikely that they would molest the town in midwinter, when the movements of even regular troops were severely restricted. The Seventh itself, traveling over miserable roads through sleet, snow, and ice, had taken a week to cover the hundred miles from Morristown to Humboldt.

But the contemporary letters of Anthony and Chaplain Ayres make it appear that the ostensible purpose of the Jayhawkers' presence in Humboldt was not defensive; the regiment, it seems, was to be a part of a "Grand Army of the southwest" which was to march through Arkansas to some distant objective, perhaps New Orleans, or possibly Galveston.[7] The chimerical character of such objectives makes it inconceivable that there should have been such a plan in reality. Whatever may have been said about it in the orders issued to the regiment was mere twaddle. Nor is there any evidence to connect the presence of the Seventh at Humboldt and the fascinating, if rather vague, scheme for a "southern expedition" concocted at this time by the president, Senator James Lane, and Secretary Cameron, without the knowledge of Generals Halleck and Hunter, the two department commanders most closely concerned.[8] This visionary scheme, aptly called a "Newspaper Expedition," never got beyond the talking stage.

To forestall a furor among the radicals over the removal of the Seventh from Missouri, something more than window dressing was needed. The missing ingredient was supplied by the appointment of Jennison to the rank of *acting* brigadier general. The Seventh was to be joined at Humboldt by the Eighth Iowa Infantry and a battalion of the Seventh

7. Anthony to his sister Susan, February 3, 1862, in Langsdorf and Richmond (eds.), "Anthony," 359–60; also Samuel Ayres to Liman Langdon, February 17, 1862, in Samuel Ayres Collection.

8. *Official Records*, VIII, 525, 554, 829.

Missouri Infantry. While not formally brigaded together, the three units, with an aggregate strength of 1,318 officers and men, made up the equivalent of a small brigade.[9] Jennison was an ally of the powerful Senator Lane and a darling of the abolitionists. And so, on January 31, on the day that the Seventh began its toilsome march from Morristown, Jennison was appointed (not commissioned) acting brigadier general.[10] The appointment was made by General David Hunter, the recipient, ever since his own assignment to the command of the Department of Kansas on November 20, of an endless litany of complaints about the misdeeds permitted, encouraged, or committed by the selfsame Jennison. Nonetheless, Hunter wrote directly to the president to recommend the formal commissioning of Jennison to the rank of brigadier general, as "an efficient and energetic officer . . . well qualified for the position."[11]

There was a notable peculiarity about Jennison's status as an acting brigadier general. Hunter's appointment gave him command of all the troops in Kansas west of, and on, the Neosho River. Was it wholly a coincidence that Humboldt was located a little less than a mile *east* of that stream?

As a result of these complicated manoeuvers, the Seventh found itself on February 6 at Humboldt, encamped in an oak grove near the bank of the Neosho River. Before the march to Humboldt began, orders were issued "to remind the soldiers . . . that in the march about to begin . . . [they] are to pass through the country of . . . friends and not that of the enemy. Our way lies through a country inhabited by those whom it is our duty to protect and it is hoped that no person belonging to this command will so far forget his duty as to treat uncivilly any loyal citizen or

9. *Ibid.*, Series III, I, 787 (strength report of January 10, 1862).

10. Unidentified clipping, Jennison Scrapbook. The text of Hunter's order is: "Col. C. R. Jennison is hereby appointed Acting Brigadier General. He will assume command of all the troops in Kansas west of and on the Neosho, including all such friendly Indians . . . as may be called into the service." This order is not in the *Official Records*, nor is it in Jennison's service record in the adjutant general's office, possibly because it was a purely local or territorial appointment.

11. Undated clipping, Jennison Scrapbook. Hunter's letter to the president is quoted in an unsigned letter dated Paola, Kansas, December 26, 1864, to the Leavenworth *Times*. Two weeks before he wrote to the president, Hunter had written Secretary Cameron to express his belief that "Colonel C. R. Jennison, like General Lane, is one of those men particularly fitted for bringing this war to a successful termination," and recommended his promotion to brigadier general. The coupling of Jennison's name with Lane's in this letter is surely not without significance. Hunter to Cameron, December 11, 1861, in Seventh Kansas, Regimental Letter and Order Book.

molest . . . [their] property. . . . The colonel commanding is determined that should any soldier be guilty of disturbing citizens of Kansas in their persons or their property . . . the military law shall be administered in its full rigor, and the perpetrators of such offenses shall suffer death."[12]

Jennison having been advanced to brigade command, Anthony was now officially in charge of the Seventh. With all his faults of temper and judgment, he was an earnest and hardworking regimental commander. As a replacement for the excitements of the previous months, he kept the men busy with five hours of drill daily, three hours of company drill in the morning, and two hours of battalion and regimental drill in the afternoon.[13] He commanded the regimental drill himself. Besides the drill, there were dress parades, reviews, and inspections.

Anthony also made it his business to wean his men away from the free and easy jayhawking habits they had acquired in Missouri.[14] It was no easy task to get them "to respect the person and property of Loyal citizens —They have lived so long on chickens turkeys apples jellies taken from Secesh—and now they have to come down to regular army rations."[15] The threat of capital punishment for marauding, voiced in the orders issued before the departure of the regiment from Morristown, had caused the men to question whether they were intended to be taken seriously, particularly since they were Jennison's orders. To remove all doubts on that score, Anthony issued new and stringent orders of his own on the subject:

1. No officer or soldier of this command shall take any property of any description without a command from the commanding officer. . . .

2. The captains or commanders of companies will be held personally responsible for the value of property taken from loyal citizens and appropriated, burned or destroyed by soldiers under their command.[16]

---

12. General Orders No. 26, January 29, 1862, *ibid.*

13. General Orders No. 31, February 11, 1862, *ibid.*

14. There may have been a connection between Anthony's new sternness and General Hunter's order of February 8, 1862, declaring his determination to put down jayhawking "with a firm hand and by summary process." See *Official Records*, VIII, 547–48.

15. Anthony to his mother, February 22, 1862, in Langsdorf and Richmond (eds.), "Anthony," 360.

16. General Orders No. 29, February 8, 1862, in Seventh Kansas, Regimental Letter and Order Book.

Anthony's efforts to check the predatory habits of his men appear to have been reasonably successful, perhaps because the Jayhawkers realized that he meant what he said and had every intention of enforcing his orders. Webster Moses ruefully testifies to the fact that "the men [were] very orderly even pigs and chickens can run around camp with[out] being molested." [17] This was indeed the millenium, and one may doubt if Moses could have stood the test of a searching cross-examination; but it does indicate a drastic change of behavior. The men did not suffer any noticeable hardship under the new regime of austerity; they were "all well and hearty," and some of them even grew "very fleshy"—not a desirable condition for a cavalryman. [18] Anthony himself had to admit that his "living . . . [was] not half as good as when in Mo." But since his diet in Humboldt consisted of "good Beef Steaks—good hot bread & Coffee," it cannot be said that he suffered from anything worse than a lack of variety. [19]

Anthony's efforts to turn the Seventh into a well-drilled and adequately disciplined organization did not arouse universal enthusiasm. Some of the men were pleased and even expressed pride in the fine appearance of the regiment on parade, but others were less than happy about the constant drill, the strict discipline, and the enforced end of jayhawking. On the night of February 9, following one of Chaplain Ayres's infrequent religious services, five disgruntled troopers deserted in a body because, it was said, they did not like Colonel Anthony. [20] Search parties were sent out to hunt for the five deserters, but came back empty-handed. There had been other desertions earlier; on February 6 Anthony had ordered Captain Pardee to march through Lykins, Linn, and Anderson counties in Kansas, to "collect all stock" belonging to the regiment, and also to "arrest every soldier belonging to this regiment and return him to his place." [21]

A break in the drill routine came on February 22, when Washington's Birthday was celebrated with a review and patriotic oratory suitable to the day. The speech delivered by Jennison on that occasion has already

17. Webster Moses to Nancy Mowry, February 15, 1862, in Moses Letters.

18. F. E. Newton to "Dear Friends," February 3, 1862, in Holmes Collection.

19. Anthony to his mother, February 22, 1862, in Langsdorf and Richmond (eds.), "Anthony," 361.

20. George Mowry, Jr., to Nancy Mowry, February 16, 1862, in Moses Letters.

21. Special Orders No. 65, in Seventh Kansas, Regimental Order Book.

been cited. The day was further enlivened by the firing of a patriotic salute of thirty-four guns, one for every state of the Union, including the eleven whose secession the Seventh refused to recognize. The salute honored not only the Father of his Country, but also General Grant's victories at Forts Henry and Donelson in Tennessee, a state with which the Seventh was shortly to become acquainted.

Variety of a different sort was provided two weeks later when Alexander Driscoll of Company H broke out of the guardhouse and escaped on one of Anthony's valuable chargers. Anthony might have had difficulty producing clear title to the horse; perhaps for that reason, or out of a sense of delicacy as an interested party, he took no part in the proceedings against the thief when Driscoll was recaptured on the day following his escape. Jennison ordered the man to be tried by court-martial; he was condemned to death and was executed by a firing squad on March 8.

The excitement caused by the Driscoll affair had hardly died down when Anthony's insensitivity and bad temper nearly precipitated a mutiny. Probably because of Driscoll's successful escape from prison, Anthony ordered a new guardhouse to be built. While the log structure was still under construction, he ordered that when the horses of the regiment were taken to the Neosho River to be watered, they were to go at a walk. His objective was certainly praiseworthy; an overheated horse given his fill of cold water will develop a case of colic which can easily become fatal. It is greatly to Anthony's credit that, unlike the majority of cavalry officers, he should insist that his men take good care of their mounts and spare them as much as possible, for the careless or callous mistreatment of cavalry mounts and the disregard by cavalrymen and their officers of the most elementary rules of horse hygiene was one of the crying scandals of the Civil War. It is also to Anthony's credit that after he issued an order, he made certain that it was obeyed.

On the evening after these orders were issued, Anthony posted himself where he could watch the horses ridden to water. Great was his wrath when he saw Private Vaughn of Company A apparently trotting his horse down to the stream. Poor Vaughn's horse was not actually trotting; it was a particularly high-strung animal that refused to walk and went prancing along, in plain view of the irascible lieutenant colonel. As soon as Company A returned to its quarters, Vaughn was placed under arrest, led to the half-finished guardhouse where a ball and chain were attached to his ankles, and locked up. His comrades of staid and well-behaved Company A decided that a grave injustice had been perpetrated. They took their arms, liberated Vaughn, struck the ball and chain from his ankles, and set fire to the guardhouse, the symbol of shoulder strap tyranny.

At this moment, Anthony appeared, armed with a revolver, and jumping on the pile of smoldering logs, "in his peculiar screeming voice . . . began to screech, ordering the men in arrest, and the guard to be turned out to arrest them." Until then, the men of Company A had gone about their insubordinate work in silence, but now they began to abuse Anthony. Just as the situation threatened to get out of hand, Jennison, who learned of the incipient mutiny, came dashing up on horseback. "He ordered Anthony to shut up, inquired into the cause of the trouble, ordered Anthony to his quarters, and told the men there would be no more ball-and-chain business, freed Vaughn, and said there would be no more arrests." [22] This energetic and sensible intervention ended the trouble and left a feeling in the regiment that Anthony owed his life to Jennison's timely arrival. Jennison himself was of that opinion. Two years later, when he and Anthony had become political and personal enemies, he boasted that he had gotten up from a sickbed to save Anthony's skin.

Obviously, Jennison's method of settling this imbroglio did not enhance Anthony's stature in the regiment. There were other incidents also to indicate a lack of harmony between the two men. Thus, when Anthony exercised his prerogatives as regimental commander by reducing to the ranks Chief Bugler Peter Gross for disciplinary reasons, Jennison at once intervened and ordered Anthony to reinstate Gross as chief bugler, and added: "In future, you will please consult with me before reducing non-commissioned officers to the ranks." [23] Even though he now had

22. The story of the near mutiny of Company A is told in Lyman, "Reminiscences," and in a letter from Simeon Fox to W. E. Connelley, March 5, 1926, in Fox Papers. The quotations in the text are from the Fox letter. Fox was in his mid-eighties in 1926, and it is indicative of his remarkable memory that his account, written sixty-four years after the event, agrees step by step with Lyman's, written many years earlier. The propriety of Anthony's order that the horses were to be walked to water is borne out by the fact that Colonels Lee and Herrick, when they in turn succeeded to the command of the Seventh, issued similar orders.

23. Jennison to Anthony, February 18, 1862, in Seventh Kansas, Regimental Order Book.

command of a brigade, Jennison clearly looked upon the Seventh as *his* regiment and did not intend to tolerate a rival in the administration of its internal affairs. Anthony, on the other hand, was determined not to let his work as regimental commander go unrecognized. Thus, he wrote General Hunter that "our men are drilled five hours daily at officers', squad, squadron and battalion and regimental drill. Strict discipline is enforced, our horses are all shod and in good condition. Our transportation is in good order. In short, our regiment is in better condition in every particular than at any time heretofore." [24] Anthony also engaged in a correspondence with Governor Robinson concerning the affairs of the regiment, to Jennison's growing indignation, which burst forth on March 3 in orders to Anthony to transmit "forthwith" to brigade headquarters certified copies "of any and all correspondence" which had passed between him and department headquarters and the governor of Kansas "regarding any matters directly or indirectly connected with the interests or affairs" of the regiment. Anthony was instructed also that "Hereafter all communications and correspondence connected directly or indirectly with the affairs of the regiment will pass through these head quarters." [25] But Anthony was not an easy man to put in his place or to intimidate. In response to what he called Jennison's "very singular communication" he sent the Regimental Letter and Order Book to headquarters and pointed out that the order to have all communications relating to the regiment pass through brigade headquarters was in conflict with army regulations and the orders of General Hunter, which directed that certain regimental reports, acknowledgements, etc., be sent directly to department headquarters, the secretary of war, or the adjutant general. Jennison had to back down—no doubt to Anthony's great satisfaction. [26]

Flurries of spontaneous indiscipline or jealousies among officers were not peculiar to the Seventh Kansas; but in February and March, 1862, the

24. Anthony to General Hunter, March 1, 1862, *ibid.*
25. Special Orders No. 12 (signed by Lee, for Jennison), March 3, 1862, *ibid.*
26. Anthony to Jennison, March 3, 1862; Jennison to Anthony, March 4, 1862; and Anthony to Jennison, March 4, 1862, *ibid.* These letters must have provided a great deal of entertainment for the regimental clerks who had to copy them into the Regimental Order Book, and no doubt the contents of the letters became common knowledge throughout the regiment within a matter of hours.

Seventh had a much more serious problem on its hands. The survival of the regiment was in question. It was obvious to the least observant trooper that Humboldt was a military backwater, that the presence of the regiment there served no military purpose whatever, and that, in fact, they were kept there as in an isolation ward until someone in authority decided what use, if any, could be made of them. Latrine gossip had it that the regiment was to be mustered out, and one may suspect that these rumors were at least as much responsible for the renewed wave of desertions as was the resentment aroused by Anthony's injudicious severities.[27] Still, in spite of the uncertain future of the regiment, the physical hardships of life under canvas in midwinter, and the more serious strains of boredom and monotony, the great majority of the men stuck it out. This was a truly remarkable exhibition of loyalty considering that half the men were within two or three days' ride of their homes and the machinery for apprehending deserters was practically nonexistent. Webster Moses expressed the feeling of most of his comrades when he wrote: "It would suit the most of the boys if we could go home but if there is any thing for us to do we are ready to do it."[28]

What was there for the Seventh to do? This puzzled the officers as much as it did the men. Anthony suggested to General Hunter that the regiment be sent to Arkansas and the Indian Territory to attempt to recapture Forts Smith and Gibson; and on March 9, Major Albert L. Lee was sent to Fort Leavenworth to try to find out what was to be the "fate and destination of" the regiment.[29] The answer was to come shortly from General Halleck.

In the summer of 1861, Confederate General H. H. Sibley, the father of the Sibley tent, had been sent to Texas with instructions to organize a brigade there and conquer New Mexico. This was to be the first step in a

27. Webster Moses to Nancy Mowry, March 14, 1862, in Moses Letters. A tabulation of the none too reliable records in *Report of the Adjutant General of the State of Kansas* indicates that the number of desertions jumped from four in January, when the regiment was on active duty in Missouri, to thirteen in February, when it was doing nothing in Humboldt.

28. Webster Moses to Nancy Mowry, March 14, 1862, in Moses Letters. The regimental strength on March 14 and March 24, 820 on both dates, is given in *Official Records*, VIII, 615, and *ibid.*, Series III, I, 949, respectively.

29. Anthony to Aaron McLean, March 1, 1862, in Langsdorf and Richmond (eds.), "Anthony," 362.

visionary scheme looking to the conquest of California and of the northern provinces of Mexico for the Confederacy. Pursuant to these orders, Sibley departed from El Paso in January, 1862, at the head of what was called the "Army of New Mexico," and after a toilsome march up the Rio Grande, arrived on February 16 at Fort Craig, near San Antonio, New Mexico. The fort was held for the Union by Colonel (later Major General) Edward R. S. Canby, with a miscellaneous force of regulars, volunteers—including Colonel Kit Carson's First New Mexico—and unorganized militia. On February 21 the two forces clashed at Valverde, a short distance north of the fort, and the balance of inexperience and incompetence being slightly in Sibley's favor, Canby was defeated.

Except to the participants, the engagement at Valverde was utterly without meaning, and the entire campaign was a military aberration from beginning to end; but Canby's defeat, by no means his last, was to have a decided effect on the fortunes of the Seventh Kansas. For Canby, if he could do nothing else, could at least ask for help, and this he did in a despatch to General Halleck in St. Louis. On March 20, the latter telegraphed the secretary of war: "Dispatches just received from Colonel Canby . . . begging for re-enforcements. . . . Five or six regiments near Fort Scott . . . can be withdrawn and sent to New Mexico, if you approve."[30] Secretary Stanton telegraphed his approval, and the next day Halleck ordered Major W. E. Prince to assemble at Lawrence, Kansas, the First Kansas Infantry, the Seventh Kansas Cavalry, and the Twelfth and Thirteenth Wisconsin Infantry regiments in preparation for a move at the earliest possible moment to far-off New Mexico.[31] Pursuant to Prince's orders, the Seventh left Humboldt on March 26 and arrived at Lawrence three days later. Camp was pitched a half-mile west of town, on a pleasant hillside overlooking the Kansas River.

It was customary during the Civil War, as it is to this day, for a military unit to give a name to any camp it expects to occupy for any length of time. The Seventh followed this custom. Its camps had been named Camp Jennison, Camp Union, Camp Denver, Camp Johnson, and, most recently at Humboldt, its camp had been named Camp Hunter in honor of the major general commanding the department. In a piece of deliberately provocative bravado, the new camp of the Seventh at Lawrence

30. *Official Records*, VIII, 627, 628.   31. *Ibid.*, VIII, 631.

was named Camp Wendell Phillips in honor of one of the patron saints of abolitionism.[32]

It is difficult to resist the suspicion that there was more than met the eye in the decision to include the Seventh in the New Mexico expedition. True enough, the regiment was at practically full strength, well mounted, and, by the standards of 1862, reasonably well equipped. It might therefore be considered a logical choice for a long march and hard service. But the Seventh had caused General Halleck a great deal of trouble with its activities in Missouri. One can easily picture that gentleman, who was not without a share of vindictiveness, as his behavior to General Grant was to demonstrate only three weeks later, licking his chops over a neat solution to an annoying command problem. The Seventh could not be kept at Humboldt indefinitely. They could not be sent back to Missouri. They had made themselves obnoxious with their jayhawking; very well, let them try jayhawking among the Mescalero Apaches in the New Mexico desert, 850 miles from Independence, Missouri, and even further from General Halleck's desk at department headquarters in St. Louis.

The situation did not work out as General Halleck might well have intended, and in fact the expedition to New Mexico did not take place at all. It is worth mentioning, however, that on the very same day that Halleck ordered Major Prince to move the Seventh Kansas to Lawrence, he found it necessary to send the following despatch to Brigadier General James Totten at Jefferson City, Missouri: "I am receiving numerous complaints of depredations of rebel bands in Jackson, LaFayette, and Johnson counties. Your troops should immediately take the field and effectually break them up."[33] Whatever may be said about the way in which the Jayhawkers had conducted themselves in Missouri, the peace of General Halleck's mind had not been troubled by "complaints of depredations of rebel bands" while that regiment of black sheep, the Seventh Kansas, was patrolling the area.

The proposed despatch of his regiment to New Mexico produced a violent upheaval in the mind of Colonel Jennison. We have only his own

---

32. The caption of Jennison's letter of resignation read "Camp Wendell Phillips." When he submitted it to General Sturgis to be forwarded through channels, Sturgis rose to the bait and asked Jennison to change the caption to "Headquarters." Jennison of course refused.

33. *Official Records*, VIII, 632.

ex post facto and no doubt self-serving explanations of his mental and emotional perturbations between March 25, when Major Prince's orders arrived in Humboldt, and April 10, when he sent the following letter to General Halleck:

General,

I would most respectfully tender my resignation as colonel of the Seventh Regiment Kansas Volunteers, to take effect on the 1st day of May, 1862.
To the policy manifested by the government in this department I cannot conscientiously in accordance with my own feelings, and in justice to my country, serve faithfully any longer.

Respectfully yours,
C. R. Jennison[34]

In Special Orders No. 105 dated April 15—a curt, one-sentence order— Jennison's resignation was accepted, no doubt with relief.[35]

But much was to happen in the five days that elapsed between Jennison's submission of his resignation and its precipitate acceptance.

On the evening of Sunday, April 13, by which time it was common knowledge that his resignation had been sent to St. Louis, Jennison had the regiment paraded and, in a lengthy speech, explained the reasons for his decision to leave the service. Jennison was in his glory when the spirit of oratory descended upon him. Senator Lane was the unequaled master of the violent diatribe, the staple of Kansas oratory of the day; but when Jennison warmed up to his subject, he could give the senator a good run for his money. And the themes that invariably brought out the highest flights of the Colonel's eloquence were his own grievances and the iniquities of his real and fancied enemies. His speech to the regiment on the evening of April 13 was apparently one of his most powerful efforts. What he said must be pieced together from the reports of contemporary newspapers, mostly pro-Jennison, and from the brief statements of a few of the troopers who heard him; but all of these accounts, whether at first

34. Records of the Adjutant General's Office. The date of Jennison's resignation is given by most authorities as April 11, but his letter of resignation is clearly dated April 10. No doubt he wrote the letter on the tenth and submitted it the next day.

35. Special Orders No. 105, April 15, 1862, in Seventh Kansas, Regimental Order Book: "The resignation of Colonel C. R. Jennison, Seventh Kansas Volunteers, is hereby accepted to take effect 1st May, 1862."

or at second hand, are in remarkably close agreement on the general tenor and tone of the speech.

Jennison began with bitter comments on the decision to send the regiment to New Mexico. He had organized it to serve on the Kansas-Missouri border and not elsewhere. The Seventh was needed for the protection of Kansas, and there was plenty of useful work for it to do keeping in check the rebels and guerillas of Missouri. Why then send the regiment to the Southwest, where it would probably never have a chance to fight? The reason was clear. The Seventh had been recalled from Missouri two months before because of the machinations of semitraitors, and the same evil influences were now to be seen behind the decision to send it to New Mexico. Who were these semitraitors? First in the list of villains was General Denver, who hated the radicals and abolitionists of Kansas and was determined to crush them. The speaker himself was the special object of the general's insidious schemes, because in his own person he represented the spirit of freedom for all men and embodied everything that Kansas radicalism stood for, everything that Denver detested. Had not the latter's first order to Jennison, after assuming command in Kansas, been to return to the grantors the deeds of forfeiture that had been obtained from the citizens of Jackson County? Was not that order an open encouragement of treason and rebellion?

But the principal villain, outranked by Denver only in seniority, was Brigadier General Samuel D. Sturgis, appointed to the Kansas command only a week before. Was this not the same Sturgis who, in the previous summer, had a soldier of the First Kansas Infantry publicly whipped for stealing a chicken from a Missouri farmer?[36] Patriotic volunteers were not to be treated in such brutal fashion, especially not by "martinets" of the regular army. Kansas had never forgiven Sturgis for the whipping of one of its sons, nor would it ever forgive him. But this was not the worst of his sins. He was well known as an "undisguised pro-slavery-ite" who paraded his detestation of Kansas radicals for being the opposite. On the streets of Leavenworth, he had publicly denounced Germans as "abolitionist traitors." And now this selfsame Sturgis, a "secesh at heart" and a

36. Another version of the incident is that Sturgis ordered the flogging of *two* men belonging to the Second Kansas Infantry "for taking a chicken." E. S. Drought to G. W. Martin, September 8, 1911, in Kansas State Historical Society, Topeka.

drunkard besides, had been appointed to the command of the District of Kansas to lord it over men more loyal than himself, to turn a fighting war against rebellion into a political war against Kansas radicalism, and to control the war on the border so that it would not injure slavery, but instead would fill the pockets of swindlers with government gold.[37]

After a few choice comments directed against General Halleck, who had appointed both Denver and Sturgis to posts in which they could do the greatest harm to freedom, and a few more directed against an administration, the president included, that allowed such appointments to stand, Jennison came to the essence of his argument. He declared that he neither could nor would serve under such officers as Denver, Sturgis, and Halleck, men not much better than so many secessionists and traitors; and so long as such men were in power, he could best discharge his duty to Kansas by remaining in the state, where he was sure he would be needed before long.

Having explained at great length why it was impossible for a loyal Kansan, a patriot, and a lover of freedom such as himself to remain with the regiment, Jennison closed by appealing to the officers and men "to do their duty, to grin and bear it in their unfortunate position, and never do anything to disgrace themselves or him." He neglected to spell out why the reasons which justified his own resignation did not apply with equal force to his officers and men; nor did he tell them why it was their duty to remain with the colors under conditions which in his own case he considered inconsistent with honor, patriotism, and conscience.[38]

There cannot be two opinions on the import of Jennison's speech. The mildest comment that can be made on it is that it was in the highest

37. Physiognomy may not be a proper basis for judging a man, but Sturgis' lackluster career in the Civil War is quite in keeping with the considerably less than sparklingly intellectual countenance we see in the photograph reproduced in *Kansas State Historical Society Quarterly*, XXIV (1958), facing p. 401.

38. There is no full report extant of Jennison's speech. The version given in the text is an approximation pieced together from numerous, mostly unindentified, clippings in the Jennison Scrapbook, and from references in Pomeroy, "War Diary," entry for April 13, 1862; Lyman, "Reminiscences"; Fox, "Story," 24; Webster Moses to Nancy Mowry, June 2, 1862, in Moses Letters; and F. E. Newton to "Dear Friends," April 27, 1862, in Holmes Collection. Colonel Deitzler, who seems not to have had any animus against Jennison, wrote in a letter printed in the Leavenworth *Conservative* on May 9, 1862, that Jennison "expressed in unmeasured terms his utter disgust of matters and things generally. His speech to the regiment, as reported to me by several officers who heard it, was calculated to excite mutiny and sedition among the troops."

degree improper and injudicious. Most of the officers and men who heard the speech called it mutinous; and without question, notwithstanding the lame non sequitur at the end, it was calculated to incite mutiny and desertion. It was not a speech that a serving officer had a right to make.

Why, actually, did Jennison resign? Why did he make a speech that he must have known was indefensible? Jennison was a complex and in many ways a contradictory character. He was much given to self-justification. In his own eyes he was ever the soul of clairvoyant patriotism, his conduct and motives beyond reproach, his many problems and difficulties always the work of his own and, by extension, his country's unscrupulous enemies. Such self-deception is not necessarily inconsistent with complete sincerity, nor was it so in Jennison's case. Rightly or wrongly, he was convinced that the cause of freedom was not safe in the hands of conservative officers of the regular army, whose hearts were not in the fight because they had been so conditioned that they could not grasp or sympathize with its real significance and therefore did everything in their power to hinder and balk and undermine everyone like Jennison, who did. This conviction was not at all uncommon among the radicals, especially during the first year or two of the war; and it must be said that there was considerable justification for it. Take, for example, General McClellan, who wrote thus to his friend, the New York lawyer S. L. M. Barlow: "Help me dodge the nigger — we want nothing to do with him. *I* am fighting to preserve . . . the Union and the power of the Government — on no other issue. To gain that end we cannot afford to mix up the nigger question, it must be incidental and subsidiary." [39] In their own way, these much-maligned regulars were as patriotic as any radical. They can be faulted for being much too free with the expression of their conservative political opinions, but not for their failure to realize that a basic moral issue and an incipient social revolution were wrapped up in what to a professional soldier looked like just another war. They were far from being the only group in America with this same lack of insight.

But was there no other reason than this for Jennison's resignation? Apparently there was. Simeon Fox says that Jennison lost his temper

39. William Starr Myers, *General George Brinton McClellan* (New York, 1934), 235.

because on April 8 another Kansas colonel, James G. Blunt, was given a promotion to brigadier general that Jennison believed should have come to him. Fox is a hostile witness on any issue involving Jennison—he embellished his account of the colonel's resignation with the remark: "Colonel Jennison performed some acts worthy of commendation, conspicuous among which was his resignation"—but the accuracy of his surmise is supported by a letter of Colonel G. W. Deitzler and by a number of otherwise openly pro-Jennison newspaper stories.[40] It may be assumed, in justice to Jennison, that the promotion over his head of a mere colonel (it should be recalled that he himself was an acting brigadier general) merely lit the fuse and determined the date of an explosion that was bound to occur in any case, sooner or later.

The reaction to Jennison's resignation and farewell speech was quite different from what he probably expected. Daniel Anthony, who was to play an equivocal part in the events of the next few days, wrote that Jennison "got into trouble on acct of his own foolishness"; Fletcher Pomeroy commented: "He has resigned, which is no loss to the regiment"; W. A. Lyman said flatly that the regiment was glad to be rid of him.[41] These reactions may be taken as representative of a large segment of regimental opinion. F. E. Newton was probably not alone in suspecting that there was more to the resignation than met the eye; he wrote that "Jennison is a sharp man & I think he will come out all right."[42]

Lieutenant George H. Hoyt, Jennison's devoted disciple, was of a contrary opinion. He sensed an opportunity for a great propaganda coup, one that at the same time would also testify to his admiration for his hero. He sent to the newspapers a testimonial which he represented as having been voted by the officers of the regiment:

Whereas, Our beloved Colonel . . . actuated by the most praiseworthy and noble purposes, has seen fit to resign his office and return to the pursuits of civil life.

Resolved, That we assure him of our sincere regret and sorrow at the severance of a connection, which has been constantly harmonious and prolific of mutual good will.

40. Fox, "Story," 24. Cf. Deitzler letter printed in the Leavenworth *Conservative*, May 9, 1862.
41. Lyman, "Reminiscences"; Pomeroy, "War Diary," entry for April 13, 1862; Anthony to his father, April 23, 1862, in Langsdorf and Richmond (eds.), "Anthony," 365.
42. F. E. Newton to "Dear Friends," April 27, 1862, in Holmes Collection.

Resolved, That he carries with him the undivided love, confidence and admiration of both officers and men—a sentiment tainted by no partisan prejudice and which no "outside" influence can change in the least degree.

Resolved, That we approve and cordially endorse the policy of his Missouri campaign, the success of which was wholly attributable to the vigor, severity and promptitude with which he dealt out justice to those accursed traitors and assassins.

Resolved, That the charges made against "Jennison's Regiment," of pillage, arson and brutality, *are inventions of envious, designing and unprincipled liars*, than whom there are not in the service, or out of it, more contemptible and utterly abandoned objects of pity and scorn.[43]

The publication of these fulsome and somewhat less than factual resolutions led to a pretty little controversy, as absurd as it was revealing.

A few days after the appearance of Hoyt's testimonial, the Leavenworth *Times* printed a "Card" from the Seventh Regiment. The card stated that at dress parade on the eventful thirteenth, Jennison had asked the officers to meet with him at the sutler's tent. When the officers assembled, Jennison announced that the purpose for which he had called them together was to allow them to express by means of a secret ballot their preference for a successor to himself as colonel of the regiment. Ballot slips were handed out, and when the votes had been collected, Jennison stated that the result of the vote would be declared at a second meeting to be held at seven o'clock that evening. (This second meeting was not held, and the result of the vote was never announced.) When Jennison had spoken, Hoyt rose and moved "that a committee of three be appointed to draft resolutions expressive of the sentiments of the officers . . . toward Col. Jennison." The motion was carried, whereupon Anthony appointed Major Thomas P. Herrick and Lieutenant William S. Moorhouse of Company B as members of the committee, and Hoyt himself as chairman. The card to the *Times*, which had been written by Herrick and Moorhouse, then averred: "We here most positively state that this committee was never called together by its chairman; that the committee never met for the purpose of drafting the resolutions . . . nor for any other purpose; . . . that the resolutions . . . never were adopted

43. Printed in Leavenworth *Conservative*, April 17, 1862.

by the officers of the Regiment and that we, as members of the committee ignore them in toto."[44] A publication such as this would have abashed almost anyone, but it did not visibly embarrass Hoyt. He countered the card with a letter of his own. He did not deny that he had drawn the resolutions himself, but he claimed that Herrick and Moorhouse had asked him to do so; "this I did. Whether they express the sentiments of Major Herrick or Lieut. Moorehouse [sic] I neither know nor care. I do know that they represent the opinions of a majority of the commissioned officers."[45] Hoyt did not bother to disclose the basis of his certainty about the opinion of a majority of the officers, but his letter at any rate closed the war of words. It left the impression that there was not among the officers of the Seventh the degree of harmony, the band-of-brothers spirit, which makes for a happy and efficient military unit.

But this was only an entertaining side issue, and Jennison's speech was to have another and far more serious result. Whatever he may have intended to convey and whatever he may have actually said, many of those who heard him believed that he had urged them to desert and to join him in forming an "independent force" to fight the war as it should be fought, unhampered by the "red tape" orders of proslavery officers like Denver and Sturgis.[46] Many of the men were already confused and restive, disturbed by the unwelcome prospect of the expedition to New Mexico, and uncertain about the future of the regiment.[47] It says much for the effect of rank and for Jennison's hold upon the men that, in spite of his chronic absences, many of them looked to him for leadership. His speech had an undoubted effect, the more so because he told the men what many of them already believed.

What happened in the next thirty-six hours is impossible to establish with precision from the contradictory mass of pro- and anti-Jennison

44. Leavenworth Times, April 30, 1862, clipping in Jennison Scrapbook.
45. Hoyt's letter of April 22, 1862, printed in Leavenworth Conservative, April 23, 1862, clipping ibid.
46. Lyman, "Reminiscences."
47. Letter captioned "Fort Riley, May 5" printed in Leavenworth Conservative, May 10, 1862, clipping in Jennison Scrapbook; "The soldiers expect orders to move to New Mexico, and from their conversation one would conclude that a trip most anywhere else would be much more agreeable to their wishes. They say that if their services are needed to put down rebels they are willing to serve faithfully until the end . . . but if they are expected to do no service except to march up and down the country, over the plains and back again, nothing but eat rations and endure the hardships and privations of camp life, then they wish to be out of service and return to their homes."

newspaper articles, letters, reports, and orders. It would appear that a large number of Jayhawkers, perhaps as many as one hundred, took Jennison at his word and went over the hill, taking their horses and arms with them.[48] Some of them simply rode away; others played it safe and left after getting furlough papers from Jennison, who issued them to everyone who applied.[49] He granted these furloughs in direct and probably deliberate defiance of Colonel Deitzler's General Orders No. 2, issued only two weeks before, which forbade the granting of leaves to officers and of furloughs to enlisted men, except with the written approval of General Deitzler himself.[50]

By the morning of April 15, the regiment had lost a high percentage —perhaps as many as 20 percent—of its members.[51] Anthony and some of the other officers had already brought the situation to the attention of Colonel Deitzler, commanding the troops, including the Seventh, that had been assembled at Lawrence for the New Mexico expedition, "and expressed the opinion that unless something were done immediately to check . . . [Jennison] the 7th Regiment would 'be broken entirely.'"[52] Deitzler, however, refused to intervene until, as he wrote afterwards,

48. The number one hundred is from an undated clipping from the Leavenworth *Bulletin, ibid.* The number of deserters is given as ninety in Colonel Deitzler's letter printed in the Leavenworth *Conservative* on May 9. Anthony's formal letter of complaint to Deitzler, dated April 15, 1862, unidentified clipping, Jennison Scrapbook, stated that "Passes have been issued by Col. Jennison to many of the soldiers—and in consequence of his action some fifty of our men have left." The charges and specifications against Jennison, drawn up as a result of this incident, state that Jennison issued "between twenty and one hundred furloughs . . . and that he further advised one or all of the soldiers receiving such furloughs to leave with or without the approval of . . . [Colonel Deitzler]." See unidentified clipping, captioned "Charges and Specifications preferred against Charles R. Jennison," Jennison Scrapbook. These charges and specifications are not in Jennison's service record compiled by the adjutant general's office, presumably because he was not brought to trial on them.

49. According to the undated clipping from the Leavenworth *Bulletin,* cited in n. 48, above, Jennison issued three hundred passes.

50. General Orders No. 2, March 31, 1862, in Seventh Kansas, Regimental Order Book.

51. A tabulation of the data in the *Report of the Adjutant General of the State of Kansas* shows only eight desertions on April 15 and eight more in the six days following. No desertions are shown for April 14. Even after every allowance is made for Anthony's excitability, it is inconceivable that he should have made so great an issue over a mere eight desertions. Either the adjutant general's data are grossly in error, or the great majority of those who took French leave returned after a brief visit to their homes or to the fleshpots of Lawrence and Leavenworth, and those only were formally classified as deserters who failed to return. It may or may not be significant that two weeks later, the Leavenworth *Times* (hostile to Jennison) reported that the Seventh was down to half its normal strength. It is of some interest also that all eight of the men recorded in the *Report of the Adjutant General of the State of Kansas* as having deserted on April 15 were members of Company H.

52. Deitzler's letter, printed in the Leavenworth *Conservative* on May 9, 1862, in Jennison Scrapbook.

the matter had been submitted to him officially, or, as is more likely, until Jennison had committed an overt act that would place him publicly, clearly, and unequivocally in the wrong.

This Jennison obligingly did on the morning of April 15. Anthony believed that a large proportion of the men who had left, with or without Jennison's passes, were in Leavenworth, and he ordered Lieutenant Amos Hodgman, Company F, to go there with a three-man detail, round up the absentees, and bring them back to camp. Hodgman was on his way to Deitzler's headquarters to have Anthony's orders approved when he met Jennison. The latter asked to see Hodgman's orders and, having read them, tore them up as a usurpation of his authority, claiming that since his resignation was not to become effective until May 1, such orders could only emanate from him.[53] Having thus thumbed his nose at his lieutenant colonel, Jennison left for Leavenworth the next day, conveniently forgetting that "since his resignation was not to become effective until May 1," his place until then was with the regiment.

When Hodgman returned to Anthony and described his encounter with the colonel, Anthony sent a formal complaint of Jennison's actions to Deitzler, who forwarded it to General Sturgis with the following endorsement: "Respectfully referred to District Headquarters, with the request that Col. Jennison, who is now in Leavenworth, be put under arrest immediately. Col. J[ennison] has, within the past five days, done all in his power to excite mutiny in and break up his regiment. The proper charges will be prepared and forwarded in due time."[54] Deitzler's despatch presented Sturgis with a thorny problem. From a purely personal standpoint, he must have been delighted. He had his highly vocal enemy just where he wanted him. But there were other weighty factors to be taken into account. In view of the undisputed facts (as he had them) of Jennison's behavior, and on the basis of Anthony's letter of complaint and Deitzler's endorsement, any commanding officer would have been justified in at once placing the culprit in arrest. But Sturgis was already

---

53. *Ibid.* According to another account, written by a newspaperman openly friendly to Jennison, the latter tore up Hodgman's orders because in the colonel's opinion, the three-man detail given him by Anthony was "utterly inadequate" to round up the deserters. See unidentified clipping, perhaps from the New York *Times*, captioned "Our St. Louis Letter—St. Louis, April 27, 1862," *ibid.*

54. Deitzler's letter printed in the Leavenworth *Conservative*, May 9, 1862, clipping *ibid.*

unpopular with Kansas radicals and abolitionists and had to think of the certainty of bringing down upon his head their bitter enmity if he arrested one of their leading lights. With the influence that Senator Lane was known to possess at the sources of promotion and choice assignments, this was not a prospect to be faced lightly by an already more than sufficiently unpopular officer of the regular army.

It does not appear, however, that Sturgis hesitated for very long over his decision. On the afternoon of the seventeenth, Lieutenant John E. Martin was sent to Leavenworth with a detail of a sergeant and ten men, with orders to arrest Jennison and Hoyt and bring them to the fort without allowing them to communicate with each other.[55] What Hoyt was doing in Leavenworth instead of being with the regiment in Lawrence, and why he too was ordered arrested, do not appear in the surviving records. He was the first to be arrested; Jennison was apprehended an hour or two later, and by midafternoon both were in secure custody at the fort. At nine that evening, Jennison was taken across the river to Weston, Missouri, and, guarded by an escort of a lieutenant and five men, he was sent by train to St. Louis, where he was delivered to the provost marshal general, Colonel B. G. Farrar.

The lieutenant in command of the escort carried the following missive from Sturgis to Colonel Farrar:

I send Col. Jennison, of the Seventh Kansas Volunteers to St. Louis, in order that he may be placed in such close custody as will place his escape beyond the pale of possibility—and I hope you will send him at once to Alton. He is charged with very grave offenses,—such as disorganizing his regiment, and inducing his men to desert so that he can place himself at their head when the expedition leaves the State for New Mexico, &c., and become the leader of a band of outlaws whose object is to be "plunder." . . . You will find him an exceeding plausible and shrewd man, which renders him the more dangerous to this already distracted community—and if not well guarded he will escape and return to this country, where he knows every lane and bush, and all the troops in the State will be unable to recapture him.[56]

55. The details of Jennison's arrest were reported in the Leavenworth *Conservative,* April 18, 1862, clipping *ibid.* The date of Jennison's arrest is sometimes given as April 18. Jennison himself dated it at various times as April 17 or 18. The arrest actually occurred on the afternoon of the seventeenth. There is doubt also about the identity of the officer sent to arrest Jennison and Hoyt. In two different accounts, he is identified as Lieutenant John E. Martin and as Lieutenant Charles Speed.

56. Quoted in full in an unidentified clipping, *ibid.*

Colonel Farrar did not follow Sturgis' suggestion to send Jennison to the Illinois penitentiary at Alton for safekeeping. Instead, he had him placed in the Fifth Street Military Prison in St. Louis. There may or may not be a symbolic significance in the fact that before the war the prison had been the barracoon of a slave trader named Lynch.

CHAPTER VIII

The Politics
of
Command

THERE WAS enough war news and to spare to fill the columns of northern newspapers in April, 1862. McClellan's huge army had at last moved from Washington and was laying siege to Yorktown on its way to Richmond. General Grant had won the bloody battle of Shiloh by an uncomfortably narrow margin. Commodore Farragut's ships had begun the bombardment of the Confederate forts below New Orleans. And now too there was excitement beyond the Mississippi. Colonel Jennison, the "Little Chief" of Kansas radicals, the uncompromising champion of freedom, the fighting abolitionist, the Turner Ashby and John Hunt Morgan combined of the Union, had fallen victim to the malice of proslavery generals. He was under arrest on the vaguest of charges or no charges at all, and confined in a St. Louis slave pen with rebels and common criminals, for only one reason: he had properly and adamantly refused to serve the proslavery traitors in their betrayal of freedom and schemes of political fraud.

This was the theme of Jennison's friends; and thus advertised, he blossomed forth in the two weeks following his arrest as the hero of the powerful abolitionist press, and his case became the sensation of the hour. Kansas and Missouri newspapers were naturally full of it. Long articles about the case appeared also in the major metropolitan papers in New

York, Chicago, and Washington; and in that era of "exchanges," the articles were widely copied by the smaller newspapers as well.

Generally speaking, Jennison got a much better press than he deserved. The Chicago *Tribune*, the New York *Times*, the St. Louis *Democrat*, the New York *Tribune*, and, of course, the German language press were conspicuous in beating the drums in his behalf and in castigating Denver and Sturgis. The reports printed by these papers were tendentious in the extreme, even by the free-and-easy journalistic standards of the day, so much so that at length Sturgis was stung into issuing a circular in his own defense. He declared that "As there appears to be a serious misapprehension in the minds of many persons (especially at a distance) as to the grounds upon which Col. C. R. Jennison was placed in arrest, and entertaining a due regard for that proper 'Public Opinion' which takes alarm at the arbitrary exercise of military power— I avail myself of this method of disabusing the public mind on the subject." After this preface, he proceeded to explain that Jennison had been arrested on Colonel Deitzler's "earnest solicitation" and was charged "with the most serious crimes known to military law." [1] Sturgis' regard for "Public Opinion" did not extend to the disclosure of the specific crimes with which Jennison was charged, notwithstanding that much was being made in the pro-Jennison newspapers of the fact that their hero was being held in prison with no knowledge of the charges he would be required to face.

Sturgis had to be more communicative with General Halleck than he was with the public. On April 19 he sent a despatch to St. Louis, "for the information of the commanding general," to explain that it was "the disorganizing and mutinous spirit evinced by . . . Jennison" that had made it necessary to arrest him. He added:

Col. Jennison's object in resigning from the service was to get rid of military restraint and return to his previous and favorite pursuit vulgarly called "jayhawking"—which is another name for high-way robbery. To this end he has been making speeches of a highly disorganizing and disgraceful character and the consequence is that the country is now flooded with deserters from his regt, well mounted, well armed and equipped, and ready to rally around him

1. Unidentified clipping, *ibid.*

as their chief as soon as the expeditions preparing for the field shall have marched.[2]

The formal charges for which Jennison's friends were clamoring were in fact prepared, and eventually they were published; but since he was never brought to trial, they were not used. He was charged, first, with using, in his April 13 speech, "contemptuous and disrespectful language towards the President of the United States" and towards Generals Halleck, Sturgis, Denver, and Mitchell, all four of whom he denounced as "secessionists and traitors"; second, with "persuading and encouraging soldiers to desert" by granting "between twenty and one hundred furloughs" contrary to orders, advising the men to whom he granted the furloughs "to leave with or without the approval of the Colonel commanding Troops in Lawrence" (that is, Colonel Deitzler), and by tearing up Anthony's order to Lieutenant Hodgman to arrest all enlisted men of the Seventh absent without furloughs approved by Colonel Deitzler.[3]

But Jennison's press was not unanimously laudatory. The Kansas City *Journal of Commerce*, in one of the longest one-sentence editorials on record, declared it "amazing—aye . . . degrading to American society and morals" that when a "notorious freebooter . . . guilty of the blackest crimes . . . who has caused men to be taken prisoners of war, and shot down in cold blood . . . who has desolated immense districts of the land with fire and sword" etc., etc., was arrested, "he should be heralded by a venal press as a martyr."[4] It was an age when editorial vituperation was the lifeblood of journalism, and it was therefore quite in order for a Kansas Democratic newspaper to describe Jennison as a "blood-stained, murdering and thieving wretch" whose "crimes are almost unparalleled in history" and who, if the question were put to a vote of the people of Kansas, would be "hung higher than Haman."[5] Justification was even found for the failure to inform him of the charges against him on the ground that if Jennison knew what the charges were,

---

2. Sturgis to Captain J. C. Kelton, April 19, 1862, in Records of the Adjutant General's Office.

3. Unidentified clipping, Jennison Scrapbook. The charges and specifications were signed by Lieutenant John Kendal (or Kendall), Company H. Kendal was "dismissed from the service" November 22, 1862.

4. Undated clipping from Kansas City *Journal of Commerce, ibid.*

5. Unidentified clipping, *ibid.*

he and his friends would set to work "to fabricate perjury, in the shape of testimony, to refute them."[6]

The hero (or villain) of this journalistic *emeute* was in the meantime having a remarkably pleasant time of it in durance vile. He had been spirited out of Leavenworth on the evening of the seventeenth without an opportunity to bid his wife and daughter farewell, or even to pick up a supply of clean linen. There was great popular excitement in Leavenworth when news of his and Hoyt's arrest got about. A "few citizens" immediately pledged a fund of four thousand dollars and authorized Jennison to draw upon it to whatever extent he needed money for personal and legal expenses. And the "slave pen" to which he was taken in St. Louis turned out on a closer look to be far less grim, and the conditions of his imprisonment far less onerous, than might have been expected. His wife and daughter followed him to St. Louis; they were permitted to visit him at will. While undoubtedly in confinement, Jennison was installed in the keeper's own quarters and was in all respects treated with the greatest kindness and indulgence. To make time pass quickly and agreeably, he was permitted to receive guests, and his room was "thronged with a stream of visitors," among them newspapermen, "prominent citizens," the British consul, and General Sigel.[7]

Although Jennison's incarceration was of the mildest variety, he was anxious to obtain his release. On April 23 he tried a curious stratagem. On the morning of the fifteenth he had torn up Lieutenant Hodgman's orders on the ground, he said, that since his own resignation was not to take effect until May 1, he was still in command of the regiment, and only he, and not Anthony, was competent to issue them. But now, on the twenty-third, he applied to Colonel J. C. Kelton, Halleck's assistant adjutant general, for an order to be released from prison on the ground that since his resignation had been accepted, he was no longer in the army and, as a civilian, could not legally be held in a military prison.[8] In numerous communications to Colonels Kelton and Farrar, he laid great stress on the fact that no charges had as yet been preferred against him. It

6. Clipping from Leavenworth *Daily Inquirer*, April 29, 1862, *ibid.*

7. Unidentified clipping, perhaps the New York *Times*, captioned "Our St. Louis Letter—St. Louis, April 27, 1862," *ibid.*

8. Jennison to Captain J. C. Kelton, datelined "Military Prison, St. Louis, April 23d, 1862," in Records of the Adjutant General's Office.

does not appear that Kelton was greatly impressed by Jennison's sudden partiality for civilian status, but the inexplicable absence of charges proved to be decisive. On the evening of April 25, Colonel Farrar assumed the responsibility of releasing Jennison on parole; but in a significant departure from normal military practice, he required Jennison to post bond in the sum of twenty thousand dollars as a condition of his release.[9] In a demonstration of radical solidarity, twenty-five of the "wealthiest Union men" in St. Louis, whose combined assets totalled five million dollars, signed Jennison's bond.[10] Hoyt, who, it was said, contracted a severe attack of rheumatic fever from his confinement in a "damp, filthy hole" at Fort Leavenworth, had been freed four days earlier.[11]

Two days before Jennison was arrested, on the evening of April 15, the officers of the Seventh had given a "grand military ball" at the Eldridge House in Lawrence. The officers of the other regiments assembled in Lawrence to make the expedition to New Mexico were the guests of the Seventh; and of course a large turnout of the ladies of Lawrence, both young and mature, graced the occasion. Music was furnished by the band of the Twelfth Wisconsin Infantry. Supper was served on three tables, each sixty feet in length, "groaning 'neath the weight of everything that is delicious to the human palate." Toasts succeeded each other in great profusion, including a toast to the health of Colonel Jennison and a toast proposed by him to the ladies of Lawrence. The Leavenworth *Conservative* reporter who covered the ball described it as a gay and happy occasion.[12] One may wonder if even with the mollifying effect of the presence of ladies, not to mention the social lubricant provided by the numerous toasts, the atmosphere was quite so brotherly as the reporter professed to believe. Were Major Herrick and Lieutenant Moorhouse filled with benevolent feelings toward Lieutenant Hoyt, and vice versa? Did Lieutenant Hodgman's heart overflow with

9. Castel, *Frontier State*, 60, states that Jennison was released from prison as a result of "pressures from influential abolitionists, to whom Jennison and Hoyt were heroes, and perhaps blackmail threats on their part prevented a court martial." No evidence is cited, either for the abolitionist pressures, or for the threats of blackmail.

10. Undated clipping, New York *Times*, in Jennison Scrapbook.

11. Report from Leavenworth datelined June 2, 1862, undated clipping, Chicago *Tribune*, *ibid.*

12. Leavenworth *Conservative*, April 18, 1862, clipping *ibid.*

affection for his colonel, who had torn up his orders only that morning, and did the latter display nothing but a cheery camaraderie toward Colonel Deitzler?

And above all, after the events of the forty-eight hours preceding the ball, how deep was the cordiality between Jennison and his lieutenant colonel? Jennison was not a writer of letters, but Anthony was. Practically nothing is known of Jennison's attitude toward Anthony while both men were members of the Seventh. Anthony, on the other hand, has revealed a great deal about his attitude toward his commanding officer. As early as December, he had expressed the hope of succeeding to the colonelcy of the regiment if Jennison was promoted to brigadier general. In subsequent letters, he rang the changes on Jennison's short-comings, his unfitness "for any position on acct of his poor education," his habitual absence from his post, and his interference with Anthony's own efforts to instil discipline into the regiment. These strictures were not unmerited, but they were made with an unction that was somewhat excessive.

One can see also in Anthony's letters, especially those written after Jennison's appointment as acting brigadier general had made Anthony commander of the regiment in fact instead of by default, a growing self-satisfaction in his knowledge of tactics and administration and his competence to command in camp and in the field. And even more, one senses in his comments a growing pride in the regiment and in his own position as its commander.

To criticize Anthony for these feelings would be most unfair. George Waring, the articulate commander of the Fourth Missouri—the "Vierte Missouri"—described thus the spiritual rewards of being colonel of a regiment of cavalry:

To be the head of the brotherhood, with the unremitted clank of the guard's empty scabbard trailing before one's tent door day and night; with the stand-ard of the regiment proclaiming the house of chief authority; with the re-spectful salute of all passers, and the natural obedience of all members of the command . . . living in this atmosphere, one almost feels the breath of feudal days coming modified through the long tempestuous ages to touch his cheek. . . . And then the thousand men, and the yearly million that they cost, while they fill the colonel's cup of responsibility (sometimes to overflowing) and give him heavy trials—they are his own men; their usefulness is almost his own creation, and their renown is his highest glory.[13]

There is nothing discreditable in Anthony's desire to become colonel of the Seventh, especially since he believed, and not entirely without reason, that he was better qualified to command the regiment than was Jennison. Now that the latter had submitted his resignation, Anthony might expect to have his opportunity. But would he have the chance to show what he could do as colonel of the regiment? Did Jennison really mean to leave the service, or was his resignation intended only to bring political pressure on the administration to replace Sturgis, Denver, and other conservatives with officers of a more radical stripe, whereupon the resignation would be withdrawn?

Then came Jennison's speech of the thirteenth and his actions on the fifteenth, clearly endangering the existence of the regiment. Was Anthony to sit back calmly and do nothing? When every allowance is made for the fact that Anthony was not at his best under stress, that excitement brought out all his hotheaded penchant to strike out in all directions, it is nevertheless difficult to resist the suspicion that if he had been less covetous of the colonelcy of the Seventh, his pleas to Colonel Deitzler to "check" Jennison would have been considerably less urgent. It was, at any rate, commonly believed at the time that Anthony's jealousy of Jennison, and his great desire to succeed him, triggered the latter's arrest. One strongly pro-Jennison newspaperman reported that Jennison had added fuel to Anthony's jealousy by letting it be known that he favored Major Lee for the command of the regiment and was using his influence with the governor to that end.[14] It may not be without significance that while Jennison was still in prison in St. Louis, he received a letter from Anthony in which the latter apologized for, and tried to excuse, his share in bringing about the colonel's arrest.[15]

Released from prison on April 25, Jennison joined his family at Barnum's Hotel and, for the next several days, basked in the status of a "hero and martyr" of freedom, to which his zealous friends of the press

---

13. George E. Waring, Jr., *Whip and Spur* (Philadelphia, 1875), 67–69.
14. Undated clipping, New York *Times*, in Jennison Scrapbook.
15. *Ibid.*

had promoted him. On the evening of the twenty-sixth he enjoyed his apotheosis. He was tendered a serenade at his hotel by two or three thousand Germans. Kost's Band played patriotic airs. Then Jennison was introduced, with appropriate eulogies. He responded by thanking the patriotic Germans for the honor they were paying him, which, he said, he accepted as due not to himself as an individual, but to the principles he represented. After telling his audience that as an officer in the army he could not with propriety say much of what was on his mind, he explained that as an avowed abolitionist he was the victim of politically inspired hatred, and that his enemies—General Sturgis, for example—were traitors and cowards.[16] This, generally, was the tenor of several other speeches he made in St. Louis in the next four days. In all of them he took pains to emphasize that his sole aim was freedom for all men and that his only ambition was to be a soldier in a *real* fight for liberty.

A peculiar change had come over Jennison in the course of the ten days he spent in St. Louis. He had submitted his resignation two weeks before, ostensibly because he could not in honor and conscience fight the war within the ideological limitations imposed upon him by a shortsighted administration and its doubtfully loyal minions. But now, whatever the reason may have been, whether it was the adulation he was receiving, the heady effect of his own oratory, or the sobering second thoughts of levelheaded friends, Jennison decided to seek vindication and reinstatement in the army. Perhaps he had not intended his resignation to be accepted with such alacrity. In any case, on May 1 he obtained from Colonel Farrar an extension of the geographic limits of his parole, to permit him to go to Washington, and on the following day he departed for the capital under the obligation of reporting by letter daily to St. Louis.

While Jennison occupied the center of the stage, his deeply disturbed regiment, its future uncertain, its colonel under arrest after resigning, and a sizeable percentage of its enlisted personnel gone, remained in its camp at Lawrence. Jennison's departure made Anthony commander of the regiment. His most urgent task was to restore a semblance of order and

---

16. Unidentified clipping, captioned "Honors to Doc Jennison—The Martyr of Bleeding Kansas Makes a Speech," *ibid.*

discipline among his men. Fortunately, nearly all the officers remained unaffected by Jennison's example, and Anthony could rely on their help. True, Hoyt was under arrest, and Captains John L. Merrick of Company I and Horace Pardee of Company H submitted their resignations on April 15 and 16 respectively, but were persuaded to withdraw them. The rest of the officers to all outward appearances placed loyalty to the regiment ahead of whatever personal sense of obligation they may have felt toward Jennison. Confident of their support, and in the expectation that their presence with the men would allay the excitement and discontent Jennison had caused, Anthony issued orders on the eighteenth that all line officers were to live with their men and were neither to be absent from camp in the daytime, nor leave camp after retreat, without the lieutenant colonel's permission.

On April 2 General Denver had recommended to Halleck that the regiments designated for the expedition to New Mexico be moved to Fort Riley, about eighty-five miles west of Lawrence. Denver explained that there was a large amount of forage at Fort Riley "which it would be economy on the part of the Government to use up at once; and besides . . . [it is] the most convenient post in Kansas for outfitting a large expedition." [17] Jennison, in one of his St. Louis speeches, insinuated that the reason given by Denver was the cover for a corrupt plot thought up by the regular army clique at Fort Leavenworth, and that the troops were to go to Fort Riley to "consume a hay contract, which would be lost if horses were not sent up there." [18] Halleck, however, accepted Denver's recommendation; and on April 21 the Seventh broke up camp and began its march to Fort Riley via Topeka. [19] Before their departure, the Jayhawkers were forced to comply with Colonel Deitzler's humiliating order to Anthony to "cause the dead horses of his command to be buried immediately." [20]

17. *Official Records*, VIII, 654.

18. Report from Leavenworth datelined June 2, 1862, undated clipping, Chicago *Tribune*, in Jennison Scrapbook.

19. Fox, "Story," 30, gives the date as April 22, but Pomeroy, "War Diary," entry for April 21, and Ira C. Dutton, "Civil War Diary," State Historical Society of Wisconsin, Madison, entry for April 21, agree on April 21 as the date of the Jayhawkers' departure for Fort Riley. Dutton was a soldier in the Thirteenth Wisconsin Infantry.

20. Colonel Deitzler to Anthony, Special Orders No. 128, April 18, 1862, in Seventh Kansas, Regimental Order Book.

There had been heavy spring rains during the final week of the Seventh's stay at Lawrence, and all the streams in eastern Kansas were out of their banks. But the skies cleared as the week ended, and the Jayhawkers made the four-day march to Fort Riley in ideal spring sunshine. Their road westward ran along the south bank of the Kansas River, whose valley was bounded on both sides by a high, gently rolling prairie, and the only signs of human habitation were an occasional cabin near the river. The scenery was "wildly picturesque," and the leisurely march was the most enjoyable the regiment had yet made.

Fort Riley was situated near the confluence of the Smoky Hill and Republican rivers. The Seventh pitched its camp one and a half miles from the fort, on the bank of the Republican, in an area sheltered from the prairie winds by a bluff two hundred feet high. The Twelfth Wisconsin camp was on the bluff, a half-mile away; one of the Badgers wrote his sister: "We can see ten miles or twelve miles in most every direction and the wind can see us a long time before it get[s] to us and it all aims right towards us."[21] The troopers of the Seventh braved the wind to view the sunsets from the bluff and found them spectacularly beautiful; said Webster Moses: "As we gase on the beauties of nature we allmost forget the warfare we are engaged in and our minds instinctively turn toward *Home* and *loved ones left behind* but enough of this."[22] The inspiration of spring and the view of the sunset over the empty prairie made Moses realize that Nancy Mowry meant considerably more to him than the cautious "Dear Friend" salutation of his letters to her suggested.

After May 2 the Seventh was able to enjoy the sunsets without having to make a long scramble up the bluff to do so. Surgeon Joseph L. Wever condemned the regiment's riverbank camp after a number of the men came down with the "ague and kindred diseases" and insisted that a new camp be set up on healthier and drier ground on the bluff.[23]

Anthony had obtained a few days' leave in Leavenworth and did not make the march to Fort Riley with the regiment. Major Herrick was in command, and presumably he was responsible for the selection of the

21. Samuel G. Swain, Twelfth Wisconsin Infantry, to his sister, April 26, 1862, in Samuel G. Swain Letters, MS 69s, State Historical Society of Wisconsin, Madison.

22. Webster Moses to Nancy Mowry, April 29, 1862, in Moses Letters.

23. Major Herrick to Colonel Deitzler, May 2, 1862, in Seventh Kansas, Regimental Letter and Order Book.

astonishing name "Camp Sturgis" for the new camp of the Seventh. Either Major Herrick was the possessor of a puckish sense of humor, or he was making a peace offering to authority.

Army officers familiar with conditions on the plains had suggested that the march to New Mexico should not begin before May 10. By that time the grass would be high enough to feed the horses of the two regiments of cavalry and two batteries of artillery, as well as the mules pulling the 525 wagons and ambulances that were to make the trip. While waiting for the orders to start, the regiments drilled and paraded. Many of the Jayhawkers who had deserted at Lawrence returned to duty and were reinstated without fuss or penalty. The men performed the routine camp duties, replaced worn-out equipment, speculated whether the march to New Mexico would actually take place, and concluded that "the natural tendency of camp life is to make one indolent and lazy." [24] They had ample leisure, which they spent in hunting, fishing, reading their mail and the newspapers, writing letters, playing cards, and visiting the fort. They also went to view the sights and to sample the entertainments, such as they were, of nearby Junction City. An indication of the nature of these recreational facilities appears in a despatch from Major Herrick to General Robert B. Mitchell. Captain Sylvester, the officer in command at Junction City, sent to the camp of the Seventh a wagon containing five barrels of whiskey, having arrested the owner on the well-founded suspicion of selling whiskey to the soldiers. Herrick asked for Mitchell's instructions "as to the disposition to be made of the liquor, as if it is not destroyed or securely stored, the men will certainly get at it in the night." [25]

Ever since Jennison's resignation, there had been much speculation in the regiment about his probable successor. Anthony, as second in command, was the obvious choice, but he suffered under two serious handicaps. Colonelcies of volunteer regiments went by political favor; they were in the gift of the governor of the state, and it was quite unlikely that Governor Robinson, a conservative Republican, would bestow a colonelcy on Anthony, a prominent member of the radical,

24. Webster Moses to Nancy Mowry, April 29, 1862, in Moses Letters.

25. Major Herrick to General R. B. Mitchell, May 7, 1862, in Seventh Kansas, Regimental Letter and Order Book.

Laneite faction. And secondly, Anthony had made too many enemies within the regiment; a majority of both the officers and men openly preferred the junior major, Albert Lindley Lee. A native of Fulton, in north-central New York, Lee was an exact contemporary of Jennison. Educated at Union College in Schenectady, of which General Halleck was a fellow alumnus, Lee practiced law in New York until 1858, when he moved to Kansas and settled in Elwood. In 1859 he was elected district judge, and after the outbreak of the Civil War, he recruited a company which became Company I of the Seventh, of which he was commissioned major, the date of his commission being one day later than that of Major Herrick.[26]

On May 14 a petition was circulated in the regiment for presentation to the governor, asking that Lee be commissioned colonel of the Seventh; it was signed by 517 of the 520 officers and men then present. On the very next day, a fantastic contretemps occurred. Governor Robinson happened to be in Washington at the time, and the lieutenant governor, Joseph P. Root, conceiving it to be his right to exercise all the functions of the chief executive in Robinson's absence, appointed Major Charles W. Blair of the Second Kansas Cavalry to the vacant colonelcy of the Seventh. The fact that Root, in addition to being lieutenant governor of Kansas, was also regimental surgeon of the same Second Kansas, was probably not unconnected with Major Blair's promotion. The freshly appointed colonel proceeded at once to Fort Riley and formally assumed command of his new regiment on May 16.[27] Fletcher Pomeroy probably understated the case when he noted in his diary that Blair's appointment was "not well received."[28] Governor Robinson now returned to Kansas and appointed Major Lee colonel of the Jayhawkers, whereupon Lee too assumed command of the regiment. The Seventh now had *two* colonels at the same time. To settle his and Blair's conflicting claims, Lee departed for Washington to obtain an official ruling from the attorney general of the United States on the legality of Blair's appointment. Thereupon

26. Blackmar (ed.), *Kansas*, II, 130; Fox, "Story," 25. The *Report of the Adjutant General of the State of Kansas*, I, 524, gives the date of Herrick's commission as October 28, 1861, and of Lee's as October 29, 1861.

27. General Mitchell's General Orders No. 7, of May 15, 1862, assigning Blair to duty as colonel of the Seventh, and Blair's General Orders No. 68, of May 16, 1862, assuming command of the regiment, are in Seventh Kansas, Regimental Order Book.

28. Pomeroy, "War Diary," entry for May 15, 1862.

Major General James G. Blunt, Sturgis' successor in command of the Department of Kansas—Sturgis having been relieved of that post at the beginning of May, to the great joy of Kansas radicals—exercised what he believed to be his prerogative as department commander; he revoked Lee's appointment as colonel and ordered Anthony to assume command of the regiment.[29] The legality of Blunt's action was very much open to question; but with Blair having disappeared from the scene and with Lee absent in Washington, Anthony had possession, legally or otherwise, and that gave the Seventh *three* claimants to the command, each with a tainted title. To anticipate the story slightly, on May 26 the Adjutant General's Office in Washington ordered Jennison restored to the command of the regiment. At that moment, therefore, the Seventh possessed the doubtful luxury of *four* commanding officers, three colonels and one lieutenant colonel, doubtless the only regiment in the Civil War that had so confusing a superfluity of riches.

Meanwhile, on May 24, a round robin signed by Chaplain Ayres, Captains Merriman, Jenkins, Merrick, and Thornton, and twelve of the lieutenants, was sent to General Blunt. The signers declared: "Learning that an attempt is being made to deprive Colonel A. L. Lee of his command as colonel of this regiment, and feeling the deepest interest for its welfare, and knowing full well that its efficiency depends entirely upon its commander, and having full confidence in the ability of Colonel Lee, [we] would most earnestly pray that he be allowed to retain command."[30] General Blunt took a rather starchy view of this well-intentioned petition. He had his assistant adjutant general return the round robin to the regiment with the endorsement: "The commanding Genl. fails to see the right that any Regt. has to petition him in relation to who shall command them. Laws and regulations are the guidance, and that alone is sufficient."[31] A member of the regiment, witnessing the tug of war then taking place between the rival candidates for the colonelcy, and another between those contending for the privilege of making the appointment, might well have doubted if the issue was as clearly a matter of "laws and regulations" as General Blunt claimed it to be.

29. Anthony to his father, May 28, 1862, in Langsdorf and Richmond (eds.), "Anthony," 367.

30. Round robin dated May 24, 1862, in Seventh Kansas, Regimental Letter and Order Book.

31. Endorsement on the round robin, dated May 26 and signed by Captain Thomas Moonlight, *ibid.*

Jennison's "restoration" to command deserves to be more widely known than it is, for it is a classic of political skullduggery. If ever a man received what in the parlance of gambling is known as a fast shuffle, Jennison assuredly did. A special piquancy is added to the story by the fact that one of the chief actors in this interesting performance was the president himself, none other than "Honest Abe," who demonstrated that in the rarefied atmosphere of his high office, he had not forgotten the sleight-of-hand aspects of Illinois courthouse politics.

After a three-day sojourn in Chicago, Jennison arrived in Washington on the evening of May 5.[32] The following morning he began his campaign for reinstatement by soliciting the support of the two Kansas senators, Lane and Pomeroy. It is not without interest that for the next three weeks, most of the daily reports of his whereabouts that he was obliged to send to Colonel Farrar under the terms of his parole were written on "Thirty-Seventh Congress—Senate Chamber" stationery. These reports make it evident that Jennison was getting the attention he undoubtedly considered to be his due. They also show that his case was receiving consideration at the highest level. On May 9 he wrote to Farrar in his inimitable grammar, spelling, and handwriting, that "the President & Sec. of War are at the great army. Many here think that they will remain there untill the capture of Richmond. There is a great many that thinks that McCleland is not as [illegible] as he should be. I have all things Right As soon as the President arives The House and Senate have recommended to the President my appointment as Brig. Genl. Sturgis has arrived at this city I wish you would advise me if there has any thing been done in my case."[33]

The president, accompanied by Secretary of the Treasury Chase and Secretary Stanton, had gone to visit Fortress Monroe and was absent from Washington for a week. While awaiting his return, Lane and Pomeroy obtained the signatures of "forty or fifty of the best members of Congress" to a petition to the president, requesting him to appoint Jennison a brigadier general. But Jennison's presence in Washington and the object of his visit had become widely known, and his enemies too got busy. Caleb Bingham's charges against him were reprinted as a pamphlet,

32. Jennison to Colonel Farrar, May 2, 4, and 6, in Records of the Adjutant General's Office.
33. Same to same, May 9, *ibid.*

copies of which were distributed to all members of Congress. Jennison was forced to defend himself with a pamphlet of his own, obviously ghostwritten, wherein all of Bingham's charges and accusations were branded as falsehoods inspired by malice stemming from Jennison's denunciation of Bingham as a coward to General Hunter. This pamphlet too was distributed to all members of Congress.

Notwithstanding the hostility against Jennison, Lane's influence at the White House was sufficiently potent to "satisfy the President of the groundlessness of the charges against" his protege—at least so it was believed.[34] On May 26 the following order was sent by Adjutant General Lorenzo Thomas to Brigadier General W. Scott Ketchum, acting inspector general at St. Louis:

The President desires that Col. Charles R. Jennison, of the Seventh Kansas Volunteers, may remain in the service, with the rank of Colonel.

If his resignation has been accepted, you are directed to muster him into his original position, as Colonel of the Seventh Kansas Volunteers, to date from the day of original muster.[35]

It was widely reported that restoration to his rank and command was but the first step toward higher things for Jennison; that, in fact, he was to receive shortly the command of a brigade to operate in western Arkansas and Indian Territory, with formal promotion to the rank of brigadier general to follow.

But in some mysterious fashion, Jennison's triumph over his enemies turned out to be as short-lived as the flowers that bloom in May on the prairies of his adopted state. No sooner did it become known that his reinstatement had been ordered than the Missouri delegation in Congress waited in a body upon the president to protest, an event that it is impossible to believe the president had failed to anticipate. The Missourians gave the president their version of Jennison's character and record and represented that his return to the border or anywhere near it at the head of a regiment of United States troops would have a deeply disturbing effect on the loyal people of Missouri. They left the White House with what they understood to be a positive assurance that Jennison would not be given a command.[36]

34. Unidentified clipping, datelined "Washington, May 26, 1862", in Jennison Scrapbook.
35. *Ibid.*
36. Kansas City *Journal*, June 5, 1862, clipping *ibid.*

Jennison in the meantime had departed for St. Louis, no doubt rejoicing in the successful outcome of his Washington journey. Arrived at his destination, he presented himself to General Ketchum to complete the formalities of his reinstatement. To his astonishment, Ketchum refused to muster him in. And why not? Because General Thomas' order, as received in St. Louis, instructed Ketchum to muster in "Charles R. Jennings" as colonel of the Seventh Kansas, whereas the gentleman then standing before General Ketchum's desk was, by his own statement, named Jennison, and not Jennings.[37] A regrettable error, due no doubt to clerical carelessness; but unless a correction came from Washington, General Ketchum was powerless to act . . . and that was the end of Jennison's connection with the Seventh Kansas.

One may well wonder why the story ended, as it did, on this unsatisfactory note. Surely a telegram to General Thomas could have brought about a rectification of the "clerical error." Why did the intrepid colonel, or ex-colonel, as he now was, give up so easily? A possible explanation is that Jennison did not actually crave the colonelcy of the Seventh, and that the real purpose of his trip to Washington was merely to prove to his friends and enemies that he could have his job back if he wanted it. Or again, Jennison may now have realized that even with the apparent backing of Lane and the president, he could not hope to prevail against the regular army clique; that, in short, he could not hope to "fight City Hall" and win. A third, and perhaps the most likely, explanation stems from the fact that by the time Jennison returned to St. Louis, the Seventh had been removed from Kansas, as will be related shortly. The regiment would now have to fight hundreds of miles from Kansas as a small cog in General Halleck's huge army. Gone were the days of the "Independent Kansas Jay-Hawkers." The colonel of the Seventh would have to follow orders instead of being a law unto himself, and whatever the regiment did in the future, it would not perform in the front yard, as it were, of an admiring public of its fellow Kansans. The theatrical possibilities of being colonel of a regiment of Kansas cavalry serving on the Kansas-Missouri border had clearly been an important

37. A "Card" dated June 24, from Jennison, printed June 25, 1862, in Leavenworth *Conservative*, clipping *ibid.*

factor in Jennison's desire to organize and lead the Seventh. The opportunity to make a splash, to show off, had appealed to his vanity. That opportunity was now gone, and all the glamor of being colonel of the Seventh was gone with it. New and better opportunities to impress a Kansas audience would surely come his way if he remained in the state and made it his business not to allow his fellow citizens to forget that Jennison the Jayhawker, the victim of a foul conspiracy of proslavery, prorebel army officers, remained among them, ready for new enterprises.

The peaceful life the Seventh had been leading at Fort Riley came to an abrupt end on May 18 with the arrival of orders cancelling the New Mexico expedition and directing the troops assembled at Fort Riley to march to Fort Leavenworth in preparation for a move to Corinth, Mississippi, where they were to join General Halleck's army.[38] The prospect of the march to New Mexico had been accepted with resignation by the men of the Kansas and Wisconsin regiments, and the change in orders was greeted with rejoicing.[39] Mississippi was a long way from Kansas, but it stood for a change in scenery; and ever since General Grant's capture of Fort Henry in early February, it was the area in which things were happening. And so the Jayhawkers were in high spirits when they set off on their march to Fort Leavenworth on the nineteenth.

The regiment had a few days' rest at Fort Leavenworth while it waited for the arrival of the boats that were to take it down the Missouri and Mississippi and up the Ohio and Tennessee to Pittsburg Landing, whence they were to march overland to Corinth. Before its departure, the entire regiment, and especially Company K, was saddened by the resignation of Captain John Brown, Jr., because of ill health, and the Seventh left for Mississippi without him.[40]

Three boats were required to transport the nearly eight hundred officers and men of the regiment, its horses, and baggage. The first section left on May 27 aboard *The New Sam. Gaty.* On the following morning the rest of the men marched aboard their ships and departed for

38. Special Orders No. 16, May 16, 1862, in Seventh Kansas, Regimental Order Book.

39. F. E. Newton to "My Friend Mr. Holmes," May 26, 1862, in Holmes Collection.

40. Brown had submitted his resignation on May 12. See Brown to Governor Robinson, May 22, 1862, in Robinson Papers. The resignation was accepted May 27, 1862. See *Report of the Adjutant General of the State of Kansas*, I, 637.

Dixie. Webster Moses, on board the *Emma*, reported that "unbounded enthusiasm" prevailed among his comrades. As the boats churned past the riverside settlements, they were greeted with the waving of handkerchiefs, flags, and even aprons, and the men responded with "cheer after cheer . . . from all parts of the boat." The general euphoria on board the *Emma* was not visibly dampened by a fatal accident on the second morning out; Private Richard Key, Company B, "slightly intoxicated," fell from the hurricane deck into the Missouri River and was never seen again.[41]

The New Sam. Gaty was already on its way up the Tennessee River, and the second and third boats were still on the Mississippi, when orders arrived in Cairo from General Halleck, directing the regiment to report to Columbus, Kentucky, a few miles downstream from Cairo, instead of to Pittsburg Landing. The second and third boats were notified of the change in destination when they arrived at Cairo, but *The New Sam. Gaty* proceeded on its way in ignorance of the new orders. Encountering another boat going upstream, the Jayhawkers participated in a race of sternwheelers and entered into the spirit of the race by contributing their entire supply of bacon to provide extra heat for the boilers of their boat and thus gain a little added speed. As a result, they were first at Pittsburg Landing, but they were also hungry and out of rations. They would have remained hungry except for the kindness of the Seventh Missouri Infantry; it learned of the predicament of its numerical namesake from Kansas and contributed its own rations to feed the starving cavalrymen. After a quick tour of the Shiloh battlefield, still littered with the debris of the desperate fighting of two months before, the Jayhawkers boarded their ship and on the following day joined the rest of the regiment at Columbus.

Anthony had been serving on a court-martial at Fort Leavenworth while the regiment was at Fort Riley. After completing the assignment, he was granted a thirty-day leave; but when orders came for the Seventh to move to Corinth, he decided to give up his leave and commanded the

---

41. Webster Moses to Nancy Mowry, June 1, 1862, in Moses Letters. Cf. *Report of the Adjutant General of the State of Kansas for the Year 1864*, 238. The *Report of the Adjutant General of the State of Kansas*, I, 517, erroneously shows Key as drowned on January 1, 1862.

regiment on its journey south. A minor mystery involving him arises from a statement in a chronicle of the Seventh printed by the Leaven-worth *Conservative* on the occasion of the return of the regiment to Kansas on veteran's furlough in February, 1864. On May 20, 1862, said the *Conservative*, "Col. Anthony [was] acquitted by a court martial of all charges brought against him." [42] Naturally, Anthony had his best foot forward in his numerous letters to members of his family. For example, one will not find in these letters any mention of the near mutiny of Company A at Humboldt. He does mention serving on and presiding over a court-martial at the end of April, but neither in his letters, nor in his service record, nor anywhere else except in the brief and mysterious note in the *Conservative* is there any reference to his appearance before a court-martial as the accused, or of any charges being preferred that might have led to court-martial proceedings against him.

June 2 found the Seventh assembled at Columbus, where with other Federal troops it occupied the extensive fortifications that Confederate General Leonidas Polk had constructed in 1861 and was compelled to evacuate when the position was flanked by Grant's capture of Forts Henry and Donelson. Camp sanitation was far from being the greatest of the Confederacy's military virtues; and on Anthony's orders, half of the Seventh spent the first two days at Columbus performing a badly needed policing of its camp area, removing a large accumulation of "brick—burnt logs—mud—old Hay—Tents clothing Beef Bones and other Bones—all half rotten and putrid." [43]

The Jayhawkers had now been in the service for eight months with practically no opportunity or need to perform the duties that in the first half of the Civil War were considered to be the proper function of cavalry. The Seventh had never been a part of an army on active service. It had not served as the eyes and ears of the infantry. It had no experience in protecting the front and flanks of an advance or the rear of a retreat. In short, except for a modest amount of scouting in Missouri in the

42. Leavenworth *Conservative*, February 6, 1864, clipping in Jennison Scrapbook. *Cf.* articles in the Leavenworth *Conservative*, May 4 and May 23, 1862, *ibid.*

43. Anthony to Aaron McLean, June 6, 1862, in Langsdorf and Richmond (eds.), "Anthony," 368.

winter of 1861, it had only a textbook knowledge of traditional cavalry doctrine when it reported for duty in Columbus. But now it was about to absorb knowledge through experience, as most military knowledge was acquired in the Civil War.

The regiment was given only one day to enjoy the camp at Columbus that it had labored so hard to clean up. On June 5 orders came to send two companies to Moscow, Kentucky, twelve miles to the south, to do picket duty for a regiment of infantry that was rebuilding a trestle, destroyed by the Confederates, on the Mobile & Ohio Railroad. Companies D and K were assigned to the job, with Major Herrick in command. On the march to Moscow, the men of the two companies had their first view of what to them was a foreign land, namely the South. The boys from Illinois and Ohio were not impressed by what they saw. The countryside itself seemed strange. They saw steep, densely wooded hills, broken by occasional patches of flat land, cleared and under cultivation. The clearings were obviously fertile, but not well cultivated. The inhabitants were "very lazy." As a member of a superior civilization, Webster Moses decided that the natives were clearly in need of "a little yankee enterprise . . . to make this one of the finest countries in the world but Slaveries curse is upon the country and its blighting effects can be seen all around." [44]

Lazy or not, the people of southwest Kentucky had their good points; even though they were "nearly all secesh they are all friendly and peaceable they do not skulk round through the brush and shoot us every chance they get like the Missourians but stay at home and mind their own business." [45] This was a boon the men could appreciate. The nearest body of rebel cavalry was a safe thirty miles away, which made picketing easy, pleasant, and quite free from danger. Even an earthquake on the sixth that shook windows and stopped pendulum clocks did not disturb the general feeling of contentment, although it did inspire the wish "that it had been hard enough to have shaken the 'Secesh Kingdom' into atoms and made the inhabitants thereof loyal to the government"; but, said Moses, the Seventh would accomplish what the earthquake had failed to

44. Webster Moses to Nancy Mowry, June 6, 1862, in Moses Letters.
45. *Ibid.*

do: "We will give them some physic that [will] make them loyal if they continue the war."[46]

On the day of the earthquake, the entire regiment was ordered to march to Union City, Tennessee, a few miles south of the Kentucky-Tennessee border. With the Twelfth Wisconsin Infantry and the Eighth Wisconsin Battery, it was to help rebuild the railroad to Corinth. That city had been evacuated by Beauregard's Confederates and occupied by Halleck's army. The Seventh remained at Union City for ten days, and then moved twenty-two miles to the southeast, to Dresden, Tennessee.

The Seventh Kansas was at this time one of the regiments composing Brigadier General Robert B. Mitchell's First Brigade of the Fourth Division, Army of the Mississippi, the latter commanded by Brigadier General William Rosecrans. General Mitchell was himself a Kansan, and the fortuitous association between him, General Rosecrans, and the Seventh Kansas was about to produce some odd and unexpected results.

46. *Ibid.*

CHAPTER IX

Exit Anthony

THE LAVISH amount of publicity the Jayhawkers and Jennison had received from the moment of their entry into the service of the United States had a serious drawback. The regiment and its colonel had become notorious, and they had made "jayhawking" a household word. The gamey reputation of the Seventh had preceded it to Kentucky and Tennessee. Moreover, finding themselves in "secesh" country once again after four months of an uneasy restraint, the Jayhawkers lost no time in living up to their reputation. Trouble began on the very first march south from Columbus, and General Halleck, already more than sufficiently well acquainted with the deviltries the Seventh Kansas Cavalry was capable of perpetrating, became the recipient of anguished despatches from his subordinates about the atrocities the Jayhawkers had committed on the way from Columbus to Union City and Dresden. It was the old familiar story of livestock and feed taken, of henroosts, smokehouses, and orchards robbed, of the theft of money and watches, of Negroes enticed from their masters, and of the loyal and disloyal victimized indiscriminately.

It was reported to headquarters that on their passage through Ripley, Tennessee, the Jayhawkers had plundered the town. Colonel Lee was to protest later that the accusation was a lie, that only one company of the Seventh had entered Ripley, that "they did not touch an article improperly," and that a trooper of the Second Iowa Cavalry had confessed to one of Lee's sergeants that the dirty work in Ripley had been done by the Hawkeyes, who, quick to take advantage of the ill repute of the Kansans, had told the townspeople that they belonged to the Seventh Kansas Cavalry.[1]

The provost marshal of Trenton, Tennessee, reported that a foraging party of the Seventh, commanded by Captain Marcus J. Parrott, assistant adjutant general of Mitchell's brigade, met near Union City a funeral procession, "with the remains of a respectable widow lady of the neighborhood, and unmindful of the remonstrances of Mr. Parrott, stopped the procession and demanded what they had in the wagon. Being told that it was a dead woman, they burst [open] the coffin and examined the contents and then left, saying, 'Go on with your d——d secession b——.' This was reported to General Mitchell, but he took no measures to punish it."[2]

Colonel Deitzler, Jennison's old antagonist, who was now in Tennessee at the head of the First Kansas Infantry, improved on the story by adding that the foraging party arrested the Reverend Mr. Koyle, a loyal citizen of Union City, and was about to possess itself of the minister's mules and buggy. Koyle then told them that he was about to conduct a funeral, and after the Kansans had made sure that he was telling the truth, which they did by breaking open the coffin and inspecting the contents, they told him "to go to hell with his d——d secession corpse."[3] Deitzler added that he had "heard of other outrages equally atrocious perpetrated by these wretches" and that they ought to be "punished or mustered out of the service to which they are a disgrace." There were even reports that the Jayhawkers "in some instances attempted to force the women to cohabit with them when found at home alone"; and the post commandant of Bethel, Tennessee, who made this report, was provoked into remarking that "the conduct of this command since it came in this vicinity had been such that it makes one ashamed of the volunteer service of the U.S. Army."[4]

1. Colonel Lee to Lieutenant George Lee, August 12, 1862, in Seventh Kansas, Regimental Letter and Order Book.
2. *Official Records*, XVII, Pt. 2, 53–54.   3. *Ibid.*, 35.
4. *Ibid.*, 94.

General Halleck informed the secretary of war of the trouble that the "robbery, theft, pillage and outrages upon the peaceful inhabitants" committed by the Seventh were causing him.[5] He represented that Anthony "actually encouraged his men in committing outrages along the road, on the ground that they were 'slaveholders' who were plundered."[6] What was to be done with the incorrigible Kansans? Halleck was plainly at a loss for an answer, for he wrote Secretary Stanton a few days later: "Measures have already been initiated to reduce these troops to order and discipline, but I have no doubt that Senator Lane and others will attribute any measures of restraint or punishment which may be adopted to political influences and will heap unmeasured abuses upon any officer who shall attempt to keep them in order."[7] Evidently the significance of General Sturgis' removal from the command of the Department of Kansas was not lost upon General Halleck.

It is at least a lefthanded tribute to the prowess of the Seventh that at a time when General Halleck was about to leave for Washington to assume the duties of general in chief of the "whole land forces of the United States," and while he was still responsible for the administration of a huge department and had an army of nearly 150,000 men under his immediate command, he should have found it worth while and indeed necessary to concern himself with the misdeeds of a single regiment of seven or eight hundred cavalrymen.

It should be said on behalf of the Seventh that the kind of misconduct General Halleck had complained of no longer represented its normal behavior toward the civilian population. For a number of reasons—the absence of guerilla activity mentioned by Webster Moses certainly made a difference—the feelings of the men towards the local citizenry were considerably less vindictive than they had been in Missouri, and their behavior toward them correspondingly less hostile. There were times, indeed, when the relations between the Jayhawkers and the Tennesseans about them were positively cordial. While General Mitchell's brigade was encamped near Dresden to "recruit the teams," a notice was circulated throughout Weakley County inviting the populace to a great pro-Union celebration on June 19. The people began to arrive bright and

5. *Ibid.*, 77.   6. *Ibid.*
7. *Ibid.*, 91.

early on the nineteenth, their wagons and buggies loaded with good things to eat; and as a preliminary to the patriotic exercises, the entire brigade was treated to a colossal picnic. This was not by any means the kind of reception the Seventh might have expected in a seceded state, nor was it what they had been accustomed to receiving in Missouri. The picnic would have been welcomed with enthusiasm had it done nothing more than provide the men with home-cooked food as a relief from army rations and camp cooking; but in addition, in the large crowd assembled for the festivities, some from as much as twenty miles away, "the Ladies were well represented."[8] With this essential ingredient added, the picnic was a great success, and deservedly so. After the food had been eaten, the soldiers and citizens adjourned to a pleasant grove of trees nearby and were treated to a stirring oration on the state of the Union by the same Marcus J. Parrott who had been involved in the secessionist funeral incident a few days earlier. General Mitchell and others also spoke, and the celebration closed with the singing of patriotic songs by the ladies, accompanied by the band of the Seventh.

The good feeling between the Seventh and the people of Weakley County that had been engendered by the picnic of the nineteenth is well illustrated by a remark in one of Webster Moses' letters. On the Sunday following the picnic, Sergeant Frank Newton and Moses went out into the country for a ride; "stoping at noon we got our dinner at a rich planter's house then after feasting on plumbs Apples cherries &c we bade our friends goodbye and started for camp."[9] To have a Jayhawker refer to a rich Tennessee planter, clearly a slaveowner, and hence by definition an enemy, and his family as "our friends" is little less than miraculous.

These pleasant events, however, did nothing to solve the command problem the Seventh had hanging over its head. And, to add to their difficulties, the Jayhawkers had succeeded, within a little more than two weeks of their arrival in the new theater, in drawing down upon themselves the wrath of a large part of the military hierarchy, up to and including the department commander. For most regiments, these troubles would have been more than enough to cope with at one time,

8. Webster Moses to Nancy Mowry, June 26, 1862, in Moses Letters; *Cf.* Pomeroy, "War Diary," entry for June 19, 1862, and Lyman, "Reminiscences."
9. Webster Moses to Nancy Mowry, June 26, 1862, in Moses Letters.

but the stalwart Seventh had a few more cards up its sleeve and proceeded to play them in a manner calculated to create the maximum of disturbance in military circles.

The principal protagonist in what can only be termed the next dramatic performance staged by the Jayhawkers was Lieutenant Colonel Anthony.

Colonel Lee returned to the regiment on June 7 from his visit to Washington. Perhaps it was by coincidence, and perhaps not, that on the same day, Anthony wrote his sister: "I desire to get out of the Army at an early day on account of some little differences in the Regt in reference to who should be colonel—Gov. Robinson wont commission me for the reason I have always belonged to the Lane party as its called—Some 20 of the officers are for me—and some 15 for Lee." [10] Attorney General Bates had not as yet handed down his ruling on the conflicting claims of Lee and Blair to the colonelcy of the regiment; but whatever his decision, Anthony's days in command of the Jayhawkers were clearly numbered. He had given up an increasingly prosperous insurance and real estate business, sold the *Conservative*, and jeopardized his lucrative postmastership to serve in the army. However sincere his devotion to the Union and freedom, it would have been unreasonable to expect that having commanded the regiment for nearly seven months, he should have been willing to stay on as second-in-command after one of his subordinates, or an outsider holding lower rank than his own, had been promoted over his head to the colonelcy of the regiment. His letter to his sister makes it evident that he had already made up his mind to leave. The question now was when and under what circumstances he would do so.

Jennison had managed to get the maximum amount of personal publicity out of his resignation and had shown, for the benefit of anyone who needed a lesson in the fine art of self-advertising, how a spectacular exit should be managed. Anthony now proceeded to demonstrate that he stood in no need of such lessons. In fact, he went Jennison one better.

From the very first days of the war, the question of what to do with, and about, the Negroes who took advantage of the proximity of Federal

10. Anthony to his sister Susan, June 7, 1862, in Langsdorf and Richmond (eds.), "Anthony," 370.

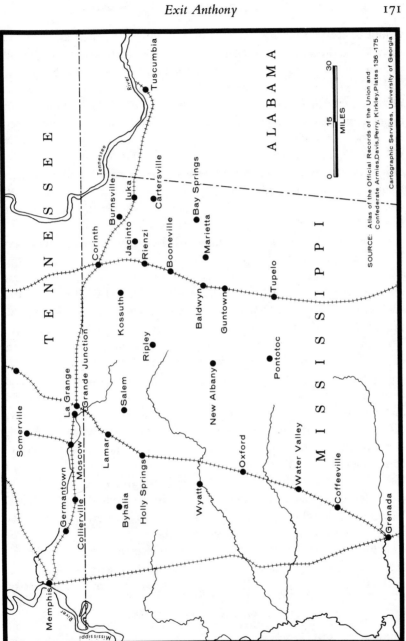

SOURCE: Atlas of the Official Records of the Union and
Confederate Armies.Davis,Perry, Kirkley,Plates 136 -175.

Cartographic Services, University of Georgia

troops to escape from slavery, had been a source of embarrassment and vexation to the national government. To permit such Negroes to remain within the Union lines was a flagrant violation of the Fugitive Slave Law and a gross breach of the laws of property; to allow their masters to recover them or (what would normally amount to the same thing) to expel them from the sanctuary of a Federal camp, was to force them back into slavery, which outraged the moral sense of even those northerners who were far from being abolitionists. To facilitate or to connive at the escape of the slaves of loyal southerners was to raise up new enemies against a government that had too many of them already; it would also serve to jeopardize the shaky allegiance of the slaveholding border states. But to permit or help secessionists to recover their slaves was to aid rebellion and place a premium on disloyalty. General Benjamin Butler had dealt with this aspect of the problem and added a word to the vocabulary of the Civil War by declaring the runaway slaves of disloyal masters "contraband of war." President Lincoln had tried to solve the problem in a more fundamental fashion by offering the border states a program of compensated emancipation, which they chose not to accept. Thus the problem remained in being, to harass and plague the officers of every Union army operating in or near slave territory.

In November, 1861, General Halleck, in General Orders No. 3, had forbidden the admission of fugitive slaves within the Union lines and directed that those already there be expelled at once.[11] General Orders No. 3 were in force in western Tennessee, which lay within Halleck's Department of the Missouri. More recently, General Isaac Quinby, commander of the district in which the Seventh now found itself, had forbidden the admission of escaped slaves within the lines of any post or encampment in his district, and ordered "all commandants of Brigades, Regiments, detachments and companies . . . to see that . . . this order is rigidly enforced."[12] Commissioned officers permitting or countenancing a violation of the order were to be punished with dismissal from the service.

Both these orders were in force when the Seventh, as a part of

11. *Official Records*, VIII, 370, order dated November 20, 1861.
12. Quoted in Langsdorf and Richmond (eds.), "Anthony," 459. Quinby's direction was his General Orders No. 16.

General Mitchell's brigade, made the march from Columbus to Union City. The regiment camped one evening on the plantation of one Sims and "learned beyond a doubt" that their unwilling host was an "active and notorious seccessionist" whose slaves had been hired out all fall and winter to work on the Confederate fortifications at Columbus and Island No. 10. The regiment departed the next morning, and so did eight of Sims's Negroes. Two days later the aggrieved slaveowner appeared in the camp of the Seventh at Union City, accompanied by Captain W. W. H. Lawrence, who had taken Parrott's place as assistant adjutant general of Mitchell's brigade, to search for his escaped property. He was met by one of the officers of the Seventh and told that it would be "unhealthy" for him to try to search the camp. He appealed to Captain Lawrence, who produced his orders to expel Sims's Negroes from the camp so that they could be rounded up by their owner. Lawrence was then told that the orders would be obeyed, but that first of all Sims would be "hung higher than Haman." The discussion had attracted a large and increasingly restive audience of Jayhawkers, who gave every indication of being eager to make good on the threat. As the situation promised to get ugly, Lawrence wisely retired, taking Sims with him.[13]

This incident was reported to General Quinby, who was probably already aware of an order Anthony had just issued to his regiment, reading as follows: "As there has been some doubt in the minds of some of the officers and soldiers of the regiment as to their duty in regard to returning Fugitive Slaves, they are hereby instructed not to return them, and should anyone do so, they will be severely punished."[14] Faced with this defiance and violation of army orders, General Quinby proceeded to send the following instructions to General Mitchell:

Mr. A. G. Sims, who lives near Hickman, Clinton county, Kentucky, reported to me that there are now within your lines eight of his colored servants, who were taken from him by some portion of your command. . . . These persons must be placed without your lines, and the parties that brought them in, or allowed them to pass in, punished. This disregard of positive orders from the Headquarters of the Department of the Mississippi, and from the Headquarters of this District, cannot be permitted. If there is within this District a regiment

13. Undated clipping from the Missouri *Democrat*, datelined "From the Kansas Brigade . . . June 18, 1862," in Jennison Scrapbook.
14. Special Orders No. 197, June 12, 1862, in Seventh Kansas, Regimental Order Book.

or detachment within which the sentiment is such that these orders and instructions cannot be enforced without riot and mutiny, such regiment or detachment will be reported for mustering out of the service.[15]

Mitchell directed that these orders be read to every regiment in his brigade at dress parade on the evening of June 17. The guilty regiment was not identified in Quinby's orders, but it was plain to everyone in the brigade, from drummer boy to general, that the Jayhawkers were meant.

After issuing instructions to have Quinby's orders read to the brigade, Mitchell departed on a two-day leave. The highest ranking officer in the brigade at that moment was none other than Anthony, and upon Mitchell's departure, command of the brigade automatically devolved upon him. Here was a conjunction of circumstances made to order for a melodramatic gesture. There was, first, Anthony's perfectly sincere hatred of slavery and slaveowners, coupled with the equally strong antislavery feelings of the majority of his officers and men. Then there was Anthony's knowledge that he would shortly be superseded in command of the regiment. And now a perfect opportunity presented itself for making a spectacular exit in a manner that would arrest the attention of all Kansans and of abolitionists and radicals everywhere. Anthony was not the man to fail to take advantage of a chance so incredibly favorable.[16]

On June 18, therefore, he issued General Orders No. 26 to what was at the moment *his* brigade:

1. The impudence and impertinence of the open and armed Rebels, Traitors, Secessionists and Southern-Rights men of this section of the State of Tennessee in arrogantly demanding the right to search our camp for their fugitive slaves has become a nuisance, and will no longer be tolerated. Officers will see that this class of men who visit our camp for this purpose are excluded from our lines.

2. Should any such parties be found within the lines, they will be arrested and sent to Hd. qu.

3. Any officer or soldier of this command who shall arrest and deliver to his

15. Undated clipping from the Missouri *Democrat*, datelined "From the Kansas Brigade . . . June 18, 1862," in Jennison Scrapbook.

16. See his letter of June 20, 1862, to his sister Susan, in Langsdorf and Richmond (eds.), "Anthony," 461: "It is most fortunate that this opportunity occurred."

master a fugitive slave shall be summarily and severely punished according to the laws relative to such crimes.[17]

The fat was now in the fire. Anthony's order was a firm, unmistakable thumbing of his nose at General Quinby, General Mitchell, General Halleck, the whole military hierarchy, and beyond it at the overcautious government, and the timid and conservative everywhere.

General Orders No. 26 was "heartily supported" by the surprised and delighted Seventh; and in one stroke it earned for Anthony the "highest respect and admiration" of his men.[18] This might have been anticipated. But the crucial question was what General Mitchell would do about this act of defiance when he returned to Union City and resumed command.

Mitchell got back to the brigade on June 19, and we may be sure that the first piece of news his staff reported to him concerned the order Anthony had issued in his absence. The lieutenant colonel was at once requested to present himself at brigade headquarters. Mitchell was a Kansan himself, a conservative by conviction, and his political antennae were reasonably sensitive. He knew that a large segment of opinion in the North, and in all probability the overwhelming majority in Kansas, shared Anthony's revulsion against any policy whose effect was to force escaped slaves back into bondage. As brigade commander, he could have expunged Anthony's order out of hand, but what he now did made it perfectly clear that he did not want to incur the odium of doing so. He ordered Anthony to countermand his own order. Thereupon the following conversation is supposed to have taken place, a colloquy that assuredly stands in a class by itself in all of American military history:

Anthony: As a subordinate officer, it is my duty to obey your orders, but you will remember, General, that "Order No. 26" is a brigade order; and I am not now in command of the brigade. Of course you are aware that the lieutenant-colonel of a regiment cannot countermand a brigade order?

17. Manuscript copy, Kansas State Historical Society, Topeka. Also quoted in John A. Logan, *The Great Conspiracy: Its Origin and History* (New York, 1886), 397–98. Interestingly enough, the order does not appear in the one place where one would expect to find it, namely, the Regimental Order Book (or Regimental Letter and Order Book) of the Seventh.

18. Pomeroy, "War Diary," entry for June 23, 1862. Arthur T. Reeve to John Brown, Jr., June 26, 1862, copy in Kansas State Historical Society, Topeka. "Our boys all say if we are to catch Negroes muster us out."

Mitchell: Oh, that need not stand in the way, Colonel Anthony. I can put you in command long enough for that.

Anthony: Do you put me in command of the brigade?

Mitchell: Yes, sir.

Anthony: You say, General Mitchell, I am now the commanding officer of this brigade?

Mitchell: Yes, sir; you are in command.

Anthony: Then, sir, as commanding officer of the brigade I am not subject to your orders; and as to your request that "Order No. 26" be countermanded, I respectfully decline to grant it. "Brigade order No. 26" shall not be countermanded while I remain in command![19]

If this conversation actually took place and followed the course here reported, General Mitchell had clearly been outmanoeuvred and outfaced. Anthony did not countermand his order, and the records do not indicate by whom, or when, if ever, the offending order was cancelled.[20] Nevertheless, in a confrontation between a brigadier general and a lieutenant colonel, the brigadier general holds all the cards, and in the present instance, Mitchell had the last word. After a most significant delay of two weeks — one can picture the anxious high-level deliberations that took place in these two weeks, to decide on the best and safest way to handle so explosive an issue — Anthony was ordered to report in arrest to General Halleck's headquarters and, of course, was relieved of the command of the Seventh.[21]

19. The Anthony-Mitchell conversation is quoted from Admire, "Early Kansas Pioneer," 698–99. It is also given in Langsdorf and Richmond (eds.), "Anthony," 459–60. The latter cites as its source *United States Biographical Dictionary: Kansas Volume* (Chicago, 1879), 57. One cannot be certain that the colloquy has been reported with literal accuracy. The drawingroom suavity of Anthony's remarks is so little in character, and his ripostes are so pat, that it is impossible to resist the suspicion that the story has had the benefit of editorial burnishing. Nonetheless, this is one case wherein the striving for strict historical accuracy must yield to an irresistible impulse to let a good story stand.

20. Simeon Fox suggests that General Orders No. 26 was never formally revoked, and he may well be right. He writes, "The order being in direct conflict with both department and division orders, was without force and void . . . and simply expunged." See Fox to W.E. Connelley, March 8, 1926, in Fox Papers. Captain B. P. Chenowith of the First Kansas Infantry, who was about to have an encounter of his own with the Seventh, reported that "when General Mitchell returned, he took no notice of [Anthony's order] so that [it] still stands on the books of the brigade as law." See *Official Records*, XVII, Pt. 2, 54.

21. Simeon Fox, no friend of Anthony, wrote many years later that "General Mitchell hesitated to act . . . until he received peremptory orders from higher authority to place Anthony under arrest." See Fox to W. E. Connelley, March 5, 1926, in Fox Papers.

Meanwhile, following the example of their lieutenant colonel, the Jayhawkers continued to vex the high command with their persistent defiance of orders favoring the owners of slaves. Since A. G. Sims had been conspicuously unsuccessful in recovering his chattels, his wife tried her hand at it, relying on the advantages she would enjoy as a female. On June 24, while six companies of the regiment, with Captain Merriman of Company D in command, were on the march from Trenton to Humboldt, Tennessee, Mrs. Sims appeared on the scene with Captain B. P. Chenowith of the First Kansas Infantry, provost marshal of Trenton, at her elbow, and with her husband and "one or two other traitors" discreetly in the background. Exhibiting an order from General Quinby authorizing her to search all camps and trains in the district for her slaves, she asked that the regimental train be stopped and proceeded to search the baggage wagons. In one of them, well hidden under tarpaulins, she found a Negro woman and her two children, whom she claimed to be her property. The unfortunate woman and the two children were removed from the wagon and marched off to slavery. It says much for the discipline of the regiment that the search could be made and the woman and children led away, without provoking violence. Captain James L. Rafety of Company H was the only Jayhawker to become obstreperous, and he was sent back to Columbus, Kentucky, in arrest for his pains, but one of the eyewitnesses wrote afterwards that this shameful incident would not have been permitted to occur if Companies G, H, and K had been present.[22]

Mrs. Sims retired in triumph with her recaptured property, oblivious, probably, of the fact that in vindicating her property rights, she had driven another nail into the coffin of the peculiar institution. For, as was the case with many another northern regiment, exposure at first hand to

22. The search of the wagon train by Mrs. Sims is described in a report datelined "Camp 7th Kansas, Humboldt, Tenn., July 3, 1862," in the Leavenworth *Conservative*, July 11, 1862. See Jennison Scrapbook. Captain Rafety's arrest is noted in *Official Records*, XVII, Pt. 2, 66–67 (Rafety's name appears as Rafferty). The comment on the "shameful incident" is in a letter from A. T. Reeve to John Brown, Jr., June 26, 1862, copy in Kansas State Historical Society, Topeka. The date of the incident cannot be fixed accurately. The Leavenworth *Conservative* report of July 11 implies that it occurred on July 2. The Reeve letter, written on June 26, says that it occurred "a few days since." General Dodge's report, *Official Records*, XVII, Pt. 2, 66–67, is dated July 2. It does not mention the date of the incident, but it must obviously have occurred prior to July 2. Webster Moses states in a letter to Nancy Mowry, June 26, 1862, in Moses Letters, that the regiment arrived in Trenton on June 24. Presumably, then, the search occurred on June 24 or 25.

some of the unlovely realities of slavery turned into confirmed abolitionists soldiers who had until then been uncommitted, lukewarm, or
conservative on the subject. There was little if any exaggeration in the
report that when the Seventh resumed the march interrupted by Mrs.
Sims, every man present was "ashamed of the officers who control
them . . . and every man disgusted with a service which has dwindled so
low that it requires the soldiers . . . to bolster up the institution which lies
at the bottom of the rebellion."[23] Anthony himself certainly remained
unrepentant; on the same day that the regimental wagon train was
searched by Mrs. Sims, he aided the escape of two slaves from Trenton by
permitting them to be admitted to the camp of the Seventh.

It might have been predicted that Hoyt, now captain of Company K,
would sooner or later step into the limelight in these stirring antislavery
activities. When the regiment reached Humboldt on June 25, he was
appointed provost marshal of the town and was promptly besieged by
the owners of runaway slaves for assistance to recover their Negroes.
Thereupon he posted the following notice on the door of his headquarters:

Slave hunting at this post or within the jurisdiction of the undersigned is
strictly prohibited.

Persons from whom bondsmen have escaped are hereby notified that all men
are regarded as "*Free* and *Equal*" at this office, and will therefore desist from
invoking the military power in aid of their efforts at rendition.[24]

General Mitchell caused the notice to be torn down, relieved Hoyt of
duty as provost marshal, and appointed a more tractable officer in his
place. But Hoyt had made his point.

Bruce Catton makes the penetrating comment in his *Grant Moves
South* that "what happened in Western Tennessee in the middle of 1862
was important, not just because it meant unlimited woe for plantation
owners and ordinary farmers, but because Western soldiers had, in effect,
ratified the Emancipation Proclamation before it was even written. They
did this by instinct rather than by thought. Back of Grant, Sherman and
the others was the vast, still shapeless body of enlisted men, whose

23. Report datelined "Camp 7th Kansas, Humboldt, Tenn., July 3, 1862," in Leavenworth
Conservative, July 11, 1862. See Jennison Scrapbook.
24. *Ibid.*

emotions were beginning to be dominant for the entire war."[25] The Seventh Kansas can properly claim credit for having played a leading role, and indeed a pioneering role, in steering the Civil War into this unlooked-for, revolutionary direction, which was recognized as inevitable after it had already changed the entire character and meaning of the war. And Anthony, his motives a hodgepodge of idealism and self-seeking, led the Seventh along this path, just as he had led them on their marches in Missouri and Tennessee.

For the moment, it was unlikely that Anthony would ever again lead the regiment, either physically or spiritually. On June 20 word was received from Washington that Attorney General Bates had resolved in favor of Governor Robinson the jurisdictional dispute with Lieutenant Governor Root over the appointment of a colonel to command the Seventh. Albert Lee's status as colonel of the regiment was thus legalized; on July 9 he received instructions from the War Department to assume command of the Jayhawkers and did so on the following day.[26]

Would Anthony stay on as second-in-command under his former subordinate? For the time being, the question was academic; while under arrest, he could exercise no command whatever. But he made it quite clear that he wanted to leave the regiment. He professed to have a poor opinion of Lee, claiming that Lee was "ignorant of the tactics & the men have not confidence in his capacity to lead," and declared: "I do detest serving under a man who has violated every obligation he owed me. I dont respect him as a man or as an officer or honor him either."[27] Later, he described Lee as "a man who lied himself into the colonelcy by the warmest professions of friendship toward me—He has a place that belongs by right to me—I earned it—The men want me—he knows it—and I hate him—I look upon him as a liar a disho[no]rable man—a coward & poltroon and so told him to his face—but he intends to intrigue himself through."[28] Anthony's harsh words, his adjectives and accusations, were clearly the product of disappointment, jealousy, and anger. Lee was actually an active, energetic, capable officer. Anthony to the contrary, Lee

25. Bruce Catton, *Grant Moves South* (Boston, 1960), 292–93.

26. Pomeroy, "War Diary," entry for July 10, 1862.

27. Anthony to his father, July 27, 1862, in Langsdorf and Richmond (eds.), "Anthony," 465–66.

28. Anthony to his sister Susan, September 2, 1862, *ibid.*, 473.

already had the confidence of the men, and in time they came to speak of him as the best and most soldierly commanding officer the regiment ever had.[29] Anthony, however, felt justified, and not without reason, in tendering his resignation; and he was sufficiently honest to give as his reason for doing so the promotion of Lee over his head. This was not thought to be an adequate ground for resigning, and his application was disapproved. Willy-nilly, he had to remain as lieutenant colonel of the Seventh, but he also remained under arrest, with no indication as yet of the course of action the army intended to pursue in his case.

Ordinarily, Anthony's actions on June 18 would have brought about his trial by court-martial, and the charges and specifications—the military equivalent of an indictment—against him were actually drawn up. He was charged by General Mitchell, who signed the charges and specifications, with disobedience of orders and with conduct unbecoming an officer and gentleman. Interestingly enough, his issuance of General Orders No. 26, in deliberate defiance of Halleck's and Quinby's orders respecting the treatment of runaway slaves, was not mentioned among the specifications on which he was to be tried. It was evidently felt that to charge Anthony with this act would provide him with the opportunity to base his defense on a challenge of the policy of the government and of the army high command toward slavery. Regardless of the outcome of a trial in which this issue was introduced, Anthony would inevitably emerge as the hero of the occasion, and those who prosecuted him as the villains. To forestall such a possibility, he was charged with a series of relatively trivial offenses—that, for example, "while in command of his regiment [he] habitually failed to post a camp guard . . . in consequence of which numerous and diverse depredations were committed by soldiers of his command," and that he entered the "negro quarters adjoining the house of . . . [one] Martin and did persuade four or more negroes to run away and to take with them mules, horses and other stock."[30]

Anthony had a pretty shrewd idea that nothing very serious was likely to happen to him. He wrote from General Halleck's headquarters at the beginning of July: "I think the matter will be kept under advise-

29. Pomeroy, "War Diary," entry for July 10, 1862. *Cf.* Utt, "Seventh Kansas"; Lyman, "Reminiscences"; and George Mowry, Jr., to Nancy Mowry, November 4, 1862, in Moses Letters.

30. The charges and specifications against Anthony are printed in full in the Leavenworth *Conservative*, July 8, 1862. See Jennison Scrapbook.

ment for a time, and then I will be discharged [.] I have demanded an immediate trial as all the witnesses against me are now here. The most that can be done will be a court martial—and cashiered—in that case I shall go to Washington for redress and shall get it too—They well know their weakness [.] They know the whole country would side with me and do not care to bring the issue before the country to[o] prominently."[31] Nevertheless, he took no chances. He made all the political capital he could out of the situation. He had already sent copies of his General Orders No. 26 to the Kansas newspapers. Now he informed the two Kansas senators of the affair and arranged through his father for the republication, in the Rochester newspapers, of articles from the Leavenworth *Conservative*, the St. Louis *Democrat*, the Chicago *Tribune*, and "from other papers which may contain favorable notices of the cause of [his] arrest." He even offered to pay to have such favorable articles set in type for republication and asked to have sent to him two hundred copies of "each paper containing anything as to the case."[32] No doubt these copies were to be distributed in and about Halleck's headquarters to impress everyone with the unwisdom of prosecuting an officer who was the subject of so much laudatory publicity. To make certain that the Rochester *Express* and the Rochester *Democrat* reprinted the right articles, he sent his brother-in-law clippings to be passed on to their respective editors and offered to write, or to have written for them, "letters" from the camp of the Seventh. As a newpaperman himself, Anthony knew well the value of extensive and favorable newspaper publicity.

In writing to Senators Lane and Pomeroy, whom he had every reason to believe to be predisposed in his favor, Anthony concentrated on the story of his General Orders No. 26. He told them that he had "been in arrest for two weeks, and no trial granted by General Halleck. The charges against me are allowing negroes within my lines [and] issuing an order (Brigade No. 26) prohibiting rebels from coming within my lines to hunt for their fugitive slaves."[33] His recital, though it was

31. Anthony to his father, July 8, 1862, in Langsdorf and Richmond (eds.), "Anthony," 461–62.

32. Same to same, July 9, 1862, *ibid.*, 463.

33. *The Congressional Globe: Containing the Debates and Proceedings of the Second Session of the Thirty-Seventh Congress* (Washington, 1862), 5334.

grossly inaccurate, was sufficiently impressive to cause Lane to introduce a resolution in the Senate "That the President of the United States be directed to communicate to the Senate any information he may have as to the reasons for the arrest of Lieutenant Colonel D. R. Anthony of the Seventh Kansas regiment, if in his opinion, such information can be given without injury to the public service."[34] The resolution was adopted on July 15. Behind its courteous words stood the ominous shadow of the Committee on the Conduct of the War. The prospect of an invitation to appear before that formidable body for a discussion of the Anthony case in all its bearings was not to be faced lightly by any officer who valued his reputation or his shoulder straps. Anthony was undoubtedly correct in reporting from Halleck's headquarters that "they are very sensitive here in regard to the arrest and a general desire not to meddle much with it."[35]

There is nothing in the records to indicate how, when, why, or by whom the final decision was made, but shortly before July 27, Anthony was discharged from arrest and ordered to report back to his regiment. By this time, Lee had assumed command of the Seventh, and Anthony's resentment over Lee's promotion was well known. It must have occurred to someone that the best way to solve the problem of what to do about Anthony was to place him in a situation where his hot temper would inevitably get him in trouble sooner rather than later; failing that, the daily and hourly humiliation of having to obey the orders of his former subordinate would without doubt cause him to use the first plausible excuse to resubmit his resignation, which this time would certainly be accepted. Either way, the army would be rid of him, and in a way that no abolitionist senator could turn into a political issue.

The scheme worked to perfection. On his return to the Seventh, Anthony was greeted by the entire regiment with three cheers, followed by three cheers for Jennison and the same for Senators Lane and Pomeroy, and he was serenaded by the regimental band; but these conventional expressions of esteem did not alleviate his discontent. He hoped that he

34. *Ibid.* As originally introduced by Lane on July 14, the resolution was directed to the secretary of war. At the suggestion of Senator H. B. Anthony of Rhode Island, it was changed to call upon the president to furnish the information concerning Anthony's arrest.

35. Anthony to his father, July 9, 1862, in Langsdorf and Richmond (eds.), "Anthony," 464.

might be offered the colonelcy of any newly raised Indiana, Illinois, or New York regiment, or that something else would occur to give him a graceful excuse to resign. No offer of a colonelcy materialized, but within two weeks after his discharge from arrest, Anthony found the pretext for resigning that he was looking for.

On July 25 the Cincinnati *Gazette* had noted Anthony's release from arrest in a brief article, which also stated that "his offense, as will be remembered, was refusing to expel negroes from his camp, agreeable to the infamous Order No. 3 by General Halleck." [36]

At the time of Anthony's arrest, the Seventh had become a part of General Rosecrans' Army of the Mississippi. Shortly after the publication of the note concerning Anthony's release from arrest, the *Gazette* received the following letter from Captain J. H. Odlin, General Rosecrans' acting assistant adjutant general:

I am requested by Gen. Rosecrans to correct a statement in your paper . . . that the offense of Lieutenant Colonel D. R. Anthony, was refusing to expel negroes from his camp, agreeable to Order No. 3 of General Halleck. This is false. He was under arrest for allowing his men to rob and steal from private families, and for allowing his men to break into private houses and break open wardrobes, closets, etc. You will confer a favor on this army by not allowing a set of worthless, lying officers to lead you astray. These fight not for the love of their country, but to rob and steal from the citizens. It is the rule, and always has been, to take all negroes that come into our lines, and set them to work. There is now a large number in the employ of the Government here. [37]

On August 7, within twenty-four hours after the arrival in Rienzi, Mississippi, where the regiment was then in camp, of the issue of the *Gazette* containing Captain Odlin's letter, Anthony resigned his commission. His letter of resignation read as follows: "I hereby tender my resignation as lieutenant colonel of the Seventh Kansas Vols. My reasons for so doing are; First: the promotion of a Maj. to the colonelcy over my head without cause. Second, important business at home involving thousands of dollars, houses and lots in Leavenworth the titles of which are in dispute." [38] It will be noted that there is no reference in this letter to the conflict with General Mitchell over the issuance and withdrawal of

36. Cincinnati *Gazette*, July 25, 1862.   37. *Ibid.*, August 4, 1862.
38. Anthony to Lieutenant F. W. Emery, August 7, 1862, in Seventh Kansas, Regimental Letter and Order Book.

General Order No. 26, nor does it make any reference to Captain Odlin's letter to the Cincinnati *Gazette*. Nonetheless, Anthony would have been fully justified in basing his resignation on the publication of Captain Odlin's letter, for the statements made therein, on the authority of the commanding general, were not merely offensive and insulting in the highest degree, but also untruthful on the essential point of the official reason for his arrest. General Rosecrans himself was apparently disturbed by Odlin's letter, for on August 8 he himself wrote to the *Gazette* that "in Capt. Odlin's note . . . which note was not submitted to me—he does injustice to Lt.-Col. Anthony of the Seventh Kansas Cavalry. There are thirty or forty complaints against the 7th KC for outrages committed by them on their march to Corinth. . . . Colonel Anthony . . . informs me he was not in command of the regiment at the time these outrages were committed; and I find his charges were for alleged derelictions anterior to that march."[39] No doubt the public was now thoroughly befuddled by the conflicting stories of the *Gazette's* own reporter, Captain Odlin, and General Rosecrans; and everyone could believe whatever he chose as to the reasons for Anthony's arrest.

But Anthony himself had his mind made up to leave the army, and he made sure that his resignation would be accepted; he himself obtained the favorable endorsements of his brigade, division, army, and department commanders. It may be taken for granted that he obtained these endorsements with a minimum of trouble. No doubt his task was facilitated by Colonel Lee's not entirely flattering endorsement, which read: "Colonel Anthony's feelings are such that I am fully persuaded he will be of little value to the service in his present position. My own wishes, his own, and, I believe, the efficiency of the regiment will be consulted by an acceptance of his resignation."[40] The resignation was forwarded to Washington, and after a long wait Anthony was notified that it had been approved by the War Department also. On September 12, no longer an officer of volunteers, he was free to leave for home. As he was about to depart, the "Boys assembled impromptu"; he then "made a few parting words[.] Three times three went up . . . the band

39. Cincinnati *Gazette*, August 12, 1862.
40. Colonel Lee's endorsement is dated August 7, 1862. See Seventh Kansas, Regimental Letter and Order Book.

played," and the ex-lieutenant colonel rode away "with an occasional 'God Bless you' from the boys." [41] At the last, he said, he "hated to leave the regiment and yet I could not be hired to return for a Brigadiers pay [.] Although a Colonels or Brigadier Generals *rank* would be a great inducement—in fact I should then be glad to go." [42]

Given the lawless record of the Seventh in Missouri and Tennessee while under Anthony's command, and the highly inconvenient declarations of his views respecting the goals for which the Civil War should be fought and of the way in which the war should be conducted, few lieutenant colonels in the western armies had a lesser chance for promotion to colonel or brigadier general. The summer of 1862 was still too early to proclaim, as Anthony was in the habit of doing in and out of season, the desirability of arming Negroes, creating slave insurrections, and confiscating the private property of rebels. On the other hand, the summer of 1862 was almost, if not quite, too late for politicians in uniform; the Union army was already well along in the process of becoming an organization of soldiers.

Rightly or wrongly, Anthony advocated a remorselessly tough war. He was convinced that a mild, conciliatory policy would fail to end the rebellion. To restore the Union, the Confederacy would have to be smashed and slavery destroyed. Much of General Sherman's fame rests on his recognition in 1863 and 1864 of facts that were obvious to Anthony in 1862 and even earlier. The latter paid the penalty for the double offense of being right prematurely and proclaiming from the lowly position of a lieutenant colonel views which, as they happened not to square with administration policy, could be voiced only from loftier levels of the military hierarchy. It is not without instruction to compare the logistics of Sherman's March to the Sea with the strictures on official army policy toward rebel barns and smokehouses in Tennessee that Anthony voiced in the summer of 1862 in a letter to his father:

To me it seems that the presence [of] our army here is doing more to strengthen the rebel cause than to suppress it—No matter how outrageous and damning may have been the course of the rebels here—if they only take the oath they are indemnified for past and present losses of Hay oats corn and even rent for lands

41. Anthony to Aaron McLean, September 14, 1862, in Langsdorf and Richmond (eds.), "Anthony," 475.
42. *Ibid.*

and Houses occupied by our troops . . . Our men are employed in watching rebel's onions, Green Peas & Potatoes[.] And if a poor soldier chances to allow his appetite to wander from the Hard Bread & Side Meat so far as to appropriate a rebel onion to his Stomach—woe unto him. . . . The soldiers . . . cannot see why they should suffer and die while guarding the property of their enemies—The soldiers are right.[43]

In order to present the story of Anthony's resignation as a continuous narrative, it has been necessary to pass over two of the Jayhawkers' most characteristic exploits, both of which occurred while Anthony was in the midst of his difficulties. They cannot be omitted from a history of the regiment.

It will be recalled that in the middle of June, the Seventh camped for some time in Union City, Tennessee. Guerillas were reported to be operating along the railroad running south from there through Trenton and Humboldt, Tennessee, and beyond; and a detachment consisting of Companies A, E, and K of the Seventh, under command of Colonel Lee, and three companies of the Second Illinois Cavalry was ordered out to scout as far south as Trenton and drive them away from the railroad. In command of the expedition was Colonel Silas Noble of the Illinois regiment. The six companies found and chased off a few small bands of rebels and, on the afternoon of June 17, reached Trenton, where they encamped in and about the railroad station. The men were without rations and, on Colonel Noble's orders, were "billeted" on the inhabitants.

In a storage shed at the station, there were several hogsheads of tobacco and barrels of sugar "waiting for shipment to the Confederate army" by one account, or, by another, belonging to rebels who had fled Trenton on the approach of the Union cavalry.[44]

On the morning of June 18, Colonel Lee and Lieutenant Colonel Hans C. Heg felt impelled, for reasons not stated, to inspect the sugar and tobacco. They found, Lee said, that a single barrel of sugar had been broken open, and $25 worth of sugar removed, as well as "a very small portion of the tobacco."[45] It may not be without significance that among

43. Anthony to his father, July 8, 1862, *ibid.*, 462–63.
44. Colonel Lee to Lieutenant George Lee, August 22, 1862, in Seventh Kansas, Regimental Letter and Order Book.
45. *Ibid.*

the members of the Seventh who were not at Trenton, it was variously understood that "Col. Lee let his men have what sugar and tobacco they wanted," or that the amount of sugar and tobacco taken was a mere trifle, "not $100 worth." [46] Later on the eighteenth, the three companies of the Seventh moved their camp to the outskirts of the town and, on the following morning, left Trenton to look for a band of guerillas reported to be camped thirty-five miles away.

Next to appear on the scene were five companies of the Eighth Kansas Infantry. The footsoldiers followed the example of the cavalry-men and helped themselves to sugar and tobacco at the station. The bulk of these desirable commodities was, however, still in the shed when the three companies of Jayhawkers returned to Trenton from their expedition against the guerillas; but before they left the town—and this is a point that neither Colonel Lee nor any other Jayhawker thought it necessary to mention—they destroyed all the sugar and tobacco that was left.

The aggrieved owners made a great outcry over their loss, which they blamed principally on the Seventh. Their representations made their way through channels to headquarters, and General Grant, who had taken over a large part of Halleck's old command, not only decided that the owners were entitled to compensation but that the incident should be used as a means of curing the Seventh of its jayhawking habits and to teach the hard-bitten Kansans that they were not to behave in Tennessee as they had in Missouri. As a result, on August 19 Colonel Lee received the following order, signed by General Rosecrans: "By direction of the district commander, the pay of the Kansas 7th cavalry and of companies B., D., H., I., and K. of the 8th Kansas infantry, shall be stopped until they shall have, by subscription or otherwise, paid the sum of $1,053.55, the value of sugar and tobacco destroyed by them at Trenton, Tenn. Paymasters are directed not to make any payments to the troops herein named, until notified that this order is complied with." [47]

As might have been anticipated, General Rosecrans' order stirred up a hornet's nest of anger and resentment. Even before the arrival of this

---

46. Webster Moses to Nancy Mowry, August 22, 1862, in Moses Letters.
47. The order, captioned "Special Order Number 212," is quoted in Pomeroy, "War Diary," entry for August 19, 1862.

iniquitous order, the Seventh felt that it had been imposed upon and discriminated against ever since its arrival in Tennessee, and the order was doubly resented because the men were convinced that they were being punished unjustly. The punishment of the entire regiment for the guilt of only three of its ten companies might have been endured, but to have visited upon the Seventh the principal part of the penalty for an offense committed partly by two other regiments, was intolerable. Colonel Lee declared that "his right arm shall wither before his money shall chink in rebel coffers."[48] Company K—one of the guilty three— stacked its arms and went on strike; only with the greatest difficulty were the indignant Ohioans persuaded to return to duty. The regiment let it be known that every man in it "has determined to forfeit all his wages before giving one cent . . . to rebels for sugar and tobacco," and that even as soldiers they had rights which they were fully resolved to maintain.[49] Adding to the Jayhawkers' sense of grievance was the fact that the families of many of the men depended for all or most of their livelihood on the pittance of thirteen dollars a month that the private soldiers received for serving in the army, and even this was usually many months in arrears.

Colonel Lee sent a dignified protest to headquarters, giving his own not entirely candid version of the events at Trenton, as soon as he received General Rosecrans' order. Relying on the virtues of a soft answer to turn away official wrath, he expressed his confidence that his exposition of the "facts" would "at once bring from the justice of [the] commander a revocation of an order which could only have been issued in the haste and press of business which hindered an investigation and so worked . . . an involuntary wrong."[50]

In the Civil War volunteer armies, disciplinary problems like this hardly ever failed to involve the political friends and allies of the men sought to be punished, and Colonel Lee thought it proper to solicit the help of the two Kansas senators to obtain relief from the objectionable order. But in writing to Senators Lane and Pomeroy, Lee was much less restrained than he had been in his letter to headquarters. He explained

48. *Ibid.*   49. *Ibid.*
50. Colonel Lee to Lieutenant George Lee, August 22, 1862, in Seventh Kansas, Regimental Letter and Order Book.

that the Jayhawkers had come to Tennessee "burthened with a false reputation for robbery, rapine and all crimes," and that "almost every corps" near which the Jayhawkers happened to be camped laid upon the Kansans "the burthen of their own villainy, and the Seventh Regt was the 'scape-goat'" of the entire army. In self-defense, every officer and man in the regiment "was making a persistent effort to give a lie to the slanders" against them, and were accordingly on their best behavior. After receiving Rosecrans' order, Lee went on, he called the regiment together and, having explained the order, requested his men "to inform [him] on consultation what course they should pursue. A resolution was unanimously adopted to the effect that they would never pay a dime of this proposed forced assessment." [51]

The paymaster made one of his infrequent visits to the regiment in September. The Seventh was informed by a message from General Grant's headquarters that if it consented to the stoppage of two dollars from each man's pay as reimbursement for the sugar and tobacco, the regiment would be paid—and not otherwise. The messenger was told to carry word back to headquarters that "General Grant . . . [could] go to hell." [52] And that was the end of the Trenton sugar and tobacco incident. Nothing more was heard about withholding the men's pay, but the Seventh was not paid for the month of June, 1862, until February of the year following.

The second of the Jayhawkers' characteristic feats occurred on July 3, as the regiment was on its way from Humboldt to Corinth. Late in the afternoon of a hot, dusty day, the Seventh marched into Jackson, Tennessee, the headquarters of General John A. Logan. Simeon Fox tells the story:

While the regiment was halted in a shady spot . . . waiting for details to fill canteens at a well near by, an aide-de-camp rode up and said, "General Logan orders this regiment moved immediately outside his lines," and rode away. The regiment did not move with any great degree of alacrity, and . . . some twenty minutes later . . . the same aide-de-camp dashed up in great wrath and said: "General Logan orders this d——abolitionist regiment outside his lines or he will order out a battery and drive it out!" . . . And the answer came

51. Colonel Lee to Senators Lane and Pomeroy, August 22, 1862, *ibid.*
52. Fox, "Story," 31.

promptly back, "Go and tell Gen. John A. Logan to bring out his battery and we will show him how quick this d——abolition regiment will take it." The officers tried to move the regiment but the men sat grim and silent and would not stir. . . . Finally a compromise was made; the regiment moved around General Logan's headquarters by a street to the rear and marched back past his front door with the band playing John Brown. The command moved out and camped on a stream just south of town, but *inside* General Logan's lines.[53]

Neither in July, 1862, nor at any other time, did the Seventh cultivate the art of ingratiating itself with high-ranking officers. Whether they were volunteers or West Pointers made no difference to the Seventh, and neither did their rank; whether they had one star or two, no one endowed with a little brief authority was ever allowed to forget that the Seventh Kansas Volunteer Cavalry, a regiment made up of the free citizens of a free country, knew its rights and intended to have them respected.

53. *Ibid.* Fox specifically dates this incident as occurring on July 3. Pomeroy, "War Diary," entry for July 4, suggests that it may have occurred on the fourth.

CHAPTER X

A Season
in
Mississippi

CORINTH, MISSISSIPPI, was evacuated by Beauregard's Confederates and occupied by General Halleck's armies on June 1, 1862. Halleck possessed an overwhelming numerical superiority over the enemy, but he lacked any clear notion of what to do with it. Hence, for six weeks he did nothing. On July 17 he left for Washington to assume the duties of general in chief. The command of what by then had become a badly disorganized army, and the problem of deciding what use to make of it, fell to his successor, Ulysses S. Grant. The nucleus of the force Grant inherited was Rosecrans' 32,000-man Army of the Mississippi, which, in mid-July, occupied a long line to the south of the Memphis and Charleston Railroad, from Corinth in the west to Cherokee, Alabama, in the east. The main Confederate concentration lay at Tupelo, Mississippi, fifty miles to the south, protected by clouds of cavalry and irregular horse operating between the two armies and harassing Grant's line of communications with Memphis and the North.

The Jayhawkers were now a part of the Army of the Mississippi. June 26 found them encamped in a beautiful grove of trees a half-mile from Humboldt, Tennessee, near a large spring of sweet, cool water. In the two following weeks they marched southward by easy stages to join Rosecrans' army. Their way led through Jackson, where they shocked the sensibilities of General Logan, to Corinth, where Daniel Anthony, then under arrest, was living at the Tishomingo Hotel. At Corinth the regiment was assigned to another excellent campsite. Located some four miles south of the town, the new camp lay on the bank of Clear Creek, in which the men watered their horses and bathed. For drinking and cooking they had sparkling clear water from a spring that discharged a barrel of water a minute. In a Mississippi July, the creek and the spring were treasures to be cherished.

Colonel Lee was now in command of the regiment and was exercising the prerogatives of a new broom. On July 12 he laid down a demanding schedule of drill: two and a half hours of squadron drill dismounted and mounted each morning, an hour each of squadron drill dismounted and battalion drill mounted in the afternoon, and dress parade at 6:30 P.M. every day. Then he ordered a school for officers to be held at 9:30 A.M. daily, "for perfection in tactics and regulations," and a school for noncommissioned officers "in tactics and their duties" every afternoon, with commissioned officers acting as instructors; company commanders were to see to it that the schools were properly conducted.[1]

The busy routine of camp was disturbed by only one untoward incident. On July 13 Lee discovered that "a very large amount" of whiskey had been sold by the brigade commissary to his officers; in fact, Lee reported, the commissary quarters had been turned into a "Grog shop," with the result that "a considerable number" of officers not only went on a two-day spree themselves, but shared their abundant supplies of whiskey with their men, many of whom became intoxicated also. Lee first punished the culprits, and then saw to it that the sale of whiskey by the commissary was prohibited by a brigade order.[2]

On July 20 the Seventh was ordered to leave its pleasant camp on Clear Creek and move to Jacinto, fifteen miles southeast of Corinth, where it was to become part of the cavalry brigade of a young colonel named Philip Henry Sheridan. A West Pointer and a captain in the regular army, Sheridan had recently manoeuvred his way from behind a desk

---

1. General Orders No. 87, July 12, 1862, and No. 89, July 17, 1862, in Seventh Kansas, Regimental Order Book.

2. Lee to Colonel Hans C. Heg, commanding Mitchell's Brigade, July 13, 1862, in Seventh Kansas, Regimental Letter and Order Book.

at Halleck's headquarters in St. Louis into the colonelcy of a Michigan regiment of volunteer cavalry. Two weeks later he had command of a two-regiment cavalry brigade, and on July 1, at Booneville, Mississippi, with barely eight hundred troopers of the Second Michigan and Second Iowa, he defeated Chalmers' Confederate cavalry division of between five and six thousand men. He was at once, and deservedly, recommended for a brigadier general's commission by General Rosecrans.[3]

The attitude of the Seventh toward brigade, division, army, and department commanders was one of aloof scepticism when it was not one of downright hostility. The bullet-headed, hard-faced, diminutive Sheridan may have impressed Rosecrans with his abilities, but the Seventh was harder to win over; it did not give its allegiance lightly. George Mowry declared that if "Col Sherdin . . . dont do better than he has done I dont think he will carry with him the good wishes of the troops."[4] He was given the courtesy of a serenade by the regimental band—an honor he may well have preferred to do without—but that was as far as the Seventh was ready to commit itself for the moment.

On July 23, as a result of a discussion between Sheridan and Brigadier General Gordon Granger, commanding the Fifth Cavalry Division, to which Sheridan's brigade belonged, the Seventh was moved from Jacinto to Rienzi, ten miles to the west and on the direct route from Corinth to Tupelo. Jacinto was held in strong force by Union Brigadier General Jefferson C. Davis' Fourth Infantry Division, making the presence of the Seventh at that location superfluous. Moreover, Sheridan wanted the Seventh under his own eye, at Rienzi.[5]

The Seventh remained at Rienzi, at the southernmost point, nearest the enemy, of Rosecrans' line, for more than two months. Its campsite, in a grove of trees as protection from the heat, was comfortable enough, but the location, on the edge of a low-lying, swampy stretch of land, "filled with pools of Tadpole water," was unhealthy.[6] One of Anthony's vir-

---

3. Sheridan's report on Booneville in *Official Records*, XIII, Pt. 1, 19–20. Rosecrans not only recommended Sheridan's promotion to brigadier general, but also issued General Orders No. 81, praising the "coolness, determination and fearless gallantry" of Sheridan and his command, and directed that the order be read to every regiment in his army. See *ibid.*, 17–18.

4. George Mowry, Jr., to Nancy Mowry, August 14, 1862, in Moses Letters.

5. *Official Records*, XVII, Pt. 2, 111–12.

6. Anthony to his mother, August 31, 1862, in Langsdorf and Richmond (eds.), "Anthony," 471.

tues as regimental commander had been a fanatical insistence on camp sanitation, sufficiently rare among commanding officers to excite comment. Because of the extra work that proper camp sanitation required, Anthony's insistence upon it was not popular. Lee being far less exigent on the subject, the result was an epidemic of typhoid fever which carried off nineteen men in the regiment and disabled many more.[7] Those who escaped the contagion bore as well as they could the multiple discomforts of the great heat, insect bites, and heat rash, and the depressing effect of a countryside nearly deserted by its inhabitants, "the fields . . . all grown up to weeds and every thing bear[ing] the marks of stern war."[8]

But it was not Colonel Sheridan's idea of war to allow cavalry to enjoy the comforts or endure the discomforts of a sedentary life in a camp. The main task of the cavalry of an army occupying an extended defensive line, as Rosecrans' troops then were, was to scout and picket every road and byway between its own army and that of the enemy, to learn all it could of the dispositions and numbers of the hostile force, to deny as much as possible of the intervening country to the enemy cavalry, and to give timely notice of any hostile advance. These functions were doubly important, and of course far more difficult, in enemy country, a large part of which was wooded, and whose roads, where there were any, were mostly cart tracks and paths meandering through the wilderness.

Sheridan kept his three regiments constantly on the prowl, probing and scouting to the south and west. On July 27-29, Colonel Lee led four hundred Jayhawkers to Ripley to attack the Third Alabama Cavalry, which was reputed to be there; but the Alabamians evacuated their camp "hurriedly" an hour before the Kansans arrived. The only tangible result of the three-day expedition was a bag of three prisoners.[9] On August 19-21, Lee took three hundred of his men southeast to Marietta. His advance was disputed by rebel pickets, but the main body of the enemy, two companies of Mississippi cavalry, alerted by the picket fire, retreated southward. They were pursued for five miles by the Jayhawkers; one rebel was wounded, but he was carried off by his comrades.[10] A few

7. Fox, "Story," 32.
8. Webster Moses to Nancy Mowry, August 22, 1862, in Moses Letters.
9. *Official Records*, XVII, Pt. 1, 25. *Cf.* Anthony to his father, July 27, 1862, and July 30, 1862, in Langsdorf and Richmond (eds.), "Anthony," 465 and 467.
10. *Official Records*, XVII, Pt. 1, 35.

hours later, at Bay Springs, Lee attacked another rebel camp, but with an equal lack of success. The enemy ran, and on horses worn out at the end of a hard day, Lee was unable to pursue. He turned over to brigade headquarters the trophies of the expedition: three horses, three guns, and one saber. His report closed with the disgusted remark: "I wish in conclusion to say that to fight small forces of the enemy in the region immediately below . . . [Rienzi] I consider impracticable unless they desire to fight. The posting and vigilance of their pickets is perfect, and their knowledge of the country enables them to evade an attack when evasion is desirable."[11] The enlisted men had a simpler and more self-satisfied explanation of their inability to make the enemy stand and fight. Webster Moses declared that the Seventh was "the best Regiment in the armey here. . . . The Secesh are affraid of the *Jayhawkers*"; and again, "We will proberly see some fighting before long if we can catch up to the Rebbels and make them stand[.] The name of Jayhawkers is a terror to the Rebbels here."[12]

A week after the Marietta-Bay Springs expedition, a detachment of the Seventh was involved in a much more costly affair, and one which had most unpleasant consequences. On August 27 a battalion of the Seventh and a battalion of the Second Iowa were ordered out under the command of Major Datus E. Coon of the Iowa regiment to scout the country to the northwest, as far as Kossuth, Mississippi. Having reached the town, Major Coon directed Captain Francis M. Malone of the Seventh to advance another ten miles westward to the Hatchie River. Malone took two companies of his regiment with him. They reached the Hatchie without incident, but on the way back to Kossuth they were ambushed. Four men were killed and eight wounded by the first rebel volley, but the Jayhawkers were not the novices they had been at Columbus, Missouri, seven months before. Instead of stampeding, they rallied at once, charged the rebels, drove them out into the open, and killed two and wounded several before they could scatter into the brush.

Some time after this scout, General Grant was informed by Brigadier General John McArthur of the Sixth Division, Army of the Tennessee, that Malone had left his dead and wounded on the field "in a shameful

---

11. *Ibid.*, 36.
12. Webster Moses to Nancy Mowry, August 22, 1862, in Moses Letters.

manner." On September 26 Colonel Lee was ordered to submit a full report, and he replied the next day. Lee described the ambush and asserted that after the fight Malone had obtained an ox-drawn wagon, in which he brought back to Kossuth his four dead troopers and those of the wounded who were unable to ride their horses. The dead were decently buried at Kossuth and the wounded sent forward in ambulances to the regimental camp in Rienzi. Lee ended his report, and paid his respects to General McArthur and his talebearing, with the remarkably restrained comment: "Of course General McArthur cannot be personally cogni- zant of the assumed facts he reports. His informants are guilty of propa- gating a vile slander. The Seventh Kansas in their history of a year have never left on a field their dead or wounded, or left a field before an enemy."[13] The unfortunate aspect of this incident was that the com- manding general once again had to deal with a report of misdeeds claimed to have been committed by the notorious Seventh Kansas Cav- alry. From General Halleck he had inherited the thorny problem of Lieutenant Colonel Anthony; then came the unpleasantness of the Tren- ton sugar and tobacco affair, and now this. And there was to be more.

While Captain Malone and his two companies were on their way to Kossuth, the rest of regiment had a lively adventure of its own. The rebel cavalry were not a passive breed to sit back and allow themselves to be harassed by the Federal horse. On August 26 they did a little harassing of their own. At two in the afternoon, the peace of the Jayhawkers' camp was rudely broken by the sound of gunfire and the cry, "the Secesh are right on us." In command of the camp at that moment was Anthony. He had the bugler sound "To Arms" and as the men ran to get their weapons, about thirty rebels galloped by, driving the Seventh's pickets before them. When they saw the Jayhawkers' camp and the Kansans assembling, the rebels halted and then began to retreat. Anthony now had "To Horse" sounded; in three minutes the horses were saddled, and the eight companies, led by Company H, which moved off without waiting for orders, set off in a hot pursuit in which the other two regiments of the brigade, alerted by the firing, also joined.[14] The main body of the enemy,

---

13. *Official Records*, XVII, Pt. 1, 42–43.

14. Anthony to his father, August 31, 1862, in Langsdorf and Richmond (eds.), "Anthony," 469.

seven or eight hundred strong, was encountered a quarter-mile away.[15] The rebels did not make a stand; after firing a few shots, they broke and fled and were chased for fifteen miles, almost to Ripley, leaving behind them a road strewn with two hundred shotguns and large numbers of pistols, blankets, hats, coats, and dead horses.[16]

In reporting on this affair, Sheridan was charitable enough not to mention that the surprise of the Seventh came about because the picket on the road toward Ripley, a detachment of the Second Iowa, ran when the rebels attacked. On the other hand, a statement Sheridan did make in his report deserves to be quoted: "The loss of the enemy I am unable to state. It was understood that they were guerillas. Unfortunately, 11 prisoners were brought in." [17]

Only a very few of the scouts and skirmishes, which were now the daily fare of the Seventh, were thought to be of sufficient moment to call for the writing of a formal report. They were so much an everyday occurrence and usually so uneventful, or so insignificant, that even the letter writers and diarists of the regiment seldom bothered to mention them. Fox recalled one lively skirmish just at dusk with a band of guerillas, "a dashing, picturesque engagement . . . the flashing of small arms was exciting and beautiful." [18] The leader of this guerilla band bore the improbable name of Funderberger; and forever after, this skirmish was known in the regiment as "the battle of Funderberger's Lane." One member of the regiment thought that Sheridan worked the Seventh to the limit of its endurance; another, perhaps a more hardy individual or of a more phlegmatic temperament, complained that there was "very little excitement," and that outside of standing picket and scouting, the regiment led a lazy life.[19] A third Jayhawker, a fervent patriot, wrote: "I hear that some of the Copperheads are preaching up that this war is ruining the country becaus the boys in the Army will get to lazy to work when they get out if some of them would take a scout with us I believe it would not be for want of exercise that would make them lazy." [20]

15. *Official Records*, XVII, Pt. 1, 39–42. Anthony says, in a letter to his father, August 31, 1862, in Langsdorf and Richmond (eds.), "Anthony," 469, that the rebels numbered four or five hundred.

16. *Official Records*, XVII, Pt. 1, 39–42.   17. *Ibid.*

18. Fox, "Story," 32–33.   19. Utt, "Seventh Kansas."

20. George Mowry, Jr., to Nancy Mowry, August 20, 1862, in Moses Letters.

Sheridan's remark about the guerillas taken prisoner on the twenty-sixth is indicative of a gradual hardening of attitude toward the enemy that became noticeable in the summer and fall of 1862 among the higher echelons of the army as well as in Washington. As Bruce Catton has observed, "It was becoming more and more apparent that Grant's army was precariously established in a land where the civilian was as devout an enemy as the soldier in gray."[21] One result of this realization was the issuance of Grant's General Orders No. 60, which laid it down that "persons acting as guerillas without organization and without uniform to distinguish them from private citizens are not entitled to the treatment of prisoners of war when caught and will not receive such treatment"; furthermore, the order said, whenever the government sustained loss as a result of guerilla attacks, the loss should be made good by "seizure of a sufficient amount of personal property" from rebel sympathizers living in the immediate neighborhood of the attack.[22]

Even General Halleck, who had tried to fight rebellion with a rifle in one hand and the Bill of Rights in the other, began to see the light and directed Grant to handle all active supporters of secession "without gloves, and take their property for public use."[23] What both Grant and Halleck should have known, and probably did know, was that when official policies such as these filtered down to the regimental level, in armies made up of imperfectly disciplined volunteers, not all the officers, provost marshals, and court-martials on earth could keep it within limits. Let it once become known that the property of "rebel sympathizers" was no longer sacrosanct, the bars were down, and such property would be taken by the soldiers whenever and wherever they found it, and no questions asked.

If any trooper of the Seventh had had the opportunity to discuss these matters with Generals Grant and Halleck, he could have told these highly placed gentlemen that "had the whole Union Armey adopted Col Jennisons plan of handling the Rebbels the war would have stoped before this time"[24] or, with a nearer approach to literacy: "As to the property of the rebels which could be used for the support of the rebel cause, we felt it

---

21. Catton, *Grant Moves South*, 290.   22. *Official Records*, XVII, Pt. 2, 69.
23. *Ibid.*, 150.
24. Webster Moses to Nancy Mowry, August 5, 1862, in Moses Letters.

was good military tactics to use what we needed and destroy what we could not use. . . . Our regiment was about a year and a half ahead of the government in our methods. It is now doing what it condemned us for doing four months ago."[25] But even in the sometimes excessively democratic Union army, major generals were not in the habit of consulting with enlisted men on questions of policy; Grant and Halleck were thus spared the mortification of hearing "I told you so" comments.

The Seventh, still at times called "Jennison's men," and not as a compliment, did not at once benefit from this easing of restrictions on the taking of rebel property. It suffered from the backlash of a well-established unsavory reputation. "Everything," Fletcher Pomeroy wrote, "that is stolen is laid to our regiment. The 2nd Iowa and 2nd Mich. regiments, which are in our brigade, go out into the country and take everything they want and lay it to our regiment."[26]

The Jayhawkers were distinctly unhappy about the situation, and their indignation over what they considered grossly unfair treatment was shared by Colonel Lee. Early on the morning of August 11, he received the following characteristic order from General Sheridan: "Some of your men are in a corn field a short distance from your camp. They have defied the provost guard. I want them moved instantly or I will do it forcibly."[27] Not at all intimidated by Sheridan's brusqueness, Lee protested the next day:

The provost guard who have been charged with the protection of these fields, have been conveniently blind when soldiers of their acquaintance and regiment desired to enter them. They have been excessively vigilant when a Kansas soldier appeared and repeatedly informed my men that they are located there to keep them out. I see and my men see, passing . . . our camp through the whole day men of the Second Iowa and Second Michigan regts . . . carrying to their camps, sacks well filled with fruit, and themselves and horses loaded with huge bundles of corn. What shall I say to my officers who point to those glaring violations of your order? Frequently these men pass themselves among strangers whom they rob as Seventh Kansas men, Jayhawkers.[28]

25. Pomeroy, "War Diary," entry for February 1, 1863.

26. *Ibid.*, entry for August 11, 1862.

27. Lee to Lieutenant George Lee, August 12, 1862, in Seventh Kansas, Regimental Letter and Order Book.

28. *Ibid.*

The Seventh was also convinced to a man that the brigade provost marshal showed a discriminatory zeal in rounding up and lodging in the guardhouse Jayhawkers away from camp without passes. But for all their grumbling and indignation and protests, the Jayhawkers lived well, and not by any means on army rations alone. There were "lots of hogs running around, and plenty of green corn in a field nearby," and the men did not go hungry for want of either.[29] The curious habit of the fat hogs and beef cattle of Mississippi of seeking out the camp kettles of the Seventh Kansas, became the subject of mildly humorous jokes. Peaches and apples were plentiful and orchard fences easy to climb. At the beginning of August, Colonel Lee got permission to send his wagons "under the charge of a competent officer" to bring in green corn and fruit "once or twice a week," to benefit the health of his men and improve their monotonous fare.[30] Placing a liberal interpretation on his authority, he sent four wagons into the country every other day to gather fruit and vegetables. No doubt they were relished more than were the desiccated potatoes issued by the quartermaster at this time. Nor did the horses go hungry; whenever the hay and corn issued by the quartermaster ran short, the nearest fields were laid under contribution, whether General Sheridan liked it or not.

Among the first of the old restrictions to go by the board under the new dispensation was Halleck's General Orders No. 3 concerning the treatment of escaped slaves. "Contrabands" were now accepted, cared for, and given work to do. Their numbers grew steadily; more came every day, and every detachment of the brigade returning from a scout was followed into camp by a jubilant "tail" of runaways, more than sixty on one occasion. Freed from the indignity of having to "catch Negroes" for the benefit of secessionist owners, the Jayhawkers indulged in the complacency of prophets honored in their own country. One of them wrote: "The secesh think that it is to bad for us to take all their *Negroes*[.] *How I pitty their lazy souls* let them go to work now."[31]

On July 14 George Hoyt submitted his resignation as captain of Com-

29. Pomeroy, "War Diary," entry for July 29, 1862.

30. Lee to Lieutenant George Lee, July 30, 1862, in Seventh Kansas, Regimental Letter and Order Book.

31. Webster Moses to Nancy Mowry, August 15, 1862, in Moses Letters.

pany K. Lee forwarded it to department headquarters with a surprisingly flattering endorsement: "In recommending its acceptance, I cannot forbear adding that in this retirement, the service will lose one of its most valuable officers, and myself . . . one of my bravest coadjutors in the field and most efficient aides in the care and discipline of the regiment."[32] Hoyt gave extreme ill health as the reason for his resignation, and Colonel Lee explained that his favorable endorsement was prompted by the conviction that "any considerable stay in this climate, burdened by the duties of his position, would prove fatal to Capt. Hoyt's life."[33] Indeed, five days later Lee informed Brigadier General Granger in an urgent despatch that Hoyt was risking his life by remaining any longer in Mississippi. He wrote that the "surgeon thinks three or four more days here will so prostrate him as to render him unable ever to leave this camp. Immediately to go may keep him alive."[34] Granger's response is not on record, but evidently Hoyt was permitted to leave at once for Kansas, where he staged one of the fastest recoveries in medical history.

There is certainly no reason to doubt Colonel Lee's veracity or good faith in the matter of Hoyt's resignation; one must therefore conclude that he was hoodwinked. The virtual abandonment of Halleck's "proslavery" policy made Hoyt's abolitionist heroics redundant. An officer of the Seventh had in prospect only the duty of performing the wearisome, monotonous, and prosaic task of fighting rebellion. Back in Kansas, on the other hand, spacious opportunities remained to beckon an enterprising patriot; Missourians still possessed livestock that had not been jayhawked, houses and barns that had not yet been plundered and burned, and slaves that had not been freed. Hoyt's good friend Jennison was even then organizing a regiment of Negroes, a project that might well provide better avenues for notoriety and profit than fighting rebellion in Mississippi. Moreover, a new organization called the Red Legs was now in the field in Kansas and gave promise of becoming a wellnigh perfect instrument for the exercise of George Hoyt's talents. He was in Kansas in August and was about to demonstrate that the disability

32. Lee to Colonel [*sic*] John C. Kelton, July 14, 1862, in Seventh Kansas, Regimental Letter and Order Book.
33. *Ibid.*
34. Lee to Brigadier General Gordon Granger, July 19, 1862, *ibid.*

that had him at death's door and made it impossible for him to continue as an officer of cavalry in Mississippi did not hamper his activities in the more salubrious Kansas climate.

Hoyt's resignation became official on September 3 and was followed by Anthony's departure on September 12. On the twenty-fifth, Captain James Rafety left, "discharged by Special Order No. 319," for reasons not given. The change in personnel most closely affecting the Seventh was, however, the departure of Colonel Sheridan for Kentucky on September 4.[35] Colonel Lee was ordered to take command of what had been Sheridan's brigade, reduced to two regiments owing to the transfer of the Second Michigan to Kentucky with Sheridan. The division commander, General Granger, was also transferred to Kentucky, and command of the attenuated Cavalry Division of the Army of the Mississippi, consisting of a mere three regiments, fell to Colonel John K. Mizner of the Third Michigan Cavalry.

The Seventh began the month of September with a false alarm. One of the pickets rode into camp at top speed at ten in the evening of the first, with the breathless report that his post was even then in a skirmish with an enemy force of unknown size. "To Horse" was sounded, and "in less than five minutes every man including lame halt and blind were drawn up in line of battle awaiting orders"; these orders were never given because a second picket arrived with the information that the "enemy" was an old horse that had blundered into the picket post and had been mistaken in the dark for an enemy raiding party.[36] A few days later the regiment was ordered to move its camp inside the earthworks that had been built around Rienzi and was assigned an area that had been occupied previously by other troops and needed a great deal of laborious policing to make it clean and habitable.

No sooner had the regiment settled down in its new camp than it experienced an event which did not acquire a suitable name until World War II, namely, a typical army snafu. The men were aroused at midnight on the night of September 7 and ordered to strike tents and pack up as rapidly as possible in preparation for an immediate move. Within an hour the regiment was ready to go, but the orders to march did not come.

35. *Official Records*, XVII, Pt. 2, 200.
36. Anthony to his sister Susan, September 2, 1862, in Langsdorf and Richmond (eds.), "Anthony," 473.

September 8 passed with the regiment standing by for marching orders due "any minute." Then the night of September 8 passed. September 9 came and went, with the wagons loaded, the teams harnessed, and the horses saddled, ready for departure at a moment's notice. Then came the night of September 9, with no change in the situation. At last, on the morning of September 10, the orders arrived . . . to unload the wagons, unsaddle the horses, and reerect the tents. The contemplated move, whatever it may have been, was cancelled.

The regiment, or parts of it, made a few scouts during the early part of September, northwest to Kossuth, to Jacinto, south toward Booneville, and to various other places in the area. Then, toward the middle of the month, it became evident that the Confederates were astir. Generals Braxton Bragg and Edmund Kirby Smith were already far into Kentucky with the main Confederate forces, on a campaign that was to take them nearly to the Ohio River at Cincinnati, but was to end in futility and retreat. The armies of Generals Earl Van Dorn and Sterling Price, which had been brought across the Mississippi to Corinth in April, were given the task of holding Grant in check in northern Mississippi. On September 14 Price occupied Iuka, on the Memphis and Charleston Railroad west of Corinth. Colonel Mizner's three weak regiments of cavalry shadowed Price and kept Rosecrans fully informed of his movements.

The Seventh was not in good condition at this time for an active campaign. In addition to a year's losses in the ranks, one lieutenant, one sergeant, and fifteen enlisted men were absent, having been detailed for service with the Seventh Kansas Battery. There was also an acute shortage of officers. Colonel Lee complained that a number of his officers were overstaying sick leaves and that delays in the adjutant general's office in Washington in approving the resignations of other officers prevented him from filling their places. On August 25 he had promoted Sergeant Edward Colbert of Company F to acting first lieutenant of Company I and Sergeant William Weston of Company I to acting second lieutenant of the same company.[37] Nevertheless, he declared that the efficiency of his command was crippled by his inability to fill the places "of a lot of sick men and dolts."[38] But with Van Dorn and Price advancing, Lee had

37. General Orders No. 97, August 25, 1862, in Seventh Kansas, Regimental Order Book.
38. Lee to [illegible], September 19, 1862, in Seventh Kansas, Regimental Letter and Order Book.

to make do with what he had. Two companies of the Seventh had been stationed at Iuka and remained there until Price arrived. The rest of the regiment had to do picket duty on a fifteen-mile front; from two to four companies were constantly absent on patrol, and those that remained in camp had to cut and haul forage for the horses of the entire regiment.[39]

Colonel Mizner, to make certain that his own and his men's strenuous activities and services were neither overlooked nor undervalued, later wrote:

It is due to the cavalry to remark that, although the nature of their service in this wooded country is such that they are frequently denied a participation in general engagements, yet those whose praise and approbation is most to be desired do not lose sight of the invaluable services performed by them. No service is more arduous, yet, with patience and even a spirit of indifference to fatigue, has their labor been performed. . . . The distance traveled, the labor performed, and the fatigue endured by the cavalry is almost incredible, and all this, so cheerfully performed and with such alacrity and spirit, entitle all to the highest commendation.[40]

Grant now determined to attack Price at Iuka. His tactical plan called for Rosecrans with nine thousand men to come in on Iuka from the south on the morning of September 19, while Major General E. O. C. Ord, with eight thousand men, attacked from the west. Had the twin attacks gone according to plan, Price's small army would have been trapped. However, the plans went awry; Rosecrans was delayed and did not attack until late in the afternoon, and Ord did not attack at all. After a brisk fight at nightfall with Rosecrans' lead division, Price decided to evacuate the town and made his escape before daylight. Throughout these operations, two companies of the Seventh covered the flanks of Rosecrans' advance and, on the next day, harassed Price's retreat as well as they could, with sharp attacks on the flanks of his marching column. Captain Fred Swoyer of Company B was singled out for special praise in Colonel Mizner's report, for having performed these duties " with great energy."[41]

Before the fight at Iuka, Price and Van Dorn had discussed an attack on Rosecrans' base at Corinth and now proceeded to put their plan into

39. Letter from Rienzi, Mississippi, dated September 12, 1862, in the Leavenworth *Conservative*, reprinted *ibid.*, February 6, 1864. See Jennison Scrapbook.
40. *Official Records*, XVII, Pt. 1, 244–45.   41. *Ibid.*, 75, 113.

execution. The two Confederate armies met at Ripley and on October 1 began their march northeastward to Corinth, where Rosecrans was waiting for them. Price's and Van Dorn's combined armies numbered about twenty thousand. Rosecrans' force, slightly larger, occupied the extensive fortifications and entrenchments around Corinth that had been constructed after the battle of Shiloh to accomodate Beauregard's much larger army. Price's and Van Dorn's strategic objective was to unhinge Grant's loosely held defensive line running west to east from Memphis to northern Alabama; if Rosecrans were driven out of Corinth in defeat the Federal line would be breached and Grant would be forced to evacuate all of northern Mississippi and western Tennessee. Price and Van Dorn would then be free to march northward to join Bragg and Smith in central Kentucky.

Rosecrans, not sure whether the Confederates intended to attack him in Corinth or bypass him to the northwest, stationed his cavalry, including the Seventh Kansas and a part of the Seventh Illinois, at Kossuth and Bone Yard, where they could detect, and be on the flank of, any Confederate advance in his direction.[42]

Since September 25, the Jayhawkers had been somewhat better equipped to hold their own against the rebels, for on that day, Companies E and G exchanged their muskets for five-shot Colt repeating rifles.[43] From his position at Kossuth and Bone Yard, Colonel Lee sent out strong patrols to the south and west, and was the first to discover and report that the enemy was advancing; the Confederates, their right shielded by the Hatchie River, were marching north through Ruckersville and Jonesboro. Lee crossed the Hatchie to ascertain the enemy's strength, and after a sharp skirmish with its rear guard at Ruckersville on the evening of October 1, in which he captured fifty prisoners, he retired to the east bank of the river to guard the crossings and to keep a sharp eye on the Confederate advance. On the evening of the third he was ordered to retreat to Corinth and to take position within the fortifications on the southern or left flank of the Union army.

The ensuing battle of Corinth was a hard-fought, two-day affair. Rosecrans gained a victory at the cost of nearly 2,200 killed and

42. *Ibid.*, 167.
43. Pomeroy, "War Diary," entry for September 25, 1862.

John Brown, Jr.

Daniel R. Anthony

James H. Lane

James Montgomery

Samuel Pomeroy   Charles Robinson

The Planters Hotel in Leavenworth

wounded.[44] The Confederates attacked from the north and west. On October 3, the first day, the divisions of Union Generals Thomas A. Davies and Charles S. Hamilton were pushed back two miles from their position in the outer ring of entrenchments, to an inner chain of fortifications and batteries of heavy guns located close to the outskirts of the town. It was well after dark when the fighting stopped. The Confederate attack was resumed in heavy force on the morning of the fourth. Battery Robinette, the key to the Federal defenses on the west, was twice taken by Dabney Maury's Confederates, and twice retaken; on the right, Price's men succeeded in penetrating the Union line and reached the streets of the town, but the Federals rallied and drove them out. By two in the afternoon the Confederates were fought out and Van Dorn gave orders for a retreat.

It was not the function of cavalry to take an active part in a pitched battle fought in the midst of fortifications. The Seventh, however, did what it could. On the evening of the first day, with the Union army in serious danger, the regiment deployed dismounted and fought as skirmishers and sharpshooters. In the severe fighting of the second day, six companies of Jayhawkers, again dismounted, were in the firing line to the left of Battery Robinette, while Major John T. Snoddy, with four companies, drew off to the south to harass the Confederate right flank; he was engaged twice with rebel flank guards and routed them both times. Simeon Fox and several other Jayhawkers were detailed as orderlies, couriers, and despatch riders at Rosecrans' headquarters. Fox was in the general's suite on the late afternoon of the second day, when Rosecrans rode along his lines and thanked each regiment of his army for the victory they had helped to win. Sergeant Bayless S. Campbell of Company C earned a battlefield commission for volunteering to carry an order through a belt of fire so intense that Rosecrans would not order any of his orderlies to cross it.[45] Another Jayhawker, Corporal Edward Sanders, was tendered the general's thanks for delivering one of Rosecrans' orders in conditions of grave peril.[46]

44. *Official Records*, XVII, Pt. 1, 176.

45. Pomeroy, "War Diary," entry for October 4, 1862. *Cf. Report of the Adjutant General of the State of Kansas*, I, 554.

46. Leavenworth *Conservative*, February 6, 1864, clipping in Jennison Scrapbook.

At one stage of the fighting around Battery Robinette, three companies of the Seventh, including Company H, were ordered to form line in support of a regiment of infantry. The men of Company H, not satisfied with this relatively passive role, pushed to the front and fought side by side with the infantrymen until the battle ended. Company A, separated for a time from the rest of the regiment and stationed in front of Battery Phillips on College Hill, on the left of the Union line, used its Sharp's carbines to good effect. Lying under cover of log breastworks and firing an average of eighty rounds per man, they inflicted heavy punishment on Major General Mansfield Lovell's division, "swarming in their front at a distance of two or three hundred yards."[47]

When the fighting ended, the entire Union army had been in motion for two successive nights, and had had two days of severe fighting in temperatures well up in the nineties. Rosecrans, lacking the killer instinct, decided that his men needed a night's rest before they could begin the pursuit of the beaten Confederates, who had undergone the same hardships as his own men. When the pursuit got under way on the morning of the fifth, Colonel Mizner divided his cavalry into two sections. Colonel Edward Hatch of the Second Iowa led one group, composed of his own regiment, the Third Michigan, and a section of artillery, to the north of the Chewallah Road, which the Confederates were using to get to the Hatchie River. At the same time, Colonel Lee, with his Jayhawkers, the Seventh Illinois, two companies of infantry, and a section of artillery, marched parallel to the Chewallah Road to the south. Both groups stabbed repeatedly at the flanks and rear of the retreating rebels. Captain Levi Utt and Company A particularly distinguished themselves in these operations and were singled out for commendation by Colonel Lee and Major General James B. McPherson.[48]

After driving the Confederate rear guard out of Kossuth and skirmishing with it through Ruckersville all the way to Ripley, Lee's group occupied the latter town after a heavy skirmish in the outskirts, in which they took thirty-five prisoners.[49] Another large bag of prisoners was captured during the ensuing night by Captain David W. Houston, Rafety's successor as captain of Company H. At nightfall, Houston was

47. Utt, "Seventh Kansas."   48. *Ibid.*
49. *Official Records,* XVII, Pt. 1, 244.

ordered to picket the road running south from Ripley with his company. He thought that he might be attacked during the night, so he had a large fire built, and around it he placed rolled-up blankets to represent sleeping troopers. Then he posted his men in the underbrush, away from the road and a short distance south of the campfire. At two in the morning, a company of rebel infantry came up the road and, seeing the campfire ahead, advanced cautiously upon it. Houston and his men stealthily followed, and when the Confederates reached the campfire and called upon the dummies to surrender, Houston quietly suggested that the rebels surrender instead, which they did, and Houston returned to Ripley with over forty prisoners.

At Ripley, the pursuit was called off by order of General Grant. Rosecrans, convinced that he had a "defeated, routed and demoralized" enemy to deal with, begged for permission to go on, but Grant refused and ordered him to return to Corinth. W. A. Lyman of Company G, Colonel Lee's orderly, was sent to Ripley with a message for Rosecrans, and got there just after the General had received Grant's order to break off the pursuit. Lyman found Rosecrans "tramping back and forth in his office, cursing like the proverbial trooper that he should thus be prevented from proceeding any further."[50] Nevertheless, he was forced to obey, and his army, including the Seventh, marched back to Corinth. His irritation at Grant's orders is understandable, for he believed, and was not alone in believing, that if Grant had allowed him to go on, he could have captured Vicksburg.[51]

The Jayhawkers had put in a strenuous thirty days since mid-September and had reason to be satisfied with themselves and their accomplishments. And so they were. George Mowry, Jr., wrote his sister after the regiment returned to Corinth, "We have a fine man for Col now. . . . I think we have as good field officers in this Regt as any Regt I know of and as good a Regt."[52] And astonishingly, after the events of June–August, the Jayhawkers' good opinion of themselves was shared by Rosecrans. He had sent a requisition for cavalry arms to the War Department and was greatly displeased to learn that the arms he asked

50. Lyman, "Reminiscences."
51. Robert U. Johnson and Clarence C. Buel (eds.), *Battles and Leaders of the Civil War* (New York, 1884–87), II, 755.
52. George Mowry, Jr., to Nancy Mowry, November 4, 1862, in Moses Letters.

for were delivered "to little detachments, split up and performing picket duty in . . . [the] rear," units for which, Rosecrans declared, the rebels did not care a pin; and he asked that the new weapons be given first to the regiments which "alone have made the enemy afraid and whipped them in force . . . [the] brave men, who had not less than three fights per week for the last thirty days."[53] He listed five regiments which he considered worthy of this priority, and the Seventh Kansas was one of the favored five; the others were the Second Iowa, the Third Michigan, and the Seventh and Eleventh Illinois. In another despatch the next day, he went even further; he specifically requested that the Seventh be supplied with 250 new revolvers and 500 Colt revolving rifles, "all with slugs, pistol pouches, cap boxes and ammunition complete."[54] His energetic representations brought results, and eventually, five more companies of the Seventh received Colt revolving rifles, giving the regiment seven companies armed with the revolving rifle and three armed with the Sharp's carbine; in addition, all the men now had sabers and Colt navy revolvers. Since the regiment did practically all of its fighting dismounted, the sabers were an ornament at best, if not an encumbrance, and in fact it was not until October, 1864, that the Seventh made its first and, as it turned out, its only saber charge of the entire war. Nevertheless, Companies A, B, and H retained their designation as the "saber companies."[55]

One Jayhawker who was not at Corinth to share the complacent self-satisfaction of his comrades was Nancy Mowry's chief correspondent, Webster Moses. Stricken with a mysterious malady, he had left the regiment on September 22 and entered the hospital at Corinth; and four days later, he was shipped with several hundred other invalids to the base hospital at St. Louis. The journey north took nine days, and during the entire trip the sick and wounded lived on a diet of hardtack, raw bacon, and coffee.[56]

Notwithstanding the unsatisfactory ending of the pursuit following the battle of Corinth, the Confederate defeat in that battle, coupled with the failure of Bragg's invasion of Kentucky, opened up new strategic

53. *Official Records*, XVII, Pt. 2, 284.
54. *Ibid.*, 287.
55. Utt, "Seventh Kansas."
56. Webster Moses to Nancy Mowry, October 13, 1862, in Moses Letters.

possibilities for the Union armies in Tennessee and Mississippi. Since June they had been tied to a static defensive role, protecting the east–west railroads behind them for use in an eventual invasion of East Tennessee. But now an aggressive strategy became feasible. Grant was given authority to proceed with a plan that involved the destruction of the railroads about Corinth, the moving of his force forty miles west to Grand Junction, Tennessee, at the intersection of the Memphis and Charleston and the Mississippi Central railroads, and a drive south from that point to Holly Springs, Granada, and Jackson, Mississippi, to get at Vicksburg through the back door, using the Mississippi Central as his supply line. Every mile of his proposed two hundred-mile advance, and every mile of the single-track railroad on which he was to depend for his supplies, ran through enemy territory. The campaign thus promised to provide ample work for his cavalry.

The army with which Grant was to make his campaign had received powerful reinforcements. It was to consist of two "wings," a two-division right wing commanded by Major General James B. McPherson, and a three-division left wing commanded by Brigadier General Charles S. Hamilton. The Seventh Kansas was now part of the cavalry brigade, commanded by Colonel Lee, attached to Hamilton's wing; the brigade consisted, besides the Seventh, of the Second Iowa, the Third Michigan, and one company each of the Eleventh Illinois and the Fifth Missouri. Lee being in command of the brigade, the Seventh was commanded by Lieutenant Colonel Thomas P. Herrick, who had been promoted to that rank on September 3, upon Anthony's resignation.[57] The "aggregate present for duty" in Lee's brigade on November 10 was 1,896 officers and men; the brigade of cavalry attached to McPherson's wing numbered a mere 1,267 officers and men "present for duty."[58] It was to become apparent very shortly that 3,163 cavalry, subject to daily wastage by casualties, illness, resignations, discharges, and the giving out of horses, were far from enough for the ambitious campaign Grant proposed to wage.

It will have been noticed that Rosecrans was not one of Grant's wing commanders; on October 23 he was given command of the Army of the

57. *Report of the Adjutant General of the State of Kansas*, I, 524.
58. *Official Records*, XVII, Pt. 2, 338.

Ohio in succession to Don Carlos Buell, and Grant was thereby relieved of the burden of a difficult and uncongenial subordinate. But the Seventh was to meet Rosecrans again, two years later.

JENNISON THE CIVILIAN

The war had drifted away from Kansas since the spring of 1862. The cockpit of the first winter of war had become a backwater. But with guerillas still rampant in Missouri, the irrepressible Lane in Washington and Jennison back in Leavenworth, there was little chance that the Kansas backwater would ever become completely stagnant. At the end of June Jennison found it expedient to explain, in a "card" to the Leavenworth *Conservative*, why he was not in the army. Halleck's General Orders No. 3 was then still in effect, and Jennison declared: "I am informed officially that Gen. R. B. Mitchell uses my regiment principally in the capacity of Kidnappers. . . . I did not enlist to return slaves or protect rebels, but to crush slavery and to kill rebels, and while in the service, I gave a good deal of attention to these two points. When the Government adopts that policy, I shall be again a soldier; until that time, I shall be a citizen." [59]

To make his living, or at least a part of it, as a civilian, Jennison formed a partnership with one Losee to exploit what was known as the Pike's Peak Trade. Gold had been discovered near Denver in 1858. The Colorado gold rush, stimulated by additional strikes in 1859, raised the population of the territory in two years from a few hundred fur trappers and prospectors to 34,000 and created a rapidly growing market for the agricultural and manufactured products of the East. Much of this trade funneled through Leavenworth. In the traveling season of 1862, notwithstanding that the Civil War was going on, a steady stream of emigrants and supplies flowed westward from Leavenworth to the gold fields; at least one wagon train, and usually several, left Leavenworth every week for Denver. The firm of Losee and Jennison did a general freighting business to the gold fields and also traded for its own account, buying and selling horses and mules and hauling as many as fifty thousand bushels of corn at a time to be sold in Colorado.

---

59. "Card" dated June 24, 1862. See undated clipping from the Leavenworth *Conservative*, in Jennison Scrapbook.

Jennison's involvement in an enterprise requiring large numbers of draft animals has a suspicious aptness about it. Earlier in the year, Generals James G. Blunt and Thomas Ewing, Jr., had organized a body of scouts to operate on the Missouri border, to give warning of rebel guerilla raids into Kansas and, when possible, to drive them off.[60] These scouts, headed by "Captain" William S. Tough, a native of Baltimore, Maryland, (or by another account, of Savannah, Georgia), acquired the name of "Red Legs" or "Red Legged Scouts" from their habit of wearing sheepskin leggings dyed red.[61] Also, in short order they acquired an evil reputation that to all appearance was thoroughly well deserved. The Red Legs were not the kind of military body that keeps records and makes reports, and if its members were given to writing letters or keeping diaries, which is quite unlikely, these contemporary documents have not survived. Hence the history of the organization, and even its actual composition, are full of uncertainties. One tradition has it that the official body of Red Legs has been sadly maligned, and that most of the sins laid to its door were committed by Kansans who were not Red Legs at all, but adopted the costume and name of Red Legs as a convenient means of carrying on their nefarious activities with impunity.

It may be mentioned here that Wild Bill Hickok, later a pillar of the law, was at one time a Red Leg; and Buffalo Bill Cody, the putative author of one of the most wildly unreliable "autobiographies" ever published, claimed that he too was a member of the "Red Legged Scouts, having joined in the summer of 1861," which is several months before the Red Legs were organized.[62]

The original breed of jayhawkers had made a profession of robbing, burning out, and murdering rebels in arms against the government. The Red Legs, on the other hand, whether of the official or pretended variety, stole, robbed, burned, and killed indiscriminately, and not in Missouri alone. One may wonder if after a year of raiding by Lane's brigade, the "Southern Kansas Jay-Hawkers," the Seventh Kansas, and other groups, there was anything left in northwest Missouri worth stealing; apparently

60. William E. Connelley, *Quantrill and the Border Wars* (Cedar Rapids, 1910), 411–12, n.
61. In an order dated November 15, 1862, General Blunt stated that the Red Legs had been "organized under the auspices of Capt. Stout, late Provost Marshal." See unidentified clipping, Jennison Scrapbook. Russell, *Buffalo Bill*, 59, gives Savannah, Georgia, as Tough's birthplace.
62. William F. Cody, *An Autobiography of Buffalo Bill Cody* (New York, 1920), 61.

there was. General Blunt, who, it may be assumed, was fully familiar with the Red Legs's activities, wrote:

Whatever had been the primary object and purpose of those identified with . . . [the Red Legs] its operations had certainly become fraught with danger to the peace and security of society. The organization embraced many of the most desperate characters in the country, while the inducements of easy gain had allured into it many persons who, in ordinary times, would never have consented to be connected with such an enterprise. Officers, soldiers and citizens had become infected until the leaders became so bold as to defy interference with their operations . . . [which] extended into Colorado, Nebraska and Iowa. A reign of terror was inaugurated, and no man's property was safe, nor was his life worth much if he opposed them in their schemes of plunder and robbery. . . . I considered it my duty to interfere for the protection of honest and peaceable citizen . . . notwithstanding I daily received anonymous letters threatening me with assassination if I did not desist arresting and punishing these offenders.[63]

It was a foregone conclusion that Jennison, once he was free of his ties with the army, would become involved in some manner with the Red Legs. They were only practicing what he had advocated from the start as the proper method of dealing with rebels. If in the process non-rebels and even antirebels and Kansans suffered the same treatment, Jennison was not the man to boggle over technicalities. Doubtless too, some of his old jayhawkers, and men who had deserted from the Seventh and never returned, were now Red Legs and would welcome a renewed association with their like-minded and enterprising former leader. One cannot point to any concrete and unquestionably reliable evidence to prove Jennison's connection with an organization that General Blunt aptly called "The Forty Thieves," but there can be little doubt that from the time of his return to Kansas in late May or early June, 1862, he was not only a Red Leg, but actually one of the leaders of the band. It is not unreasonable to assume that his role was to dispose of the loot. It is a fact, in any case, that from the summer of 1862 on, both friendly and hostile newspapers repeatedly referred to Jennison as a Red Leg, and these statements were never contradicted, then or later.

Leavenworth and Lawrence were the two principal markets in which

63. James G. Blunt, "General Blunt's Account of His Civil War Experiences," *Kansas Historical Quarterly*, I (1932), 239.

the Red Legs sold their plunder. One may assume that some of it found its way to Colorado through the instrumentality of the firm of Losee and Jennison, or if it was loot of the four-legged variety, that it traveled to Colorado harnessed to the wagons of that firm.

If Jennison's association with the Red Legs is no matter for surprise, George Hoyt's is even less so, for Hoyt could have said to Jennison as Ruth said to Naomi, "Intreat me not to leave thee, *or* to return from following after thee; for whither thou goest, I will go." There is ample evidence to substantiate the universally held belief of contemporary Kansas that Hoyt was the leader of the Red Legs; it is not clear, however, whether he was head of the organization in his own right or as a front and deputy for Jennison.[64] One of the minor ironies of Kansas history is the fact that within three years from the end of the Civil War, the attorney general and hence the chief law officer of that straitlaced state was none other than George Hoyt, former leader of what was nothing better than a band of highwaymen, arsonists, and murderers.

The Red Legs and the affairs of Losee and Jennison were not sufficient to claim all of Jennison's abundant energies, and in July and August he took on another assignment. Senator Lane had been authorized some time before to raise a regiment of Negroes, enlisting ex-slaves who had escaped to Kansas. He in turn appointed Jennison as his recruiting agent; Jennison naturally chose Hoyt to assist him in the task. The inducement, express or implied, that at least partially influenced Jennison to act for Lane was that he would be appointed colonel of the regiment. It may be taken as a mercy of Providence that the regiment never came into being, for the presence of Jennison and Hoyt in Missouri at the head of a regiment of armed Negroes only a few months removed from slavery, and disciplined according to Jennison's conception of that term, would have added greater horrors to a war already more than sufficiently disgraced by the atrocities of Missouri guerillas and Kansas jayhawkers of the Marshall Cleveland-Red Leg variety.

64. According to Henry E. Palmer's account, Hoyt resigned his commission in the Seventh Kansas to "raise a band of over 300 red legs, an organization sworn to shoot rebels, take no prisoners, free slaves and respect no property rights of rebels or of their sympathizers." See "Black Flag Character," 464. It is beyond doubt that for a time Hoyt was the (or one of the) leaders of the Red Legs. But Palmer's statement that he raised the band is almost certainly erroneous, and his list of the things the Red Legs were "sworn" to do is surely exaggerated.

Jennison, at any rate, threw himself into the recruiting campaign with his customary enthusiasm and energy. There are strong indications that the project aroused his genuine sympathy. His scrapbook contains clippings of newspaper articles on the employment of Negro troops in the Revolutionary War and the War of 1812, as well as the printed record of the proceedings of a mass meeting held in Philadelphia to encourage the enlistment of Negroes in the Union army; his own speeches to potential recruits hammered away at the theme that the government offered Negroes a chance to fight for their own freedom, and if they were not willing to fight, they did not deserve to be free.[65]

Whatever activity Jennison happened to be engaged in, he was sure to become the center of controversy in the process. So it was with this recruiting campaign. James Montgomery, his Linn County neighbor and rival of Free State days, protested vehemently against Jennison's appointment as colonel of the Negro regiment; he wrote Governor Robinson:

Your Excellency is aware that a regiment of Col^d men is being formed at Mound City. These men are nearly, or quite, unanimous in their preference for me as their Colonel.

Their second choice is Jennison.

Now, Governor, allow me to say that with my *personal* knowledge of Jennison, I cannot imagine any greater calamity that could befall the blacks than the appointment of Jennison to command them. I have been solicited by the *honorable portion* of our Citizens—Those who wish to see the Negro elevated instead of being made a thief and a pest to society, to take command of them.[66]

Montgomery's opposition was not the only stumbling block in the way. Lane, apparently, had the right to appoint the colonel of the regiment, but it is evident from Montgomery's letter, and the citation which follows, that the governor too had a voice in the matter; and to be known, as Jennison was, as a confederate of Lane was not the way to Robinson's heart. Hence, Jennison made use of George Hoyt's pen, for neither the first nor the last time, to protest to the governor:

Gen Lane *voluntarily* gave him the authority he has, to organize the colored

---

65. Speech in Doniphan County. See unidentified clipping, Jennison Scrapbook.
66. Montgomery to Robinson, August 3, 1862, in Robinson Papers.

regiment. . . . It was an *unsolicited position*, but *being hedged about with no conditions of any sort could not well be refused*. In view of what has heretofore transpired it is unnecessary to say that Col. Jennison takes hold of this work, *not* as a Lane man, but altogether on the Jennison basis. . . . He wishes to say frankly . . . that in the exercise of any influence or power he may have in the premises, he will be governed by a policy to which you can urge no objection.[67]

It will be observed that getting a military command in Kansas was far from being a simple affair.

Nor was Jennison's recruiting invariably of a conventional variety. Toward the end of August, a group of fifteen Kansans appeared in Clay County, Missouri, across the Missouri River from Kansas City, "to enlist negroes." They took "forcible possession" of twenty-five Negroes and—a characteristic touch—of about forty horses. They were intercepted by a detachment of Missouri State Militia as they were about to recross the Missouri River; the Negroes and horses were recovered, and eight of the recruiting agents were captured and lodged in the jail at Liberty, Missouri.[68] A day or two later a man appeared at Liberty with a written demand, signed by Jennison, for the release of the eight prisoners, coupled with the threat that "he would hold the county responsible if they were not released and given up." The demand was nevertheless refused. A "United States detective" who later examined the prisoners declared that they were "outlaws and thieves of the worst description."[69] Jennison claimed them as his men. Were they Red Legs? The records are silent on the subject, but the affiliations of these most unusual recruiting agents are not unduly difficult to guess.

It is no cause for wonder that even though Jennison had retired from the wars, ostensibly to lead the life of a peaceful civilian, Major General Samuel R. Curtis, who now had command of the Department of the Missouri, which embraced the state of Kansas, wrote that he hoped to send him against the rebels and Indians in the southwestern corner of Missouri, so that he would not be "loose, to carry on guerilla warfare, which drives good people out of Jackson and Lafayette [counties]."[70]

67. Hoyt to Robinson, August 12, 1862, *ibid.*
68. *Official Records*, XVIII, 619.   69. *Ibid.*, 713.
70. *Ibid.*, 688.

CHAPTER XI

A Road South

NOVEMBER BRINGS good campaigning weather to northern Mississippi. It is the season between the heat of summer and the winter rains. On the second of the month, in 1862, Grant began to assemble his troops at Grand Junction in preparation for his campaign, whose first objective was the capture of Jackson, the capital of Mississippi. The Seventh left Corinth on the fourth and, on the afternoon of the fifth, went into camp four miles south of Grand Junction, on the left wing of Grant's army. On the next day, Colonel Lee assumed command of the cavalry brigade of General Hamilton's wing, and Lieutenant Colonel Thomas P. Herrick took over command of the Jayhawkers.

Grant's move forward began at once, and on November 8 Lee's cavalry had its first brush with the enemy at Lamar, twelve miles southwest of Grand Junction. The Seventh, leading the advance of the cavalry brigade, some two miles ahead of the infantry, came upon Colonel W. H. Jackson's Confederate cavalry. Captain Charles H. Gregory, in the lead with his Company E, had learned well the first commandment of the cavalryman's decalogue; as soon as he caught sight of the enemy, he attacked. He was followed by the entire regiment. Jackson was caught on the march and had no time to deploy from column into line before the attack of the Seventh, coming in from the flank, struck the center of his column. The Confederates stampeded—one Jayhawker, possibly prejudiced, wrote that they "fled like sheep"—leaving dead, wounded, prisoners, arms, and horses in the hands of the victorious Kansans.[1] It is of some interest as an illustration of the difficulty of establishing the truth in such matters, that three different Federal accounts of this encounter give the number of Confederates killed as 7, 16, and 36, respectively, and the number of prisoners as 75, 134, and "400 or 500."[2] Whatever Jackson's actual losses may have been, the Seventh undoubtedly had a small but satisfying victory to its credit. Grant was well pleased and telegraphed General Halleck: "Colonel Lee is one of our best cavalry officers. I earnestly recommend him for promotion."[3]

Within two months, Lee had the brigadier general's stars that his Jayhawkers had won for him. And when the Seventh returned to camp after the fight with Jackson, it had the heartening experience, probably unique in the none too glamorous career of the Federal cavalry prior to the summer of 1863, of being cheered by the infantry for its victory.

Grant's advance continued against weak opposition, and at daylight on the thirteenth, Lee occupied Holly Springs. Obviously feeling that he was entitled to do a little crowing, Lee indulged in some unmilitary language in reporting to Grant that his pickets were "polluting the 'sacred soil' " some two miles beyond the town and that the five regiments of Jackson's cavalry that tried to contest his advance had "skedaddled."[4] The word "skedaddled" proved to be somewhat premature, for before the day was over, Lee had to report that he had been skirmishing with the Confederate cavalry all day and that, in midafternoon, *they* had attacked *him*. He was able to beat off Jackson's attack; and as night fell, he remained in possession of Holly Springs.

The campaign now came to a brief halt while Grant pulled forward his administrative tail. The Seventh used the pause to do some foraging, and on the nineteenth it went on a scout to Ripley, thirty miles to the east, where it broke up Colonel W. W. Faulkner's regiment.[5] Sixty

---

1. Pomeroy, "War Diary," entry for November 8, 1862.
2. *Ibid.* Pomeroy gives the number of killed as seven and the number of prisoners as seventy-five. General Grant, *Official Records*, XVII, Pt. 1, 469, reports sixteen killed and 134 prisoners. Fox, "Story," 34, is responsible for the count of thirty-six killed and four to five hundred prisoners.
3. *Official Records*, XVII, Pt. 1, 469.   4. *Ibid.*, 488.
5. *Ibid.*, 490–91. The Confederate commander's name is given as "Falkner."

prisoners were taken, and on the return march the inhabitants of Tippah County were relieved of eighty-one horses and sixty-seven mules, those being the numbers turned over by Lee to the divisional quartermaster; it may be taken for granted that in addition to the animals officially accounted for, those of the Jayhawkers whose horses were not fully satisfactory exchanged them for better ones. In doing so, they were merely following their colonel's example, for when Holly Springs was captured, Lee appropriated a "very fine bay horse. The owner offered him $1,000 to leave the horse, but the Col. was not interested."[6]

Grant's advance resumed on November 27, and on the next day, with the Seventh again in the lead, the rebels were driven south of Holly Springs to the Tallahatchie River. There, protected by strong field fortifications garnished with forty pieces of artillery, they made a stand and gave the Seventh a hot reception. The shelling gave Lee the opportunity to exhibit the kind of cool courage under fire that goes far to account for the high regard his men had for him. He was sitting at the foot of a tree, writing a despatch, and had just risen to hand it to an orderly when a rebel shell crashed into the root on which he had been sitting. He looked around calmly and remarked, "Rather disagreeable proximity!"[7]

During the night, Sergeant William Henry of Company D, with two of his men, crept inside the Confederate fortifications and came back with the report that the enemy was in the process of evacuating the position and crossing over to the south bank of the stream; Sergeant John H. Wildey of Company C made the same perilous trip at another point in the lines and confirmed Sergeant Henry's report. Another Jayhawker, identified only as "a little Irishman belonging to the 7th," had an adventure, quite possibly imaginary, which appears with various changes of detail in numerous Civil War regimental histories, usually

6. Lyman, "Reminiscences." General James H. Wilson, then a member of Grant's staff, encountered the Seventh in November, 1862. "On our way back," he wrote, "with all the horses and mules we could gather in the country, I was not surprised to see that our Kansas 'Jay-hawkers' had but little respect for the people of the country and none for their property. Just outside of Ripley I saw a trooper carrying a Yankee clock and, of course, asked him where he got it and what he was going to do with it. He replied at once: 'I got it in town and I am going to take it to camp and get a pair of the little wheels out of it for spur rowels.'" See James H. Wilson, *Under the Old Flag* (New York, 1912), I, 141.

7. Lyman, "Reminiscences."

with an Irishman as the hero. The Jayhawker from the Auld Sod is reported to have gone awandering by his lonesome after dark and to have come upon a party of rebels occupying a log hut. In a loud voice he commanded the nonexistent force he had with him to guard the doors; and then, going up to a window, revolver in hand, he ordered the rebels to surrender and throw their arms out to him. This they obligingly did. They also obeyed his next order and came out the door one at a time, to the number of five. The Irishman marched his prisoners back to camp. While he was turning them in to the officer of the guard, he was asked how he had managed to take five prisoners singlehanded. He replied, "I surrounded them." [8]

The rebels having withdrawn across the Tallahatchie during the night, the Seventh followed them across the river at 3 A.M. Lee's brigade, now consisting of the Seventh Kansas, the Fourth Illinois, a battalion of the Second Iowa, and temporarily, the Third Michigan, then pressed forward on the direct road toward Oxford, delayed more by the deep mud than by the rebel rear guard. Early in the afternoon, the Confederates made a strong stand about a mile north of Oxford. Captain Swoyer was sent forward with Company B in a mounted charge, but he was checked by a heavy fire. The entire regiment then deployed and made an attack dismounted with its revolving rifles and carbines and drove the enemy through and beyond the town. The fighting was sharp, the rebels losing eight killed and many prisoners. Two of the latter were flushed out of hiding in a corncrib beside the road and captured by the diarist of Company D, Fletcher Pomeroy.

The Seventh remained in occupation of Oxford long enough to lay in a "bountiful supply of tobacco at the expense of the Oxford merchants." [9] The pursuit then continued against stiff opposition. At nightfall the next day, the brigade reached Water Valley, and the Seventh was given the job of guarding the nearly one thousand prisoners who had been captured. Discovering that "the prisoners were destitute and fainting for a chaw . . . [the Jayhawkers] began to pitch whole plugs of 'flat' to the suffering Johnnies. It created a transformation; despondency disappeared . . . three cheers for the jayhawkers were given with a gusto." [10]

8. *Ibid.*   9. Fox, "Story," 36.   10. *Ibid.*

By December 5 the Confederates opposing Grant's advance—Mansfield Lovell's division of infantry—had retreated to Coffeeville, nearly thirty miles south of Oxford. Lovell's scouts had alerted him to the fact that there was a gap of several miles between Lee's cavalry and Hamilton's infantry, and at Coffeeville he took advantage of the opportunity thus presented to him. He laid a trap for the overly confident Federal horsemen. He posted his infantry in timber, a mile north of the town, on a ridge running perpendicular to the road on which the Federals were advancing. Behind the infantry, and well screened by the woods and underbrush, he placed a four-gun battery, and three hundred yards further to the rear and on higher ground, he positioned two Parrott guns of Captain W. H. Hedden's battery.[11] The trap was sprung by the artillery at two in the afternoon, when Lee's men came within easy range of the guns. Companies A, G, I, and K of the Seventh were at once ordered to dismount and go forward as skirmishers. The other six companies of the Seventh, also dismounted, were deployed in support of the skirmish line. Lieutenant Isaiah J. Hughes of Company D, in command of his company, violated an unwritten but firm rule by sending his men into the firing line under the command of First Sergeant Nathan B. Hinsdale, while he himself remained behind as a horseholder. Hinsdale was killed in the action. Hughes came out of the fight with a whole skin, but his standing among his men was irretrievably ruined. A month after the fight, he had to be transferred to Company G, and five months later he resigned.[12]

As Companies A, G, I, and K advanced across an open field toward the Confederate infantry, they were met by a "withering volley" and were forced to fall back on their supports. The Confederates now moved forward to the attack against the heavily outnumbered cavalrymen and pressed them steadily back. The fighting ranged through alternating bands of timber and clearings. As the cavalrymen were forced back to the northern edge of each belt of timber, they mounted their horses,

---

11. *Official Records*, XVII, Pt. 1, 504. Fox, "Story," 36, claims that the Seventh was fired on by two full batteries.

12. Lieutenant Hughes's first name is given as Isaac by Fox, "Story," 21; as Isaiah in *Report of the Adjutant General of the State of Kansas*, I, 566; and as Josiah in *Report of the Adjutant General of the State of Kansas for the Year 1864*, 244. Hughes was transferred to Company G on February 2, 1863.

galloped across the clearing to the next patch of woods, dismounted and took position along its southern edge, held on as long as they could, and then repeated the process. Brigadier General Lloyd Tilghman, who directed the Confederate attack, said in his report on the engagement that "the tactics of the enemy did them great credit."[13] Nonetheless, the Federals were forced out of each successive position, but not until the much longer Confederate line, curving inwards at both ends, had them practically surrounded—if the somewhat partial accounts of Simeon Fox and Fletcher Pomeroy are to be believed.

The fighting went on until dark, and when it ended, the Federals had been pushed back two miles. Casualties were heavy, especially so in the Seventh, which had been in the forefront of the fight, both in the advance and in the retreat. Eight of the ten killed in the entire cavalry division, and forty of the sixty-three wounded, belonged to the Seventh Kansas.[14] Lieutenant Thomas J. Woodburn of Company K was one of those killed, and among the wounded were Lieutenant Edward Colbert of Company F and Private Christopher M. Ford of Company A. The latter was hit five times before he could be induced to leave the field. In addition to the nearly fifty killed and wounded, seventy Jayhawkers were missing when the action ended. These were men who, in the confusion of the successive changes of position under fire, were unable to find or reach their horses and hid in the woods as the action swept past them. A few of them were taken prisoner, but the majority escaped and eventually rejoined the regiment, some as many as five days after the fight.

The action at Coffeeville had been fought under difficult conditions. Colonel T. Lyle Dickey, in command of the cavalry division, commented in his report:

The road was narrow and muddy, lined nearly all the way on both sides by a dense and almost impenetrable growth of oak trees and underbrush, running over a broken and impracticable country or through river bottoms of a miry character. It was impossible to see the enemy's position or note his strength till we were upon him. It was equally difficult to show a strong front or properly dispose of the wagons and ambulances and the horses of the dismounted men.[15]

13. *Official Records*, XVII, Pt. 1, 505.
14. *Ibid.*, 496.
15. *Ibid.*

Nevertheless, this engagement added to Colonel Lee's already excellent reputation. Colonel Dickey commended his handling of his troops, and General Tilghman's praise of his tactics was an unusual tribute from an enemy. But Lee also demonstrated that he was something more than an able tactician. He took personal charge of one of the twelve-pounder guns that had been attached to his brigade, and in the intervals of directing the movements of his cavalrymen, he himself aimed and fired the gun.[16] This was not among the duties the manuals prescribed for the commander of a cavalry brigade, but it was the kind of personal leadership under fire that captured the imagination of Civil War volunteers and made for the success of a commander.

The check at Coffeeville imposed a halt upon the hitherto carefree advance of Grant's army and provided the Confederates the breathing space for a devastating counterstroke. Grant had been building up Holly Springs, captured by Lee's cavalrymen in mid-November, as his forward supply base. By mid-December Grant's army was some fifty miles south of Holly Springs, which was guarded by a scratch force of Wisconsin and Illinois infantry and a detachment of the Second Illinois Cavalry. Earl Van Dorn, much more at home in the command of a cavalry division than of an army, now proceeded to redeem his defeat at Corinth. He started out from Grenada, Mississippi, at the head of about 3,500 troopers—his numbers were variously exaggerated in Federal reports as being anywhere from five to seven thousand—and making a wide circuit to the east, he captured Holly Springs at daybreak on December 20. Because of the incompetence of the Federal officer in command, who was later cashiered, Van Dorn captured the place without a fight and destroyed the ammunition, quartermaster stores, and supplies of all kinds Grant had accumulated there to nourish his advance. Grant reported that supplies to the value of $400,000 had been burned; Van Dorn claimed a much more probable figure of $1,500,000. In addition, Van Dorn paroled about 1,500 prisoners and carried off large quantities of arms and supplies.[17] On the same day, Nathan Bedford Forrest raided

---

16. Lyman, "Reminiscences."

17. Grant's $400,000 figure in *Official Records*, XVII, I, 478; Van Dorn's $1,500,000 *ibid.*, 503. Pomeroy, "War Diary," entry for December 21, 1862, states the loss as $3,000,000, mostly rations and clothing. It may be doubted that the loss of a mere $400,000 worth of supplies would have caused Grant to call off his campaign, as in fact he did.

Jackson, Tennessee, at the intersection of the Mobile and Ohio and the Mississippi Central, seventy miles north of Holly Springs, and spent the next five days destroying trestles and many miles of track on both railroads.

Grant's campaign down the line of the Mississippi Central was intended to be one branch of a two-pronged move whose goal was the capture of Vicksburg and the opening of the Mississippi River. He hoped to draw upon himself the main strength of Confederate General John C. Pemberton's forces defending Vicksburg, thus opening the way for the capture of the "Gibraltar of the West" by General Sherman's assault on the bluffs overlooking Chickasaw Bayou, to the northeast of the city. Van Dorn's capture of Holly Springs and Forrest's raid on Jackson made a shambles of the campaign and convinced Grant of the impracticability of an overland march south to Vicksburg, with a supply line several hundred miles long unrolling behind him. As Van Dorn and Forrest had just demonstrated, it was impossible to protect even a much shorter line from Confederate raiding parties which, with little effort, could put the line out of commission for days or even weeks.[18] The twin raids of December 20 also demonstrated that a few hours' or even a full day's forewarning of a Confederate raid, its strength nearly always exaggerated and its exact destination hidden in the fog of war, was of no avail. The space and distances were too great, the Union armies were too weak in cavalry, and the raiders, especially when led by a near genius like Forrest, were too wily and fast moving; furthermore, the raiders also enjoyed the inestimable advantage of operating in territory where nearly the entire population was willing and anxious to help them.

Van Dorn's destruction of the supply base at Holly Springs is a classic example of these conditions. Grant learned of Van Dorn's move north nearly twenty-four hours before the latter struck the railroad and did what he could to counter it. Rumor credited Van Dorn with a much larger force than he actually had, his destination could only be guessed at, and Grant was woefully weak in cavalry. Nevertheless, every Federal post along the railroad as far north as Bolivar, including Holly Springs,

---

18. Grant reported to Halleck's chief of staff on December 25, 1862, *Official Records*, XVII, Pt. 1, 478, that "It is perfectly impracticable to go farther south by this route, depending on the road for supplies, and the country does not afford them."

was alerted, and all of the available Federal cavalry—a mere 1,500 troopers—was at once ordered to proceed north by forced marches to try to intercept the raiders. Lee's brigade, including the Seventh, was in camp at Prophet's Bridge on the Yocknapatalfa River, whither it had retreated after its defeat at Coffeeville. Company A had been sent back on a scout to Coffeeville on the fifteenth or sixteenth of December (the exact date is not given) and, according to Simeon Fox, obtained full information about Van Dorn's movement north, which had just then started. Colonel Dickey was informed at once, but he "received the report with incredulity and neglected to report to General Grant until eight hours later." [19] Fox's story is cited as a specimen of a large class of Civil War legends, of the type in which the organization the writer belongs to is exalted at the expense of the higher echelons of command. There is no reason to question the accuracy of Fox's statement that Company A got wind of Van Dorn's expedition and at once reported it. But he has maligned Colonel Dickey, for at the time when the Company A scout presumably occurred, Dickey, with half of the cavalry division, was off on a six-day raid of his own to the Mobile and Ohio Railroad, sixty miles or more to the east of the camp of the Seventh; in fact, on his return march, he brushed against the rear of Van Dorn's column and informed Grant of the Confederate threat immediately upon his arrival at Oxford on the afternoon of December 19.[20] By that time Grant already knew of Van Dorn's advance and his cavalry had started north to intercept it.

The Seventh was as usual in the advance of the forced march north of Lee's brigade. In less than twenty-four hours the brigade marched nearly fifty miles over abominable roads; the crossing of the low, marshy valley of the Tallahatchie, north of Abbeville, was especially difficult; the Jayhawkers needed three hours to negotiate a two-mile stretch of road, at that point. The Seventh rode into Holly Springs just before noon on the twentieth, a little more than an hour after Van Dorn's departure, and spent the afternoon collecting government property to which the citizens had been invited to help themselves while the raiders were setting fire to the warehouses. The brigade then set off in pursuit

19. Fox, "Story," 37.
20. *Official Records*, XVII, Pt. 1, 497–99.

of Van Dorn, who had chosen to make his escape not the way he had come, but northward along the railroad toward Bolivar, Tennessee, where he turned to the southeast and returned to his base at Grenada by way of Pontotoc, Mississippi. During the pursuit, Lee's brigade was commanded by Colonel Benjamin Grierson of the Sixth Illinois Cavalry, whose preparation for commanding mounted troops had consisted of teaching the piano, cornet, clarinet, guitar, and voice in the college town of Jacksonville, Illinois; he was also a band conductor, piano tuner, composer and arranger, amateur painter, poet, and song writer. Grierson assumed command of the brigade when his regiment joined in the pursuit, by virtue of a few days' seniority as colonel over Lee. The Jayhawkers, from Lee on down, were convinced that Grierson mishandled two successive opportunities at and near Bolivar to bring Van Dorn to battle and thus allowed the raiders to escape. By the winter of 1862, Jayhawkers were expert tacticians to a man and could distinguish between good leadership and bad with an unerring eye; they had little charity for what they conceived to be errors in tactics. After a long chase which accomplished nothing except to keep Van Dorn moving, the brigade returned to Holly Springs and went into camp. The Seventh had left Holly Springs with two days' rations; it pursued Van Dorn for nine days and was on the move every day from long before daylight until long after dark, the last five days in an almost continuous, bone-chilling, cold rain.

The behavior of the Seventh at New Albany, Mississippi, on the last day of the pursuit, once again got it into General Grant's black books. It was reported to him that the regiment had stopped "to plunder the citizens instead of pursuing the enemy."[21] Grant took no action on these reports for the moment, other than to call them to General Hamilton's attention. With his campaign in ruins, he had more important problems to worry about than the misconduct of a Kansas cavalry regiment. But the information was filed away for future use in his excellent memory.

W. A. Lyman, who served as Colonel Lee's orderly throughout this period, had lived in wet clothes for five days and nights, and on the day the regiment returned to Holly Springs, he caught a chill which rapidly developed into pneumonia. For a few days he was looked after by a

21. *Ibid.*, Pt. 2, 575.

kindly housewife, but when Grant evacuated Holly Springs in early January, he was taken in an ambulance to the army hospital at LaGrange, Tennessee. He was more fortunate than the majority of the sick and wounded at Holly Springs, most of whom were shipped to LaGrange "in freight cars or anything, some of them lying at the railroad station for 24 hours without attention"; it is not surprising, therefore, that men were dying in the hospital at LaGrange at the rate of eight or ten a day.[22] While still bedridden in the hospital at LaGrange, Lyman was given food suitable for a seriously ill patient, but after he was allowed to get out of bed and began to take his meals with the other convalescents in the dining room, his diet consisted of "a bowl of bean soup with a piece of pork measuring about a cubic inch floating in it, and a slice of bread."[23]

On the last day of the old year, twenty-four hours after its return from the fruitless pursuit of Van Dorn, the Seventh was ordered to move north, to Moscow, Tennessee, on the Memphis and Charleston Railroad, a few miles above the Tennessee-Mississippi border. A short time later the regiment was ordered to move fifteen miles to the west, to Germantown, Tennessee, and there it settled down for the winter.

With bands of Confederate cavalry and guerillas prowling about in southwestern Tennessee, "settling down" in winter camp did not mean a long period of idleness. The Seventh had its base at Germantown for nearly three and a half months, and it made itself as comfortable as possible, stockading the tents and building stables for the horses. Camp duties and the care of the horses, plus a little drill when the weather permitted, helped to pass the time; but in addition, some part of the regiment was out on a scout nearly every day, sometimes a single company, sometimes more, and other detachments had to go out for forage in an ever-widening circle. These scouts and foraging expeditions were anything but child's play. The roads were knee-deep in mud or snow or both. The men had to sleep, or try to, in wet clothes, on ground saturated with moisture, with but a single blanket for cover and the available wood too green to burn. These conditions fully justified Pomeroy's rueful comment: "On the whole it is very difficult soldiering."[24]

The first scouting expedition the Seventh made from Moscow,

22. Lyman, "Reminiscences."
23. *Ibid.*
24. Pomeroy, "War Diary," entry for January 18, 1863.

before its move to Germantown, produced one of the most disgraceful episodes in its frequently unedifying history. Confederate Colonel R. V. Richardson's brigade of West Tennessee cavalry (inevitably called "Richardson's guerillas" in the Jayhawkers' chronicles) was reported hovering about Somerville, Tennessee, thirteen miles north of Moscow.[25] On January 2 Lee was ordered to destroy them or at least drive them away.[26] He started out the same afternoon with ten companies of the Fourth Illinois Cavalry and his own regiment. In the evening, fires being forbidden, the men made a cheerless bivouac three miles short of their destination. The command was called at 3 A.M. on the third, "without the sound of bugle or loud orders and . . . [was] not allowed any fires or lights."[27] A cold January rain began to fall while the horses were being saddled, and by the time the command arrived at Somerville at dawn, everyone was well soaked, thoroughly chilled, hungry, and in a foul humor.

Upon reaching the town, Lee appointed Lieutenant Colonel Herrick provost marshal and directed him to institute a search for Confederate officers and soldiers and to seize all the horses, mules, and harness he could find. Herrick and his provost guard rounded up a large number of citizens on suspicion of being members of the Confederate army. All of these were interviewed by Lee and released. In another respect, however, Herrick's search proved to be entirely too much of a success. His men found large quantities of whiskey; Lee later reported that "the town was literally full of intoxicating liquors."[28] The inevitable result ensued. Within a short time, the majority of the men, who had started

25. *Ibid.*, entry for January 2, 1863.

26. The chronology of the Somerville incident is thrown into confusion by Colonel Lee's report, *Official Records*, XXIV, Pt. 3, 141. Lee stated that he left Moscow on January 5 and arrived at Somerville at dawn on January 6. Lee, however, did not write his report until March 5, and then only because he had been ordered to do so. The January 2 and 3 dates given in the text are based on Pomeroy's diary entries, whose language makes it evident that they were actually written on those dates. Pomeroy's accuracy is borne out by the historian of the Fourth Illinois Cavalry, P. O. Avery, *History of the Fourth Illinois Cavalry Regiment* (Humboldt, 1903), 112, and by the *Report of the Adjutant General of the State of Kansas*, I, 543.

27. Pomeroy, "War Diary," entry for January 3, 1863.

28. The story in the text of what happened at Somerville is based on Lee's report, *Official Records*, XXIV, Pt. 3, 141–43. The incident is mentioned briefly in a letter of George Mowry, Jr., to his sister, dated January 11, 1863, in Moses Letters, and in Avery, *History of the Fourth Illinois*, 112. Neither Webster Moses nor W. A. Lyman were with the regiment on January 2–3, and Fox and Pomeroy are, respectively, completely or very nearly silent on the subject.

out well before dawn from a fireless bivouac and had marched three miles in a cold rain, were drunk, or, as Lee preferred to call it, intoxicated.

Company B of the Seventh was stationed as a picket on the southern edge of town. Captain Swoyer found a quantity of "commissary stores" in a building near his post and, after stationing a guard at the entrance, rode away to a nearby house and asked to have breakfast served him. He was given a meal liberally laced with whiskey, and as a result became, again in Colonel Lee's words, "somewhat exhilerated." The sequel makes it evident that during the captain's absence, his men too had succeeded in locating a supply of whiskey. When Swoyer returned to his post, the guard he had placed over the commissary stores reported that two of the men had tried persistently to get into the building, in violation of the captain's orders. Swoyer ordered the company to mount and fall in, and then, in language that was "harsh and peremptory in the extreme," he commanded the two culprits to give up their arms and submit to arrest. One of the two "demurred, and attempted to explain." Swoyer ordered him to be silent and, drawing his pistol, threatened to shoot if he said another word. The trooper continued talking, whereupon Swoyer fired and wounded him.[29] Now Timothy Mullen, another member of Company B, fired at Swoyer but missed. Swoyer rode at Mullen, who turned his horse and galloped away with the captain in hot pursuit. The latter, on a better mount, drew abreast of Mullen in a few bounds. He and Mullen fired at each other in the same instant. Swoyer's bullet struck Mullen in the head, killing him instantly. Mullen's bullet passed through Swoyer's body, inflicting a wound from which he died the next day.

During the few moments while Swoyer rode in pursuit of Mullen, "many" shots were fired at him by his men. Whether these shots were fired in anger, or whether they were fired by men too drunk to know or care what they were doing, was never established. Whatever it was, the regiment had a full-fledged, murderous mutiny on its hands.

Colonel Lee, meanwhile, was at the courthouse in the center of town, doing his best to cope with the riot of insubordination, robbery, and plundering in which a large part of his brigade was engaged, its discipline almost completely destroyed by alcohol. When word reached him of

29. The name of this man does not appear in the records.

the mutiny of Company B, he sent Herrick to deal with it. The troopers of Company B had been shocked into a state of relative sobriety by the killing of Mullen and the wounding of their captain, and Herrick had little difficulty in restoring order, "though the men remained much excited." In the meantime, Lee, realizing that his command had gotten completely out of hand, and seeing his officers actually risking their lives in trying without much success to control several hundred well-armed and drunken troopers, wisely decided that his only safe course was to call off the search for Richardson and get his men out of Somerville and back to camp as quickly as possible. By this time, the effects of alcohol may have begun to wear off, or perhaps the men were not so far gone in drink that they could not realize what would probably happen to them if they were left behind when the brigade left Somerville. Lee, in any case, managed to get them started back to Moscow.

When the Seventh reached Moscow, Lee ordered that all the Jayhawkers who had been intoxicated and insubordinate in Somerville be tried by regimental court-martial. Captain Merriman headed the court in his capacity of regimental provost marshal and sentenced more than two hundred culprits to loss of a month's pay; more severe punishment was meted out in some cases.[30] George Mowry proudly informed his sister that of the more than two hundred men punished, only one belonged to Company D, and he was a Kansan and not a member of the original contingent from Illinois.

On January 20 Grant sent a despatch to General Hamilton to inform him that he had received complaints from Somerville "of the outrageous conduct of the Seventh Kansas." It is worthy of note that no mention was made in this despatch of the Fourth Illinois, whose men had behaved

30. *Official Records*, XXIV, Pt. 3, 141. Pomeroy, "War Diary," entry for January 4, 1863, says that the sentences varied from loss of a half-month's to two months' pay. Utt, "Seventh Kansas," says that all the sergeants of Company B were sentenced to death, "but their sentences were commuted by the President." This statement is not substantiated by any other source. Seventh Kansas, Company Order Books, show that Captain Merriman sentenced one corporal and five enlisted men of Company C and one corporal and four enlisted men of Company F to the loss of one month's pay for drunkenness at Somerville. The regimental records do not indicate what sentences, if any, were meted out to members of other companies.

just as badly at Somerville as had the Jayhawkers.[31] Hamilton was instructed to have Lee placed in arrest and tried for incompetence and to have the regiment dismounted and disarmed if any more complaints were received. He was told also, in words clearly intended to be transmitted to the Seventh, that "all the laurels won by the regiment and their commander on the pursuit of the enemy from Holly Springs to Coffeeville have been more than counterbalanced by their bad conduct since. Their present course may serve to frighten women and children and helpless old men, but will never drive out an armed enemy."[32] The instructions to Hamilton, unlike the majority of Grant's orders and despatches, were neither clear nor firmly worded. Hamilton was not given positive orders to do anything. Major General Stephen A. Hurlbut, in command of the District of West Tennessee, and, as such, Hamilton's immediate superior, had been conducting a running feud with the latter and saw in the vagueness of Grant's despatch an opportunity to take a fall out of his enemy. He reported in March to Lieutenant Colonel John A. Rawlins, Grant's chief of staff, that "Major-General Hamilton seems disposed to provoke my good nature, to which there are limits. . . . I shall probably have to arrest . . . [him] . . . because of his neglect to comply with the order in relation to the Seventh Kan. I have directed him to report on this subject, which he has not yet done."[33] As matters turned out, there was no need for Hurlbut to make good on his peevish threat, and his good nature was not pushed to its limits. On March 20 Hamilton sent him Colonel Lee's report on the Somerville affair, and himself added, "I am well assured that Col Lee exerted himself to the utmost in repressing all disorders. That disorders occurred, and more or less plundering took place, cannot be denied, but I believe Colonel Lee did all that any man could have done under the peculiar circumstances to

31. The historian of the Fourth Illinois Cavalry writes, *History of the Fourth Illinois*, 112, that "Many of our boys were under the influence of liquor who I never saw in such a condition before or afterwards. It was very difficult to get the command together to leave town. . . . A few of us that were sober . . . formed in line by the side of the road, others fell in as they came along, drunk or sober."

32. *Official Records*, XVII, Pt. 2, 575.   33. *Ibid.*, XXIV, Pt. 3, 137–38.

control his men. I am disposed to think that the severe censure contained in General Grant's letter is unmerited."[34]

Lee's own report was a reasonably factual and objective recital of the events at Somerville, but the excuse he gave for the drunkenness of his men fell considerably short of complete candor. Said Lee, "The people of the town treated the soldiers well, and offered them in singular profusion wines and liquors of all kinds. . . . As a result of this unfortunate profusion of strong drinks, many soldiers, who had neither supper nor breakfast, and laid on the ground without shelter, through a night of pelting storm, were induced to drink and as a consequence . . . many were intoxicated."[35] Unfortunately for Lee's posthumous reputation for veracity, Fletcher Pomeroy's diary entries explicitly state that the Seventh left its camp on the afternoon of January 2 with two days' rations; hence the men had food for both supper and breakfast. Pomeroy also noted, contrary to Lee's claim of "a night of pelting storm," that it did not begin to rain on the night of January 2 until the men had already been roused to prepare for their predawn march to Somerville.

Colonel Lee's and General Hamilton's reports apparently satisfied General Hurlbut's *amour propre*. By the time they were turned in, Grant was busy with his plans for the spring campaign and allowed the matter to drop. The last word on the Somerville incident was spoken in 1867 by the adjutant general of the state of Kansas, who, as has been mentioned, reported that Captain Swoyer had been killed in action at Somerville; to keep even the scales of pious misrepresentation as between officers and enlisted men, Mullen's death was recorded in the same words.[36]

It was a chastened and crestfallen regiment that returned from Somerville to the camp at Moscow. The Somerville culprits were duly punished. Then, orders were issued forbidding, and not for the first time, the wearing of "citizen's clothing or rebel uniform" by enlisted men.[37]

34. *Ibid.*, 140.   35. *Ibid.*, 141–42.
    36. *Report of the Adjutant General of the State of Kansas*, I, 542 (Swoyer) and 548 (Mullen). The adjutant general also reports, *ibid.*, 581, that John McCabe died on February 17, 1863, "of wounds received in action [*sic*] Jan. 3, 1863, Somerville, Tenn." And the January 4 morning report of Company B, Seventh Kansas, Regimental Letter and Order Book, states that Samuel Graves was also wounded at Somerville. The records are silent on the circumstances in which McCabe and Graves were wounded.
    37. General Orders No. 9, January 11, 1863, in Seventh Kansas, Regimental Order Book.

In December, 1861, Jennison had issued strict orders on the subject: "Soldiers will wear the prescribed uniform in camp and garrison and will not be permitted to keep in their possession any other clothing."[38] But the wearing of improper garb on duty continued to give offense and was the subject of repeated prohibitions. Thus, in August, 1863, Colonel Herrick announced that "any carelessness of company commanders in making their estimates for clothing and in executing existing orders forbidding the wearing of clothing not uniform is a grave offense. Notice is hereby given that hereafter, the failure of any company commander to . . . prevent [his men] from wearing prohibited articles of citizens clothing, will subject the offender to arrest and trial for disobedience of orders and neglect of duty."[39] A year and a half later, Lieutenant Colonel Francis M. Malone found it necessary to order each of his company commanders to "make a thorough inspection of [his] command and cause all officers and citizens clothing in possession of the enlisted men to be destroyed and see also that each man is furnished with proper uniform. The 'not wearing prescribed uniform' was a point against the regiment on the last inspection report."[40] These complaints and orders were not at all peculiar to the Seventh Kansas, nor were they caused by any perverse dislike of volunteers for the army uniform. The clothing furnished by the quartermaster was often of a shockingly poor quality and at best was not sturdy enough to withstand for more than a short time the hard usage of active service. Each trooper had a clothing allowance of $3.50 per month, or $42.00 per year.[41] With cavalry hats charged to the men at $1.55, jackets at $5.84, trousers at $4.00, boots at $3.33, overcoats at $9.75, and blankets at $2.95, it did not take very long to use up the $42.00 considered

38. General Orders No. 14, December 30, 1861, in Seventh Kansas, Regimental Letter and Order Book.

39. Circular to all company commanders, August 10, 1863, in Seventh Kansas, Regimental Order Book.

40. Orders, not numbered, dated January 31, 1865. On February 9, 1865, Major Hillyard, post commandant at Pilot Knob, Missouri, where a part of the Seventh was then stationed, deemed it necessary to order that "Commanding officers will see that none of the enlisted men will wear commissioned officers' insignia of rank, such as gold cords on hats, nor white hats, nor anything not their proper uniform." See Seventh Kansas, Company Order Books.

41. General Orders No. 11, Quartermaster General's Office, July 10, 1863, in Seventh Kansas, Regimental Order Book.

by the army as adequate to clothe a man for a year.[42] And when their clothing allowance was used up, any new gear the men needed to replace articles that had been lost or were worn or damaged beyond repair had to be paid for out of their niggardly wages of thirteen dollars a month; instead, they naturally took to wearing clothing sent from home or taken wherever they could find it.

What was left of January following the Somerville expedition passed in comparative quiet, and so did February. Webster Moses returned from his long stay in the army hospital in St. Louis, "glad to be with the Boys again," and resumed writing letters to "Dear Friend Nancy"; he told her that returning to the regiment "seemed like getting home," that he was not homesick (a comment that Nancy probably did not relish), but that he and most of the boys in the regiment were tired of the service and longed to return "to the civilized world or as some of the boys call it 'the Old Country.'"[43] Such expressions were usually the product of boredom, of the dull routine of winter quarters, and were never heard when active campaigning was in progress.

The paymasters' appearance on February 1—their first visit to the regiment since September, 1862—provided a more than welcome diversion. Each man received four months' pay, amounting to fifty-two dollars for the privates who had not been sentenced to loss of a part of their pay for their misconduct at Somerville. But the pay of the regiment was still five months in arrears. Then there was a little trouble with the Fifth Ohio Cavalry, now a part of Lee's brigade and camped nearby. The Jayhawkers' many scouts had provided the opportunity of improving the quality of their horses by the exchange of unsatisfactory animals for better ones taken from rebel sympathizers. Suddenly, in mid-February, horses belonging to the Seventh by right of conquest began to disappear in the night, and the finger of suspicion pointed squarely in the direction of the unscrupulous horsemen from the Buckeye State. Suspicion became

42. The clothing prices shown in the text were established on March 4, 1861, and were in effect at the start of the war. See *ibid.* Nearly all these prices were increased materially by General Orders No. 220, Adjutant General's Office, July 1, 1864. See *ibid.* Hats were now $1.80, jackets $6.25, trousers $4.15, overcoats $10.55, and blankets $3.60. Boots, however, selling at $3.25 a pair, had become a little cheaper. One may add, as a historical curiosity, that the plumes worn on cavalry hats cost fifteen cents, the cord and tassels fifteen cents also, the eagle and the crossed swords insignia two cents each, and the forage cap sixty-five cents.

43. Webster Moses to Nancy Mowry, January 26 and February 1, 1863, in Moses Letters.

certainty when, as a crowning insult, even Colonel Herrick's charger disappeared, and was located in the possession of one of the Ohioans. It became necessary for the Jayhawkers to post a guard over the regimental stables and horselines at night. The threat to the security of Kansas property was at length removed when the Ohioans were ordered to move their camp far enough away to make nocturnal raids on the Kansans' horselines impractical.

Another, and potentially more serious, incident occurred in February also. On the twentieth, Colonel Lee notified Captain H. Binmore, assistant adjutant general of the XVI Corps, that a private of the Fourth Illinois Cavalry, just returned to the Federal lines after being paroled, had reported that General Tilghman had ordered three of his prisoners at Jackson, Mississippi, placed in irons. The three prisoners were Jayhawkers —James M. Tefft, Marcus L. Underwood, and William W. Reed, all of Company G—who had been captured near Germantown on January 23. They left camp without permisson and were captured in a farmhouse where they had gone "to get leather for mending boots."[44] Tilghman had the three chained together, hand and foot, and refused to parole them because "they belonged to the Kansas troops and . . . had in their possession some facsimiles of Kansas notes."[45] Lee requested authority to send his men out to hunt for three Confederate officers, whom he proposed to put in chains as soon as they were captured; he would then open a correspondence with Tilghman for the reciprocal release of the prisoners from the cruel indignity of being held in irons.[46] No reply to Lee's request appears in the records, but apparently he was not permitted to put his harsh plan into execution. As for the three captured Jayhawkers, Tilghman kept them in irons until they were transferred to Castle Thunder in Richmond.

Spring came late in 1863. The Jayhawkers, most of them country boys and sensitive to the seasons, noticed that none of the spring farm work was under way in the fields around the camp because of the lateness of spring. But it was apparent also that even if the time for plowing and

44. Herrick to [name of addressee missing], June 6, 1863, in Seventh Kansas, Regimental Letter and Order Book.

45. *Ibid.* The present writer is unable to offer an explanation of the mysterious phrase "facsimiles of Kansas notes." Perhaps facsimiles (*i.e.*, counterfeit) of Confederate notes were meant.

46. *Official Records*, XXIV, Pt. 3, 61.

planting had come on schedule, it would have been nearly impossible for the farmers around Germantown to raise a crop in 1863. Their slaves were gone, their draft animals had been taken, their fences burned for firewood, their cattle, hogs, and poultry eaten by the soldiers, and their hay and corn taken to feed the animals of both armies. But at length spring did arrive. March 1, a Sunday, was a memorably lovely day. And Fletcher Pomeroy celebrated it in a lyrical passage in his diary: "All nature is clothed in beauty. The pleasant sunshine, the fragrant fresh grass, and the sweet notes of feathered songsters combine to excite praise and gratitude to God for his continued goodness. Though Civil War is raging amongst us we still have seed time and harvest." [47]

But the advent of spring also brought with it grazing for cavalry horses and dry roads; it meant the start of another campaigning season and the start too of the third year of the Civil War.

The Seventh had now been in the service for a year and a half. It was made up, in the spring of 1863, of the survivors of a formidable weeding-out process; the physically weak had been carried off by disease or, if more fortunate, had been discharged for disability; the spiritual and emotional weaklings had deserted. In spite of a trickle of recruits, the regiment was greatly depleted in numbers. Company D, for example, had but twenty-three men present for duty on March 20, not even a third of the eighty-three mustered in the fall of 1861. [48] Some good men were gone, but the Jayhawkers who answered the daily roll call at this midpoint of the war were tough, battle-hardened professionals, inured to every hardship, unruly as ever, but, as became old campaigners, wise in the ways of authority, of the army, the elements, and above all, of the enemy. A few weeks later, when General Hurlbut was ordered to send his two most efficient regiments of cavalry to Corinth, his first choice was the Seventh Kansas. [49]

The colonelcy of the Seventh had once again become vacant in January through the promotion of Colonel Lee to brigadier general. As a compliment to his able handling of the cavalry on Grant's abortive drive in November, his commission was predated to November 29,

---

47. Pomeroy, "War Diary," entry for March 1, 1863.
48. Webster Moses to Nancy Mowry, March 20, 1863, in Moses Letters.
49. *Official Records*, XXIV, Pt. 3, 189.

1862. In actual fact, he had held brigade command since September, 1862, and Lieutenant Colonel Thomas P. Herrick had been in command of the regiment in his stead. In the normal course of events, Herrick, a competent officer, could have expected to succeed to the colonelcy as a matter of course. But Kansas politics was a complex affair, and the colonelcy of a volunteer regiment was considered to be a political plum of some consequence. Hence Herrick's promotion, albeit logical, well deserved, and eminently proper, was not at all inevitable. And thus we find Thomas Carney, who had succeeded Charles Robinson as governor of Kansas, writing in the following terms to one of his political cronies:

I have been thinking of appointing Anthony in the place of Lee just to get him out of Town, as I believe it would add to the peace of . . . [Leavenworth]. Herrick is now Lt Col & entitled to the place. I do not know him, some say he has but little influence at home. Anthony is said to be popular in the regiment which if I thought to be true would feel inclined to appoint him—he would be pleased and flattered with the appointment. Think the matter over and should you meet Tom Osborne ask him about Herrick, as I understand he is from the same neighborhood. . . . I have just seen Tom Osborne and he says that Herrick is no act. and says by all means take any one [else] if I can make an excuse for it.[50]

Such were the considerations which, nearly two years after the start of the Civil War, governed some, but fortunately not all, appointments to regimental command. Eventually, Governor Carney must have learned that Herrick was of some account after all in and around Highland, Kansas, and for that, or possibly for some better reason, he decided to appoint him to the colonelcy. Herrick was commissioned colonel on June 11, 1863.[51] Whatever the extent of his political influence in Doniphan County may have been, perhaps the fact that he had already exercised regimental command over a period of nine months with respectable competence and success had some bearing on Governor Carney's decision to appoint him to the colonelcy of the Seventh.

While Grant and his armies made ready for the campaign which, after some false starts, was to result in the surrender of Vicksburg on July 4, 1863, the Seventh made an occasional scout to harry the bands of

50. Carney to General McDowell, March 16, 1863, in James L. McDowell Collection, Kansas State Historical Society, Topeka.
51. *Report of the Adjutant General of the State of Kansas*, I, 524.

partisan rangers, guerillas, and Confederate cavalry that, in company and battalion strength, hovered about the neighborhood of the Memphis and Charleston Railroad as far east as Corinth. For the most part, these scouts were uneventful. The entire regiment, or some part of it, had many a futile chase after the usually better mounted Confederates; occasionally, when the enemy chose to make a stand, the Jayhawkers fought a brief skirmish.[52] At long intervals, a little spice was added to these usually monotonous expeditions. On March 11 the regiment crossed to the north of the Wolf River, which was out of its banks. Much of the bottom land along the river was flooded, deep enough in places to swim the horses. Many of them fell in the slippery going, and their riders got a good ducking, greatly to the amusement of Major William S. Jenkins. Poetic justice was done when the Major's horse too went down, and Jenkins in turn received a total immersion in the cold, muddy water, to the unanimous delight of the Jayhawkers.

On one of these scouts, Private Samuel Donaldson of Company A was killed by a guerilla party of eleven men.[53] Whether the killers were actually guerillas as the Jayhawkers believed, or regularly enlisted Confederate cavalrymen, can no longer be determined; and in any case, the line between the two in southwestern Tennessee and northern Mississippi was usually so blurred as to be undistinguishable. At daybreak on April 2, the day after the killing, Captain Levi Utt with thirty men of Company A took off after the killers. He followed their trail to the Wolf River, which, near Germantown, is a deep stream fifty yards wide. There being no fords nearby, Utt found a canoe, and he and three of his troopers paddled across, with their horses swimming alongside. On the far side, they captured a two-man vidette the Confederates had left behind. Utt then trailed the rest of the party, and a short distance from the river, he surprised and captured six of them. That left three more of the enemy unaccounted for. Leaving one of his three men to guard the eight prisoners, Utt with his two remaining troopers found the last three guerillas eating breakfast at a farmhouse. Ordering his two men to keep

52. See, for example, *Official Records*, XXIV, Pt. 1, 427–28 and 429, and Utt, "Seventh Kansas."

53. Donaldson was killed near Germantown on April 1, 1863. See *Report of the Adjutant General of the State of Kansas*, I, 532.

up a steady fire on the front of the house, Utt slipped around to the back, where he caught the owner of the farm. Pushing the man before him as a shield, Utt broke into the house and, with his pistol aimed at the rebels over the farmer's shoulder, persuaded them to surrender. The three guerillas had eight Colt's revolvers between them. The records are silent on the fate of Utt's eleven captives. If they were able to convince him that they were properly enlisted members of the Confederate army, it is quite likely that they were taken back to the Jayhawkers' camp as prisoners of war and subsequently paroled. If they were not able to prove their status as soldiers, their fate is not too difficult to guess.[54]

The battle of Murfreesboro had been won by the Union army under Rosecrans against Braxton Bragg's Army of Tennessee, a victory described by a southern writer in the classic euphemism, "the tide of battle did not turn in . . . [Bragg's] favor."[55] Following the battle, Bragg settled down for the winter in Tullahoma, Tennessee. He drew supplies for his army through Chattanooga, where the Memphis and Charleston Railroad met other railroads running southeast to Atlanta and northeast to Knoxville. Early in the spring Colonel Abel D. Streight of the Fifty-First Indiana Infantry came to Brigadier General James A. Garfield, Rosecrans' chief of staff and later president of the United States, with an ingenious but only remotely practical plan to break up the railroads behind Bragg, as Forrest and Van Dorn had done behind Grant, and thereby force him to retreat to Georgia. In essence, he proposed taking four regiments of infantry by boat up the Tennessee River as far as Eastport, Mississippi, where they would be mounted on mules; and then, following a belt of sparsely inhabited, mountainous country running across northern Alabama south of the great loop of the Tennessee River, he would march southeast toward Gadsden, Alabama, and Rome, Georgia, to strike the Western & Atlantic Railroad, connecting Chattanooga and Atlanta, at some point north of the Etowah River. An

54. The story of Captain Utt's exploit is told in Utt, "Seventh Kansas," a source not likely to minimize the captain's prowess. It should be noted that this, the only source for the incident, speaks of it as having occurred "In February," whereas the *Report of the Adjutant General of the State of Kansas*, I, 532, shows Donaldson as killed on April 1. Either source, or both, may be in error on these dates.

55. John Allan Wyeth, *That Devil Forrest: Life of General Nathan Bedford Forrest* (New York, 1959), 165.

essential feature of Streight's plan was an attack to be made in strong force by General Grenville M. Dodge on the Confederates holding Tuscumbia, Alabama. This attack, to be made just before Streight's start, was to drive the Confederates up the valley of the Tennessee toward Decatur, Alabama, to sweep them away from Streight's path and keep them fully occupied until he was too far east for effective pursuit.

The ultimate fate of Streight's raid does not form a part of the story of the Seventh Kansas, which was involved only in the preliminaries of the raid, as a part of General Dodge's forces. The raid was a failure, and nearly all of Streight's two thousand men were taken prisoner by General Forrest. The fiasco was due in part to a series of mischances and in part to the relentless energy of Forrest's pursuit; but the basic flaw of Streight's plan was something that the knowledgeable veterans of the Seventh were prompt to recognize; as Fletcher Pomeroy put it, *not* with the benefit of hindsight, "We think that mounted infantry, with a cumbersome pack train, is a poor outfit for a raid. It is our opinion that our best cavalry should have been sent." [56]

The preliminary moves connected with the Streight raid ended the generally pleasant stay the Jayhawkers had enjoyed at Germantown. Orders came from General Hurlbut early in the second week of April, for the regiment to prepare for the march to join General Dodge's force of about four thousand infantry and seven hundred cavalry at Corinth.

Hurlbut's orders found the Seventh in poor condition for an active campaign. Its strength had been reduced to a little over four hundred officers and men.[57] Moreover, the horses had had a hard winter. Many had died, the survivors were in poor shape, and with the country around Germantown long since picked clean of serviceable animals, there were no replacements to be had for the taking. In a situation that was typical of the Union cavalry throughout the war, half the Jayhawkers were without mounts or were riding weakened, diseased, or broken-down animals unfit for cavalry duty. Nevertheless, inspired by the spring sunshine and the dry fields, the Jayhawkers occupied their leisure by arranging impromptu horseraces. The sport did nothing to improve the condition of their animals and caused Colonel Herrick to issue stringent

56. Pomeroy, "War Diary," entry for April 28, 1863.
57. *Official Records*, XXIV, Pt. 3, 193.

orders forbidding the racing of horses "under the severest penalties"; and he promised that the order would be "rigidly enforced."[58] General Hurlbut, complaining bitterly of being "horribly crippled for want of horses" and of "the gross neglect of the quartermasters at St. Louis," managed to get two hundred horses from that source, far fewer than the number he had asked for, and turned them over to the Seventh; but there was no time to have these horses shod before the regiment left Germantown, with the result that a sizeable proportion developed sore hooves within a few days and had to be abandoned.[59]

The Jayhawkers were far from happy about their imminent departure from winter camp. As is the way of soldiers, it had not taken them long to strike roots in Germantown. They had formed "some pleasant acquaintances" in the neighborhood of camp and, now that they were about to leave, discovered that their stay there had been "as pleasant as a volunteer soldier life can be expected to be."[60] In fact, as Webster Moses wrote on April 13, after the men had been told that they were to march at sunrise the next day, "We hate to leave this place for we are well fixed here[.] it seems like leaveing home to leave here."[61]

To add to the wrench of leaving surroundings that had become familiar and friendly, Albert L. Lee, wearing the brigadier general's stars the Seventh had helped him win, came to say goodbye to the Jayhawkers. He too was about to leave, to take command of an infantry brigade.[62] In the fashion of the time, he made a farewell speech. He commended the Jayhawkers in the most handsome terms for their services and for their loyalty to him, and in his peroration he declared: "They have called you all the hard names they could think of, but they have never called you *cowards!*"[63]

At daybreak on April 14, the Seventh departed on a march of

58. Circular order, not numbered, March 27, 1863, in Seventh Kansas, Regimental Order Book.

59. *Official Records*, XXII, Pt. 1, 242.

60. Pomeroy, "War Diary," entry for April 13, 1863.

61. Webster Moses to Nancy Mowry, April 13, 1863, in Moses Letters.

62. After commanding a brigade of infantry for a time, Lee served as General John A. McClernand's chief of staff at the siege of Vicksburg. He was severely wounded while leading an assault on the Confederate lines. Upon his recovery, he was given command of the cavalry division of the XIII Army Corps, and then, as Chief of Cavalry, Army of the Gulf, he commanded the cavalry in Nathaniel P. Banks's Red River Campaign.

63. Lyman, "Reminiscences."

seventy-five miles, eastward to Corinth. Many of the troopers, as they filed out of the abandoned camp, must have shared the fatalistic feeling that Fletcher Pomeroy recorded in his diary the evening before: "We go out to enter upon another campaign with the fortunes of war, so unknown and uncertain, before us."[64]

64. Pomeroy, "War Diary," entry for April 13, 1863.

CHAPTER XII

The
Home Front
in Kansas

IF ANYONE seeking a peaceful and quiet existence in the early spring of 1863 had been asked to choose between the life of a civilian in Leavenworth and that of a trooper of the Seventh Kansas in its winter camp in enemy country, he would have been well advised to choose the latter. For, with the Civil War about to enter its third year, with partisan emotions keyed to a high pitch, and with Anthony, Hoyt, and Jennison in residence in the city, Leavenworth was anything but a restful place in which to live.

To edit and publish a Democratic newspaper in Leavenworth during the Civil War would have been a risky occupation at best, and doubly so if the newspaper happened to be of the Peace Democrat or "Copperhead" persuasion. The Leavenworth *Inquirer* was an avowedly Democratic newspaper, and its editorial policy was of the Peace Democrat variety. It was therefore a "Copperhead sheet," and a stench in the nostrils of all patriotic and decent Republicans and unionists in the city, and to none more so than to Messrs. Anthony, Hoyt, and Jennison.

There were several ways in which the disloyal machinations (as Jennison would have called them) of the objectionable newspaper could have been foiled. One such method was used on the occasion when the *Inquirer* called upon the Democrats of Leavenworth to hold a meeting to endorse the proposals for peace that had been made by Clement Vallandigham in January, 1863; the meeting was also to act on the call for the "Louisville Peace Convention" that the Democrats of Kentucky proposed holding, to concert a common course of action among the Peace Democrats of the Middle West. The meeting called by the *Inquirer* took place on February 7. When the session was called to order, it became apparent that the Republicans had "packed the house" and were determined not to allow the meeting to proceed. A motion was therefore made to adjourn to the following Saturday. As soon as the motion had been carried, Jennison arose. He was not only present at the meeting, but it may be taken for granted that he had had a considerable share in seeing to it that there was a large and vocal attendance of Republicans. He now proposed that an "unconditional Union meeting be held" there and then; "he was interrupted by a few, but he told them that he had come there for the purpose of shooting down the first man who uttered a disloyal sentiment, and quiet was immediately restored." The precise limits of free speech having thus been established, Daniel Anthony, who was also present, was called to the chair "amid uproarious cheers," and the unconditional Union meeting proceeded. In his introductory remarks as chairman, "Col. Anthony stated the purpose of the *Inquirer*'s call to be the assembling of a meeting of traitors, in order to pass resolutions in favor of a Peace Convention and to send delegates to Louisville. He said he had come there *prepared to shoot down* the first traitor who dared give utterance to his cowardly thoughts." Anthony's address was followed by speeches from Jennison and Hoyt, and it was editorially stated afterwards that "the meeting was one of the greatest victories ever achieved in Kansas. The rebels in Leavenworth are cowed, and will do well to remain so."[1]

But the rebels of Leavenworth did not remain cowed. The editor of the *Inquirer*, Burrell F. Taylor, was evidently a man of mettle who refused to be frightened out of his convictions by Jennison's and Anthony's rodomontades, or by the less belligerently expressed but equally strong hostility of the great majority of his fellow citizens. He continued to print opinions at variance with the prevailing public sentiment of

1. Leavenworth *Conservative*, February 8, 1863, clipping in Jennison Scrapbook.

Leavenworth and relied for the protection he obviously needed on the city police and on a volunteer guard of Peace Democrats. It is quite unnecessary to add that his guard was armed; at least one pistol, revolver, or bowie knife was, so far as one may judge, an ordinary and indispensable part of male costume in Leavenworth in 1863, irrespective of the wearer's political affiliations.

On Monday evening, February 9, editor Taylor's guard of about thirty men, "armed . . . with muskets, revolvers and knives," stationed themselves in and about the *Inquirer* office. The accounts of what now ensued appeared in newspapers uniformly hostile to the *Inquirer*, and must therefore be viewed with a careful and suspicious eye both for what is said and what is omitted, if one is to gain a reasonably accurate idea of what actually happened. By midnight, it is said, the guard had become "boisterous, abusive, and guilty of such manifestations as usually result from bad whiskey."[2] One should note, however, firstly, that the leaders of the *Inquirer* guard were the city marshal and several policemen, and, secondly, that between ten and eleven in the evening, "five or six men assembled on the opposite side of the street—sang 'Old John Brown,' and fired several shots in the air." One can easily imagine the taunts and name-calling that preceded and followed the singing of "John Brown's Body," and it is more than likely that the "boisterous" and "abusive" conduct of the guard was in retaliation for this, and a reaction to the firing of "several shots in the air," rather than the result of "bad whiskey."

At this point enter Anthony in the role, unusual for him, of peacemaker. The boarding house in which he lived was located across the street from the *Inquirer* office. Arriving on the scene, he "began efforts to pacify the 'John Brown' boys; after considerable persuasion, he induced them to go home." Having done so, he retired to his chamber. An hour or so later, between one and two in the morning, his slumbers were disturbed by a renewed commotion outside. Feeling no doubt that a resumption of his peacemaking efforts was called for, Anthony went out

2. Leavenworth *Conservative*, February 11, 1863, clipping *ibid.* The reference to "bad whiskey" is very much to the point, for it was said that there were at this time two hundred saloons in Leavenworth to serve the needs of a total population of twenty thousand men, women, and children.

into the street armed with a revolver, only to be greeted with the cry, "There is Col. Anthony, shoot the damn scoundrel!" followed at once by the firing of "a half dozen" or "twenty-six" shots (the two accounts of the incident are in disagreement on the count) in his direction, all of which missed their mark and struck the building behind him. Evidently the guard had no confidence in the pacific character of Anthony's intentions. The latter of course returned the fusillade with his revolver, but hit no one. After this demonstration of amazingly inept marksmanship on both sides, Anthony returned to his bed, the troubles of the night ceased, and peace descended upon the streets of Leavenworth.

Early in the morning of the tenth, news of the events of the night spread with great and in fact astonishing rapidity over the city, and "by nine o'clock, a large and excited crowd had collected in front of the *Inquirer* office, demanding that the rebel sheet be destroyed." Characteristically, both Jennison and Anthony were prominent in the crowd, and Jennison supplied the leadership the mob needed to set about the business of the day. He mounted a box and declared: "Yesterday, this establishment was a Printing Office, and I proposed to protect it—this morning it is a *rebel fort*, and I propose to gut it!" With this, the crowd rushed into the building, "and in less than half an hour the whole establishment was a complete wreck." The presses were smashed, the type thrown out into the street, and the cases burned. The unfortunate editor, Taylor, like the prudent man of Proverbs, looked well to his going and hurriedly left town.[3]

The Leavenworth *Conservative* concluded its report of the gutting of its Democratic rival with the declaration: "We have no better citizens than those engaged in putting an end to the treasonable organ. If this was a mob, it was such a mob as threw the tea into Boston Harbor." And three days later Anthony told another unconditional Union meeting that "when the Inquirer office was destroyed, real estate in Leaven- went up ten per cent."[4]

The destruction of the objectionable newspaper was only one aspect of Jennison's and Anthony's participation in the civic affairs of Leaven-

3. The story of Anthony's nocturnal adventures, and of the wrecking of the *Inquirer* office the next day, is from an unidentified clipping, *ibid.*

4. The editorial comment is in Leavenworth *Conservative*, February 11, 1863, clipping *ibid.* Anthony's remark is in Leavenworth *Conservative*, February 14, 1863, clipping *ibid.*

worth and Kansas. Jennison in particular was active in politics and played a prominent part in the affairs of the Republican party at both the local and the state level. In September, 1862, he had been a delegate to the convention of the Republican State Central Committee, and following the convention, he stumped for the so-called "Topeka Ticket," making ten speeches in eleven days, throughout the state.[5] A member at this time of the all-powerful Lane faction of the Republican party, Jennison modeled his oratory upon that of Lane and even copied some of the senator's platform mannerisms, such as the step-by-step removal of coat, vest, cravat, and shirt, with the appropriate oratorical flourishes, as he warmed up to his subject. By this time he had become a practiced and fluent speaker and a great popular favorite. He drew large crowds wherever he spoke, and if we may believe the frankly pro-Jennison newspaper reports, he never failed "to keep his audience in a constant uproar of applause and laughter."[6] However, in the faction-ridden politics of the day, he also attracted his share of brickbats. One editor announced that it was "considerable of a joke" that Jennison, of all people, should endorse anyone as honest, capable, or honorable.[7] Another asked the plaintive question: "Will Kansas never be rid of Jim Lane and Jennison? If kind Providence still continues to take an active part in the affairs of the United States and Kansas in particular, now is a good time for her to show her loving kindness to us by relieving the State of these two men. I shall always think that we have committed some grievous sin for which we are now being punished by their existence in our midst."[8]

There is no reason at all to question the perfect sincerity of Jennison's devotion to the Union, but if it was anything more than a shibboleth, if it stood for a body of reasoned principle, he gave no sign of it. Nor did he give any indication that his involvement in politics was founded on any set of principles, on anything more than a liking for power, notoriety, and excitement, a taste for the complicated manoeuvering of factional jobbery, and a craving for the material rewards of influence and wire-pulling. Jennison in the role of a politician was not hampered by idealism,

5. Unidentified clipping, *ibid.*
6. Report datelined Mound City, August 22, 1863. See unidentified clipping, *ibid.*
7. Unidentified clipping, *ibid.*
8. Unidentified clipping, *ibid.*

or even by personal loyalties, any more than he had been hampered by army rules in his role of a soldier. But in his own lighthearted way he enjoyed himself; or perhaps it would be more accurate to say that he enjoyed his own performances. He certainly managed to communicate his enjoyment to others, as evidenced by the following notice that appeared one day on the masthead of the Leavenworth *Conservative*:

> For President
> Until 2000,
> Charles R. Jennison,
> of Kansas
> For Vice-President,
> Forever,
> Wendell Phillips,
> Of Massachusetts.[9]

This obvious jape was taken seriously and commented upon with indignation by the editor of the St. Joseph, Missouri, *News*, who thereby drew upon himself the following retort from the *Conservative*:

The creature who edits the St. Joseph Mo. News . . . is clearly a Copperhead and evidently a fool. . . . Miller, the idiotic editor of the News . . . is one of the "poor whites" of the South. He used to eat Clay. His pauperism is paternal, his ignorance is inherited, and his treason the legitimate result of bogus birth and breeding. . . . We raised the names of Jennison and Phillips because we knew that neither could be elected . . . and we wished to testify to their gallantry and devotion to the great abolition principle which is hereafter to be the corner stone of our regenerated Republic.[10]

In June, 1863, Jennison was a member of the Kansas delegation to the Great National Ship Canal Convention in Chicago, whose purpose was to agitate for the building of a canal to connect the Mississippi with Lake Michigan, and thence, via the Great Lakes, with the Atlantic. He was, or made himself, one of the leaders of the delegation; and without doubt he was its best known member. The Lawrence *State Journal* reported that at nearly every station between St. Joseph and Chicago, "prying eyes were searching for 'Jennison the Jayhawker.'"[11] The

9. Leavenworth *Conservative*, June 30, 1863, clipping *ibid.* Editor Miller is not the only one taken in by the obviously tongue-in-cheek notice. See Castel, *Frontier State*, 113.
10. Undated clipping, Leavenworth *Conservative*, in Jennison Scrapbook.
11. Undated clipping, *ibid.*

convention assembled in a tent on Michigan Boulevard on the morning of June 2, with Vice President Hannibal Hamlin in the chair. The next day Jennison spoke on behalf of Kansas. The speech was in his best patriotic vein, and he was interrupted "at frequent intervals with most frantic applause." [12] He made much of the interest which all Kansas felt in the canal project as both an economic and a military necessity, and he had an answer ready for those who deprecated the starting of a costly public works project in the midst of a fabulously expensive war. He dismissed the objection as irrelevant; "Honest Old Abe" could carry on the war, he said, and win it too, even if there were not a cent in the treasury, by putting it on a self-sustaining basis. The audience was evidently already familiar with the meaning of the term "self-sustaining" as Jennison was wont to use it, and his sally was greeted with "immense applause." [13] The reporter for the Cincinnati *Gazette* who covered the meeting described Jennison as "a young man, of slight build, with sharp features and a sanguine expression," and added: "As he stood there in the midst of the audience . . . greeted with the heartiest applause I ever heard, he was master of the situation, and he knew it." [14]

While the Ship Canal Convention was holding its sessions, Senator Lyman Trumbull of Illinois, a Conservative Republican, was in Chicago; he delivered, or more accurately attempted to deliver, a speech criticizing the government for the arbitrary and illegal arrest of Peace Democrats by the War Department. His audience was hostile and he was heckled unmercifully with cries of "Give us somebody else . . . Jennison . . . Give us Jennison the Jayhawker . . . Give us our man of blood!" After Trumbull had been silenced, Jennison, who was present, made a speech more to the taste of the audience. He said that no man had the right to live a moment who had "a drop of traitorous blood in his veins." He told the assembly: "We of Kansas, for the last nine years, have been battling with this same rebellion. We have had our turn at the war in advance. . . . In Kansas we hang traitors, and there is not one

12. Article from the Missouri *Democrat*, reprinted in Leavenworth *Conservative*, June 6, clipping *ibid.*
13. *Ibid.*
14. Unidentified clipping, *ibid.* The present author, after a diligent search, has been unable to find the comments in the Cincinnati *Gazette* on Jennison and his speech. The attribution of the original article to the Cincinnati *Gazette* appears to be erroneous.

left now to hang—and if you will send us your traitors by express, we'll hang them for you." He reminded his hearers that, having eight bullets in his body, he was qualified to speak as a "practical Union man." [15] The New York *World*, reporting Jennison's speech, spoke of its "murderous malignity" and described the speaker as worse than a Sioux warrior; his hearers in Chicago, however, were delighted.[16] He had caught their mood exactly and told them just what they wanted to hear.

In March, 1863, Anthony ran as the Republican candidate for mayor of Leavenworth. He had the cordial backing of Jennison and Hoyt and, on April 6, was elected to the post by a large majority. In the ensuing year—mercifully for Leavenworth, its mayors were elected for one-year terms—the city experienced an administration that can have few equals in the frequently bizarre annals of American municipal government. Anthony announced that he intended his administration to be vigorous and determined, and that he would see to it that loyal and law-abiding citizens were no longer terrorized by "the rebel desperadoes and gangs of lawless characters that had committed acts of violence almost without number." [17] One of his first acts as mayor was to burn down "houses of ill-repute, in which thieves, cut-throats and murderers were wont to congregate . . . the inmates being given a brief warning to vacate." [18]

Protecting the loyal people of Leavenworth, as that function was interpreted by Anthony, made it seem necessary to him that he arrest David H. Bailey, editor of the Leavenworth *Times*, for printing an article criticizing the generalship of Joseph Hooker at Chancellorsville, and fine him twenty dollars for "disturbing the peace." Bailey obtained his release on a writ of habeas corpus, sued Anthony for false arrest, and won a judgment against him of fifty dollars and costs.[19] There was a well-founded suspicion in Leavenworth that some of the "houses of ill-repute" put to the torch by the energetic mayor were nothing worse than the homes of southern sympathizers; this, however, did not prevent Anthony from lumping all his political opponents together under the blanket designation of "pimps" when he ran for reelection in 1864.

15. Unidentified clipping, Jennison Scrapbook.
16. Quoted in an unidentified clipping, *ibid.*
17. Admire, "Early Kansas Pioneer," 699.
18. *Ibid.*, 694.
19. Castel, *Frontier State*, 213.

Setting Leavenworth by the ears with his ill-directed energy and arbitrary conduct represented only one facet of Anthony's activities as mayor. It was generally believed that he was hand-in-glove with the Red Legs and brigands of all descriptions who infested the eastern counties of Kansas as much as they did northwestern Missouri. A hostile newspaper later wrote that the people of Brown and Doniphan counties, in the northeastern corner of Kansas, were convinced that Anthony was connected with a gang of horse thieves headed by one Bennett and that his active collaboration or behind-the-scenes support made it possible for the gang to dispose of its stolen livestock in Leavenworth.[20] The likelihood that Anthony was involved in some manner with such gangs does not rest solely on the suspicions of the people of Brown and Doniphan counties. Jennison and Hoyt, who broke with Anthony before the end of his term of office, openly accused him of protecting or at least tolerating these illegalities; they said that "a very large number . . . [of horses and mules] stolen from loyal men, both in Kansas and Missouri . . . [had] found convenient and secret stables and a ready market in Leavenworth."[21] And this was a subject on which both Jennison and Hoyt could speak with a great deal of authority. Even more to the point, General Thomas Ewing, Jr., commanding the District of the Border, who had already denounced "men in Kansas who are stealing themselves rich in the name of Liberty," imposed martial law in Leavenworth on July 19 because of Anthony's interference with his efforts to put down the traffic in stolen livestock in the city.[22] Anthony retaliated in characteristic fashion by arresting a well-to-do friend of Ewing's and fining him twenty dollars for vagrancy.

But politics as usual in Kansas was about to receive a rude shock. The surrender of Vicksburg and the Union victory at Gettysburg were duly celebrated in Leavenworth with a splendid bonfire of tar barrels, a "peculiarly felicitous" speech by Jennison, and "the grandest display of fireworks ever witnessed" in the city; but the unionists of Kansas were given little time to revel in this unaccustomed feeling of joy over Union triumphs.[23] In late July rumors began to filter into the state from across

20. Leavenworth *Times*, February 28, 1865, clipping in Jennison Scrapbook.
21. Undated clipping, Leavenworth *Conservative, ibid.*
22. Castel, *Frontier State,* 113.
23. Unidentified clipping, Jennison Scrapbook.

the border that the dreaded guerilla, Quantrill, was planning a raid to
Lawrence. On August 1 a correspondent in Lawrence, who signed
himself "Ivory," sent to the Leavenworth *Conservative* a report whose
blithe humor is in gruesome contrast with the fate that befell the city
only three weeks later:

Lawrence is safe. The beleaguered City of Martyrs, at last, due to the exuberant
energy of its people, is in such condition of defence that we only fear that the
cowardly guerilla will not penetrate even to the suburbs. . . .

These formidable defenses were made for two reasons: *First*, to save us from
surprise from Quant[rill]. *Second*, to prevent Jennison and Hoyt from coming
to our rescue.

In the sudden terror of the first news of Quantrile's [*sic*] meditated advance, a
messenger came to us and reported that twelve Red Legs, headed by the two
Jayhawkers, would reach and reinforce us by midnight. The Red Legs were
happy. . . .

They demanded of the mayor that the freedom of the city and a fine contraband mule be presented to Jennison on his arrival, and that a procession of
young and comely virgins present the youthful Hoyt with sprigs of the
graceful sunflower. . . .

A meeting of the "property holders and all those opposed to martial law" was
called.

It was decided that although great danger to the city existed, still, a just regard
to the insecurity of property, especially stock, demanded that Jennison and
Hoyt be excluded.[24]

This jovial despatch shows much more clearly than would a more sober
recital, Jennison's reputation among his fellow Kansans, and it illustrates
as well the attitude of amused toleration that made Jennison's and the
Red Legs' criminal activities possible.

Three weeks to a day after "Ivory" penned his sprightly despatch
to the *Conservative*, at daybreak on August 21, Quantrill did appear in
Lawrence at the head of 450 men. He left the town two hours later,
leaving behind 150 men and boys murdered in cold blood, many more
wounded, 182 buildings burned to the ground, and the survivors
robbed of money, jewelry, and all the portable valuables the raiders

24. Leavenworth *Conservative*, August 4, 1863, clipping *ibid.*

could carry.[25] For concentrated loathsomeness, the Lawrence Massacre is approached among the atrocities of the Civil War only by the slaughter of Negro prisoners at Fort Pillow by Bedford Forrest's troopers.

In the first shock of horror produced in Kansas by the massacre, Governor Carney called upon Jennison to organize a force to protect the state. He wrote: "The State of Kansas is invaded. To meet the invasion, you are hereby authorized to raise all the effective men you can. I call upon all Loyal Kansans to aid you. Kansas must be protected at all hazards! The people of Leavenworth, and of every county in the State, will rally to avenge the lawless sacking of Lawrence, and to punish the rebel invaders of the State."[26] It is not without interest that despite his murky past and unsavory reputation, Jennison was Carney's immediate choice to take in hand the defense of the state in a moment of apparent danger. The governor's call must be set beside "Ivory's" despatch to the *Conservative* in any assessment of the position Jennison held in the estimation of his fellow Kansans. One does not often find, and certainly not in a normal atmosphere, one and the same individual being a tolerated brigand and the strong right arm of the community simultaneously.

Carney had actually received authorization in the course of a visit to Washington in early July to raise a regiment of cavalry to be known as the Fifteenth Kansas, which was to be used to defend the eastern counties of the state from the incursions of Missouri guerillas. It is said that he offered the colonelcy and lieutenant colonelcy of the new regiment to Jennison and Hoyt, respectively, in exchange for their promise to abandon the Lane faction of the Republican party and to use their influence among the radical elements in southeastern Kansas in behalf of Carney's faction.[27] Whether or not there was such a bargain, Jennison

25. Connelley, *Quantrill*, 315. Concerning the figure of 150 killed, Connelley adds in 385, n., "but as many bodies were consumed in the flames, the exact number can never be known." Contemporary accounts, as well as present day historians, vary widely in their reports of the number of men Quantrill had with him, as well as in the number of victims. Thus, Castel, *Frontier State*, 132, gives the number killed as "an estimated" 150, and in his *General Sterling Price and the Civil War in the West* (Baton Rouge, 1968), 168, he gives the number killed as 180. After describing the killings, Brownlee adds, *Gray Ghosts*, 124, "Not one Lawrence woman was injured or physically violated"—admirable self-restraint, indeed, on the part of Quantrill and his merry men.

26. Governor Carney's letter is dated August 21, 1863. See Leavenworth *Conservative*, August 23, 1863, clipping in Jennison Scrapbook.

27. Castel, *Frontier State*, 120.

sold his interest in the firm of Losee and Jennison and began to organize
the new regiment prior to the Lawrence Massacre. The thirty-six line
officers were all appointed by Carney on the basis of political considerations instead of being elected by the men. They were evidently a sorry
lot, for during the two-year life of the regiment, fourteen of them were
dismissed from the service, compared to only three officers of the
Seventh dismissed from the service in four years.[28]

On the evening following the sack of Lawrence, "an immense con-
course of people" assembled in front of the Mansion House in Leavenworth to deliberate on the frightful event. Anthony and Jennison were
the principal speakers, and the tenor of their remarks may be inferred
from the headlines of the newspaper report of the meeting: "A Policy of
Extermination Demanded . . . The Lex Talionis Urged."[29] At another
meeting at the same place on the evening of the twenty-seventh, Senator
Lane was the principal orator. He had been in Lawrence on the morning
of the massacre, and to kill him was one of Quantrill's principal objectives. Only by the narrowest of margins had he managed to escape, clad
only in his nightshirt. At Leavenworth a week later he spoke with real
feeling of the slaughter of his friends and neighbours. Then he asked what
the department commander, General Schofield, had been doing while
Quantrill and his fiendish followers were murdering the innocent citizens
of Lawrence. Schofield, Lane said, was administering oaths of allegiance
to Quantrill's allies in Missouri, trying to woo them back to loyalty to
the Union, instead of exterminating them as they deserved. That led
Lane to the climax of his oration; he said:

Not for mere butchery—not for the gratification of mere prejudice, but for
self-preservation, we believe in a war of extermination. . . . I repeat here that
for self-preservation there shall be extermination of the first tier of counties in
Missouri, and if that won't secure us, then the second and third tier, and tier on
tier until we are secure. . . .

There is no such thing as Union men in the border of Missouri where these
bushwhackers stay. . . . I want to see every foot of ground in Jackson, Cass

28. *Report of the Adjutant General of the State of Kansas,* I, XXXV (Seventh), and XLIII
(Fifteenth).

29. Leavenworth *Conservative,* August 28, 1863, clipping in Jennison Scrapbook.

and Bates counties burned over — everything laid waste. Then we shall have no further trouble.[30]

Following Lane's address, Anthony offered a series of resolutions holding the people of Missouri responsible for the losses of life and property in Kansas. These resolutions were adopted by acclamation. Jennison was then "loudly called for." He announced that in response to Governor Carney's request, he was raising the Fifteenth Kansas Cavalry, whose motto would be "Death to traitors and freedom for all men." He declared that when he had command of the Seventh and was in the process of "cleaning out" the rebels from western Missouri, he had been recalled to Kansas through the influence of semitraitors; but, he said, he had learned his lesson, and this time he would take the Fifteenth so far into the enemy's country that no recall order could reach him.[31]

By reason of the wave of bitterness and fear engendered by the Lawrence Massacre, as well as the undoubted drawing power of Jennison's name and his tireless campaigning for recruits, the ranks of the Fifteenth filled up rapidly. With his lieutenant colonel-to-be, George Hoyt, ever at his elbow, Jennison spent the better part of September touring the state and making recruiting speeches in towns and villages. He spoke in Wyandotte, Osawatomie, Mound City, Fort Scott, Prairie City, Garnett, Lawrence, Topeka, Oskaloosa, and Atchison, and the gist of his fiery speeches was everywhere the same; the whole duty of the Fifteenth would be to exact vengeance; let those who desired to avenge the martyrs of Lawrence join the regiment; he would lead them into Missouri "to shoot, kill, burn and confiscate until Lawrence and her murdered citizens were avenged."[32] There would be no quarter for bushwhackers, and everything disloyal from a Shanghai chicken to a Durham cow would be "cleaned out." And he promised the widows and orphans of Lawrence that "*they* should cry 'Hold!' before he stayed his arm from the work of a Kansan's vengeance."[33]

These speeches were explicit enough, but not more so than Jennison's recruiting posters, which announced: "No Compromise with Rebels!

---

30. *Ibid.* 31. Unidentified clipping, *ibid.*
32. Report datelined "Olathe, Sept. 3, 1863." See unidentified clipping, *ibid.*
33. Report datelined "Lawrence, Sept. 11." See unidentified clipping, *ibid.*

No Quarter to Bushwhackers! Desolation Shall Follow Treason Wherever This Regiment Marches! . . . It will be raised for the protection of Kansas, and the destruction of Bushwhackers and Rebels."[34]

At no time did Jennison inform the people of a fact he must surely have known, namely, that the Fifteenth, based on an agreement between Governor Carney and General Schofield, was to be used solely for the protection of Kansas within that state and would not be permitted to cross the border into Missouri.

Jennison's violent speeches and proclamations were the subject of laudatory notices in the Kansas newspapers. One of them told its readers: "We do not endorse Jennison in some respects. He is too wild and reckless. But one thing is certain; when Jennison was in Missouri, we did not have rebel raids into this state. He generally made enough work for them at home, to keep them there. Nothing short of the complete depopulation of the border of Missouri will rid the country of bushwhackers. They must be driven out root and branch—women, children and all. . . . There must be nothing left for them to come back to."[35] Another declared:

[Jennison] is the most effective commander we have ever had on our border . . . and we rejoice that the Union cause is once more to have his services. . . . Gov. Carney has shown the best judgment in selecting a man of military experience and of great personal popularity to put the new cavalry regiment into the field. Col. Jennison is known everywhere for his valor, vigor and determined opposition to every form of treason. He can fill a regiment quicker than any man in Kansas, and he will use it to some purpose when he gets to the head of it.[36]

And in truth, within two weeks from the time recruiting began, nearly eight hundred men enlisted in the Fifteenth Kansas; in another week or ten days the regiment had its full quota of men; and on October 17 it was mustered in 1,015 strong.[37] Recruits continued to present themselves even after the muster-in, until, with a surplus of 400 men on hand and visions of a brigadier general's stars in his mind's eye, Jennison requested authority to use the surplus as the nucleus of a second regiment

34. Quoted in an unidentified clipping, *ibid.*
35. Unidentified clipping, *ibid.*   36. Unidentified clipping, *ibid.*
37. *Report of the Adjutant General of the State of Kansas for the Year 1864*, 18.

of cavalry and a battery of horse artillery, but his proposal was not approved.

There was even a superfluity of applicants for the post of chaplain of the new regiment, which led Jennison to send the following open letter to the newspapers:

Rev. Gentlemen:

Your applications for the Chaplaincy of the Fifteenth are received. In opposition, however, to the Scriptural injunctions, we are attending more closely just now to our temporal than our spiritual requirements and are not in a position to appoint a chaplain. We are commanded to watch and pray, and the Fifteenth is inclined to the opinion that the more we have of the former the less we need the latter. . . . If your fighting qualities are in excess of your pastoral capacities, we shall be happy to enlist you in the Fifteenth. We already have two ministers in a single company, one of whom may be detailed at any time when the regiment requires the interposition of their services.[38]

By the late summer of 1863, the shortages that had existed two years earlier of everything needful to equip and arm a regiment of cavalry were only an entertaining memory. As fast as the recruits for the Fifteenth assembled in Leavenworth, they were uniformed and outfitted under Jennison's personal supervision at his "commissary depot" on the corner of Shawnee and Second streets, where a reporter saw him "dealing out good clothes with a lavish hand. He says his boys have got to dress well or he won't have 'em around."[39] The only supply problem was the shortage of horses. The governor himself made an urgent request to the quartermaster at Fort Leavenworth for one thousand mounts for the Fifteenth, but the records suggest that he was no more able to supply a large number of horses for the new regiment than his colleague in St. Louis had been when the Seventh needed horses a few months earlier. For it was reported in the Kansas press that "a number of men in different parts of the state have recently been caught stealing horses, and reported themselves as belonging to the 15th regiment; and one party is said to have remarked that the regiment was to get horses in this way."[40]

It is difficult to resist the suspicion that the Leavenworth *Conservative*

38. Unidentified clipping, Jennison Scrapbook.
39. Unidentified clipping, *ibid.*
40. Unidentified clipping, *ibid.*

was not being wholly objective in dismissing these reports with the comment: "We are satisfied that these robbers are not soldiers, but are the same class of depredators who, for the last twelve months, have been engaged in this business in the guise of 'Red Legs' . . . generally wearing soldier clothes. We have information which leads us to believe that no men are or have been absent from the Fifteenth, and moreover, that that regiment is in a state of strict subordination and discipline." [41] If, as is likely, the basis of this disclaimer was information supplied by the colonel of the Fifteenth, then it falls short by a considerable margin of being worthy of implicit belief. Any knowledgeable Kansan would have had his doubts about the state of "subordination and discipline" of any newly organized regiment, especially one commanded by Jennison; and he would have been sceptical also of the grounds on which the *Conservative* saw fit to distinguish between Jennison and Hoyt on the one hand and the Red Legs on the other.

After the excitement occasioned by Quantrill's attack on Lawrence had died down, the Fifteenth, for all of Jennison's furious promises, found little enough to do. The troopers who had enlisted in the expectation of carrying fire and sword into Missouri were in for a disappointment; for General Schofield, convinced, rightly or wrongly, that the activities of Missouri guerillas were largely a reaction to aggressions from Kansas, was determined to break the chain of mutual retaliation by keeping Kansas troops out of Missouri. Hence the Fifteenth and its fiery colonel had to remain peacefully on the Kansas side of the line. Nevertheless, the mere fact that Jennison was once again at the head of a Kansas regiment caused great disquiet in Missouri, so much so that a loyalist newspaper in Kansas City printed the mocking report that "all kinds of stories are afloat in regard to Jennison coming down here with various numbers composed of whites, niggers, Red Legs, Blue Legs and Blue Bellies, with orders to sack, burn, destroy, tear to pieces, &c., &c." [42]

IN COLONEL CORNYN'S BRIGADE

The march of the Seventh from Germantown on the morning of April 14 coincided with General Dodge's departure from Corinth for Tus-

---

41. Undated clipping, *ibid.*   42. Unidentified clipping, *ibid.*

cumbia, Alabama, to push the Confederates out of the path of Colonel Streight's raiders. Dodge had with him 4,000 infantry, 1,500 cavalry and horse artillery, and two batteries.[43] His mounted brigade was commanded by Colonel Florence M. Cornyn of the Tenth Missouri Cavalry. Cornyn was "a red headed Irishman, absolutely fearless" and equally pugnacious, as evidenced by the fact that his career ended in the fall of 1863 when he was killed in a duel by the second-in-command of his regiment.[44] Except for a strong tendency to rashness, which cannot be accounted a serious fault in a cavalryman, Cornyn was a competent tactician and a capable leader. His reports of the operations of his brigade, colorful and redolent of Hibernian eloquence, make interesting reading notwithstanding their overly generous length.[45]

The march of the Seventh to Corinth was not without incident. On April 15 two men of Company D, Privates Oscar G. Porter and Perry Allen, straggled from the regiment. As they approached Saulsbury, Tennessee, a rebel soldier, who happened to be passing through on his way home on furlough, stepped out of one of the houses and opened fire on them. Porter fell from his horse, fatally wounded; Allen simply ran away and rejoined the regiment.

The Seventh arrived in Corinth on April 17 and was at once hurried forward to join Colonel Cornyn at Big Bear Creek, just east of the Mississippi-Alabama border.[46] On April 23, three days after the Seventh reached Big Bear Creek, Dodge's entire force, with Cornyn's cavalry in the lead, took up the march for Tuscumbia, which was captured the next day. Having entered the town without meeting serious opposition, Dodge directed Cornyn to follow the retreating Confederates eastward, along the line of the Memphis & Charleston Railroad, and to destroy as much as possible of the road as he went. Cornyn had with him at that moment only two of his regiments, the Seventh Kansas and the Tenth Missouri, about eight hundred men in all. He ordered the Jayhawkers to take the lead, with the three saber companies under the command of

---

43. *Official Records*, XXIII, Pt. 1, 245.   44. Fox, "Story," 40.

45. General Dodge compressed into a report covering four pages of the *Official Records* the operations of his entire force over a period of not quite three weeks. Colonel Cornyn needed exactly twice as much space to report the operations of the cavalry brigade alone.

46. Fox, "Story," 38, states that the Seventh arrived in Corinth April 17. The same date is given in Adjutant General's Office, Kansas, *Official Military History of Kansas Regiments* (Topeka, 1870), 95. The April 18 date given in *Official Records*, XXIII, Pt. 2, 251, appears to be incorrect.

Captain Levi Utt to be in the advance. Cornyn himself rode at the head of the column, knee to knee with Utt. The rebels—Colonel P. D. Roddey's division of Confederate cavalry—greatly outnumbered Cornyn's two regiments; Roddey's strength is variously given as 1,200 to as high as 3,500.[47] Utt struck Roddey's rear guard a mile east of Tuscumbia and drove it at a trot along the road for about two miles, toward Leighton. Suddenly, as Utt's three companies came around a sharp bend in the road, they rode full tilt into a discharge of grapeshot from a rebel battery that was waiting for them in a good position a short distance beyond. Fortunately for Utt and his men, the rebel volley was poorly aimed and the bullets crashed into a fence on the left of the road. Cornyn called out to the men to scatter, but Utt, using better judgment, ordered them to ride straight at the fence to the left of the road, which they did, and they crashed through it just in time to escape a second volley of grapeshot. Utt then led Company A in a charge against the guns and forced the battery to limber up and withdraw to a large cotton field some distance to the rear, where Roddey had formed his line of battle.

The rest of the command having arrived on the scene, Cornyn deployed his two regiments, placing the Seventh to the left of the road and the Missourians to the right. He ordered Utt to keep his three companies mounted and to charge in column the right flank of the rebel line, while the rest of the brigade made a frontal attack, dismounted. Utt attacked as ordered, but his charge was brought to a halt two hundred yards short of the rebel position by a deep drainage ditch with a line of fence on either side of it. Ordering his men to dismount, and using the drainage ditch as a trench, Utt "opened fire on the enemy whose battery and support were within easy shooting distance." The Jayhawkers held their horses by their halters as they fired, and "being veteran sharpshooters and well protected . . . their well directed fire soon threw the mounted men in their front into confusion." But, at this moment, tragedy intervened:

47. Adjutant General, Kansas, *Official Military History*, 95, says that Roddey's command, reinforced by a portion of Forrest's cavalry, "outnumbered Cornyn's brigade two to one." Cornyn's own report, *Official Records*, XXIII, Pt. 1, 254, describes the rebel force opposing him as consisting of "Forest's, Roddey's, Baxter's and Julian's commands, amounting . . . to about 3,500 men." On the other hand, R. S. Henry states, "*First With The Most*" *Forrest* (Indianapolis, 1944), 142, that Roddey had only 1,200 men to oppose Cornyn, and that, *ibid.*, 144, Forrest did not leave Spring Hill, Tennessee, nearly ninety miles north of Tuscumbia, until "before daylight on the twenty-fourth," and did not join Roddey until four days after the fight at Leighton.

John Smith of Highland, an excitable Irishman, boldly mounted to the top of the fence in front where he could have a better chance to hurl epithets at the enemy. In his excitement he let his horse go. Utt ordered the man down and caught his horse but at this moment, a shrapnel shell landed in the earth directly under Utt's feet, where it exploded, blowing him up in the air some distance, and tearing off his left leg at the ankle. The hind leg of the horse was torn off also. The poor creature in its agony hobbled up to its master and whinnied for relief. The men of Co. A took hold of the captain and attempted to draw him out of the fire into the ditch but the agony was so great that he begged them to leave him alone.[48]

The combined pressure of Utt's attack from the flank and the frontal attack of the rest of the brigade forced Roddey to retreat to another position five hundred yards further east, and from it he opened fire on Cornyn's line with his batteries. Cornyn countered with the fire of his light howitzers, and as his dismounted cavalrymen resumed their advance under cover of the artillery duel, Roddey retreated again, to a position at the western edge of the town of Leighton. After more shelling by Cornyn's howitzers and another charge by his dismounted troopers, the Confederates withdrew once more, to a point four miles east of Leighton; and there, at sunset, the action ended.

Cornyn's elaborate and voluminous report on the fighting at Leighton would have done credit to one of the decisive battles of the Civil War. It misled the adjutant general of Kansas into calling what was in fact a minor engagement, "the memorable cavalry battle of Leighton."[49] If with a total force of 800, from which the horseholders must be deducted, Cornyn was able to drive Roddey's 1,200–3,500 men from one position to another for a distance of well over ten miles, it is fair to conclude that the Confederates did not put up an unduly determined resistance and that they held their successive positions only long enough to slow down the Federal advance. The casualty figures Cornyn reports hardly suggest desperate fighting; the losses sustained by his two regiments in a whole day of shelling, small arms fire, and repeated charges, totalled one killed and fourteen wounded. The eloquent prose of Colonel Cornyn's reports unquestionably outran the true scale of his military accomplishments.

48. Utt, "Seventh Kansas."
49. *Official Records*, XXIII, Pt. 1, 255–56; also Adjutant General, Kansas, *Official Military History*, 95.

As soon as the firing had died down at the drainage ditch, an ambulance was brought forward for Captain Utt. He was thrown into the vehicle, and "the cowardly hospital attendant ran the team at full speed over rough plowed ground" for two miles to where Assistant Surgeon Joseph S. Martin of the Seventh had set up his dressing station.[50] Utt's shattered ankle was bandaged and he was driven back to Tuscumbia, where he lay in shock for three days before his foot could be amputated. When General Dodge's army retreated to Corinth, Utt was still too weak to be moved, and he was left in the hotel at Tuscumbia under the care of one of his men, O. C. Whitney of Company A. Owing to Whitney's devoted nursing and the kindness of Mrs. Inman, the landlady of the hotel, Utt began to recover. The good lady ransacked the town for wine and delicacies for the wounded officer, and "pretty girls brought him strawberries and cream."[51] Colonel Roddey, when he reoccupied Tuscumbia, saw to it that the wounded man was left undisturbed; and when Utt was strong enough to travel, Roddey paroled him and sent him to the Union lines at Corinth with an escort to protect him from guerillas. A short time later Utt was able to repay the kindness of the pretty girls of Tuscumbia by persuading General Dodge to grant several of them passes through the lines to Corinth so that they could buy "the various articles dear to the female heart" which were no longer obtainable in the Confederacy.[52]

From Corinth Utt returned to Kansas to regain his health and strength. As soon as he was able to move about, he had himself fitted with a wooden leg and rejoined the regiment in the field on July 31, 1864, ready once more for active service notwithstanding his wooden leg.

On the day following the fighting at Leighton, Cornyn was ordered to return to Tuscumbia, and after resting there on April 26, he advanced to Town Creek, a small stream a short distance east of Leighton, running northward to the Tennessee River. When he arrived, he found Roddey's men deployed on the east bank of the stream. Cornyn formed line of battle and advanced. Some ammunition was expended, but neither side was anxious for a fight, and after a few hours of desultory sharpshooting

50. Utt, "Seventh Kansas."   51. Ibid.
52. Ibid.

which the adjutant general of Kansas called a "heavy engagement," Cornyn retreated.[53] While the shooting was in progress, the mail arrived. Webster Moses described to Nancy Mowry a few days later how he and the other Jayhawkers who had gotten letters from home seated themselves behind a pile of logs to open their mail and "read [their letters] while occasionally a ball would whistle past us from the Rebble Sharpshooters. It was amusing to see some of the boys reading letters and others watching for a glimpse of the Butternuts behind the trees to get a shot at them."[54]

Colonel Streight and his raiders slipped south on the night of the twenty-sixth, past the protective shoulder formed by Dodge's forces, whose task was now completed. Dodge and his infantry marched back to Corinth, while his cavalry made a wide detour to the south, with orders to burn all the forage it could find in order to deny its use to the enemy. A secondary object of the cavalry march was to attract the attention of the Confederates away from the route Colonel Benjamin Grierson was taking on his six hundred-mile raid from LaGrange, Tennessee, to Baton Rouge, Louisiana, with his own Sixth Illinois Cavalry, the Seventh Illinois, and the Second Iowa. After two years of war the Federal cavalry was beginning to apply the lessons administered to it by Forrest, Van Dorn, and Morgan in the West and by Stuart in the East, and it was making some raids of its own. Streight's raid ended in failure and in the capture by the enemy of nearly all his men, but Grierson's raid was successful and incidentally demonstrated the soundness of Fletcher Pomeroy's dictum that to achieve success, a cavalry raid required the employment of good cavalry.

Cornyn's brigade accomplished both halves of the mission assigned to it. Marching through one of the most fertile stretches of farmland in the South, a land filled with corncribs, smokehouses, and haystacks, its trail was marked with columns of smoke at every hand as 1,500,000 bushels of corn, large quantities of oats, rye, and fodder, 500,000 pounds of bacon, three tanyards, and five mills went up in flames.[55] General

53. *Official Records*, XXIII, Pt. 1, 256; also Adjutant General, Kansas, *Official Military History*, 95.
54. Webster Moses to Nancy Mowry, May 12, 1863, in Moses Letters.
55. *Official Records*, XXIII, Pt. 1, 245, 249.

Dodge reported that Cornyn's troopers had been guilty of but one act in disobedience of orders; they burned some houses between Town Creek and Tuscumbia, "on the discovery of which [Cornyn] issued orders to shoot any man detected in the act."[56] The route taken by the cavalry was that "between Town Creek and Tuscumbia"; and indeed, as Webster wrote Nancy Mowry, on the way back from Town Creek they "burned all the corn and most of the houses[.] we found the country beyond Tuscumbia about the best and richest I ever saw and left it nothing but a wilderness with nothing scarcely but the chimneys left to show where once had been the habitations of man."[57] Whatever the Seventh may have done in disobedience of orders—and Webster Moses' letter makes it evident that its derelictions were far greater than General Dodge was aware of—the regiment had earned the general's good opinion for its behavior in the brief campaign. In his report on these operations, Dodge wrote: "The fighting of the cavalry was excellent. The Tenth Missouri, Seventh Kansas, Fifteenth Illinois, and First Alabama all did themselves credit; they invariably drove the enemy, no matter what their force."[58]

56. *Ibid.*, 250.
57. Webster Moses to Nancy Mowry, May 12, 1863, in Moses Letters. *Cf.* Pomeroy, "War Diary," entry for April 28, 1863.
58. *Official Records*, XXIII, Pt. 1, 250.

CHAPTER XIII

The
Veteran
Seventh

TO THE HISTORIAN the Civil War is a symmetrical curve, its chronology neatly divided by the grand climacteric of Gettysburg and Vicksburg into two segments of nearly equal length. To a participant lacking the perspective of a hundred years, for example to a Jayhawker saddling his horse (or perhaps the fractious mule he had picked up when his horse foundered) in preparation for still another scout into Alabama in May or June, 1863, the war stretched ahead in a seemingly endless vista. He may have had the momentary thought, as did Webster Moses after the successful operations around Tuscumbia and Leighton, that "Jeff Davis is about played out," but if he did, he was prompt to qualify his optimism by adding "we hope so at least." [1] But whether an optimist or a pessimist, he had become an experienced soldier who took the good and the bad as they came, with the same phlegmatic acquiescence. He had learned that not half the rumors with which the army was rife were true and that each day's living was to be accepted as a brand-new gift from fate. If there was enough food to eat and coffee to drink, if it was neither too hot nor too cold, neither too muddy nor too dry, if he had a decent animal to ride, if there was enough but not too much to do, if the mail and newspapers from home came regularly, then army life was quite tolerable after all.

1. Webster Moses to Nancy Mowry, May 12, 1863, in Moses Letters.

There was the enemy, of course, but unless he was the skulking bushwhacker, Johnny Reb was simply an accepted nuisance, no worse than a bout of the Tennessee quickstep or than the chiggers, fleas, graybacks, and other insects of which the South had so bountiful a supply.

If our Jayhawker came from a religious home, as most of them did, he might alternate between the comforting belief that he and his comrades had not been contaminated by "any of the vices that often follow a soldiers life" and the conviction, when in a more despondent mood, that "there is a great deal of vice and wickedness. . . . For soldiering is a very bad school." [2] He would deplore the absence of the familiar ritual of his churchgoing Sundays at home and would write, "No sunday is known in the armey and allmost no God. We have no Meeting and no Chaplain and sunday often passes without our knowing it." [3] For the Seventh had been without a chaplain since the resignation of Samuel Ayres on August 31, 1862. [4] For some months before, Ayres had been chaplain in name only; his last recorded appearance with the regiment was on August 3, when he preached a short sermon, and it was noted then that he had been "sick for some time and is quite feeble now. There were but a very few out to hear preaching." [5] But on April 12, 1863, after a hiatus of nearly eight months, a new chaplain, in the person of Reverend Charles H. Lovejoy, joined the regiment. He bore the family name of the martyred Elijah Lovejoy, murdered by a proslavery mob in Alton, Illinois, in 1837; but even aside from having a name revered by all abolitionists, Lovejoy's credentials for serving in the Seventh as chaplain were impeccable. Three days after joining the regiment in Corinth, he wrote: "Never was I so deeply impressed with a sense of the great wickedness of this causeless rebellion, as now, yet I can view it in no other light than as the legitimate fruit of the Godless system of human bondage, which has diffused its poisonous miasma through the entire body politic." [6]

Lovejoy demonstrated that he was a practical abolitionist in a sense different from Jennison's and Montgomery's use of the term; for, in

2. Same to same, April 24, 1863, *ibid.*   3. Same to same, February 1, 1863, *ibid.*
4. *Report of the Adjutant General of the State of Kansas*, I, 526.
5. Pomeroy, "War Diary," entry for August 3, 1863.
6. C. H. Lovejoy to "Bro. Scott," April 22, 1863, in "Letters of Julia Lovejoy, 1856–1864," *Kansas Historical Quarterly*, XVI (1948), 192.

addition to the zealous performance of his duties as chaplain of the regiment, he also organized a school for the contrabands who had "adopted" the Seventh; and he taught eighty of them, men, women, and children, to read and write. He was assisted in these labors by his wife Julia, who became an enthusiastic Jayhawker. The Seventh became *her* regiment, and her glowing reports about it to the *Zion's Herald*, a Methodist newspaper published in Boston, would have delighted the heart of a modern-day public relations officer; she informed the "Dear Old Herald" that "when the history of the war shall have been written by an impartial historian, it will no doubt be found that the 'jay-hawkers,' that have so long been a terror to the border ruffians in Missouri and the rebels in Mississippi and Alabama, have exceeded all other Western regiments in daring exploits and continous skirmishing and hard toil, being almost constantly in the saddle in pursuit of the enemy."[7] Julia Lovejoy was forced to concede, however, that with respect to the "morality of the regiment," even her otherwise peerless Seventh left something to be desired, and she admitted that there was "room for improvement in this respect as well as in other regiments which have so long been severed from the restraining influence of home."[8]

On May 1 the Seventh, forming a part of Cornyn's brigade, reached Burnsville, Mississippi, about halfway between Iuka and Corinth, on its return march from Town Creek. Here the brigade was joined by four companies of the Ninth Illinois Mounted Infantry and received orders to go to Tupelo, more than fifty miles to the southwest, to join Colonel Hatch's brigade. His numbers having increased to nine hundred by the addition of the Illinois battalion, Cornyn started out on May 2 with ten days' rations and made the march to Tupelo in three days via Jacinto, Booneville, Cartersville, Baldwyn, and Guntown. There was some skirmishing en route with scouting parties of rebels, but no serious opposition. On the second night out the Seventh camped at Twenty Mile Creek, in "Parson Yates' dooryard."[9] The parson was elsewhere, but his womenfolk were at hand; and being intense and vocal secessionists, they exercised their wit at the expense of the uninvited visitors from the

7. Julia Lovejoy to "Mr. Editor" [of the *Zion's Herald*], February 11, 1864, *ibid.*, 204–205.
8. *Ibid.*, 205.   9. Pomeroy, "War Diary," entry for May 3, 1863.

North. They intimated that however gay the Jayhawkers might feel on the way south, they would inevitably return faster than they went and would be singing a different tune to boot. The mention of a different tune suggests that the ladies had had to endure a serenade in which, not without malice, such northern airs as "John Brown's Body" and "Yankee Doodle" were prominently featured.

Tupelo was held by General S.J. Gholson's Mississippi militia, both infantry and mounted infantry. Regular Confederate troops, consisting of the Second Alabama Cavalry, the Thirteenth Alabama Battalion of Partisan Rangers, Major W. M. Inge's Battalion, and the Second Tennessee Cavalry, were at or near Verona and were ordered to Tupelo by General Gholson as soon as he heard of Cornyn's approach. The total Confederate strength was probably considerably short of Cornyn's estimate of 3,500.[10] Gholson was fully informed of Cornyn's strength and route by his scouts and friendly civilians.[11] To reach Tupelo, Cornyn had to cross the "dense and almost impassable" bottom land to the east of Old Town Creek, and having negotiated the swamp, he had to cross the creek itself on a narrow bridge.

In retrospect, Cornyn's men thought that the engagement which now ensued was based on a carefully laid trap concocted by the Confederates. The plan, as they reconstructed it, called for a portion of the regular Confederate troops, all of which belonged to the command of Brigadier General Daniel Ruggles, to defend the bridge across Old Town Creek and thereby force Cornyn to deploy to fight his way across. Ruggles' men were then to retreat slowly, drawing the yankees after them. Cornyn's ranks, already disorganized by the crossing of the physical obstacle of the swamp and the fight for the bridge, would be attacked from the flank and rear by Gholson. Trapped by the Confederate cavalry in front and to the right, with Gholson's militia to the left, and the stream to the rear, Cornyn would either be smashed or forced to surrender.[12]

10. Official Records, XXIII, Pt. 1, 257–58. Cf. Fox, "Story," 38–39, and Adjutant General, Kansas, Official Military History, 95.

11. Colonel C. R. Barteau, Second Tennessee Cavalry, CSA, knew as early as May 4 or 5 that Cornyn (whom he calls "Colonel Quinine") had three regiments of cavalry and some artillery, a total of not over nine hundred men. See Official Records, XXIV, Pt. 1, 693.

12. Fox, "Story," 38.

If Gholson had had such a plan, it might well have worked to perfection, for it had the terrain and the Confederates' numerical superiority in its favor; however, the plan existed only in the imagination of the Federals, who not unnaturally ascribed to a prearranged plan the successive attacks of the Confederate cavalry on their right and of Gholson's militia on their left and rear. In the end, the Federals prevailed because of Cornyn's energetic leadership and the superior battle discipline of his seasoned troopers.

The crossing of the bridge over Old Town Creek, held by Inge's Battalion, was effected in five minutes by a charge in column of the Seventh. As soon as Inge began to retreat, he was charged by four dismounted companies of the Seventh and was thrown into confusion. He was then subjected to a saber charge by four companies of the Tenth Missouri and driven back. At this moment, Lieutenant Colonel James Cunningham's Second Alabama Cavalry, W. A. Hewlett's Battalion of Partisan Rangers, and Lieutenant Colonel C. R. Barteau's Second Tennessee Cavalry moved down under cover of a patch of timber to attack from the right flank the advance of the eight companies of Kansans and Missourians, but were themselves struck in the flank by a mounted charge of Company A of the Seventh led by First Lieutenant Bazil C. Sanders, driven down on the Tenth Missouri, and scattered. A short while later Gholson made his attack from the other flank. He was met head-on by the battery of mountain howitzers of the Tenth Missouri, supported by two companies of dismounted cavalry, and was struck from the flank by a charge of Company C of the Seventh. Gholson's attack was spirited, but his men were largely untrained and poorly armed militia, and the artillery in their front and the revolving rifles of the Jayhawkers on their flank were too much for them. They wavered, retreated, and finally fled, pursued by the cavalry.[13]

The fighting ended with Cornyn in possession of the field. He had taken more than eighty prisoners, including three commissioned officers,

---

13. Typical of the difficulty of arriving at the truth about these minor engagements is the conflict of evidence on the identity of the two companies of dismounted cavalry supporting the mountain howitzers of the Tenth Missouri. Cornyn says, *Official Records*, XXIII, Pt. 1, 257, that these were two companies of the Fifteenth Illinois Cavalry. Fox, on the other hand, says, "Story," 39, that Companies I and K of his own regiment had this assignment.

and the field of battle was covered with "immense quantities" of discarded Confederate arms, coats, and blankets, which were collected and burned.[14]

In the exultation of what was undoubtedly a victory for the Union, Fletcher Pomeroy wrote in his diary, as the sun set at the end of the day: "We are the victors with one killed and three wounded. . . . We captured 84 of the enemy thus striking another death blow to treason. We will continue to 'strike till the last armed foe expires,' till our country is saved, and until our glorious old flag waves triumphantly over every foot of our Union."[15] Colonel Cornyn, on the other hand, had second thoughts about his victory. The enemy had been defeated and driven from the field, but the rebels, now protected by darkness, were still in superior strength by a substantial margin and might well be preparing for another fight in the morning. No reliable news was to be had of General Hatch's whereabouts, and Cornyn, with a few hundred men, was deep in enemy country fifty miles from help. After consultation with his senior officers, he decided on an immediate retreat. The men were given time to feed their horses and to eat supper, and after building numerous camp-fires to deceive the enemy (a fact Cornyn did not think it necessary to mention in his report), the brigade left Tupelo and headed north toward Corinth.

The brigade marched all through the night of May 5, and after a brief pause for breakfast at sunrise, it marched all day and long past sunset on the sixth. At last a halt was called . . . at Parson Yates's door-yard. The eighty-four prisoners were installed for safekeeping in the parson's house, and the ladies who had had their fun taunting the yankees three days before were requested to prepare supper and then breakfast

14. *Official Records*, XXIII, Pt. 1, 258. Colonel Cornyn reported eighty-one prisoners. Webster Moses, in a letter to Nancy Mowry, May 12, 1863, in Moses Letters, puts the number at eighty-three. Pomeroy, "War Diary," entry for May 5, 1863, says there were eighty-four. Fox tops them all with the claim, "Story," 39, that the "prisoners numbered several hundred," and he adds that "many of the prisoners bore marks of the saber." For the Confederate reports of the fight at Tupelo, see *Official Records*, XXIV, Pt. 1, 689–94. General Gholson made no report, but the three officers who did stated that their losses totalled three killed, twelve wounded, and only ten missing. Colonel Barteau, having said that Cornyn's strength had been reported by a prisoner as no more than nine hundred, blithely ends his report with the claim that the "force of the enemy was not less than 1,500." See *Official Records*, XXIV, Pt. 1, 694.

15. Pomeroy, "War Diary," entry for May 5, 1863. The Jayhawker killed was Corporal Edwin M. Vaughan, Company A, of Hiawatha, Kansas, shown incorrectly in *Report of the Adjutant General of the State of Kansas*, I, 530, as killed on May 6.

for their unfortunate fellow rebels—all eighty-four of them. Not surprisingly, the ladies were not jubilant at this turn of events. Out of danger after his twenty-five hour march, Cornyn was in no hurry to leave the Yates plantation on the morning of the seventh. The Fifth Ohio Cavalry arrived with orders for Cornyn to return at once to Corinth and brought with them news of "glorious Union victories under Hooker on the Rappahannock," which the gallant Colonel Cornyn made haste to announce to the ladies. The yankees then marched away, and, said Pomeroy, "if the ladies shed any tears at our departure, they were certainly not in our behalf." [16] But the parson's ladies had the last laugh after all, for Hooker's glorious victories on the Rappahannock turned into Lee and Jackson's greatest triumph at Chancellorsville.

The Jayhawkers arrived in Corinth on May 9, and for eight months, until mid-January, 1864, Corinth remained their home base. In the latter half of 1863 the northeastern corner of Mississippi became an island of relative peace. There was fighting to the southwest, around Vicksburg, and to the northeast, where Rosecrans and Bragg dueled for the possession of Chattanooga. The Jayhawkers were a part of the cavalry, commanded by Grierson, of the XVI Army Corps, and were assigned to the First Cavalry Brigade, consisting, besides themselves, of the Third Michigan, Tenth Missouri, Fifth Ohio, and First Alabama, with the senior colonel, John K. Mizner of the Michigan regiment, commanding the brigade.[17] Governor Carney at length overcame his reluctance to make a politically unprofitable appointment, and Thomas P. Herrick was commissioned colonel of the Seventh. The appointment gave "entire satisfaction" to the men.[18] But Herrick became colonel of a regiment greatly diminished in numbers. Its losses from all causes were far from being made good by the trickle of recruits picked up among the unionists of Tennessee or forwarded from Kansas, and the regiment usually numbered well under four hundred officers and men present for duty.[19]

---

16. Pomeroy, "War Diary," entry for May 7, 1863.

17. *Official Records*, XXX, Pt. 3, 82.

18. Pomeroy, "War Diary," entry for June 11, 1863. On July 1, Captain David W. Houston of Company H was jumped a grade and promoted to the lieutenant colonelcy vacated by Herrick. See *Report of the Adjutant General of the State of Kansas*, I, 524.

19. *Official Records*, XXX, Pt. 3, 75. On October 4, 1863, the Seventh reported twenty-three officers and 370 enlisted men present for duty.

The duties the regiment was now called upon to perform were neither novel nor onerous. With the main rebel armies concentrated out of range to the east and west, the Federal garrison at Corinth had only militia, irregulars, and occasional small bands of regular Confederate horse to deal with. Scouts and expeditions, sometimes lasting a week or even longer, were made in various directions. Opposition was usually slight, and what contacts there were with the enemy led to nothing more serious than skirmishes. There was a dreary sameness about these excursions, the same tale of mills, cotton gins, tanyards, blacksmith shops, corncribs, and barns burned, a few prisoners taken, a few dozen horses and mules captured to replace the animals that had given out on long marches in the midsummer heat, and always a dozen or two, sometimes as many as a hundred, Negroes following the column back to Corinth and freedom.[20] There was little of interest and even less of pleasure for the men in these forays. To return to Corinth, which the men now thought of as home, after one of these expeditions was always pleasant, and while the Jayhawkers were wise enough in the ways of war to question the value of these wearisome marches up and down the countryside, after a few days' rest in camp they were ready for yet another trip into "Dixie."[21]

Camp life was agreeable enough, especially when something unusual occurred to relieve the tedium. On June 4 there was a "dreadful storm of rain and wind" that blew down most of the tents and uprooted a good many trees; two men of the Tenth Missouri were killed by falling timber, and many of the Jayhawkers narrowly escaped serious injury or death when branches and trunks of trees came crashing down all around them.[22] A month later, on July 4, there was excitement of a more pleasant variety. The brigade was awakened at daybreak by the Jayhawkers' regimental band playing the "Star Spangled Banner" and "Hail Columbia," and the stirring strains "inspired all with a higher patriotism

20. For examples of these scouts, see Colonel Cornyn's report of the expedition to Florence, Alabama, May 26–31, in *ibid.*, XXIII, Pt. 1, 349–51, and of a "reconnaissance in force" to Iuka, July 7, in *ibid.*, XXIV, Pt. 2, 663–65. There were other expeditions, too uneventful to justify the submission of formal reports. See, for example, the ten-day scout from July 26 to August 6, mentioned in Pomeroy, "War Diary," entry for August 6, and by Webster Moses in a letter to Nancy Mowry, August 9, 1863, in Moses Letters.

21. Webster Moses to Nancy Mowry, August 9, 1863, in Moses Letters.

22. Pomeroy, "War Diary," entry for June 4, 1863.

and a desire to put forth greater efforts to crush rebellion."[23] At one o'clock in the afternoon a national salute of thirty-five guns was fired; then the Jayhawker band was ensconced on one of the regimental wagons fitted up for the purpose, "and with the Old Flag floating to the breeze... [the] band visited each regiment in Corinth and gave them a sample of 7th Kansas music."[24]

Then came the news of the fall of Vicksburg, followed shortly by the first brief reports of "the victory of Gen Meads armey in the east."[25] The glad tidings were received with the greatest enthusiasm and gave rise to the hope that the twin victories heralded the beginning of the end of the war. But whatever the outlook, the men were willing to stay out their time and then return "home and fight Copperheads for another year if necessary."[26] The Jayhawkers' willingness to see the war through to the end was not mere brave talk to impress the home folks, as they were to demonstrate shortly, and as Fletcher Pomeroy demonstrated on August 8. He received word that day that he had been granted a thirty-day furlough to visit his home in Illinois and was told at the same time that he could have the post of regimental quartermaster sergeant. To obtain the promotion, he would have to forego his furlough. The choice was not easy, for it was now only a month short of two years since he had left Wyanet, and this was to be his first leave. Pomeroy made his decision without feeling the need to parade his virtue, even in his diary; he accepted the promotion and turned over his furlough to his brother Emerson, who was also a member of Company D.

On September 3, while commanding the regiment in the absence of Colonel Herrick, Lieutenant Colonel David W. Houston thought it necessary to remind the men that "the safety of the army depends upon well-regulated guards, pickets and outposts, faithfully and efficiently carried into effect. The lives of thousands of soldiers often depend upon the vigilance and bravery of one sentinel."[27] The occasion for this homily was an attack on the previous night by a large force of guerillas on a ten-man picket of the Seventh, stationed on the road between Corinth and Kossuth. Houston praised the brave conduct of Sergeants

---

23. *Ibid.*, entry for July 4, 1863.   24. *Ibid.*
25. Webster Moses to Nancy Mowry, July 13, 1863, in Moses Letters.
26. Same to same, July 21, 1863, *ibid.*
27. General Orders No. 41, September 3, 1863, in Seventh Kansas, Regimental Order Book.

James G. Wright and Patrick Hollarn, and of Privates William Leiber, John Mitchell, J. P. D. Mouriquand, and Jacob Shaiffer, all of Company I, who "gallantly stood their ground" and "repulsed and drove the enemy." "They have," said Houston, "the thanks of the commander of the regiment and the congratulations of the brave throughout the army." On the other hand, four other members of the picket, Privates John A. Gillen, Aaron McSparren, James P. McCrum, and John Miller, also of Company I, who had "disgracefully abandoned their station and comrades at the approach of danger," had their "disreputable conduct" publicly pilloried in the same order.[28]

Four weeks later, Major William S. Jenkins, who evidently had a more sensitive ear than either Colonel Herrick or Lieutenant Colonel Houston, ordered that the buglers of the regiment, while in camp, were to practice two hours daily under the supervision of the same John A. Gillen of Company I who had deserted his post and comrades a month before.[29] Gillen may well have felt that he was being subjected to excessive punishment for his misconduct. Colonel Houston had chastised him with whips, but Major Jenkins was chastising him with scorpions.

On October 1 the Seventh returned to its camp at Corinth from a five-day expedition along the Tennessee River to break up the guerilla bands that were operating in the area and were becoming increasingly troublesome. In command of the expedition was Colonel Richard Rowett of the Seventh Illinois Mounted Infantry. The Kansans came to the conclusion that Rowett, an infantryman by trade, had "no sense about marching cavalry," and it is impossible not to agree with them. Having covered nearly 110 miles in four days of rain and muddy going, and with the horses already jaded, Rowett marched his column forty-five miles on the last day out, although there was no reason to hurry. This would have been a long day's march for cavalry, even on fresh horses. But at least the expedition had something tangible to show for its exertions. On September 30 Rowett had caught a portion of Colonel W. W. Faulkner's Confederate cavalry crossing the Tennessee River and

28. *Ibid.*
29. Special Orders No. 33, October 3, 1863, *ibid.*

attacked them with Company A and C of the Seventh in the lead. With the loss of one Jayhawker killed, two seriously wounded, and three lightly wounded, he captured twenty of the enemy, including a major.[30]

In late September, Brigadier General James R. Chalmers, commanding the Confederate cavalry in northern Mississippi, decided to raid the Memphis and Charleston Railroad. Word of his intentions filtered across the lines to LaGrange, Tennessee, where Colonel Edward Hatch, then in command of the cavalry division of the XVI Army Corps, had his headquarters. Not until October 4, however, did Hatch receive fairly definite information about Chalmers' strength and probable destination. Four days later, on the morning of October 8, with 750 men, including the Seventh, he marched against the raiders, whom he expected to intercept at Salem, Mississippi, about fifteen miles south of LaGrange. At Salem Hatch learned that Chalmers had been heavily reinforced and now had at least three thousand men and nine or ten guns under his command.[31] Deciding that the odds against him were too great, Hatch returned to LaGrange to collect the rest of his division and pick up his artillery. In the meantime, Chalmers veered off to the northwest, toward Collierville, Tennessee. Hatch was being urged on by General Hurlbut's telegraphic injunction to "pursue with vigor and break ... up [the enemy] thoroughly."[32] After marching fifty-two miles in twenty-four hours, Hatch caught up with Chalmers, who had already begun his retreat, near Collierville.

As Chalmers moved south, Hatch maintained contact with him and pressed his retreat with sufficient vigor to force him to stand at bay to beat off his pursuers. Chalmers chose a strong position on a line of hills with a swamp protecting his front, three miles south of the town of Byhalia, Mississippi. His line was held by Colonel R. V. Richardson's West Tennessee Brigade of about eight hundred men, with two 6-

30. *Official Records*, XXX, Pt. 2, 662. *Cf.* Fox, "Story," 41. The Jayhawker killed was Thomas Graham, Company C, of Leavenworth. See *Report of the Adjutant General of the State of Kansas*, I, 556.

31. *Official Records*, XXX, Pt. 4, 147. One of the reports reaching Hatch credited Chalmers with a force of 7,100.

32. *Ibid.*, 201.

pounder guns in the center.[33] Hatch deployed his attacking line with the Ninth Illinois Mounted Infantry on the left, the Seventh Illinois Cavalry in the center, the Jayhawkers on the right, and the Sixth Illinois Cavalry in support. Driving Richardson's skirmishers out of the swamp, the Federals opened on his main line with artillery and, after repulsing a spirited attack by Richardson's Tennesseans on their center, went over to the attack themselves. The Seventh Kansas and the Seventh Illinois advanced on the run; Richardson's line broke at the first onset, and his men were driven by the Federals until late in the evening.

The pursuit was resumed before daylight the next morning. The Confederate rearguard was met within a mile from the start, and a running fight developed as Chalmers retreated southward toward Wyatt, on the north bank of the Tallahatchie River about twenty miles below Byhalia. There was a bridge across the river at Wyatt, and Chalmers had to accept battle just north of the town to protect the crossing. His force had been reduced by "straggling and other causes" to not more than 1,600, most of his ammunition had been expended in the fight at Byhalia and the almost constant skirmishing since, and only three of the nine or ten cannon with which he had started were still in condition to be brought into action. Nevertheless, Chalmers put up a stout fight. The Federals concentrated their attack on his right, which they succeeded in forcing back. This enabled them to close in on the river and gave them a position from which they could enfilade the bridge with their artillery. Four separate times Chalmers sent his right forward in counterattacks to dislodge the Federals from their position on his flank, but all four attacks were repulsed with loss. After the fourth Confederate charge had been broken up, at nine o'clock in the evening and in the midst of a heavy thunderstorm and driving rain, the four regiments of Hatch's left went forward to the attack. In the pitch darkness, with the enemy's position indicated only by the flashes of his guns, the dismounted cavalrymen rushed forward, over fences, across ditches, and through the mud, and drove the Confederates out of their position and across the bridge.[34]

33. The description of the actions at Byhalia and Wyatt is based on the reports of Colonel Hatch, *ibid.*, Pt. 2, 740–43, and of Lieutenant Colonel George Trafton, Seventh Illinois Cavalry, *ibid.*, 749; and, on the Confederate side, the reports of General Chalmers, *ibid.*, 761–62, and of Lieutenant Colonel James A. Barksdale, Third Regiment, Mississippi State Cavalry, *ibid.*, 771.
34. Fox, "Story," 41; *Cf. Official Records*, XXX, Pt. 2, 742. General Chalmers claimed in

The first of Chalmers' four counterattacks, led by the Third Regiment, Mississippi State Cavalry, had struck the Seventh Kansas, which formed the skirmish line in front of Hatch's left wing. The Jayhawkers were driven back on their supports, and Captain Amos Hodgman of Company H was severely wounded and taken prisoner. This gave Lieutenant Colonel James A. Barksdale, in command of the Mississippians, the opportunity to boast in his report of the capture of "Captain Hodgman, of Seventh Kan. notoriety."[35] Hodgman died of his wound shortly after he was captured.

As Colonel Hatch tells the story, his command crossed the bridge over the Tallahatchie on the morning after the fight, pushed forward for some distance, and finding no enemy in sight, returned to Wyatt.[36] With Chalmers well on his way to his base and his men scattering to the four winds, there was no work left for the Federal cavalry to do in the area, and Hatch marched back to his camps in Tennessee. But before the Federals left Wyatt, they set fire to the town. In his report on this brief campaign, Hatch singled out the Seventh Kansas for special praise; the Kansans, he wrote, "dashed at the enemy splendidly."[37]

A short time after these events, rumors spread in western Tennessee that the redoubtable Nathan Bedford Forrest was coming to northern Mississippi to supersede Chalmers. "If so," wrote General Hurlbut, "there will be more dash in their attacks."[38] The rumors were well founded. In mid-November Forrest set up his headquarters in Okolona, Mississippi, and within ten days of his arrival, he was on his way north into Tennessee with 450 poorly armed men to round up an army out of the small independent bands of Confederate horse operating in the area, deserters from other commands, recruits, and conscripts. To distract the attention of the Federals, Major General Stephen D. Lee led his mounted

---

his report that his men "held their position firmly for more than three hours, and until night put an end to the firing, when they withdrew quietly across the river without loss." See *Official Records*, XXX, Pt. 2, 762.

35. *Official Records*, XXX, Pt. 2, 771.

36. *Ibid.*, 742. But here again there is a direct conflict of testimony, for General Chalmers maintained that "On the next day, our troops were drawn up in the intrenchments on the south side of the river to resist any attempt of the enemy to cross, but . . . they . . . retired without making any attempt to follow us." See *ibid.*, 762.

37. *Ibid.*, 743.   38. *Ibid.*, XXXI, Pt. 3, 694.

forces in a raid on the section of the Memphis and Charleston Railroad between Moscow and Pocahontas. Colonel Mizner, with a small brigade consisting of three hundred men of the Seventh Kansas, three hundred of the Third Michigan, and two hundred of the First Alabama, was ordered to march south and block Lee as far from the railroad as possible. Lee had only a fraction of the six to twelve thousand men he was credited with having; still, Mizner was greatly outnumbered. The Michigan colonel spent four days, from the twenty-sixth to the thirtieth of November, hunting for the enemy. He finally located Lee near Ripley on December 1, but in an all-day running skirmish, he was unceremoniously brushed aside. Mizner was later blamed for falling back against orders, thus allowing Lee to strike the railroad at Saulsbury, where he destroyed a stretch of track.

Forrest and Lee's move into Tennessee occurred at an inconvenient time for the Jayhawkers, who were busy building their winter quarters at Corinth when the alarm came. There was not a single tent left in the regiment, and in an area that had been occupied by one army after another for two years, materials for building shelters were no longer easy to find. However, Fletcher Pomeroy, in his role of quartermaster sergeant, was equal to the occasion. On November 16 he took the five regimental wagons on an expedition for building materials. Two miles from Tuscumbia, enough brick to fill three of the wagons was salvaged from the ruins of a house that had been burned. A few miles further on, at Kossuth, a deserted house yielded two wagonloads of planks and timbers. In another respect, on the other hand, the period of active duty was beneficial to the regiment, for the comparatively easy life in camp had as usual produced misbehavior and indiscipline. On December 11, for example, Sergeants Jackson T. Lavery of Company A, Theodore Krause of Company B, John Daley of Company E, and William Taylor and J. G. Wright of Company I were all reduced to the ranks for "drunkenness on duty." [39]

In the latter part of December the regiment was sent out on a scout toward Purdy. The expedition was uneventful until, on the evening of the twenty-first, Colonel Herrick got word that there was to be a "rebel dance" at a house two miles away. Herrick sent Captain Edward Thorn-

---

39. General Orders No. 51, December 11, 1863, in Seventh Kansas, Regimental Order Book.

ton of Company G with a detachment of twenty-five men to join the
fun. As Thornton and his men approached the house, where the dance
was already in full swing, the male revelers rushed out and greeted the
uninvited guests with a volley of musketry. There was a brief fight in
which two of the rebels were killed. The rest escaped into the woods,
but Thornton returned to camp with a prize haul of twenty-one horses.

Three days later, on Christmas Eve, there was more serious work
to be done. General Hurlbut had decided to break up Forrest's recruiting
activities in the interior of West Tennessee by having no fewer than five
Federal columns, a total of nearly 15,000 men, converge on Forrest's
3,500 raw and partially armed troops. Receiving timely warning of the
Federal move from his scouts, Forrest started back to Mississippi on the
twenty-third, sending one detachment forward to secure the crossing
of the Hatchie River and another, under Lieutenant Colonel D. M.
Wisdom, to fend off the Federal column led by Brigadier General Joseph
A. Mower that was closing in from the southeast to intercept him. A
portion of Mower's force, including a battalion of the Seventh, met
Wisdom's detachment in the vicinity of Jack's Creek, Tennessee. In an
all-day fight with the Federals, Wisdom accomplished his objective; he
prevented them from advancing. Employing his usual combination of
imagination, guile, speed, and energy, Forrest escaped the trap Hurlbut
laid for him and brought his 3,500 men, 40 wagonloads of bacon and
supplies, 200 beef cattle, and 300 hogs to Holly Springs and safety.

The Seventh spent Christmas Day in the saddle, scouting in the
vicinity of Jack's Creek. Webster Moses ruefully wrote to Nancy Mowry
that "every Christmas since we have be[en] in the service we have been
on active duty in the field but we complain not."[40] It was some comfort
that Christmas Day was bright and sunny. The following day, however,
it began to rain, and soon the rain turned into a downpour. At times it
rained so hard that it was impossible to see more than two or three
hundred yards. Forrest, a native of the area, wrote that he had never
experienced worse weather or roads.[41] Then, on the thirtieth, with 240
men of the Seventh—all those who had serviceable horses—away from
camp on a scout to Moscow and LaGrange, the rain turned to snow. On

40. Webster Moses to Nancy Mowry, undated, in Moses Letters.
41. Henry, *Forrest*, 212.

New Year's Eve there was a thick mantle of snow on the ground, and the temperature began to drop. The Jayhawkers, without a single tent, went into camp at dusk and welcomed in the New Year on as miserable a night as any of them had ever spent. The next day was remembered for many years throughout the country as "The Cold New Year's Day," and nowhere was the temperature lower than in the usually mild South. The regiment started back to Corinth in the morning, but it was so bitterly cold that the men could not ride for more than a few minutes at a time; they had to dismount and lead their horses most of the way. After a short march in nearly impossible conditions, the Seventh went into camp long before dark, a few miles from LaGrange. There was a large field nearby with a rail fence around it. The rails were used to build lean-tos, which the men covered with their rubber ponchos. Before the open side of each lean-to, a blazing fire was built, and with the liberal use of dry fence rails for fuel, the men managed to get through the night without freezing to death.[42]

It was in this camp, and under these grim conditions, that the Jayhawkers were told that the War Department, faced with the imminent loss of nearly all the trained men in the Union armies, soldiers whose three-year terms of enlistment were due to expire in the summer and fall of 1864, had announced a program to keep them in the service. Every man who reenlisted for a new term of three years or the duration of the war was to receive a thirty-day furlough at home and a bounty of four hundred dollars upon his discharge; if three-fourths or more of a regiment reenlisted, it would retain its organization and identity and would be authorized to add the word "Veteran" to its name. It says much for the morale, the corporate spirit, and the patriotism of the Jayhawkers that in the midst of the most severe physical hardships, and without compulsion of any kind, nearly four-fifths of them reenlisted before nightfall.[43] Webster Moses expressed their attitude, as he frequently did, in his own matter-of-fact fashion: "The general opinion is that we will have about one year to serve or less[.] We think that the Confederacy is

42. The following day, when General Grierson was asked by Colonel Mizner to supply tents for the Seventh, the latter telegraphed that the regiment was "without a single tent" and that "quite a number" of the men had been "frost bitten and all were suffering from the intense cold." See *Official Records*, XXXII, Pt. 2, 15.
43. Fox, "Story," 42. *Cf.* Lyman, "Reminiscences."

about *'played out*[.]' I have no doubt that you will be surprised and perhaps pained at our reenlisting[.] the Most of Co. D have reenlisted and we wanted to go all together and want to see the war over and then we will come home to stay[.]" [44] No doubt, as the historian of another cavalry regiment wrote, "there were . . . as many motives for reenlistment —in addition to patriotism pure and simple—as there were individuals. With a few it was a 'fad.' . . . Some hesitated till the example of others carried them over the ripple." [45] The Seventh, nevertheless, was particularly and rightfully proud of the fact that it was the first regiment in the XVI Army Corps to reenlist. It was no less proud of the distinction of being the only Kansas regiment to reenlist in a body and thus to maintain, as veterans, its regimental organization intact.

For reasons that are not at all difficult to account for, the Jayhawkers attached a condition to their reenlistment. They declared that they would remain in the service if the government allowed each man to supply his own horse and paid him for the use of the animal at the standard rate of forty cents a day. It was well known that this arrangement was the normal practice in the Confederate cavalry, and no doubt the Jayhawkers also knew that a few volunteer regiments in the Federal service had a similar arrangement with the War Department. [46] The forty cents a day allowance would have nearly doubled each trooper's monthly pay; moreover, he would have been entitled to be paid the value of his horse if it were killed in battle or captured by the enemy. To be paid upwards of $120 for a horse that had cost no more than the trouble of taking it from its lawful owner had, from the trooper's point of view, much to recommend it. True, the loss of the animal by disease was not reimbursable by the government, but with the regiment operating in rebel territory, dead or broken-down horses were not too difficult to replace, and no one suffered except the Tennessee or Mississippi farmer whose horse would probably have been taken anyway, if not by the Federals then by the Confederates. Nonetheless, when the conditional reenlistment of the Seventh came before General Sherman, he ruled that the

44. Webster Moses to Nancy Mowry, n. d., in Moses Letters.

45. William R. Hartpence, *History of the Fifty-First Indiana Veteran Volunteer Infantry* (Cincinnati, 1894), 199. The Fifty-first Indiana was a regiment of mounted infantry.

46. *E.g.,* the First New York, Second Illinois, First Iowa, Third Indiana, First Kentucky, and Twenty-second Pennsylvania.

Kansans would have to reenlist unconditionally or not at all. On January 12, accordingly, a vote of the regiment was taken, and with a few exceptions all those who had previously signed up to reenlist agreed to stay in without conditions.

With this problem settled, the regiment received on January 15 the eagerly awaited orders to turn in its horses and equipment and proceed to Memphis by train. There, on January 21, firearms were surrendered to the quartermaster, and those members of the regiment who had "veteranized" were mustered into the veteran service as of January 1. The Seventh thereby became the Seventh Kansas *Veteran* Volunteer Cavalry. Each reenlisted veteran was given, as a badge of honorable distinction, a "service chevron," consisting of a red worsted braid twelve inches long and nearly an inch wide, on which was centered a strip of blue worsted braid of the same length but only a half-inch wide. The badge, doubled in the shape of a "V," was to be sewn on the left coat sleeve. There was a host of other formalities to be attended to; company commanders and clerks had to make out their muster rolls so that the men could be paid; those members of the regiment who had decided not to reenlist and the recent recruits not eligible to do so—all of whom had acquired the name of "bobtails"—had to be turned over to the Second Iowa Cavalry for safekeeping. But at last all these chores were completed, and on January 25 the Seventh was ready to start for home.[47]

The bustle of activity at Memphis, the ostentatious happiness of comrades about to start for their homes, and the prospect of having to serve for two months under strange officers in a strange regiment, had an inevitable effect on the holdouts. Many of them "who could stand it no longer, reenlisted at the last moment" and qualified themselves for a trip home with the regiment.[48]

At eleven at night on January 25, the steamer *Belle of Memphis* cast off from the levee and began the two-day journey upriver to Cairo. She was "one of the most splendid boats that ply on the waters of the Mississippi River." But on this trip her splendors were difficult to discern, for she was jammed to capacity and even beyond. Besides nearly four hundred Jayhawkers, there were on board a part of an Ohio regiment of infantry,

47. According to *Official Records*, XXXII, Pt. 2, 229, the "bobtails" of the Third Michigan and the Seventh Kansas were to be turned over to the Second Iowa Cavalry.
48. Fox, "Story," 42.

the families of numerous officers and soldiers, plus miscellaneous passengers and a full crew, as well as sixty horses and sixty bales of cotton. The weather was fine, and the men enjoyed themselves, notwithstanding the crowding. In the excitement of going home, they did not even mind having to live on army rations, a great comedown from the more varied diet to be had by foraging in Tennessee and Mississippi. The main hazard of the journey came from the stream of sparks spewed forth by the smokestacks, and raining down on the piles of soldiers' bedding and baggage heaped on the upper deck:

The deck once caught fire and blazed, and almost every combustible matter on the upper deck, even the soldiers' hats, overcoats and blankets caught fire, so that numbers were entirely ruined, and in repeated instances the fires in the bedding could not be extinguished, and they were committed to the deep a flaming mass; and many a soldier cast a last lingering look at the remnant of his pallet, as it smoked in the wake of the boat and then disappeared, like all sublunary enjoyments, forever.[49]

But a near approach of eternity, in the shape of a boat on fire, was not sufficient to recall to a becoming gravity the lighter minded among the passengers. Julia Lovejoy, who made the trip North with her chaplain-husband and the regiment, tells us:

Would you believe . . . that even then, when some watchful ones were turning pale with fear, and the soldiers were shouting from the deck, "Fire, fire," that a dance was proposed in the cabin, and entered into with zest, even by some who had once borne the profession of Christianity. . . . Wives participated, whose husbands had just bid them farewell as they joined the fleet that was to sail the following day, and many of them their eyes beheld for the last time. Deep-seated sorrow, how easily art thou dissipated by mirth, in a volatile spirit![50]

Need it be said that Mrs. Lovejoy was above such thoughtless levities? She, her husband, and some like-minded fellow passengers retired to her stateroom "to sing old-fashioned Methodist hymns, strangely contrasted with the violin and the guitar at the door entrance."[51]

On January 27 the *Belle of Memphis* tied up at Cairo, "a town built on

---

49. Julia Lovejoy to "Mr. Editor" [of the *Zion's Herald*], February 11, 1864, in "Letters of Julia Lovejoy," 202.

50. *Ibid.*, 202–203.

51. *Ibid.*, 203.

a foul morass, with almost every house labeled Hotel, the streets bar-
ricaded by mud, the sidewalks on stilts"; and there the Seventh was
forced to remain for several days until the officers succeeded in chartering
a train of sufficient length to haul the regiment, its baggage, and the
officers' chargers to Quincy, Illinois. And indeed the train was long; it
needed a locomotive pulling in front and another pushing and snorting
in the rear to keep it in motion. Rank had its privileges; the first passenger
coach at the head of the train was reserved for the officers. As the train
chugged through the loyal towns and villages of Illinois, it was greeted
with much huzzaing and waving of flags and feminine handkerchiefs,
and the Jayhawker band returned the compliment by playing "Yankee
Doodle" and other patriotic airs of a lively nature.

The journey of the Seventh to its home was not lacking in memorable
incidents. The first of these occurred at Decatur, Illinois, which the train
reached just at dinnertime on the thirtieth. The Copperhead proprietor
of the station hotel and eating house, seeing several hundred hungry
soldiers deposited on his doorstep, discerned an opportunity to make
economic hay and to express his political convictions at the same time.
He announced that the charge for the table d'hote dinner was seventy-
five cents per man. About a hundred of the soldiers had already eaten and
paid when they learned from a patriotic, or perhaps merely disgruntled,
employe that the normal charge for dinner was only fifty cents. The
reaction was instantaneous and violent. The landlord, threatened with
mayhem or worse, fled for his life and hid in the attic; but he was
found, dragged out, and given the choice of making instant restitution
of the overcharge or having his hotel burned down with himself in it.
He chose the less painful alternative and agreed to the refund, whereupon
the hundred men who had partaken of his expensive hospitality, followed
by the rest of the regiment, fell into line; and as fast as each man reached
the head of the line and received his twenty-five cent shinplaster, he fell in
at the end of the line for another go at the unfortunate proprietor. With
ruin staring him in the face, the landlord begged for mercy, and the
soldiers, who were by that time a little tired of the game, agreed to waive
all further claims provided the landlord distributed free cigars to the
regiment as compensation for the injury to their feelings; the injury to
their pocketbooks had already been made good two or three times over.

But not everyone in Decatur was a Copperhead. Word of the Jay-hawkers' presence at the station, and of their difficulties with the hotel proprietor, spread rapidly through the town, and in less than an hour the patriotic ladies of Decatur collected a barrel of apples and liberal supplies of other eatables and distributed them among the soldiers to tide them over until their next stopping place.

On January 31 the regiment arrived at Quincy, where they had to leave their train and cross the Mississippi by ferry. The river was clogged by an immense flow of ice set free by the January thaw, and the crossing was dangerous and slow. Three days were required to get the entire regiment, the horses, and baggage across the river. Still another problem cropped up in connection with the short trip by train from the west bank of the Mississippi to Palmyra, Missouri; the only locomotive available was too small for the weight of the train behind it, and it had to stop after every mile or two, to get up stream. At Palmyra, however, a better train with a more powerful engine was made available, and the remainder of the trip across Missouri to St. Joseph and Weston was uneventful.

The final difficulty of the trip arose at the crossing of the Missouri from Weston to Leavenworth. The owner of the ferryboat had encountered a variety of bureaucratic snags in getting paid by the government for ferrying another regiment across the river some time before, and he firmly refused to take the Seventh across unless he was paid then and there, and in advance. The Jayhawkers had come too far, and had been away from home too long, to be thwarted thus at the final stage of their journey. The ferryman and his crew were carried bodily ashore, Lieutenant DeWitt C. Taylor of Company A took the wheel, the mechanics and blacksmiths of the regiment manned the boiler and engine, and in no time at all, the entire regiment was ferried over to the Kansas side. It was met at the landing by a large delegation of the leading citizens of Leavenworth and the highest ranking officers from the fort, and it was escorted to Fort Leavenworth by two squadrons of cavalry amid the "booming of cannon and almost deafening demonstrations of joy." [52]

The reception the regiment received at the ferry landing above Fort Leavenworth was only a small foretaste of the glories to come. It had

52. *Ibid.*, 204.

been known in Leavenworth for some days that the Seventh was coming home, or, as Julia Lovejoy put it, "the tell-tale wires had told the citizens of Leavenworth that the 'jayhawk regiment' would soon be in their streets." [53] The city fathers, in an expansive mood, had voted the sum of eight hundred dollars to cover the expenses of a fittingly splendid reception, and a committee of civic leaders was appointed to draw up the programme. And so, when the Jayhawkers reached Fort Leavenworth all was in readiness to receive them.

February 6 was a gala day in the history of the Seventh Kansas and of the city of Leavenworth. The town was astir at an early hour. Flags were flying from housetops and hanging from windows, and hotels and stores were decorated with bunting. At nine o'clock, the First Regiment, Kansas State Militia, boasting no fewer than four colonels on its roster, marched up Broadway and took station at the city limits to await the arrival of the honored guests. Shortly thereafter the Seventh, preceded by a military guard of honor, emerged from the main gate of Fort Leavenworth to the sound of cannon and began its march to the city. At the head of the parade was Colonel Jennison "on a richly caparisoned horse, who seemed to understand the pomp and pride of war as well as his rider." [54] The guard of honor consisted of Jennison's Fifteenth Kansas, a section of artillery, and a detachment of the Invalid Corps. The Jayhawkers brought up the rear. When the parade reached the city limits, the militia regiment fell in at the head of the line, making the procession more than a mile long. Music was supplied by three regimental bands, including the band of the Seventh, playing martial and patriotic airs. The parade moved down Broadway, Osage, and Sixth streets to Delaware, amid the cheers and applause of the citizens, and came to a halt in front of Turner's Hall for the formalities of the civic welcome.

The committee in charge of planning the reception had decided by a majority of one that Anthony should welcome the Seventh on behalf of the city. As chief magistrate of Leavenworth and former lieutenant colonel of the regiment, he had a double claim to the privilege of making the principal speech of the occasion. But as mayor, Anthony had made bitter enemies. He was a candidate for reelection against powerful

53. Ibid.   54. Ibid.

opposition, and in that day in Kansas, political alliances and enmities governed much less important affairs than the choice of a speaker to occupy the center of the stage at a major civic event. The minority of the committee refused to accept the choice of the majority and proposed instead the name of Marcus J. Parrott, former member of the House of Representatives from Kansas. "To secure harmony" (or under pressure) the majority gave way, and the honor of welcoming the Seventh thus fell to Parrott.[55]

The ex-Congressman's speech was in every way worthy of the great occasion. He spoke at length of the regiment's gallant services, touched fittingly upon the battles of Corinth, Iuka, Byhalia, and the score of other hard-fought fields on which the Seventh had covered itself with honor; and in a few graceful words, he spoke of the fallen. Then, speaking directly to the Jayhawkers standing before him, he said: "If there have been those who censured you, let them remember your gallant services and be forever silent. . . . You have secured a prestige which makes you a terror to the foe wherever you may march. How noble is your example compared with those who remain at home and content themselves with censuring the Government that you are risking your lives to save."[56] Colonel Herrick, as was only fitting, responded on behalf of the Seventh to Parrott's welcoming address. He reminded the audience:

The efforts of Hunter and Fremont to strike at the root of the rebellion were over-ruled by the Government, which did not then recognize the fact that Slavery was the cause of the war. Since then the President and people have declared that they will extend the Constitution over every foot of national soil and obliterate slavery in every State. The praise which I award the Seventh Kansas is that they were the first of all to recognize the great fact which was at the bottom of this rebellion. This regiment stood alone for months in refusing to return fugitive slaves. . . . We left Kansas under a ban as anti-slavery men. But we lived it down and fought it down. The army now all believe what we believed then.[57]

The selection of ex-Congressman Parrott to welcome the Seventh on behalf of the city had not been effected without a struggle, but the choice

55. Unidentified clipping, Jennison Scrapbook.
56. Leavenworth *Conservative*, February 7, 1864, clipping *ibid.*
57. *Ibid.*

of Jennison to welcome the regiment on behalf of "The Soldiers of Kansas" was unanimous. When Herrick had responded to Parrott's welcome, Jennison addressed the "Soldiers and Brothers of the Seventh":

This to me is a pleasure beyond expectation. When I stand here and attempt to talk to my old soldiers it almost unmans me. The times are changed since eight years ago when you and I were denounced as outlaws and thieves for sustaining the principles of Freedom. Let us carry this title of "Jayhawker" to glory and honor. . . . I claim that the Seventh Kansas is one of the bravest and best regiments that have ever entered the field. . . . I have another regiment now, the Fifteenth. They are not equal to the Seventh, but Jennison will soon cultivate them. The Fifteenth is organized on the Jayhawking principle. Some men are inclined to weaken on Jayhawking. I am not. When properly construed it simply means the most speedy and effectual way of putting down the rebellion.[58]

Jennison's speech brought the oratory to a close. And now the Seventh marched to Laing's Hall, where a sumptuous dinner, described as being "as fine as the best hotels could furnish," awaited them and the six hundred invited guests. The hall had been decorated for the festive event; the Stars and Stripes were festooned along the walls and over the ceiling, and shields bearing the names of the states in which the Seventh had fought, and the names of the principal battles in which it had participated, were affixed to the national ensigns. At one end of the hall was a large streamer bearing the legend: "Jennison—Lee—Herrick— Always in the Front"; and facing it on the opposite wall was another, with the words "D. R. Anthony, Mayor—Welcome Gallant Seventh— Again to the Field—New Triumphs Await You" blazoned upon it.[59]

The dinner, which contrary to the customs of a later day was not followed by oratory, concluded the official festivities for the enlisted men. It was understood that for the rest of the day and evening, the freedom of the city was theirs, to enjoy the more than ample facilities for the entertainment of returning heroes that Leavenworth had to offer. Simeon Fox remarks, no doubt justly, that any formal bestowal of the freedom of the city on the Seventh would have been superfluous, "for the boys would have taken it anyhow."[60] But for the officers there was another treat in store. The officers of the First Kansas Militia Regiment

58. *Ibid.*   59. *Ibid.*
60. Fox, "Story," 42.

gave an "impromptu hop" in honor of their "brethren of the sword," the officers of the Seventh Kansas. The pleasures of the evening can best be described in the words of a contemporary newspaper report:

The boys of the Seventh were as gallant and agreeable to the ladies, as they are brave and fearless in the field, the softer sex smiling their welcome and approbation with a fascination that could not be otherwise than agreeable to the brave fellows, whose devotion and courage have been tried upon many a hard contested field. We noticed in the assemblage representatives of all the military and civil dignitaries of the city, interspersed with our most prominent citizens. The gallant little jayhawker was conspicuous among the sea of crinoline and regulation blue. Dancing was kept up to the enlivening strains of stirring music, until the hour hand of the clock warned the merry meeting that another morn had ushered in its pleasures, vicissitudes and sorrows.[61]

For the Veteran Seventh, reassembled at Fort Leavenworth and quartered in comfortable new barracks furnished with stoves for cooking and heating, the morn of the new day—the seventh of February—brought neither vicissitudes nor sorrows, but only pleasures. The morning was devoted to the issuance of furlough papers, and by the end of the day the regiment had disbanded and all its members were homeward bound to enjoy, in Fletcher Pomeroy's words, "peace, comfort and rest after the marches and conflicts of $2\frac{1}{2}$ years."[62]

61. Unidentified clipping, Jennison Scrapbook.
62. Pomeroy, "War Diary," entry for February 7, 1864.

CHAPTER XIV

Return
to
Battle

THE FUNCTIONS of the regimental historian are necessarily in abeyance while the men of his regiment are scattered far and wide, enjoying a long furlough. Letters to be saved for posterity are not written and no entries are made in diaries while the troopers revel in the comforts of home in the villages and farmhouses of Kansas, Illinois, and Ohio, and support as best they can the solicitous ministrations of families and friends. But a furlough of even a month passes swiftly, and on March 13 the Jayhawkers began to reassemble at Fort Leavenworth. In keeping with his position of regimental quartermaster, Fletcher Pomeroy was one of the first to return. After arriving at the fort on Sunday, March 13, he tried to have issued to him the blankets and mess boxes belonging to the regiment that had been left there in storage, but the officers on duty refused to transact business on a Sunday. Pomeroy was himself a sabbatarian, but the prospect of having to sleep without blankets in unheated barracks made him wish that the observance of the Sabbath on the part of the officers at the fort had been rather less strict. His own furlough had been a happy one—he called it "the happiest period of [his] life"—but perhaps not surprisingly, he found that it felt good to be back in harness, and many of the Jayhawkers shared his feeling.[1] It says much for the morale

1. Pomeroy, "War Diary," entry for March 10, 1864.

of the regiment that Pomeroy could write: "It seems good to meet again as a regiment. It is like a family of brothers meeting. The first question of all is how did you enjoy your furlough, and the invariable answer is, the best kind." [2]

Certain of the comrades may not have shared completely the pleasurable feelings with which the Jayhawkers resumed their companionship-in-arms. Webster Moses was probably one of the exceptions. In September, 1861, he had written the first of his many letters to Nancy Mowry, back in Bureau County, Illinois. Nancy's two brothers, George and Welcome, were members of the Seventh, but it was not their presence in the regiment that made Moses so regular a correspondent. Far from it. The cheerful, chatty letters he wrote Nancy in a beautifully disciplined Spencerian hand over a period of more than two years nearly always bore the restrained superscription "Dear Friend," expanded in more daring moments to "Dear Friend Nancy." But in the case of Webster Moses and Nancy Mowry, absence had indeed made the heart grow fonder. Their long separation, followed by his furlough, had wrought a special miracle, and the first of his postfurlough letters, written on the very day of his arrival at Fort Leavenworth, is addressed to "Dearest Nancy." In the succeeding months of a renewed separation, Moses retreated to a more cautious and reserved "Dear Nancy" or "My Dear Nancy." But the furlough had brought him and Nancy to an understanding, and in due course "Dear Nancy" blossomed into "My own dear Nancy" and eventually into "My dear wife." But that happy consummation was another long year away, and in the meantime, the only one of his letters addressed to "Dearest Nancy" said: "I will not attempt to describe my feelings when I left you. I knew not how much I loved you and I hope we may not be separated *very* long. I look forward to the future hopefully and shall spend my life in making you happy." [3]

Those of the Jayhawkers who had the opportunity to do so during their furlough, had endeavored to obtain recruits to fill up the sadly shrunken ranks of the regiment. Their efforts were conspicuously successful; when the veterans reassembled at Fort Leavenworth, 120 recruits were already there to greet them. One of the newcomers, signed up

2. *Ibid.*, entry for March 15, 1864.
3. Webster Moses to Nancy Mowry, March 13, 1864, in Moses Letters.

under rather unconventional circumstances, was an eighteen-year-old lad who had enlisted on February 19; he was mustered in on February 24 and assigned to Company H.[4] His name was William F. Cody, a name that became internationally famous under the variant of "Buffalo Bill" Cody. Buffalo Bill had been a Pony Express rider at the age of fifteen. In the fall and winter of 1861, aged sixteen, he was a member of an "independent company" of Kansans, organized by one Chandler, "for the purpose of invading Missouri and making war upon its people"; needless to say, the real object of the Chandler gang was the large-scale stealing of horses and cattle in Missouri, in imitation of Marshall Cleveland's exploits in the same line of endeavor. After the Chandler gang was broken up by government detectives, Cody worked for a time for Wild Bill Hickok, and then, in the winter of 1862–1863, he joined the Red Legs. The following winter he was in Leavenworth, and in the words of his autobiography, he "entered upon a dissolute and reckless life . . . and associated with gamblers, drunkards and bad characters generally. I continued my dissipation about two months and was becoming a very hard case."[5] Cody had several friends and old neighbors in the Seventh who did their best to persuade him to enlist in the regiment. He would have none of it, but the Jayhawkers were too much for him. "One day," his autobiography continues, "after having been under the influence of bad whiskey, I awoke to find myself a soldier in the Seventh Kansas. I did not remember how or when I had enlisted."[6] Having waited until February, 1864, to contribute his assistance to the restoration of the Union, Cody could not properly claim patriotism as the reason for his enlistment; nonetheless, the candor of his account is as impressive as it is unconventional, especially in the light of the general unreliability of his successive "autobiographies." Having exhausted his severely limited stock of veracity with the story of his enlistment, Cody's tales of his exploits as a member of the regiment become pure fantasy, tainted only slightly by reality.

While the Seventh was still on furlough, Major General Samuel R. Curtis, in command of the Department of Kansas, applied to the War Department for authority to retain the regiment in his department when

4. *Report of the Adjutant General of the State of Kansas*, I, 625.
5. Quoted in Russell, *Buffalo Bill*, 61.   6. *Ibid.*

it reassembled. General Halleck, to whom Curtis' request was ultimately referred for decision, had evidently not forgotten the tribulations the Jayhawkers had caused him two years before and had no intention of allowing them to be stationed in the tempting proximity of Missouri. General Curtis' request was firmly denied, and he was directed to return the Seventh to its "former command."[7] Meanwhile, the Jayhawkers had reassembled and, amid rumors that they were to be sent to New Orleans, were having a pleasant rest while awaiting their departure. There was much dancing in the mess hall; Webster Moses complained that the music of the violin and the "heavy tramping of the dancers" confused his mind while he was trying to write to Nancy; but, he added, "soldiers have to get used to most everything."[8] Those with more sedentary inclinations played cards or sat around the stove telling stories. As old campaigners, the Jayhawkers had "become used to delays and disappointments" and they had learned that "part of the disaplin of a good soldier [is] to be contented any where and under any circumstances."[9]

The period of waiting ended on March 21. At noon that day the regiment left Leavenworth aboard the steamer *Isabella* "amid the cheers and blessings of the citizens who thronged the shore."[10] It was given out that the regiment was to proceed to St. Louis to pick up new arms, horses, and accoutrements, and was then to go on to Memphis. The journey down the Missouri was made in the period of low water between the January thaw and the summer rise caused by the melting of the snow in the Rockies and was not free from difficulties and dangers. One can do no better than to let Fletcher Pomeroy tell the story of the five-day trip:

[March 21] We stopped a short time at Kansas City. About dusk we reached Independence Landing where we have tied up for the night as it is dangerous to run on this river after dark, on account of the numerous snags, and the ever shifting channel, and bars. It has been cold all day. The boiler deck, and upper deck, have been crowded with our men, and some are on the hurricane deck. [March 22] It snowed some last night and those who slept out on the decks were covered with two inches of snow. . . . Sandbars in the river are covered with

7. *Official Records*, XXXIV, Pt. 2, 606.
8. Webster Moses to Nancy Mowry, March 19, 1864, in Moses Letters.
9. Same to same, March 20, 1864, *ibid.*
10. Pomeroy, "War Diary," entry for March 21, 1864.

wild geese, ducks, geese, brants and swans; they are so numerous that when they rise on our approach they fill the air. [March 24, below Jefferson City] At 10:30 our boat grounded on a bar and it was 3:40 P. M. when she got afloat again. [March 25] At 10:30 A. M. got on a sand bar which delayed us two hours and a half. After getting afloat we proceeded with but little trouble till 3 P. M. when we got aground again and were till after dark getting loose. [March 26] We were under headway at daylight, and soon after sunrise passed St. Charles. About 10 A. M. we struck heavy on a sandbar, but our boat swung around and got loose. She then landed and we all went ashore and walked around the bar and thus lightened of her load she passed over it all right. At 11 A. M. we entered the Mississippi and at 1 P. M. reached St. Louis.[11]

There was one untoward incident on this trip which Pomeroy does not mention at all and which Moses refers to only in a roundabout fashion. The latter wrote that there had been "some trouble with a fiew drunken raskalls" on the way.[12] The "trouble" was rather more serious than one would gather from Moses' casual mention of it. It appears that Privates George D. Bate, Henry S. Cline, and John Ratliff, all of Company B, celebrated their imminent return to the wars with more enthusiasm than discretion. On the first day out from Leavenworth they got drunk, or perhaps were already drunk when they came on board. In their drunken state, they decided that they had a grievance against Colonel Herrick and invaded the cabin of the *Isabella* with "loud and threatening" cries of "Down with Herrick . . . Throw him overboard . . . Let's put him off the boat, by God!" and other expressions of a similarly mutinous import. Eventually they were quieted down, and in May, while the regiment was still in St. Louis, they were tried before a general court-martial on charges of drunkenness, disorderly conduct, and resisting the lawful authority of their commanding officer. All three were found guilty. Bate and Cline were sentenced to a year's imprisonment at hard labor in the military prison at Alton, Illinois, and "to wear a ball and chain weighing fifty-six pounds attached to . . . [the] left leg, the chain to be not more than six feet long, and to forfeit to the government all pay and allowances for . . . one (1) year." Ratliff too was sentenced to a year's imprisonment, but without the added severity of the ball and chain. On review, the penalty of having to wear a ball and

11. *Ibid.*, entries for March 21, 22, 24, and 25, 1864.
12. Webster Moses to Nancy Mowry, April 24, 1864, in Moses Letters.

chain was stricken from Bate's and Cline's sentences also.[13] Nevertheless, the punishment meted out for a drunken frolic was severe enough.

The fate of the Seventh for the two months following its arrival in St. Louis can only be described as deplorable. Scheduled to pause there only long enough to receive weapons, equipment, and horses, the regiment had to remain in St. Louis in idleness for two months because neither weapons, nor equipment, nor horses were to be had. In the meantime, Generals Hurlbut, Grierson, and Washburn, beset by Forrest in western Tennessee, were proclaiming in a stream of doleful despatches their inability to deal with the wily and aggressive Confederate chieftain because of the absence of their veteran regiments of cavalry, the Seventh Kansas prominent among them. Typical of these despatches is Hurlbut's message to Major General McPherson that "at present the force about Memphis . . . is not more than adequate for defense, and will so continue until the return to this post of the veteran cavalry."[14]

Meanwhile, the Seventh endured a life of misery in St. Louis. The same administrative breakdown that caused the regiment to be kept dangling about the city for two months before it was reequipped for the field, also caused it to undergo privations and hardships that in the fourth year of the war could and should have been avoided. Lack of adequate shelter, for example, which was excusable in the chaotic conditions of the summer of 1861, should not have been a problem in April and May, 1864, but it was. The regiment disembarked in East St. Louis on March 26, and was directed to camp on Bloody Island, where there were no quarters, shelter, or camp facilities to receive it. The inevitable result was a wave of sickness of epidemic proportions, especially among the recruits, four of whom died of smallpox and "fever."[15] Second only to the lack of proper camp facilities was the debilitating effect of sheer boredom. There was simply nothing for the men to do. Routine camp duties and

---

13. General Orders No. 5, Headquarters, West Division, Cavalry Bureau, St. Louis, May 11, 1864, in Seventh Kansas, Company Order Books. In these orders, Bate's name is spelled Bates and Cline's Kline. The presumably correct spelling of the names in *Report of the Adjutant General of the State of Kansas*, I, 546 and 548, is followed in the text. All three culprits were mustered out with the regiment in 1865.

14. *Official Records*, XXXII, Pt. 3, 317–18.

15. General Orders No. 4, April 3, 1864, in Seventh Kansas, Regimental Order Book. The orders called for reveille at daylight, officers' drill at 7:45 A.M., regimental drill at 9 A.M. and 2 P.M., noncommissioned officers' drill at 4 P.M., and officers' school three evenings a week.

a few hours of so-called drill were a poor substitute for worthwhile occupation, drill especially so, for most of the Jayhawkers were veterans with three years of service behind them.[16] And to add an extra dimension of dreariness and mockery to the drill, it had to be performed without weapons and without horses. Moses, forgetting for the moment that the mark of a good soldier was to be contented anywhere and under any circumstances, complained that "to lie in camp without any thing to do . . . is the bane of a soldiers life."[17]

The most serious shortage preventing the reequipment of the regiment was that of horses. The St. Louis quartermasters were receiving about one hundred cavalry mounts daily, but when the Jayhawkers arrived there were already six cavalry regiments in and about the city waiting for horses, and with each regiment needing about six hundred mounts, the Seventh faced a long delay. The men were thrown largely on their own resources to fill up their time, and the ways they chose or found to keep occupied were amazing in their variety. Fletcher Pomeroy, his brother Emerson, and two other members of Company D went in for self-improvement; they signed up for a penmanship course in St. Louis at a fee of three dollars per man for a course of thirty lessons. Passes to visit the sights of St. Louis—the largest city most of the Jayhawkers had ever seen—were freely granted, and Barnum's menagerie in particular was one of the principal attractions. Many a postwar fireside must have been beguiled by tales of the marvels exhibited by Mr. Barnum: the hippopotamus, the twenty-eight-year-old Asiatic giant, eight feet tall and weighing 475 pounds, the thirty-foot-long anaconda, the sixteen-year-old Illinois girl who weighed four hundred pounds, and lastly, Barnum's "celebrated 'What is it.'"[18] On May 17 the Great Mississippi Valley Sanitary Fair opened with a parade of cavalry, infantry, artillery, militia, fire companies, and citizens, and with ceremonies graced by singing, prayers, and the oratory of General Rosecrans, who had been exiled to the command of the Department of Missouri after his

16. Webster Moses to Nancy Mowry, April 14, 1864, in Moses Letters; Pomeroy, "War Diary," entry for April 20, 1864; C. H. Lovejoy to his wife and son, April 26, 1864, in "Letters of Julia Lovejoy," 206.

17. Webster Moses to Nancy Mowry, April 24, 1864, in Moses Letters.

18. Pomeroy, "War Diary," entry for April 29, 1864. In one of his rare lapses, Pomeroy spells hippopotamus "hypotamus."

defeat at Chickamauga. Singly, in groups, and eventually as a regimental unit, the Jayhawkers visited the fair.

But the frivolities and cultural diversions offered by St. Louis were not the only outlet for the Jayhawkers' energies while they waited for their gear. Perhaps as an after effect of the month they had just spent with their families, or because of the sobering prospect of returning to the hazards of active service, the Seventh experienced a collective urge for moral improvement and found itself in the grip of a religious revival. Chaplain Lovejoy happily reported to his wife and son that "there is a decided improvement in the morrals of the Reg. Quite a religious influence in Camp. At our prayer meeting 7 arose for prayer, with tears in their eyes told me that they were resolved to lead new & Christian lives. There is every prospect of a revival. . . . I expect to draw one or two Hospital tents to-day for the purpose of haveing them to hold meetings in. . . . The Col. appears willing to aid me in any thing I desin, to prosicute my work as Chap." [19] A chaplain's glowing report of a new-found dedication to morality and religion among the men entrusted to his spiritual care may be suspected of excessive optimism; actually, however, there is ample testimony to support Chaplain Lovejoy's assertions. Webster Moses wrote Nancy Mowry that there was "scarcely no drinking at all" in Company D, and that there was even "an anti-tobacco pledge in the Co and several old tobacco users have sined it." [20] There is a hint in this that there might have been words on the subject of the tobacco habit between Webster and Nancy while the former was at home and that the virtuous Webster was himself a recent convert. In any event, Webster may have been premature in concluding that "when we return home we will be *partly* sivilised at least." [21] Fletcher Pomeroy noted that on April 12 a regimental temperance meeting was held; fifty-seven Jayhawkers, "some of them of very intemperate habits," signed the temperance pledge there and then.[22] Eventually, the number of signers increased to two hundred, and even Colonel Herrick promised to add his name to the list; whether he actually did so the records do not disclose. A committee was appointed to draw up a constitution for the regimental

19. C. H. Lovejoy to his wife and son, April 26, 1864, in "Letters of Julia Lovejoy," 205–206.
20. Webster Moses to Nancy Mowry, March 19, 1864, and April 24, 1864, in Moses Letters.
21. Same to same, April 24, 1864, *ibid.*
22. Pomeroy, "War Diary," entry for April 12, 1864.

temperance society, which continued to hold regular meetings while the regiment remained in St. Louis.

However earnest and laudable such activities may have been, they contributed little if anything to the defeat of the Confederacy. While the Seventh was whiling away the time at Camp Gamble, Grant began the Wilderness Campaign against Lee's army in Virginia, and Sherman started his massive advance against Atlanta and the Confederate Army of Tennessee. Meanwhile, by order of General Rosecrans, one hundred "of the most reliable and trusty men" of the Seventh, "chosen for their sobriety, trustworthiness, and promptness in obeying orders," were armed with infantry muskets, issued a hundred rounds of ammunition apiece, and held in readiness for immediate departure to assist the authorities in enforcing the draft in Callaway County, Missouri.[23] As it turned out, the enrolling officers were adequately guarded by the Missouri State Militia, and the services of the Seventh to deal with the Callaway County Copperheads were not needed. A little later, when a squad of guerillas was reported to be operating in Franklin County, about fifty miles southwest of St. Louis, two companies of the Seventh, led by Captain William S. Moorhouse of Company B, were sent there with orders to wipe them out.[24] Unfortunately, six days were allowed to elapse between the time the guerillas were first reported in the county and the issuance of orders to the Seventh to send two companies after them, and by the time Moorhouse arrived in Franklin County the guerillas had of course disappeared.[25] The futility of such incidents fully justified Webster Moses' remark that "we might be of more service to Government if we were sent south where we are needed more than here in St. Louis."[26]

On May 11 the Seventh was at last issued its full quota of horses, saddles, and tack, but as yet it was without weapons of any kind. Five days later, Fletcher Pomeroy drew light cavalry sabers for the regiment at the St. Louis arsenal, and in the following week carbines were issued to the men. The Seventh was thus once again in condition for active duty. It was high time, for on May 27 General Halleck telegraphed peremp-

23. *Official Records*, XXXIV, Pt. 3, 348.   24. *Ibid.*, 655.
25. *Official Records*, XXXIV, Pt. 4, 33–34.
26. Webster Moses to Nancy Mowry, May 19, 1864, in Moses Letters.

tory orders in the name of the secretary of war to General Rosecrans to send the Seventh at once to Major General E. R. S. Canby, in command of the Department of the Gulf; Rosecrans was told that if the regiment could not at once be mounted and equipped as cavalry, it was to be equipped as infantry and sent forward as such; and to make certain that these orders were executed without the procrastination that generally attended the transfer of troops from one department commander to another, Rosecrans was directed to telegraph daily to the adjutant general of the army a report of the progress made in equipping and forwarding the regiment.[27] Fortunately for the Seventh, it had received its horses, cavalry weapons, and accoutrements when these orders arrived in St. Louis and was thereby spared the ignominy suffered by several other cavalry regiments in the Union army, of being turned into foot-soldiers. For Rosecrans wasted no time in acting on Halleck's orders. On May 28 Colonel Herrick was directed to get ready for an immediate departure; the following day, orders were sent to Captain Moorhouse to rejoin the regiment at once with his two companies.[28] On May 31, Companies C, G, and K marched aboard the steamer *G. W. Graham* and started downriver under command of Major Malone; they were followed the next day by Companies D, E, and F aboard the *Belle of St. Louis* and, on June 6, by Companies A and H and regimental headquarters aboard the *G. E. Hillman*. Companies B and I, which came back from the expedition to Franklin County with the credit of having "mustered out" two Missouri guerillas, had to remain behind in St. Louis until June 10, for lack of transportation.[29]

On June 11 the entire regiment, including the "bobtails" who had been left behind when the veterans went home on furlough nearly five months before, were reunited at Memphis. The orders directing the Seventh to New Orleans had been cancelled; the Jayhawkers were needed in West Tennessee. Camp was established in a grove of trees two and a half miles northeast of the city, in a location which Pomeroy described as low, damp, and unhealthy, whereas Moses thought that it was a pleasant place.

The spring of 1864 had been an evil time for the Union cause in west-

---

27. *Official Records*, XXXIV, Pt. 4, 64. 28. *Ibid.*, 85.
29. *Ibid.*, 200.

ern Tennessee, and all because of one man: Nathan Bedford Forrest. Ever since his return to the area in November, 1863, his ceaseless raids and incursions had kept the Federal command in a constant state of alarm, and their efforts to dispose of him, or at least to contain him, invariably ended in failure. Brigadier General William Sooy Smith, at the head of 7,500 well-mounted and well-armed cavalry, tried to "pitch into Forrest," only to be beaten at Okolona, Mississippi, on February 22 and forced to retreat to Memphis with his command "worn and weary, and sadly demoralized, and almost dismounted . . . broken in spirit and sadly weakened in discipline."[30] Equally unsuccessful were the poorly co-ordinated efforts of the Federals to intercept Forrest's raid to Paducah, Kentucky, in March. Then in April came the capture of Fort Pillow and the massacre of its garrison.[31]

General Sherman, busy with plans for his march to Atlanta, had Forrest as one of his major preoccupations; Forrest could not be left in a position from which he could raid the railroads from Louisville to Nashville and Chattanooga and thus interrupt the flow of supplies Sherman needed for his 100,000 men and 35,000 animals.[32] Sherman was satisfied that neither Hurlbut, in command at Memphis, nor Grierson, Hurlbut's chief of cavalry, had the energy, determination, and skill needed to hold Forrest in check. He was not at all impressed by their anguished despatches blaming all their misfortunes on the absence of their veteran cavalry regiments.[33] He decided that a change in command was necessary, and on April 18 he replaced Hurlbut with Major General Cadwallader C. Washburn. On the same day, Grierson was superseded by an officer well known to the Seventh, none other than Brigadier General Samuel D. Sturgis. Sherman's orders to Sturgis were explicit; he

30. Waring, *Whip and Spur*, 125.

31. An interesting example of "objectivity" will be found in the treatment of the Fort Pillow massacre in Henry's otherwise splendid *Forrest*, 248 *et seq.*, a fascinating exercise in the manipulation of evidence to prove a preconceived conclusion.

32. "The Atlanta campaign would simply have been impossible without the use of the railroads from Louisville to Nashville . . . [and] from Nashville to Chattanooga . . . and from Chattanooga to Atlanta." See William T. Sherman, *Memoirs* (Bloomington, 1957), II, 399.

33. *Official Records*, XXXII, Pt. 2, 217, 275, 317, and 406. General Sherman was not at all impressed with these excuses. On one of Hurlbut's despatches he commented, "Hurlbut has full 10,000 men at Memphis, but if he had a million, he would be on the defensive." See *ibid.*, 382.

was to move out, attack Forrest wherever he could be found, and whip him. The intent of Sherman's orders was plain enough; their execution, however, proved to be quite difficult. Sturgis' first expedition against Forrest, at the beginning of May, failed to bring the elusive raider to bay. On June 1, as the first three companies of the Seventh were about to arrive in Memphis, Sturgis started out on a second expedition at the head of the largest and best equipped force that had been assembled up to that time to hunt Forrest: 3,500 cavalry, 5,000 infantry (including Colonel Edward Bouton's brigade of Negro troops), 22 guns, and 250 wagons. But Sturgis fared no better than Streight or Smith had done. He suffered a crushing defeat at Brice's Crossroads on June 10, and was driven back to Memphis with the loss of 2,200 men killed, wounded, or captured, minus all his artillery, 200 wagons loaded with ammunition and rations, and his reputation.

This was the situation in West Tennessee as the successive detachments of the Seventh went into camp at Memphis. On July 12, when the first reports of Sturgis' defeat reached them, the Jayhawkers, drawing on their memories of Jennison's difficulties with Sturgis two years before, had a ready explanation for the disaster. Webster Moses wrote that "Gen Sturgis is considered a Copperhead and some think he sold his command. . . . We hope the Government will put all such Generals as Sturgis out of office that they have so long disgraced." [34] And he added nine days later, perhaps reflecting the feelings of Sturgis' own troops: "Gen Sturgis late disaster or rather traitorous surrender has not been as bad as at first supposed. . . . No one here doubts that he intended to surrender the whole force to Forrest. . . . the colored troops were especially obnoxious to Sturgis while they fought with a bravery that will stop the tale that Negroes will not fight." [35]

The unusual vindictiveness of Moses' comments is indicative of a new bitterness, reminiscent of Missouri in the winter of 1861–1862, that had crept into the fighting in West Tennessee following the Fort Pillow massacre. It was firmly believed on the Union side, and apparently with some justification, that at Brice's Crossroads also Negro

34. Webster Moses to Nancy Mowry, June 12, 1864, in Moses Letters.
35. Same to same, June 21, 1864, *ibid.*

soldiers had been refused quarter or had been killed after they surrendered.[36] It was not long before the Seventh was caught up in the
deadly business of retaliation that ensued.

On June 16 Colonel Herrick was ordered to leave Memphis at dawn
the next day, with three days' rations and one hundred rounds of ammunition per man, to patrol the roads in the neighborhood of Colliersville
and Lafayette as part of a concerted movement ordered by General
Sherman to defeat Forrest "at any cost."[37] In compliance with these
orders, the Jayhawkers set up camp near Moscow, Tennessee, and sent
out company-strength scouting parties in all directions. Within ten
days thereafter, Moses wrote Nancy Mowry that "the Rebs are getting
desperate—here they generaly shoot all the prisoners they capture espe-
cialy of our cavalry and we of course retaliate[.] some of Co B captured
a confederate captain here a few days ago and it is supposed shot him as
they did not bring him in. While we were at LaFayette Co A shot 4 men
the Rebs killed 6 prisoners near Colliersville a few days ago. They never
can take any of us alive for if they do we know our fate."[38] One is
tempted not to believe such atrocity stories and to suppose that they are
based on that most prolific source of misinformation, camp gossip. But
there was a substratum of fact in Moses' grim report, for on June 30
Forrest wrote Major General Andrew J. Smith, who had replaced the
luckless Sturgis, that "I have received information of the killing (after
capture) of several of my scouts. . . . Two of my scouts were captured
and killed by the Ninth Illinois Cavalry, and one by the Seventh Kansas,
whose major I learn has vowed to kill every man they find in Confederate
uniform. I do not intend acting hastily, but . . . I shall hold . . . all the
officers captured at [Brice's Crossroads] as hostages, and shall certainly
execute them man for man, or in any other proportion to stop it."[39]

Smith of course denied that any of Forrest's men had been killed after
being taken prisoner. He informed Forrest that he had examined "both
officers and men of the Seventh Kansas Cavalry and the Ninth Illinois
Cavalry, and they deny positively having participated in, or having any

36. See the extensive correspondence between Washburn and Forrest on this subject in
Official Records, XXXII, Pt. 1, 586–93.
37. *Official Records*, XXXIX, Pt. 2, 155.
38. Webster Moses to Nancy Mowry, June 26, 1864, in Moses Letters.
39. Official Records, XXXIX, Pt. 2, 155.

knowledge of, any such occurrence."[40] The reader will make his own choice between Webster Moses' report and General Smith's.

With Sherman moving ever deeper into Georgia—his headquarters were at Big Shanty, a short distance above Marietta, when news of Sturgis' discomfiture reached him—Forrest could not be allowed to remain as a perpetual threat to the railroads on which the success of the campaign depended. As soon as he learned of Sturgis' defeat, Sherman ordered Washburn to collect a force under General A. J. Smith to go after Forrest. He made it crystal clear that he meant business, writing to Secretary Stanton that Smith was to "go out and follow Forrest to the death if it costs 10,000 lives and breaks the Treasury."[41] Urged from all sides to make haste, Washburn acted with remarkable despatch, and as a result of his efforts, Smith was able to leave Memphis on June 25 at the head of nine thousand infantry, three thousand cavalry, and four batteries of artillery to "follow Forrest to the death."[42] Smith's plan of campaign was to march eastward along the Memphis and Charleston Railroad to Corinth and then south along the Mobile and Ohio Railroad to Tupelo and beyond, where he expected to find and strike Forrest's forces. As usual, with his scouts blanketing West Tennessee, Forrest was fully posted on Smith's numbers, plans, destination, and progress, and was quite willing to be found.

Had he but known it, Smith had an advantage in his campaign against Forrest that neither Streight nor Sooy Smith nor Sturgis had possessed. That advantage was the presence under his command of Private William F. Cody, Seventh Kansas Cavalry. Cody (but no one else) tells us:

While we were mobilizing near Memphis, Colonel Herrick of our regiment recommended me to General A. J. Smith for membership in a picked corps to be used for duty as scouts, messengers and dispatch carriers. Colonel Herrick recounted my history as a plainsman, which convinced the commander that I would be useful in this special line of duty. When I reported to General Smith . . . he instructed me to disguise myself as a Tennessee boy, to provide myself with a farm horse from the stock in the camp, and to try to locate Forrest's main command. . . . I was to gather all the information possible concerning the

40. *Ibid.*, 162.
41. *Official Records*, XXXVIII, Pt. 4, 480.
42. *Official Records*, XXXIX, Pt. 2, 139.

enemy's strength . . . and to make my way back as speedily as possible. . . . Following a wagon road that led to the south, I made nearly sixty miles the first night. . . . [Smith] was much pleased with my report, which proved to be extremely accurate and valuable.[43]

A "farm horse" capable of covering "nearly sixty miles" in a short summer night must have been a Bucephalus indeed. But Cody's contributions to the Union cause were not merely martial; they were also humanitarian. In the course of these operations, he found occasion to protect from some of General Smith's evil-disposed cavalrymen, a Mississippi plantation and its inhabitants, who, we learn with no surprise whatever, were "a handsome old lady and her two attractive daughters." By doing so, Cody earned the gratitude of the three ladies as well as the commendation of General Smith, who said to Cody: "My boy, you may be too good-hearted for a soldier, but you have done just what I would have done. My orders are to destroy all Southern property. But we will forget your violation of them."[44]

The Seventh was in camp along the Memphis and Charleston Railroad at LaGrange when Smith's movement began. Peaches were ripe and apples nearly so in nearby secessionist orchards, and new potatoes could be dug in the dark of the moon in secessionist gardens. The constant scouting was a welcome change after two months of idleness and boredom in St. Louis. The regiment lived well enough, the time passed quickly, and the news from Grant's and Sherman's armies was sufficiently favorable to cause the Jayhawkers to believe that the war could not last much longer. The Glorious Fourth was celebrated with much beating of drums and the playing of "Yankee Doodle" and other national tunes by the regimental band, "while a few of the boys more patriotic than the rest or for mischief occasionally discharge[d] their carbines and hurrah[ed] for the Union."[45]

On July 5 Smith started out on the southward leg of his march against Forrest. The Seventh, as part of the cavalry division led by

43. Cody, *Autobiography*, 63–68.

44. *Ibid.*, 70–72. The present writer is not alone in his scepticism about these tales. Russell, *Buffalo Bill*, 276, comments about this "*Autobiography*," that "of all the books signed by Cody, it would seem least likely that he should have written this one, for it contains many blunders that Bill could not have made."

45. Webster Moses to Nancy Mowry, June 24–July 4, 1864, in Moses Letters.

General Grierson, who was back in favor after Sturgis' fiasco, left its pleasant camp at LaGrange and moved forward over familiar country, through Ripley and New Albany toward Pontotoc. Forrest promptly sent forward two divisions of cavalry under Abraham Buford and James R. Chalmers to badger the flanks and rear of Smith's advance and hinder his progress as much as possible without bringing on a general engagement. Grierson's job was to cope with Buford's and Chalmers' horsemen. For the first six days of the march, as far south as Pontotoc, the Jayhawkers were detached from the cavalry division and acted as advance guard for the infantry column. Until July 11 they met with little opposition. Nonetheless, on the seventh, they came close to being disgraced forever. Seventeen men of Company H had been detailed to drive a herd of beef cattle intended to be slaughtered on the march to feed the infantry. The men of Company H had had more experience in driving beef cattle than most cavalrymen, but owing to the natural contrariness of the animals and their unwillingness to accept the axiom that a straight line is the shortest distance between two points, the seventeen cowboys pro tem fell farther and farther behind until they found themselves a considerable distance to the rear of the rear guard. They were promptly pounced upon by Confederate cavalry dogging the heels of Smith's advance. Scattered about the edges of the herd, the seventeen Jayhawkers were in no position to offer effective resistance; they were driven off, and the cattle passed into the possession of Forrest's troopers. For a regiment notorious for its cattle-rustling exploits to lose cattle entrusted to its care was an ignominy not to be borne. Before dawn the next day, Companies A, H, and I set off under command of Major Charles H. Gregory to recover the herd. Fortunately for the good repute of the regiment, the cattle had proven no more amenable to Confederate discipline than to Federal. The herd had not traveled far; Gregory and his men located it, drove off the Confederate herdsmen, and returned with the cattle in triumph.

On the tenth of July Smith's advance began to meet serious opposition. On that day, the Seventh had a sharp fight with Colonel Clark R. Barteau's Second Tennessee Cavalry of Buford's division and drove it out of the way. Forrest had the bulk of his force concentrated near Okolona. He sent Brigadier General James R. Chalmers forward to

Pontotoc with orders to take command of Abraham Buford's division in addition to his own and, with the two divisions of cavalry, to hold Smith in check for two days. Smith's advance was cautious but steady. On the morning of the eleventh, finding Chalmers' troopers blocking his way into Pontotoc, he used his cavalry, with the Jayhawkers again in the van, to brush them out of the way. This was successfully accomplished, and one of Chalmers' brigades then made a stand in the town itself. Smith ordered the Seventh, supported by a brigade of infantry, to attack the town from the north, while the main body of Grierson's cavalry attacked from the east. The two-pronged attack drove the Confederates out of the town. They retreated to Cherry Creek, six miles to the south, where they joined Forrest's main body, holding a well-prepared defensive position on a ridge protected in front by the marshy bottom land of two small creeks.

Forrest's hope that Smith would repeat Sturgis' mistake and attack him under conditions that gave him all the advantages of an excellent defensive position was to be disappointed. Smith was not only cautious, but he was also capable of a stratagem or two of his own. He scouted the Confederate position on the twelfth; and at dawn the next day, instead of playing into Forrest's hands by attacking him on ground of the latter's choosing, Smith made a ninety-degree turn to the left and, with his cavalry leading the way and his flanks well protected, marched eighteen miles to the east, to Tupelo. Smith expected that Forrest would pursue as soon as he discovered the Federal move and that the rear of the marching column would therefore be the most exposed and the most dangerous post. This post of honor was assigned to the Seventh.

Within a half-hour after Smith's army began its march to Tupelo, Forrest attacked its rear, and from five o'clock in the morning until eight in the evening, when the rearmost regiment of infantry reached Tupelo, the Seventh was constantly and heavily engaged. During the forenoon the Jayhawkers fought the Confederates singlehanded; later, Colonel Edward Bouton's brigade of Negro infantry, the only unit of Sturgis' army to come out of the battle of Brice's Crossroads with its reputation untarnished, was sent back to support them.[46] For most of the day the

---

46. Fox, "Story," 43. *Cf.* Webster Moses to Nancy Mowry, July 26, 1864, in Moses Letters; and Pomeroy, "War Diary," entry for July 13, 1864.

Confederates attacked in three widely separated columns, and it took all the skill the Seventh had acquired in its three years of service not merely to repel these attacks but also to hold off the attacking columns at an equal distance, for if one of them had been allowed to forge ahead of the others, it would have flanked the thin line of Jayhawkers blocking the advance of the other two. The Kansans occupied every hill, every grove of trees, and every patch of brush that favored the defense and held it to the last possible moment. Individual companies were detached to give the impression of a much larger force. Wherever the terrain, a bend in the road, or a stand of timber allowed, an ambush was laid to slow down the pursuit. Many of the Jayhawkers used up all their ammunition before the long day was over. Miraculously, however, not a man was killed or wounded, although they were exposed to almost constant artillery and small-arms fire; this was undoubtedly due to the fact that the men fought as skirmishers, in open ranks, and took advantage of every tree, bush, or stump that could provide some sort of shelter.

When at last the regiment was safely within the Federal lines at Tupelo and sheltered by the darkness, the men tumbled off their horses and rolled up in their blankets to sleep, too tired to start their little fires and cook supper. It had been, by general agreement, the hardest day's fighting the regiment had ever had.[47]

Smith's flank march to Tupelo had neatly turned the tables on Forrest. Now it was the Federals who occupied a strong defensive position, and it was up to Forrest, who had been joined by his official superior, Lieutenant General Stephen D. Lee, to try to dislodge them. The result was the battle of Tupelo, fought on July 14, and ending in a clear-cut victory for the Union army.[48]

If Smith had been a more aggressive commander—if, for example, he had been Forrest—he could have turned his victory into a Confederate disaster. But he was satisfied with what he had accomplished, and it must be said in his favor that he had done infinitely better against Forrest than any of his predecessors. Smith believed with some justification that he had crippled Forrest sufficiently to keep him away from Sherman's line

47. Webster Moses to Nancy Mowry, July 26, 1864, in Moses Letters.
48. The actual site of the battle was the village of Harrisburg, now a suburb of Tupelo, but in 1864 separated from the town by a mile of country. Forrest's losses in the battle were 996 killed, wounded, and missing. See Johnson and Buel (eds.), *Battles and Leaders*, IV, 421–22.

of communications for some time to come, and with his own supplies nearly exhausted, he decided to return to Memphis. He did not exaggerate his supply difficulties, for in the three days that it took his army to march to Salem, Mississippi, where he was met by a supply train that had been sent forward with rations and ammunition for his army, the Jayhawkers lived on one hardtack a man per day. The infantry fared better; they made their long marches on two "crackers" a man per day. No doubt it was expected that the cavalry would be able to get additional food by foraging. This, however, they were unable to do, for the Confederate cavalry hung on the flanks and rear of the retreating army, and the Federal troopers were too busy fending off their attacks to hunt for food.

On July 16, when Smith's retreat began, the Seventh was once again posted as rear guard. After its exertions on the march to Tupelo, it was given a rest on the day of the battle; it occupied a position in rear of the fighting line and took no part in the action. Its exposed position on the return march north made up for the comparative safety it had enjoyed on the day of the battle, for on the first day's march it had an all-day skirmish with a detachment of between three and five hundred Confederate cavalry. During the afternoon, Major Gregory was sent out along an intersecting road with two companies to intercept a threatened attack from the flank. The attack did not materialize, but Gregory stayed out too long, and when he turned back to rejoin the regiment, he found that the head of the Confederate cavalry advance was between him and the Federal column. His small detachment had not been spotted by the rebels, and Gregory could have gotten back in safety by making a wide detour, "but that was not his manner of doing things." He ordered his men to draw pistols "and charge by file down upon and along the flank of the enemy. The movement was brilliantly executed; the Confederate cavalry was taken absolutely by surprise, and our men rode by, Gregory bringing up the rear, emptying their revolvers into the rebel flank without a shot being returned." [49]

The effective performance of the Seventh on this expedition pointed up a highly significant, and from the Confederate point of view, most ominous fact. Nearly three years of service had given the Federal cavalry,

49. Fox, "Story," 44.

and the Jayhawkers along with the rest, the competence of professionals. This was true not only of the survivors from 1861, but of the more recent recruits as well; for the latter, dispersed in relatively small numbers among the veteran troopers in each company, had the benefit of expert guidance. But more important, and less obvious, was the transformation of the corps of line officers. The original lot almost without exception owed their shoulder straps to factors that did not necessarily guarantee their competence as cavalry officers. Local prominence in civilian life, political influence, ingenuity and energy as recruiters, and popularity were the passport to appointment or election to lieutenancies and captaincies in 1861. It is not at all surprising that many, if not the majority, of those selected in such haphazard and unrealistic fashion for a tremendously demanding job failed to measure up to its manifold requirements. Indeed, it is much more surprising that so many did pass the searching test and became competent and, in some cases, outstandingly able officers. But by the summer of 1864 these survivors of a harsh process of elimination were outnumbered by a new breed of officers, men who had started their military careers as enlisted men, and who had risen by ability and merit step by step to corporal, sergeant, first sergeant, second lieutenant, first lieutenant, and captain, and, in some cases, to field grade rank.

Several factors combined to assist the successful upward climb of the Federal cavalry from its lowly and despised estate of 1861–1862. The adaptation of its tactics to fit the realities of weaponry and terrain, better arms, better and more confident leadership at the top, and a vast improvement in the expertise of the rank and file were among these factors, and their importance cannot be minimized. But the key ingredient was the dramatic improvement in the caliber and competence of its line officers, resulting from the weeding out of the unfit and the taking of their places by men of ability risen from the ranks.

As a ten-company regiment, the Seventh was entitled to have ten field and staff officers (one colonel, one lieutenant colonel, two majors, an adjutant, a quartermaster, a commissary, a chaplain, a surgeon, and an assistant surgeon) and thirty line officers (a captain, a first lieutenant, and a second lieutenant for each of the ten companies). On the date of its muster-out, six of the nine captains then on the rolls, nine of ten first lieutenants, and all of the three second lieutenants, or eighteen of twenty-two officers of the line, had started their careers in the regiment as enlisted men. In addition, fifteen officers who were no longer with the Seventh on the day of its muster-out had also been commissioned from the ranks. Most of the total of thirty-five officers promoted from the ranks had already received their commissions by the summer of 1864, and it was their presence at the head of, or as second-in-command of, the ten companies, that made the Seventh the top-notch fighting organization it had become.

On July 20 the Seventh was back in LaGrange to enjoy a ten-day period of rest and recuperation. General Sherman, who had a well-founded respect for Forrest's capacity for mischief, concluded that Smith's expedition to Tupelo had not sufficiently clipped Forrest's wings, and he directed Washburn to have Smith try again, and as soon as possible. Amazingly, Smith had his command reorganized and his supplies assembled within five days after his arrival in Memphis and was ready to sally forth again.[50] Reinforced to a total strength of ten thousand infantry and artillery and five thousand cavalry, he started off on July 28 for his second invasion of northern Mississippi. This time his plan was to follow the Memphis and Charleston Railroad as far east as Grand Junction and then to march south along the route of the Mississippi Central Railroad to Holly Springs, Abbeville, Oxford, and beyond; the railroads were to be put into working order and used to send supplies after him so that he would not have to retreat with the job half done, as he had had to retreat from Tupelo, because of a shortage of food and ammunition.

On July 31 the Seventh received orders to be prepared to march with five days' rations in haversacks.[51] The Jayhawkers were now one of the four regiments, the others being the Third Illinois, Seventh Illinois and Twelfth Missouri, making up the First Brigade, First Division, Cavalry of the XVI Army Corps.[52] The division was commanded by Brigadier General Edward Hatch, whom the Seventh knew from the autumn of 1863 when he was still a colonel. In overall command of the cavalry was

50. *Official Records*, XXXIX, Pt. 2, 202, 222.
51. Webster Moses to Nancy Mowry, July 31, 1864, in Moses Letters.
52. *Official Records*, XXXIX, Pt. 2, 333.

General Grierson, also an acquaintance of long standing. The First Brigade was commanded by Colonel Herrick by virtue of his seniority, but he had shown in the fighting on the march from Okolona to Tupelo that he was fully qualified for brigade command on merit alone; in the opinion of his own men, the most severe judges in such cases, he had shown "how much genuine stuff there was in him."[53] With Herrick in command of the brigade, command of the regiment devolved on Lieutenant Colonel William S. Jenkins.

Smith's forward progress was once again cautious and slow. Forrest kept his troops in the Okolona-Tupelo area and offered no resistance to Smith's advance. Normally, August is a dry month in northern Mississippi, but it was not so in 1864, and for many years thereafter August of 1864 was remembered as the "wet August." It rained constantly and it rained hard; rivers and creeks were in spate, bottom lands turned into lakes and quagmires, and roads became so nearly impassable that Smith's men expected the campaign to be abandoned. Men and animals alike suffered. The Jayhawkers lived day and night in soggy uniforms, and they had to sleep, if they could, on the muddy ground under the useless shelter of waterlogged blankets. They tried without much success to console themselves with the reflection that after all it was midsummer, and the hardships they experienced were as nothing compared to those their revolutionary forefathers had had to endure in the winter at Valley Forge. Webster Moses suffered under a special hardship; for three weeks there was no writing paper to be had, and in consequence, there was a long hiatus in the chief consolation of his existence, the writing of frequent letters to Nancy Mowry.

The Jayhawkers' first fight on this expedition took place on August 10 when they were ordered to force a crossing of Hurricane Creek, a short distance north of Oxford, against the opposition of Chalmers' cavalry. This was a cavalry fight, with no infantry engaged on either side, and it resulted in the retreat of the Confederates.

The Hurricane Creek engagement was the scene of one of the more sprightly episodes in the history of the Seventh, an incident that can best be recounted in the words of Simeon Fox:

53. Fox, "Story," 44–45.

Just as this expedition moved from LaGrange . . . Captain [Edward] Thornton [of Company G] appeared arrayed in a pair of buckskin breeches; "Not regulation," he said, "but durable." The day before the . . . fight at Hurricane creek it rained, and we were in the saddle during the downpour and thoroughly wet through, and Thornton's buckskin breeches, soaked and soggy, became a sort of tenacious pulp. That night he improvised a clothes line and hung them out to dry. At early reveille he sought his trousers; they were there. Some evil-disposed person, under cover of the night, had stretched them until they looked like a pair of gigantic tongs—they were twenty feet long if they were an inch. The cavalry battle of Hurricane creek was fought that day, and Thornton led his company, but it was in a costume that must have made pleasant to him the knowledge that the exigencies of war debarred the presence of the female sex. . . . He turned his trousers over to his colored servant early in the morning, and the faithful darky rode that day in the wake of battle with the captain's breeches festooned about his horse, industriously employed in trying to sketch and draw them back into wearable shape. He reported progress to the captain's orderly (sent back frequently during the day with solicitous inquiries) and by the following morning, after cutting off about five feet from each trouser leg, the captain was able to appear in attenuated and crinkled [trousers] so tight and drawn that it was difficult to know whether it was breeches or nature that he wore.[54]

Having effected a crossing of Hurricane Creek, Smith had to pause to accumulate supplies. He did not resume his advance until the seventeenth, and did not occupy Oxford until the twenty-second. His men, the Jayhawkers included, set fire to all the public buildings and a number of unoccupied dwellings in the town. Simeon Fox explained this apparently senseless act of vandalism in the following words: "I wish to state . . . that the day this was done, Southern newspapers fell into our hands glorying over the burning of Chambersburg . . . and Oxford was burned in retaliation."[55] Chambersburg, Pennsylvania, had in fact been put to the torch by John McCausland's Confederate cavalry on orders from General Jubal Early to burn the town in retaliation for General Hunter's burning of the Virginia Military Institute and Governor Letcher's home in Lexington, Virginia, a month earlier.

Fighting of a minor nature with Chalmers' cavalry followed the occupation of Oxford. In a skirmish at Abbeville on the twenty-third, Orderly Sergeant Alonzo Dixon of Company H, one of the best soldiers

54. Ibid., 45.   55. Ibid., 44.

in the regiment, was killed. But in its essential purpose of beating Forrest, Smith's expedition proved to be a conspicuous failure. Outnumbered by better than three to one, with an even greater preponderance of firepower against him, Forrest realized that in a head-on fight with Smith he would probably be beaten. Guile and imagination had to take the place of the strength he did not possess. And so, on the evening of August 18, he had ridden out of Oxford at the head of two thousand of his best-mounted men on a raid of Smith's base. On Sunday morning, August 21, the day before Smith marched into Oxford, Forrest rode into Memphis. As a military operation, the Memphis raid was no more than a spectacular and successful diversion, but as a foundation for Confederate folklore it leaves nothing to be desired. It was on this occasion that Forrest's scouts, led by his brother William, rode their horses into the lobby of the Gayoso Hotel, and another group of Forrest's men, failing by an eyelash to capture General Washburn, took his two chargers and his best uniform, the latter of which Forrest returned under a flag of truce the same day; Washburn repaid Forrest's courtesy a few days later by sending him a brand-new Confederate uniform of the finest quality, which Washburn had Forrest's own tailor make to Forrest's measurements.

News of Forrest's dash into Memphis reached Smith on the morning of August 22, a bare couple of hours after he had occupied Oxford. The same afternoon, he ordered his army to do an about-face and began his retreat to Memphis, with Chalmers, who had managed with two thousand men to keep Smith's fifteen thousand in check in a manner worthy of Forrest himself, in close pursuit. In view of Smith's great numerical superiority, Chalmers could not seriously hinder his retreat, but he did snap up stragglers and parties of foragers. Thus, on August 26, one of his detachments surprised and attacked a foraging party made up of seven troopers of the Second Iowa Cavalry and three Jayhawkers. One of the Iowa men was killed and one was captured. Of the three Jayhawkers, Thomas Quirk of Company E was captured, and Nelson Rice of Company A and Henry Allison of Company E were wounded but escaped with the loss of their horses.

On August 28 the campaign was ended and the Seventh was back in LaGrange. Its old camp had not been fully satisfactory; a new site was chosen, and in the next few days the entire regiment was hard at work moving camp and garrison equipage to the new location and setting up the new camp, Colonel Herrick having issued orders to the Jayhawkers "to fix up just as though we were going to remain a year."[56] This, as it turned out, was one of the most bootless enterprises in which the Seventh was ever engaged. As far back as August 20, rumors were current that the regiment had been ordered to return to Missouri. For once, the scuttlebut proved to be entirely accurate, and in fact the orders relieving the regiment of duty in the District of West Tennessee and directing it to be "sent without delay to St. Louis, Mo., to report to Maj. Gen. W. S. Rosecrans" had been issued on August 4, but could not be executed while the regiment was many miles away in Mississippi with General Smith.[57] On August 26, while the regiment was on its way back to LaGrange, General Washburn appealed directly to Rosecrans to let him keep the Seventh; but the latter's response was apparently a firm negative, for on the night of September 6, when the Jayhawkers were still in the midst of setting up a camp suitable for a year's occupancy, they received orders to report to Memphis early the following morning "to be in readiness to go to Missouri."[58]

56. Pomeroy, "War Diary," entry for September 2, 1864.
57. *Official Records*, XLI, Pt. 2, 550.   58. *Ibid.*, 879 and *ibid.*, XXXIX, Pt. 2, 346.

CHAPTER XV

The Border in Peace and War

WHILE THE Jayhawkers were leading a dull life of leisure in St. Louis in April, 1864, the political kettle back home in Leavenworth was boiling. The chief protagonists in what developed into a more than usually turbulent episode in Kansas politics were the two ex-Jayhawkers, Jennison and Anthony; behind them stood the figures of Senator James H. Lane and Governor Thomas Carney in mutual antagonism. Anthony's term of office as mayor of Leavenworth that had begun in April, 1863, was anything but a popular success. His dictatorial temper, unpredictability, tactlessness, and bursts of ill-directed energy had embroiled him with his constituents, the state authorities, and the military administration alike. He personally, as well as his associates, was accused of corruption and of profiting from the endemic lawlessness of the Border, of which the activities of the Red Legs were merely one manifestation. And to crown his other problems and difficulties, Anthony was caught up, as any Kansas politician was bound to be, in the no-holds-barred feuding between the pro-Lane and anti-Lane factions of Kansas Republicanism. Anthony himself was a supporter of the radical pro-Lane faction; that made it obligatory for the relatively conservative anti-Lane faction headed by Governor Carney, and numbering Colonel Jennison, who had recently changed sides, among its adherents, to fight him tooth and nail.

Anthony announced his candidacy for a second term as mayor in the election to be held in April, 1864, and at once his troubles began. The turbulence of his administration had alienated the more prosperous, propertied classes. They held him responsible for the "wild and reckless system which . . . reduced the bonds of the city to sixty cents on the dollar . . . [and] emptied the city treasury."[1] They professed to believe that due to his maladministration, the good name of Leavenworth had "suffered at home, and more abroad, and its growth and prosperity [had] been seriously retarted." And finally, they also condemned "those practices by which, under color of law, but in violation of its spirit, men guilty of no offense, or pretended offense, have been wantonly deprived of their liberties, and subjected to ignominious punishments, the result of which has been that Leavenworth has obtained the reputation of being an unsafe place for a stranger to visit for the transaction of business." But unlike most political figures in a similar situation, Anthony had not gained the adherence of the Leavenworth masses in the process of alienating the "establishment." Far from it. The more raffish elements, of which the city contained far more than its fair share, were his bitter enemies. The burning of the houses of ill fame was neither forgotten nor forgiven. The attitude of this powerful segment of the community (whom His Honor habitually referred to as "thieves, bullies and pimps") toward the mayor is well illustrated by the following "card" published in the Leavenworth *Times* by one of their leading spirits, who went by the simple but striking name of Yellow Tom:

I have never wronged the innocent and confiding who have trusted me—never left to the cold charity of the world an offspring because forsooth its mother was a shade blacker in skin . . . than I was. I have never deprived a human being of life, because I knew I had the advantage, in order to make a name for bravery that is foreign to my heart. I am no murderer; nor have I ever robbed virtue of its purity, in order to satiate the brutal passions of a fiendish and bestial nature. Can you say so, D. R. Anthony? You stand before the people of this city, branded with all those marks upon your brow—the modern Cain of the world.[2]

1. This, and the two quotations which follow, arc taken from an unidentified clipping, Jennison Scrapbook.

2. Unidentified clipping, *ibid.* If we assume correctly that Yellow Tom's *nom de guerre* was indicative, among other things, of his educational attainments, it would follow that his "card" had received extensive editorial doctoring.

To the respectable working people of Leavenworth, Anthony's radicalism on the race issue gave serious offense. Everyone was in favor of freeing the slaves of Missourians in the name of humanity, but to carry solicitude for ex-slaves to the point of appointing Negroes to the Leavenworth police force, as Anthony had done, was something altogether different. It is not without significance that among the transparencies carried by Anthony's opponents in one of the preelection torchlight parades was one showing the mayor "in the act of issuing orders to his negro policemen" and another with a "representation of a negro policeman arresting a laborer with a hod upon his shoulder, with the motto 'White laborers but negro policemen.'"[3]

To oppose Anthony, the Carney faction nominated the governor's "intimate friend," United States Marshal James L. McDowell.[4] To add an extra element of animosity to what promised from the start to be a bitter campaign, Anthony declared that his reelection would be a direct vote of confidence in Jim Lane; on the other side, McDowell made much of his friendship with Governor Carney, Lane's enemy.

Jennison was an army officer on active duty and, as such, was debarred at least in theory from active participation in a strictly political contest. But, given his temperament, his prominence, and his presence in Leavenworth, it was inevitable that he should become involved in the mayoralty contest. That, in fact, proved to be the case. "Being loudly called for," he made the speech of the evening at the mass meeting that nominated McDowell. After explaining that he spoke not as a soldier but as a citizen and taxpayer, he told the audience that he had given Anthony his hearty support "although a personal enemy" when the latter ran for mayor the year before, but that Anthony's record in office made it impossible for the speaker to support him for reelection; he ended by offering to bet anyone any amount from five dollars to five thousand dollars that McDowell would win.[5]

Another pro-McDowell meeting, held a few nights later, was reported under the following high-flown headline:

Immense Gathering of the People! The Masses in their Might! The Knell of

---

3. Unidentified clipping, *ibid.*   4. *Ibid.*
5. *Ibid.* Jennison did not bother to add that in the spring of 1863, he as well as Anthony had been allied with the radical Lane faction. In the interim, he had changed sides, but Anthony had not.

the Tyrant!! Lang's [sic] Hall Overflowed! Sovereigns in Open Council! The People in Earnest! The Lord Mayor Sat Upon!! He is Found Wanting! Grand Torchlight Procession! Unbounded Enthusiasm! 3,000 People in Procession!! They Shout Hallelujahs! For McDowell and All the Rest![6]

Having thus strained the resources of typography and of his journalistic enthusiasm, the editor then proceeded to give an account of the speeches delivered to the "Immense Gathering." One orator declared that Anthony's character was "modeled upon that of Henry VIII whom he resemble[d] in more respects than one." Jennison, again the principal speaker, gazed out over the audience and declared that he could not see among them any of the "scoundrels, pimps and blackguards" who, according to Anthony, made up the ranks of his opponents; he saw only respectable citizens, "the laborer, the mechanic, the merchant, the rich and the poor." He spoke in scathing terms of Anthony's tyrannical and overbearing rule as mayor of the city. Warming up to his subject, which generally meant that he was about to speak of himself, he told of the difficulties between Anthony and himself in the days when they were both officers in the Seventh Kansas—a recital in which the speaker showed to much better advantage than did Anthony—and in his peroration, accused the mayor of telling what "some folks would call . . . lies."

Anthony, of course, retaliated in kind. He and his supporters assumed the mantle of unconditional unionism. They habitually accused McDowell of being the candidate of the Copperheads and secessionists, and they singled out Jennison as the target for their choicest abuse. In one of his speeches, Anthony asserted that "Col. Jennison had never been in a battle or where there was a shot fired by the rebels since Jennison had been an officer. Col. Jennison had never even given the simplest command to his regiment—he couldn't drill even a squad of men."[7]

Polling day came on Monday, April 4. Not surprisingly, considering the social and political climate of Leavenworth in the 1860s, and the virulence with which the campaign had been conducted by both sides, the election did not pass off without disorder and violence. So much is certain, but the accounts of the events of the day in the openly partisan

6. The headline, as well as the quotations which follow, are taken from an unidentified clipping, ibid.

7. Leavenworth Conservative, March 24, 1864, clipping ibid.

newspapers, their stories of the extent of the disorders and their apportionment of the responsibility for the trouble, are so flagrantly contradictory that one could easily conclude that they describe two entirely different elections. These stories, in any event, make a most illuminating picture of contemporary mores in municipal politics and journalism alike. The outcome of this turbulent election is the only aspect of it that is not in doubt; Anthony was beaten by a majority of nearly three to one, receiving 549 votes to McDowell's 1,534. In 1864 Leavenworth had about twenty thousand inhabitants. Assuming that between four and five thousand of them were adult males entitled to vote, a turnout of less than 50 percent of eligible voters suggests either a remarkable state of apathy among the citizenry or else a degree of disorder at the polls that caused the peacefully inclined to stay at home.

The most vivid of the pro-Anthony accounts of the events of election day is Anthony's own, written in the third person. He stated that the disorders actually began two days before the election when Yellow Tom, who has previously been introduced, and a number of his cronies "knocked down and brutally beat the City Marshal."[8] The next day, Sunday, these same men and some sixty others "paraded the streets defying the civil authorities to arrest them, showing authority from McDowell to carry arms and to defy the officers of the law . . . On . . . [election day] the polls in the various wards in [the] city were surrounded by armed men who defied the civil authorities. These men were under the command of J. L. McDowell and C. R. Jennison. McDowell as U.S. Marshal had appointed some one hundred men, mostly Roughs, Pimps, and Shysters as his deputies . . . These rioters intimidated the judges of election, and they would not permit those legally appointed to act." When he heard of these disorders, Anthony's account continues, he decided to see the situation for himself:

A gang of armed ruffians were on horse back and followed the Mayor from poll to poll threatening to kill him if he attempted to enforce the law. At the First ward poll he was struck upon the head and assaulted by a dozen of these scoundrels.

Col. C. R. Jennison was present with some two hundred of his men. . . .

8. This and the two quotations which follow are from Leavenworth *Conservative*, April 9, 1864, clipping *ibid.*

Many copperheads and secessionists were at the head of the party hooting and yelling for Carney, McDowell and Jennison.

At 10½ o'clock, A. M., the Mayor ordered the polls closed. The mob would not permit it in the Fourth ward; they forcibly took possession of the ballot box. . . . Hundreds of men voted who had no right to vote. . . . The two principal rioters and leaders of the mob were McDowell . . . and Col. C. R. Jennison. . . . But back of these two violators of law, stands Thomas Carney offering pardon to the Pimps and would be murderers. He was too cowardly to come out, but with his money to buy roughs and pimps and his power to grant pardon to all criminals, he has shown himself the worst scoundrel of them all.

It will be observed that there is nothing conciliatory about Anthony's language, and one may be certain that, characteristically, he indulged in similarly forceful epithets when he made his tour of the polling places on election day. Anthony was woefully short of judgment and prudence, but he cannot be accused of lacking courage.

Another account, published on election day by a pro-Anthony newspaper, added a number of telling details. It would appear that "Mayor Anthony and many of his friends who went to vote were knocked down and brutally beaten. . . . Armed men took possession of the polls early in the morning and defied the city authorities."[9] Whereupon Anthony issued the following proclamation: "The polls in the several wards of this city being in the possession of lawless mobs, I hereby order them closed until quiet can be restored, and all quiet and peaceable citizens allowed to vote. Judges will report with their ballot boxes at my office in the Market House." When the judges of election attempted to comply with the mayor's proclamation, "the mob followed . . . [them] to the market house, broke down the doors, and seized the ballot boxes. Since then, the election has been under the control of McDowell's friends, the friends of Anthony being intimidated, and hundreds having been refused to [sic] vote. . . . Many persons have been badly beaten, but none killed so far."

The newspapers hostile to Anthony naturally gave a drastically different account of these events. The trouble, one of them reported, had its origin more than a week before the election when "the friends of

9. This and the two quotations which follow are from an unidentified clipping, *ibid.*

Mayor Anthony became aware that he could not be elected, and . . . set their wits to work to make the election void any way they could. It was necessary to do this to save their money." [10] A follow-up story added that the mayor's friends, to put their "damnable scheme" into execution, "combined and confederated to seize the ballot box of the Fourth Ward and keep possession of it until the time for closing of the polls had passed." [11] Not one of the pro-McDowell editors saw the faintest sign of the disorder, intimidation, and mob violence that were so clearly visible to Anthony and his journalistic adherents. One of the former asserted that "at every place around the polls and in every portion of the city, the utmost quiet prevailed." [12] Another reported that "at about ten o'clock the cry was raised that Mr. Anthony's friends were intimidated. . . . We went to every Ward and found all quiet. . . . Mayor Anthony himself done [*sic*] more than all other men to get up a riot, but the people remained quiet." [13] The most circumstantial of these accounts, adorned with the partisan headline "The People Triumphant!! . . . The People Disenthralled!!" tells us that "Anthony caused the only difficulty, and that, for a while, had a threatening look. Without cause, when there was no trouble, he ordered the ballot box of the Fourth Ward seized. . . . Then he ordered the polls to be closed! . . . Then he sought to raise a mob; but he failed. During this period Anthony's life was threatened and was saved by McDowell and Colonel Jennison, on three occasions." [14] If, indeed, Anthony's life was saved on three occasions, it is evident that his life must have been in danger, a fact that it is difficult to reconcile with the atmosphere of the "utmost quiet" that the pro-McDowell newspapers professed to find throughout the city. Insofar as the truth may be glimpsed through the murky clouds of printer's ink, it would appear that Anthony's no doubt exaggerated account of an election dominated by McDowell's and Jennison's bully boys is mainly correct. [15] Summing up

10. *Ibid.*   11. *Ibid.*
12. *Ibid.*   13. *Ibid.*
14. *Ibid.*
15. There is in existence an account of the election that at least on the surface appears to be impartial. This is a report written by Brigadier General Thomas A. Davies, in command of the District of North Kansas, with headquarters at Fort Leavenworth. Davies wrote that on the day before the election he received several pleas from Anthony to send a detachment of soldiers to the city "sufficient to . . . preserve the peace" and to break up a gang of sixty or more who were parading the streets "armed with knives and revolvers" and who had already "assaulted several

these events, one newspaper declared: "This . . . was the most exciting election that has ever taken place in Kansas. Probably no canvass has ever been made in any locality in this country where the excitement was more intense, more earnest . . . or where deeper feeling possessed all parties as to its results."[16]

It is quite apparent that Jennison's military duties at this time were not so onerous as to interfere with his political activities. Through a combination of simply being present and of seniority, he had been post commandant at Fort Leavenworth since December 23, 1863.[17] Parts of his regiment were stationed in Kansas City, West Point, Missouri, Paola, Kansas, and at Fort Leavenworth, and the regiment seemed to require only a minumum of its colonel's attention and time. On his recommendation, the War Department authorized the building of a new guardhouse at the fort, and he exerted himself to refurbish its grounds and buildings; he had a new fence built around the parade ground, paved the walks, and repaired the barracks. Thanks to his efforts, "the venerable old Fort . . . put on a new countenance"; it may be added that the fort, less than forty years old in 1864, was "venerable" only by the unexacting

citizens, knocking them down." But, informed by one of his staff officers (an officer, be it noted, of Jennison's Fifteenth Kansas) that all was quiet in the city, Davies refused. Anthony then asked him to send soldiers early the next morning to each of the polling places "to protect the judges, clerks and the legal voters." Despite the assurances of Governor Carney, who visited the fort in the afternoon, that there would be no rioting "and that the civil authorities . . . were sufficient to maintain peace," Davies sent 150 of his men to Leavenworth the next morning and established his own headquarters in the center of town. On the way there, he saw "a good deal of election excitement but no rioting, and about the usual loud and threatening talk among some speakers, but no collision." Members of his staff, whom he sent through the town to investigate conditions, came back with reports that there were no disorders. The only untoward incident occurred at about 10 A.M. "The mayor had undertaken to disarm a man claiming to be acting as deputy U.S. Marshal, and . . . he was struck two or three times and knocked down in the mud; . . . the mayor ordered the closing of one of the polls, and caused the ballot-box to be removed, whereupon some armed citizens arrested him, but he was soon after released by others. . . . This was about 10'clock, and from this time till 2 o'clock everything was quiet, and the voting proceeding at the various polls without interruption. . . . I returned at 2 o'clock to the fort, and the troops soon followed." See *Official Records*, XXXIV, Pt. 3, 53–56. General Davies' report might be taken as establishing the truth as between the conflicting pro- and anti-Anthony newspaper reports, were it not for the fact that with the exception of what he saw with his own eyes on his way to the center of town, everything he reports is based on the testimony of subordinates whose objectivity cannot be taken on faith. Nor is the general's own impartiality wholly beyond suspicion. Carney's visit to him on the afternoon before the election has a distinctly odd look about it.

16. Unidentified clipping, Jennison Scrapbook.
17. Special Orders No. 29, AAAG's Office, District of the Border, Fort Leavenworth, December 23, 1863, in Records of the Adjutant General's Office. *Cf.* Elvid Hunt and Walter E. Lorence, *History of Fort Leavenworth, 1827–1937* (Fort Leavenworth, 1937), 224.

Kansas standards of the time.[18] Another Jennison enterprise was more in character than the beautification of the fort. He decided that the Leavenworth hackmen were charging too much for the three-mile trip from the city to the fort and issued a special order fixing a maximum price for the trip. The hackmen naturally testified to their devotion to the principle of free enterprise by ignoring the order, whereupon Jennison arrested nine of them in one day, and it took the personal intervention of the department commander, Major General Samuel R. Curtis, to have them released from the colonel's new guardhouse.[19]

In the middle of the summer of 1864, the large segment of Kansas lying south of the line running due west from the northeastern corner of Linn County was established as the First Sub-District of South Kansas. Jennison's regiment was moved into the area, and on August 1 he was given command of the subdistrict, with headquarters in Mound City.[20] Brigadier General James G. Blunt, Jennison's immediate superior, was in command of the district. Jennison's new assignment was welcomed with the customary journalistic hosannas and praise of his "vigilance and activity." One exuberant editor declared that "the dark clouds of danger which have so long hung over this portion of Kansas have been driven away; and the star of hope for us seems to have arisen, we trust to set no more."[21]

Jennison's new assignment did not present any military problems of sufficient consequence to place undue demands on his energies or to interfere to any extent with his leisure. He toured the area under his command to make an inspection of the condition of his regiment, which was posted in small detachments throughout the subdistrict. But neither this, nor the issuance of a circular to the regiment to remind the officers and men that $499 remained to be raised to complete payment for the instruments of "silver and beautifully engraved with the number of the Regiment and the name of its commander," that had been purchased on credit for the regimental band, was the kind of activity that his loyal

---

18. Unidentified clipping, Jennison Scrapbook.

19. Unidentified clipping, *ibid.*

20. Unidentified clipping, *ibid.* Jennison was appointed to the command of the First Sub-District of South Kansas by General Orders No. 19, District of South Kansas, August 1, 1864. A copy of his own General Orders No. 1, August 2, 1864, assuming command of the subdistrict, is *ibid.*

21. Unidentified clipping, *ibid.*

admirers expected of their favorite jayhawker.[22] He had time for an excursion to St. Louis, ostensibly on business connected with his regiment; and on one occasion he and George Hoyt went to St. Joseph, Missouri, to address the loyal inhabitants of that city. Their intention to visit St. Joseph was widely publicized in advance, but it was not universally welcomed. There were many Missourians, even among the thoroughly loyal, who did not relish the prospect of a visit by Jennison and Hoyt, peaceful or otherwise, to their state. As a result, the military authorities, to forestall any violence, "ordered the closing of all places where ardent liquors were sold."[23] On the evening of the visit, "at half past seven o'clock a crowd of several hundred persons, making one of the largest assemblages ever collected in the city, met in front of the Market House. Some came through curiosity, others to be in the crowd, others still having nothing else to do, but everybody to see the little jayhawker." Hoyt had the job of warming up the audience for Jennison; for over an hour he "kept the crowd in the highest state of loyal excitement, by the blows he showered . . . on copperheads and their rebel allies." One of his most telling points was the assertion that after the Lawrence Massacre he and his Kansas companions had killed all the "butternuts" in Jackson County, Missouri, whom they found with new (hence ipso facto stolen) coats on their backs.

With the audience brought to the proper pitch, Jennison was introduced and was received with "enthusiastic and deafening cheers." He made "one of the most patriotic and eloquent" speeches his audience had ever heard. In the course of it he advised them to carry out the immediate and unconditional abolition of slavery in their state and to send to Kansas, "to be taken care of," all their "conservatives"; for conservatism, said Jennison, was not only synonymous with copperhead tendencies, but was also a detriment to the welfare and progress of Missouri.

Jennison's pleasant existence in Mound City, and the stay of the Seventh in Tennessee, were alike ended by a new but familiar storm cloud. Kansas and Missouri were once more in danger. General Sterling Price was once again on the march, headed north from Arkansas.

22. Unidentified clipping, *ibid.*
23. This, and the quotations which follow, are from an unidentified clipping, apparently from a St. Joseph, Missouri, newspaper, *ibid.*

After the fighting at Iuka and Corinth in the autumn of 1862, Price had recrossed the Mississippi and, in the following year, was involved in military operations in Arkansas. In the spring of 1864, the Federals, led by General Frederick Steele, advanced from Little Rock with Shreveport as their goal, in a movement synchronized with Major General Nathaniel P. Banks's Red River Campaign. Banks was badly beaten and his campaign wrecked at Sabine Cross Roads in a battle which, except for the numbers engaged, was an almost exact replica of Sturgis' defeat at Brice's Cross Roads. With Banks's defeat, Steele's advance lost its strategic raison d'etre, and he retreated to his original position north of the Arkansas River, after inflicting a sharp check on the Confederates at Jenkins' Ferry on April 30.

After the conclusion of these operations, and a number of alternatives having been explored and discarded, Price was given authority to invade Missouri once again, with St. Louis as his principal objective. He spent the summer organizing his forces for the campaign. He assembled a small army, consisting of the three divisions of veteran cavalry, a total of eight thousand officers and men, under Generals J. F. Fagan, John S. Marmaduke, and Joseph O. Shelby, twenty pieces of artillery, and about four thousand unarmed men whom he expected to arm and equip with captures from the Federals, the one unfailing source of Confederate armament and supplies.

General Rosecrans, since his exile to St. Louis and the command of the Department of Missouri, had been persuaded by his provost marshal general, Colonel John P. Sanderson, of the existence in Missouri of a vast subversive organization of Copperheads, known as the Order of American Knights, or OAK for short. He learned, he said, of Price's intention to invade Missouri from the spies Sanderson had planted in the OAK lodges: "From early in the spring it was known through the lodges of the O. A. K.'s and other rebel sources that Price intended a great invasion of this State, in which he expected the co-operation of that order and of rebels generally, and by which he hoped to obtain important military and political results." [24] Rosecrans had been given command of a military backwater practically denuded of troops, and his credit with the War Department in Washington was at an all-time low, but his warnings

24. *Official Records*, XLI, Pt. 1, 307.

about Price's intentions could not be disregarded, and he was authorized to enroll ten new regiments of infantry to meet the threat. His obvious need for trained troops to support and stiffen his new levies led to the issuance of orders which the Seventh received on the night of September 6 to return to Memphis forthwith in preparation for an immediate move to Missouri. When these orders reached the Seventh, Price had already begun his forward movement; he put his army in motion on August 30, and on September 7, the same day that the Jayhawkers arrived in Memphis, his men forded the Arkansas River and took up their march northeastward on the direct road to St. Louis, via Batesville and Pocahontas, Arkansas, and Fredericktown, Missouri.

The Civil War had changed in many ways in the three years the Jayhawkers had spent in the service, but in one respect it remained unaltered. The Seventh arrived in Memphis in the forenoon of September 7, ready to march on board the transports that were to hurry it to St. Louis; but the boats were not there, and there was no prospect of their early arrival. The regiment was ordered to set up camp and wait, which it did. The men who had chosen not to reenlist as veterans in January were preparing to depart, their three-year terms of enlistment being nearly up; and in normal human fashion, many of their veteran comrades, who had reenlisted and had their thirty-day furlough, now wished they had not done so. It was not easy for men who were committed to stay in the army for the duration of the war to witness the jubilant preparations of others to go home. But on September 9 the Memphis garrison fired a one hundred gun salute in honor of Sherman's capture of Atlanta and Admiral Farragut's spectacular victory in Mobile Bay; it suggested to the disconsolate veterans that their own terms of service might also end fairly soon.

While the regiment was waiting for transportation to St. Louis, and the cynics in the ranks were telling themselves that "everything is uncertain in the army and sometimes I do not believe anything about our movements until we move," despatches concerning it were being exchanged at the highest military levels.[25] The momentous problem at issue was whether the Seventh should proceed to St. Louis with or without its horses. General Washburn, chronically short of mounts for

25. Webster Moses to Nancy Mowry, September 9, 1864, in Moses Letters.

his cavalry, wired General Rosecrans, "I will send the Seventh Kansas Cav. Can you not mount them at St. Louis, allowing me to keep the horses here?[26] General Rosecrans, thus alerted to a hostile stratagem, decided to execute an outflanking manoeuver. Going right to the top, he wired the chief of staff of the army in Washington for a decision in this vital matter. General Halleck, with whom Rosecrans was not by any means a favorite, wired back: "General Washburn must decide for himself in regard to the horses of the Seventh Kansas." Finally, in an excess of unselfishness, Washburn decided to let the Jayhawkers take their horses with them to Missouri. Urged on by Rosecrans' pleas for speed, Washburn's quartermasters eventually found transportation for the Seventh, and the regiment started north, five companies on September 12, and the others on the next two days. The journey upstream against the current was slow, and it was not until the eighteenth that the entire regiment was assembled at Camp Gamble in St. Louis.

The next few days were a busy time for the regimental quartermaster as the Jayhawkers prepared for what promised to be a hard campaign. All the horses had to be reshod, weapons inspected and repaired, worn and damaged equipment replaced, wagons reconditioned. This period of intense activity was marred by a tragic incident. John Bolton of Company H, a native of Palmyra, Missouri, who had enlisted in the regiment on June 1, 1864, was shot and fatally wounded by Sergeant James C. Service of his company while "resisting arrest for drunkenness, fighting and disorderly conduct."[27]

The Seventh prepared to take the field in considerable doubt as to just what field it was going to take. General Rosecrans had several requisitions for the services of the famous regiment. Brigadier General S. B. Fisk, at Columbia, Missouri wanted the Jayhawkers sent to him for ten days to deal with the rebels of Boone and Howard counties in preparation for the enforcement of the draft in the area.[28] Three days later, General Fisk had another idea; unable to control guerilla activity around Macon, in northeastern Missouri, he wanted the Seventh sent there: "The guerillas are all mounted on the best of horses and are well armed.

---

26. *Official Records*, XLI, Pt. 3, 141. The additional telegrams in this series will be found *ibid.*, 164, 174, and 189.
27. Pomeroy, "War Diary," entry for September 25, 1864.
28. *Official Records*, XLI, Pt. 3, 232.

We cannot make much headway against them with footmen. They range over such an extensive field, and have so many more friends than we have, that it is exceedingly difficult to operate against them with even well mounted men."[29] He felt, with considerable justice, that only a "well-mounted force of the character of" the Seventh Kansas could strike "a decisive blow at the rascals." By September 22, Brigadier General John McNeil, guarding Rosecrans' principal supply depot at Rolla, about one hundred miles southwest of St. Louis, had obtained fairly accurate information from prisoners about the location and route of Price's invading columns headed in his direction, and he at once telegraphed Rosecrans, "I must have cavalry before I can do anything effective. Can you send the Seventh Kansas right up?"[30] Here then was another claimant. And McNeil followed up his despatch with another explaining in more detail why he wanted the Seventh sent to him: "The defense, when the occasion comes, shall be to the last man, and the last gun if my troops will stand by me. You must recollect, however . . . that the infantry I have is raw and uninstructed. . . . You will see the importance of having some good troops here—troops that will fight the enemy's advance outside our works, so as to inspire our green troops to stand up to the work when assaulted inside."[31] By the time Rosecrans received McNeil's despatches, he too knew that Price was on his way north, and deeming the West Plains-Rolla-Jefferson City route the one Price was most likely to take, he ordered his chief of cavalry "to make every effort to get the Seventh Kansas off to Rolla as soon as possible."[32]

As late as September 25, the Jayhawkers did not know where they would be ordered to march, but with Webster Moses, they accepted the uncertainty philosophically: "We do not know where we will go next neither does it make much difference as one place is as good as another for a soldier."[33] Not until the twenty-sixth was the regiment ready to take the field, and Colonel Herrick received orders the same day to take the regiment to Rolla by way of Jefferson Barracks and DeSoto. Reveille was blown at 3 A.M. on the twenty-seventh, and at daybreak the total effective force of the regiment—four hundred officers and men,

29. *Ibid.*, 276.   30. *Ibid.*, 306.
31. *Ibid.*, 362.
32. *Ibid.*, 305. See also *Official Records*, XLI, Pt. 1, 307 and 323.
33. Webster Moses to Nancy Mowry, September 21, 1864, in Moses Letters.

with four days' rations, three wagons carrying ammunition and baggage, and two ambulances—marched out of camp. Two days later, beyond DeSoto, where the regiment had gone into camp for the night, a despatch rider arrived at 1 A.M. with orders of the utmost urgency; the Seventh was to make ready at once to march at a moment's notice, detailed instructions to follow. The men were aroused forthwith, the horses were fed and saddled, the teams harnessed, and the Jayhawkers stood to horse in a driving rain. At nine-thirty in the morning, eight hours later, they were still waiting for the promised orders, which never came.

On September 26 Price had been informed by his spies that the Federals in St. Louis outnumbered him two to one. The information was wildly off the mark, but, convinced that St. Louis was too strongly held to be attacked successfully, and further influenced by the bloody check he sustained at Pilot Knob the next day, he decided to bypass the city to the west and march northwestward through the middle of the state, toward Jefferson City, Independence, Kansas City, and Leavenworth, whence he would return to Arkansas by way of eastern Kansas and Indian Territory. On his march through northern Arkansas and southern Missouri he had picked up or drafted thousands of recruits, and hundreds more were joining him daily; he was arming them, as well as the unarmed men he had with him at the start, with the weapons taken from the small garrisons of Missouri militia that his columns were snapping up on the way. Price therefore felt strong enough to deal with any opposition he might meet on his long march.

During the last days of September and the first week of October, the Seventh was attached to the two small infantry divisions headed by the last commander the Jayhawkers had had in Mississippi, Major General Andrew J. Smith, who was on the way upriver to reinforce Sherman in Georgia when he was ordered to stop off in Missouri with his troops to help Rosecrans. On October 4 the Jayhawkers were at Union. Price's army had already passed through the area, inhabited mostly by loyal people, and "took nearly everything robed houses even took bedding and women's clothing," activities not entirely unknown to the Jayhawkers in their early, unregenerate days.[34] Two days later some

34. Same to same, October 11, 1864, *ibid. Cf.* Pomeroy, "War Diary," entry for October 5, 1864.

"citizens" came pelting into camp with the news that a force of from 500 to 1,500 Confederate Indians had appeared at St. Clair, about eight miles to the south, and were "killing and destroying everything in their way."[35] "Boots and Saddles" was blown immediately, and in twenty minutes the Jayhawkers were riding south at the best speed of their tired horses. Before they had gone the full distance, "reliable information brought from St. Clair developed the fact that there were no Indians or rebels either, and the excitement was all a false alarm."[36] The regiment turned about and arrived back at Union at midnight, feeling very foolish about the "Indian expedition."

Shortly after this incident, the Seventh, commanded temporarily by Major Francis M. Malone in the absence of both Colonel Herrick and Lieutenant Colonel William S. Jenkins, was detached from General Smith's command and became part of the second brigade, commanded by General John McNeil, of a newly formed cavalry division.[37] The division was under the command of Major General Alfred Pleasonton, who had been replaced as commander of the cavalry of the Army of the Potomac by General Sheridan and exiled to the West. McNeil was ordered to push along behind, and in contact with, Price's rear guard. The brigade arrived at Jefferson City on October 11, and for the next ten days it followed Price's army westward along the south bank of the Missouri River, through Boonville, Marshall, and Waverly. The brigade had halted for the night ten miles east of Lexington on the evening of October 20, and the men were already rolling up in their blankets beside the campfires when orders came to resume the march immediately. In a half hour the brigade was on the way, a battalion of the Fifth Missouri Militia Cavalry in the lead, followed by the Jayhawkers. The night was pitch dark and cold, and a storm of sleet and rain and snow was pelting down, making everyone miserable. Reaching and occupying Lexington shortly after midnight, the brigade bivouacked in

35. Pomeroy, "War Diary," entry for October 7, 1864.
36. *Ibid.*
37. Lieutenant Colonel William S. Jenkins had entered the regiment as captain of Company C. He was promoted to major on May 27, 1863, and to lieutenant colonel on March 21, 1864, and was mustered out of the service on November 21, 1864. See *Report of the Adjutant General of the State of Kansas,* I, 524. Jenkins was absent from the regiment at the time of the Price campaign.

the streets for the night, while the Seventh drew the unenviable assignment of picketing all the roads leading into the town.[38]

Early on the morning of the twenty-second, the Seventh was back in familiar territory, at the Little Blue River, a short distance east of Independence. The Confederate rear guard, two brigades of General Fagan's division, had broken up the bridge across the Little Blue, but McNeil forded the river with part of his brigade, deployed on the other side, and pressed the Confederates back to the eastern edge of Independence, where he received orders from Pleasonton to charge the enemy. As soon as the horseholders came up and the men were mounted, the Thirteenth Missouri, "brilliantly supported" by the Jayhawkers and the Seventeenth Illinois, charged the Confederates in close order. Fagan's men were driven out of the town with the loss of two guns and "a large number" killed, wounded, and captured.[39]

While Pleasonton and his cavalry were following Price, Major General Samuel R. Curtis was meeting the enemy head-on. In mid-October he organized most of the regiments he had into the First Division, Army of the Border, placed General Blunt in command, and sent him forward to Lexington. Blunt's Army of the Border was made up for the most part of Kansas State Militia, stiffened by a few regiments and batteries of U.S. Volunteers. The militia had been called out by Governor Carney as Price approached the Kansas border, but even in that moment of danger, the calling out of the militia to protect the state was the occasion for the usual vicious political fight between the Carney and Lane factions. The Sixth Militia Regiment was commanded by the veteran fighter of Bleeding Kansas days, James Montgomery. General Curtis directed that for identification the nonuniformed militiamen should wear as a distinguishing badge a strip of red cloth on their hatbands; most of them used instead sumac leaves, which are scarlet in October. Blunt placed Jennison in command of the first brigade of his division; the brigade was made up of Jennison's own Fifteenth Kansas, commanded by Hoyt, a battalion of the Third Wisconsin Cavalry, and a

---

38. Pomeroy, "War Diary," entry for October 21, 1864. Cf. *Official Records*, XLI, Pt. 1, 371.
39. *Official Records*, XLI, Pt. 1, 371. Simeon Fox, "Story," 45, says that forty rebels were killed.

battery of four mountain howitzers manned by Fifteenth Kansas and Third Wisconsin cavalrymen who had volunteered for temporary artillery duty.[40]

As soon as his division was organized, Blunt advanced to Lexington, and there, on the nineteenth, he had his first fight with Price's army, whose advance was led that day by General Shelby's division. Badly outnumbered, principally because Governor Carney refused to allow General Curtis to send Kansas militia as far east into Missouri as Lexington, Blunt was forced to retreat. On the twenty-first, he fought Price again, this time on the Little Blue, and was again driven back to the west, through Independence to the Big Blue River, where he joined the rest of General Curtis' army.

The Big Blue flows in a generally northward direction, about half-way between what were in 1864 the eastern edge of Kansas City and the western edge of Independence. General Curtis had chosen the thickly wooded, steep slopes on the west bank of the stream as his main defensive position to block Price's advance, and he used the last four days prior to the latter's arrival on the scene to have his men construct "such field-works as seemed expedient to resist the passage of cavalry and artillery."[41] When Blunt reached the Big Blue, he was directed to occupy the works on the right or southern wing of the line. Blunt in turn posted Jennison's brigade at one of the principal crossings of the river, named Byram's Ford.[42] The next day's fighting was to show that the sector assigned to Blunt was the post of greatest danger, and Byram's Ford, which Jennison and his men were to endeavor to deny to the enemy, was the key to the entire Federal position.

On the morning of the twenty-second, Price's army, minus Fagan's division, which had been left behind at Independence to block Pleasonton's cavalry, drew up in front of Curtis' position on the Big Blue. Price feinted at crossing the river on the direct road from Independence to

40. *Official Records*, XLI, Pt. 1, 572. Blunt says that Jennison had four mountain howitzers. Jennison himself, *ibid.*, 581, says that he had five.

41. *Ibid.*, 478.

42. Price's and Shelby's reports are *ibid.*, 634 and 658, respectively; Jennison's and Blunt's *ibid.*, 584 and 575, respectively. See also [Richard J. Hinton], *Rebel Invasion of Missouri and Kansas and the Campaign of the Army of the Border Against General Sterling Price* (Chicago, 1865), 128–30. The name of the crossing is variously given as Byram's, Byron's, and Byrom's Ford. "Byram's" is used in the *Official Records* reports.

Kansas City at the point covered by the left center of the Federal line, but his main effort was directed at outflanking Curtis' position by forcing a crossing of the river at Byram's Ford, held by Jennison and his small brigade. The reports of Price, and of General Shelby, whose division made the attack at Byram's Ford, imply that the crossing was forced with a minimum of effort; Blunt's and Jennison's reports, on the other hand, suggest fighting of considerable severity. Whatever the truth may be, by midafternoon the Confederates were across the river and well beyond it, and by nightfall they held a line running generally east and west— perpendicular to the line Curtis had held in the morning—some distance below Westport, now a part of Kansas City.

With his defensive line forced and outflanked, Curtis first withdrew his army to Kansas City; then, leaving a part of the Kansas militia behind as a garrison in the city, at 3 A.M. on the twenty-third, he ordered Jennison, encamped just above Westport, to move south to Brush Creek, a tributary of the Big Blue flowing in an easterly direction some two miles south of Westport and bounded on either bank by a belt of scrub and woods nearly a mile wide. The Confederate line of battle was drawn up in the woods along the right, or south, bank of the creek. Jennison was to force a crossing of the creek, and supported by Colonel J. H. Ford's and Colonel L. S. Treat's troops on his left and by Colonel Thomas Moonlight's brigade on the right, he was to attack and drive the Confederates through the woods and onto the open prairie beyond.

What was to be known as the Battle of Westport opened at dawn with the attack of Jennison's, Blunt's, Ford's, and Deitzler's Kansas troops on the right of Price's line. By seven-thirty, this attack had been driven off and the Confederates themselves advanced behind the re-treating Federals to the bank of the creek. From then until about 10 A.M., the fighting consisted of artillery and skirmish fire, with little damage to either side. A second attempt by the Kansans to drive the Confederates out of the protection of the woods on their side of the creek failed also. Then, however, General Curtis, who had taken personal charge of the battle, detected an opening and ordered a general advance, and by eleven o'clock his men had gained the southern edge of the woods and had a foothold on the open prairie beyond. A Confederate counterattack having been checked, Curtis personally ordered Jennison, in the center of the Federal line with his brigade, to make a mounted charge. Hoyt, with six companies of the Fifteenth Kansas, charged to the left of the road running straight toward the center of the Confederate line; Jennison charged to the right of the road, at the head of a mixed group consisting of one company of the Fifteenth, two companies of the Second Colorado Cavalry, four companies of the Third Wisconsin Cavalry, and General Blunt's mounted bodyguard.

Jennison's own description of the charge of his brigade does not err on the side of excessive modesty: "The brigade thus formed advanced, charging the rebel lines with an impetuousity that overcame opposition. The enemy then, confused and demoralized, broke and fled, scattering arms and equipments along the route, and covering the ground with the debris of a routed army. For more than a mile the brigade pursued, never drawing rein, while the rebels, too demoralized to attempt a halt, seemed each determined to save himself as best he might." [43] This account of a broken and demoralized enemy fleeing in confusion is a considerable exaggeration. Nonetheless, General Curtis' report makes it clear that Jennison's charge was the turning point of the battle and the key to an undoubted Federal victory. Curtis attested his approval of Jennison's contribution to victory by listing his name, as well as Hoyt's, in the "Roll of Honor" he appended to his report on the campaign, a list, he said with shaky grammar, "which I hope may be transmitted to posterity, and ask for the generous sympathy of their countrymen and from their Government the advancement due to those who have gained victories, conquered armies, saved cities, and increased the great aggregate of glorious achievements which are crushing the rebellion." [44]

Sunday, October 23, was a cold but clear autumn day. At noon, as Curtis' entire battle line, in the wake of Jennison's charge, began to emerge from the dark woods skirting Brush Creek into the bright sunlight of the open prairie, they heard artillery fire well to the rear and off to the right of the Confederate position. And as they breasted a slight rise, they saw a heavy column of cavalry a mile ahead and to the left, just

43. *Official Records*, XLI, Pt. 1, 586. *Cf.* George S. Grover, "The Price Campaign of 1864," *Missouri Historical Review*, VI (1912), 176. Grover says that "Jennison . . . rode far in advance of his line, straight at the enemy's long gray columns."
44. *Official Records*, XLI, Pt. 1, 519

emerging from a large patch of timber. At first no one knew whether these strange horsemen were friendly or hostile, but as the latter deployed from column into line and moved forward, their battle flags and guidons caught the sunlight and "were hailed with thundering cheers"—for the strangers were Pleasonton's cavalry, arriving at a perfect time and in a perfect position to complete Price's defeat.[45]

At midnight on the twenty-second, as soon as he had driven Fagan's rear guard out of Independence, McNeil was ordered by Pleasonton to take the road leading southwest from there to Little Santa Fe, on the Missouri-Kansas border about ten miles south of Westport, and to be at that point by daylight.[46] Had McNeil but known it, this order gave him the chance of a lifetime. If he had been where Pleasonton wanted him to be on the morning of the twenty-third, squarely behind the Confederate position at Westport, he might have earned the glory of bagging or completely smashing Price's army. But McNeil was not equal to the occasion. It is true that his brigade had been in the saddle, or fighting, for nineteen hours straight when he received Pleasonton's order, and to get from Independence to Little Santa Fe by daylight meant a long, hard night march for tired men on tired and hungry horses. Nevertheless, it could have been done if McNeil had been a driver, but he was not. He got as far as Byram's Ford, well short of his destination, by 4 A.M. and stopped there to feed his horses.[47] He was still there at daylight when the battle began, and then moved off "cautiously" when the occasion called for the utmost energy and daring; he rode for a distance of four or five miles to the south, looking for an opportunity to strike Price in flank.[48] Not until after 1 P.M., by which time Price's army, attacked in front by Curtis and from the flank by Pleasonton, was in full retreat, did McNeil come in sight of Little Santa Fe. And there the fates of war handed him a second great opportunity which he fumbled just as he had fumbled the first.

Instead of keeping his regiments closed up and in a compact mass, so that he could throw the full weight of the brigade into battle the instant the opportunity offered, McNeil permitted the column to become strung

45. [Hinton], *Rebel Invasion*, 166.
46. *Official Records*, XLI, Pt. 1, 341.
47. *Ibid.*, 372. 48. *Ibid.*

out on the march. The Jayhawkers were in the lead, on a branch road to Little Santa Fe, when they came to a high ridge running northwest to southeast and caught sight of the village a short distance ahead. And there, on the road running south a little to the west of the base of the ridge on which they stood, was Price's beaten army, streaming south; at the moment when the Seventh reached the ridge, Price's wagon train, guarded by a meager escort, was passing below them. Major Malone, in command, should have attacked instantly, but with a mere 310 men at hand, he thought it best to halt on the ridge and to send word back to McNeil (who should have been with the advance) that the enemy had been found. An hour went by before McNeil appeared on the scene and surveyed the situation.[49] He ordered Malone to charge and if possible to break the rebel column marching along the road. But it was too late. The Seventh had already been spotted by the enemy. The rebels had had time to set up a defensive line to protect the road and had also occupied in force a patch of timber lying between the road and the ridge, a position from which they could have taken in flank any advance by the Seventh. And as a crowning touch of ineptitude, McNeil had permitted the rest of his brigade to halt a mile back, out of supporting distance of his lead regiment. Every Jayhawker on the ridge knew that for 310 men to charge the rebels under such circumstances would have been madness. McNeil too had second thoughts and cancelled his order to Malone. For the next two hours the Jayhawkers exchanged long-range skirmish fire with the rebels and were forced to watch a large part of Price's army march past their position virtually unmolested; at dusk, the Seventh was ordered to fall back and go into camp.[50]

McNeil's weakness and incompetence enraged the Jayhawkers and General Pleasonton alike. The latter stated in his report that "instead of vigorously attacking the enemy's wagon train, which was directly in front of him with but little escort . . . [McNeil] contented himself with

49. Pomeroy, "War Diary," entry for October 23, 1864. Pomeroy's account of the missed opportunity, written on the day the incident occurred, by an eyewitness who had a sharp pair of eyes and a good mind, appears to be more reliable than McNeil's rather obviously self-serving report, written a month later. After three years in the service, a man of Pomeroy's intelligence was well able to assess a tactical situation and to judge the capabilities of his commanders. His unfavorable verdict on McNeil is quite mild in comparison with General Pleasonton's, *Official Records*, XLI, Pt. 1, 337.

50. Pomeroy, "War Diary," entry for October 23, 1864.

some skirmishing and cannonading, and the train escaped. The rebel General Marmaduke stated after he was captured that had McNeil attacked at this time they would have lost their whole train. I trust that this conduct on the part of General McNeil will meet the marked disapprobation of the major-general commanding, as it has mine."[51] Aside from prolonging the campaign and damaging his reputation, McNeil had also deprived the Jayhawkers of the chance of performing a feat of arms that would have made a bright page in the history of the regiment.

51. *Official Records*, XLI, Pt. 1, 337.

CHAPTER XVI

The Last
Post

IN THE three days following the battle of Westport, Curtis' relentless pursuit turned Price's defeat into a smashing rout. Price still had an army when he camped for the night on the twenty-third. By the evening of the twenty-sixth, he was in command of what was little more than a disorganized rabble. Some of his units kept their cohesion and did so to the end of the campaign, but he was shedding deserters by hundreds and left behind at every step artillery, ammunition, food, broken-down wagons, cattle, camp equipage, mess kits, clothing, plunder, arms, and all the other debris of defeat and flight. Price had to make a stand at dawn on the twenty-fifth to protect the crossing of the Marais des Cygnes—what the natives called the "Mary de Zene"—and was driven back. Later the same morning, forced to make another stand three miles to the south, at the crossing of Mine Creek, the Confederates were routed by simultaneous charges on their two flanks by two brigades of Pleasonton's cavalry. This two-pronged attack resulted in the capture of Generals John S. Marmaduke and William L. Cabell, between five hundred and one thousand of their men, eight pieces of artillery, and a large number of wagons.[1] A number of the prisoners wore Federal uniforms when they were captured. They were executed on the spot.[2]

---

1. *Official Records*, XLI, Pt. 1. The prisoners numbered five to six hundred according to General Curtis (496) and a thousand according to General Pleasonton.
2. *Ibid.*, 352.

The capture of rebel generals was an event of considerable note. The honor of having accepted the surrender of General Marmaduke was claimed by Private James Dunleavy, Third Iowa Cavalry, and rightfully so.[3] But when ex-Private William F. Cody of the Seventh Kansas came to write his autobiography a good many years later, *he* claimed credit for this feat of arms. Disdaining the *Official Records*, he asserted:

In carrying dispatches from General McNeil to General Blunt or General Pleasonton I passed around and through Price's army many times. I always wore the disguise of a Confederate soldier and always escaped detection. . . . Near Mound City a scouting party of which I was a member surprised a small detachment of Price's army. Our advantage was such that they surrendered, and while we were rounding them up I heard one of them say that we Yanks had captured a bigger prize than we suspected. When he was asked what this prize consisted of, the soldier said: "That big man over yonder is General Marmaduke. . . ." I was put in charge of General Marmaduke and accompanied him as his custodian to Fort Leavenworth. The general and I became fast friends, and our friendship lasted long after the war.[4]

For the sake of historical accuracy, it is necessary to contradict even the last, touching part of Cody's heroic myth. Marmaduke's captivity was not solaced by the assignment of the future popular hero to be his escort to Fort Leavenworth; General Curtis, who was not without a sense of the fitness of things, placed the captured Confederate general under the custody of the Eighteenth U.S. Colored Regiment.[5]

The valley of the Little Osage River, a few miles south of Mine Creek, is separated from the latter by a high, undulating belt of prairie. Within moments after smashing Marmaduke's division on the north side of Mine Creek, the Federals were across the stream and in full pursuit of the rest of Price's army toward the Little Osage. His aesthetic perceptions sharpened by the exhilaration of victory, General Curtis now beheld a grand panorama before him:

Being mostly in prairie country the troops of both armies were in full view, and the rapid onward movement of the whole force presented the most extensive, beautiful, and animated view of hostile armies I have ever witnessed. Spread over vast prairies, some moving at full speed in column, some in double

---

3. *Ibid.*, 603–604. Colonel Charles W. Blair, Fourteenth Kansas Cavalry, who witnessed the capture of Marmaduke, spells the captor's name as "Dunlavy" and gives his rank as corporal. *Cf.* [Hinton]. *Rebel Invasion*, 212.

4. Cody, *Autobiography*, 77–78.   5. *Official Records*, XLI, Pt. 1, 496.

lines, and others as skirmishers, groups striving in utmost efforts, and shifting as occasion required, while the great clouds of living masses moved steadily southward, presented a picture of prairie scenery such as neither man nor pencil can delineate.[6]

At the Little Osage, and for the third time on that desperate day, Price had to make a stand to protect a river crossing; but for the third time his covering line was driven across the stream and from one position after another south of it. His men set fire to haystacks and fields of dry corn-stalks along the line of march and to the dry prairie grass on both sides of the road to slow down the Federal advance, and they took advantage of every fold of ground and every fencerow along the way to try to bring the pursuit to a halt; but nothing availed, and in midafternoon the Con-federates were once again brought to bay, this time on the north bank of the Marmiton River. And here, while two of his brigades fought the enemy and pressed him back to the river with such vigor that Price ordered his remaining wagons burned to prevent their falling into the hands of the Federals, Pleasonton made the kind of decision that goes far to explain why he had been replaced as chief of cavalry of the Army of the Potomac. His men and horses were desperately tired. Their exertions on the twenty-third, twenty-fourth, and twenty-fifth climaxed a march of several hundred miles on Price's heels across Missouri. His wagons had been unable to keep up; they were miles behind and out of reach. Fort Scott, where his men and animals could be fed and rested, lay six miles away, directly to the west. So conscious of his troopers' fatigue, and perhaps even more so of his own, that he lost sight of the fact that the Confederates were in much worse straits, Pleasonton ignored General Curtis' pleas and expostulations, and leaving his two brigades on the Marmiton to fend for themselves, he departed with the rest of his divi-sion for Fort Scott. Because of a mixup in orders, Blunt followed him. As a result, Price, nearly at his last gasp on the evening of the twenty-fifth, was relieved of the pressure of the Federal pursuit, and for the next two and a half days, he went his way undisturbed.

The roads taken by Price on his retreat ran close to the Kansas-Missouri line, on the Kansas side for part of the way, and for part of the way on the Missouri side, but at no point, during the first few days of

6. *Ibid.*, 497.

his retreat, more than four or five miles on one side or the other of the boundary. Hence the two armies marched through a belt of country that for nearly ten years had been the scene of almost incessant fighting, jay-hawking, and mutual reprisals. Captain Richard J. Hinton, Second Kansas (Colored) Infantry, who took part in the campaign as aide-de-camp to General Blunt, later wrote:

The border of Missouri, through which both armies were passing, was entirely desolate; not with the grand monotony of nature, but with the ruin of civilization and cultivation. . . . During the fifty miles of this march not an inhabitant was to be seen. Where they had lived was marked by the charred remains of consumed dwellings, the only standing parts of which were brick chimneys. . . . These are familiarly known as Jennison's Tombstones. . . . Long lines of gray ashes told where fences had stood; while rank crops of unsightly weeds marked where cultivation had once smiled.[7]

Price's men, and especially the Missouri recruits in his army, reacted characteristically and predictably to the desolation they saw all around them. They added to it whenever they had the chance. Even after the stories that followed their passage are discounted for the typical exaggeration of atrocity tales, the residue is sufficiently grim. On the twenty-fourth, when Price was on the Kansas side of the line, "every house within reach . . . was robbed of everything it contained. All kinds of clothing were taken. . . . Every morsel of food . . . was consumed, destroyed or taken along; and all the stock that could be led or driven was taken."[8] Had Price's men done no more than to take forcibly the food and clothing they needed, their actions would have been no different and no worse than those of most armies operating in enemy territory. But on his march through Missouri, Price had swept into his army thousands of "buccaneers, bushwhackers, deserters and campfollowers" whom he had no means of keeping under control, and what little discipline he had established among them had been swept away by defeat.[9] Their march through Kansas left behind a trail of robbery, arson, and murder: "Six miles north of . . . Trading Post they murdered Samuel A. Long, aged fifty-six years; he was previously robbed of his money. Three miles north of . . . Trading Post, John Williams, a preacher, aged sixty years, was

7. [Hinton], *Rebel Invasion*, 186–87.
8. *Ibid.*, 190.
9. Samuel J. Crawford, *Kansas in the Sixties* (Chicago, 1911), 170.

indecently mutilated and then hung."[10] And the catalogue of horrors goes on. Richard B. Vernon murdered; John Miller, aged sixty-five, murdered. Another witness tells us:

As the rebels passed through Lincoln and Valley townships . . . the Texas troops . . . marched in close ranks in military order, while the Missourians were scattered all over the country murdering and pillaging. At old Sammy Nickel's place a visitor, just after their passage, asked Mrs. Nickel how they had fared. She said the rebels took everything—all they had left was at the end of a rope out at the barn. Jennison had caught one of the pillagers there and refused him a soldier's death and hung him.[11]

The old game of atrocities followed by reprisals was on again. The "pillager" left hanging at the end of a rope in Sammy Nickel's barn may have been one of the gang who had robbed the Nickels of everything they possessed, or he may have been a half-starved straggler looking for a meal hours after the real pillagers had left. It made no difference; in either case, he was a rebel and a Missourian and deserved to be hanged. Nor was he the first of the victims of Jennison's and Hoyt's men on this campaign. It is said that in the fighting preceding the battle of Westport, the Fifteenth Kansas gave no quarter to prisoners, and that on the day of the battle they executed four Kansas militiamen whom they mistook for Missouri bushwhackers.[12]

As Price moved south, the Seventh, last seen encamped some distance to the east of Little Santa Fe on the night of October 23, could have entertained, after the frustrations of the day, precious little respect for their brigade commander and little confidence in his leadership qualities. Indeed, General McNeil was not one of the better volunteer officers. A hatter by trade, he had failed in business in New York. A second start in St. Louis proved more successful. By 1861 McNeil possessed a large fortune. On the outbreak of war he was commissioned colonel of the Nineteenth Missouri Infantry. Later, he became colonel of a regiment of cavalry in the state militia and was given command of the District of Southwestern Missouri, where he made a name for himself by pursuing

10. [Hinton], *Rebel Invasion*, 191. Trading Post was a small settlement at the crossing of the Marais des Cygnes. Price's army halted there for the night on the twenty-fourth.
11. William A. Mitchell, "Historic Linn," *Collections of the Kansas State Historical Society, 1923–1925*, XVI, 654.
12. Palmer, "Black Flag Character," 460.

a ruthless policy against guerillas. In the fall of 1862 he discovered that fifteen of a group of forty-seven guerillas he had recently captured had previously been paroled and were in arms in violation of the terms of their paroles. He had all fifteen executed. On a later occasion, when a citizen of Palmyra, Missouri, named Allsman was taken from his home by "the guerilla Colonel Porter" and killed, McNeil hanged ten of Porter's men in retaliation.[13]

However tough he may have been in dealing with guerillas, McNeil had failed dismally in his first real test as a military leader on October 23. On the following day he caught up with Pleasonton. Ordered to take the lead of the cavalry division "and attack the enemy . . . day or night," he marched until midnight and then halted and went into camp some distance north of the Marais des Cygnes on orders supposedly in Pleasonton's name which he claimed he had received through the staff of another brigade; he learned at daylight the next morning that "no such order could have been given by the general commanding."[14] Already in deep disfavor because of his ineptitude of the twenty-third, McNeil further antagonized Pleasonton with this episode. Since the other brigades of cavalry had kept on going for some three hours when McNeil stopped for the night, the latter found himself completely out of touch with the rest of the division on the morning of the twenty-fifth; his regiments were not on hand at the Marais des Cygnes, and they were still not up with the rest of the cavalry when the fighting at Mine Creek was already over and the bulk of Pleasonton's forces had crossed the stream and were pushing the rebels across the Little Osage. Pleasonton complained to General Curtis that "McNeil seemed insubordinate or neglectful of his orders and did not come forward as directed."[15] Curtis sent his adjutant, Major Chapman S. Charlot, to McNeil, with peremptory orders to get his brigade up to the front at the utmost speed of his horses. When at last McNeil arrived on the scene, he was apparently able to convince Curtis that the delay in coming forward was not his fault and that Pleasonton's orders directing him to advance had never reached him. McNeil was

13. [Hinton], *Rebel Invasion*, 345.
14. *Official Records*, XLI, Pt. 1, 372.
15. *Ibid.*, 496. It is significant that in his report of the campaign, the only one of his brigade commanders Pleasonton did not commend "to favorable consideration" was McNeil. See *ibid.*, 342.

now in the unenviable position of having received and acted on orders which his superior officer did not send and of having failed to receive and act on orders which *were* sent, all within a space of less than twelve hours. Fortunately for him, Curtis was far more tolerant than Sheridan, for example, would have been under similar circumstances. McNeil was allowed to retain his command, and after assuring Curtis that he was "ready to obey all orders as promptly as possible," he was ordered to deploy his brigade and to take the advance.[16]

For the first time since the pursuit began, the Seventh was now in contact with the enemy, and after a brisk fight in cornfields and timber, the regiment drove the Confederates off the high ground skirting the south bank of the Little Osage. Some distance beyond, the rebels made a stand along the edge of another cornfield, and their small arms fire brought McNeil's advance to a halt. Accordingly, McNeil "formed his brigade in close column of companies, and made them a little speech while forming to the effect that it made no difference whether there was 1,000 or 10,000 men in that field, he wanted them to ride right over them and saber them down as fast as they came to them."[17] This was the kind of language Civil War cavalrymen expected to hear from their leaders. They "responded with a yell, the dismounted skirmishers tore down the fence in the face of a galling fire, and the column swept through it like a tornado."[18] A second line the Confederates formed on the prairie behind the cornfield was charged also and broken at the first onset; and so was a third line the rebels attempted to form further to the rear. General Mc-Neil's stock had now risen considerably in the estimation of his men.

McNeil's brigade was still in the lead and in close contact with the enemy when, in midafternoon, Price halted north of the Marmiton River, and formed a quadruple line of battle, his flanks resting on Little Marmiton Creek on one side and on Shiloh Creek on the other. His lines extended on each side far beyond the ends of the battle line formed by McNeil's small brigade; but made bold by his successes earlier in the day, McNeil ordered an attack as soon as his artillery had brought to a halt an advance by Price's first line. As he moved forward against the Con-

---

16. *Ibid.*, 496. 17. *Ibid.*, 605.
18. *Ibid.* The dismounted skirmishers were the troopers of the Fifth Missouri State Militia Cavalry.

federates, eight hundred yards ahead, McNeil was joined by Colonel Frederick W. Benteen's brigade. The two brigades of dismounted cavalry pressed back the center of Price's front line, and a second attack drove back his right, but as the Confederates slowly retreated, darkness descended on the field and the fighting came to an end.[19]

It was then that General Pleasonton left McNeil and Benteen to fend for themselves and took the rest of his division to Fort Scott. The Jayhawkers and the other regiments in the two brigades had marched, fought, and charged over a distance of forty-five miles since dawn. Their horses were so exhausted that in the final, mounted attack of the day, "the utmost exertions of officers and men could not move . . . [them] to a trot or a gallop," and the "charge" was delivered at a walk.[20] When at last the fighting stopped, the two brigades halted for the night in line of battle on the open prairie, with no fuel for fires and no food either for the men or the horses. General Curtis had sent one of his aides to Fort Scott with orders to have rations and feed sent on for McNeil and Benteen, and a train of wagons actually started out with supplies for the two brigades; but due to a misunderstanding, they turned back after a short march. At daylight the next morning, the Jayhawkers found enough standing corn in a nearby field to feed their horses, the first feed the miserable animals had had in thirty-two hours, during which time the regiment had marched 112 miles. The dry cornstalks made good fires for boiling coffee, and providentially, the Jayhawkers' own supply wagons arrived while the horses were feeding. Three days' rations of hardtack were issued, and the men had a feast. The last previous distribution of rations had been three days before, when each man was given two pieces of hardtack; and with the rebels before them sweeping up everything in the way of eatables along the line of march, foraging for additional food had been out of the question.

When Pleasonton marched away from the Marmiton River to Fort Scott, General Curtis at first thought that he could do nothing but acquiesce, for Pleasonton was subordinate to Rosecrans and not to himself. But during the night he decided to assert his prerogatives as commander of the department and in effect took over command of

19. General Curtis, in his report, *ibid.*, 502, calls this the Battle of Charlot.
20. *Ibid.*, 373.

Pleasonton's division. On the morning of the twenty-sixth, he sent Blunt's division, and what had been Pleasonton's division, forward to resume the pursuit. Pleasonton himself, "unable to move" because of a severe fall and exhaustion brought on by his "late arduous services," remained behind at Fort Scott.[21]

By marching day and night and double-teaming his artillery and supply wagons, Curtis was able to catch up with Price just south of Newtonia, Missouri, on the afternoon of October 28. Earlier in the day, his two divisions had marched through the town of Carthage, which had been a flourishing settlement of a thousand inhabitants until, just four weeks before, it was put to the torch by a guerilla band. Unable to resist the opportunity of displaying his classical learning, General Curtis spoke in his report of "halting . . . at the ruins of Carthage."[22]

The first contact with the enemy at Newtonia was made by Blunt at the head of Jennison's and Ford's brigades of his division. Not content with a passive defense, Price attacked as soon as Blunt deployed his two brigades and drove them back in some disorder for a distance of five hundred yards; but the timely arrival of Sanborn's brigade of Pleasonton's division enabled Blunt to stabilize his position and then to go over to the attack. He dislodged the Confederates, and in the gathering darkness Price "abandoned the field and retreated rapidly . . . in the direction of Pineville," leaving his dead and wounded in the hands of the Federals.[23] In this, the last serious engagement of the pursuit, George Hoyt, commanding Jennison's brigade in the latter's absence, greatly distinguished himself for his "coolness and courage and the excellent manner in which . . . [he] handled . . . [his] troops on the field."[24]

The Jayhawkers and the rest of McNeil's brigade were too far behind Blunt's leading units to take part in the fight at Newtonia, but with Blunt's division considerably cut up in the battle, McNeil was ordered to lead the pursuit the following morning. The victory at Newtonia caused Curtis to believe that he now had Price at his mercy: "Everything now promised complete success in view of our close proximity to the enemy, his exhausted condition, and his disastrous defeat. . . . By pressing him

21. *Ibid.*, 506.   22. *Ibid.*, 507.
23. *Ibid.*, 577.
24. *Ibid.*, 578. Captain Tough, former head of the Red Legs and General Blunt's chief scout in this campaign, also distinguished himself in this engagement. See [Hinton], *Rebel Invasion*, 268.

another day or two, he would have no time to collect supplies . . . and must surrender or starve." [25] But shortly after 3 A.M. on the twenty-ninth, just as McNeil's brigade was starting out on the day's march, a despatch rider arrived from the end of the telegraph line fifty miles north with orders from Rosecrans that the brigades of McNeil and Sanborn were to return at once to Rolla and Springfield, respectively. These orders were three days old when Curtis got them and were based on Pleasonton's representations to Rosecrans that the two brigades "were so broken down it would be impossible without fresh horses to strike the enemy another great blow." [26] Aside from ignoring the probability that the condition of the rebels was even worse, Pleasonton's statement was accurate enough. Sanborn's brigade had marched 102 miles in thirty-six hours when it intervened in the fight at Newtonia, and the Jayhawkers' horses had not been fed for forty-two hours when the regiment arrived there at midnight after the battle. [27]

Copies of Rosecrans' orders were thoughtfully provided by Pleasonton for Generals McNeil and Sanborn, and they at once proceeded to carry them out. No doubt they shared the relief and pleasure of their men at the prospect of being out of an ever more miserable campaign. The weather in the last few days had been abominable, with alternating spells of rain and snow; many of the horses had given out entirely and were abandoned, and most of the remaining animals were broken down and starving. After the campaign was over, Webster Moses wrote that at one point his horse had not been unsaddled for four straight days. And the men were in little better condition than the horses. The historian of the Fourth Iowa Cavalry, one of the regiments which took part in the campaign, relates:

In a campaign so long and active army clothing would go to pieces. Many of the men had not enough left to keep them warm. On the ice and frozen ground their cheap army boots gave out, and a large number of them were not only dismounted but barefoot. Many were hatless, all were ragged and shivering. All the remaining horses were greatly jaded, many permanently injured, and none were able to move with speed. At the end of the march there were not one hundred horses in the whole brigade able to carry their owners. . . . In

25. *Official Records*, XLI, Pt. 1, 510.   26. *Ibid.*, 314.
27. Pomeroy, "War Diary," entry for October 28, 1864.

bitter weather, without shelter, without sufficient food, that shabby and weary column dragged itself painfully along.[28]

The pleasure of the two brigades in the imminent end of their miseries was to be short-lived. His forces reduced to barely one thousand men after McNeil's and Sanborn's departure, Curtis was forced to abandon the pursuit. He had just started on the long march back to Leavenworth when at midnight on the twenty-ninth he received a despatch from Halleck to tell him that Grant, Commanding General of the Armies of the United States since February, wanted Price harried to the Arkansas River. Curtis at once sent couriers after McNeil and Sanborn ordering them to rejoin him, and himself turned about in the morning and marched toward Cassville to resume the pursuit. The Seventh had reached Springfield when Curtis's recall orders arrived. The horses were inspected on November 2; about 70 of them were condemned as unserviceable; leaving the dismounted men behind with instructions to proceed to St. Louis, the regiment, reduced now to 196 officers and men, started out for Cassville on the morning of the third, and arrived there on the sixth. McNeil reported to Curtis that his advance beyond that point would be "regulated by supplies"; he also expressed the fear "that the belly impediment" would halt his further progress—which it did.[29]

On November 8, Election Day, the Jayhawkers were still at Cassville. Kansas, unlike some other states, had made no provision to allow its soldiers in the field to cast their ballots for president; but the Seventh conducted a straw vote to allow the men to express their political convictions. Of the 196 votes cast, 186 were for Abraham Lincoln, 9 for McClellan, and one for Fremont. On the same day, what little remained of Price's army reached the Arkansas River, with Curtis hard on its heels. McNeil and Sanborn had not succeeded in catching up with Curtis. Quite clearly they had made little effort to do so and now their services were no longer needed. The campaign was over. Price, said General Curtis, "had been pursued beyond the Arkansas, carrying away with him the murderers, marauders and bushwhackers that infested Missouri, Arkansas and Kansas. He entered Missouri, feasting and furnishing his

28. Scott, *Story of a Cavalry Regiment*, 346–47.
29. *Official Records*, XLI, Pt. 4, 459.

troops on the rich products and abundant spoils of the Missouri Valley, but crossed the Arkansas destitute, disarmed, disorganized, and avoiding starvation by eating raw corn and slippery elm bark." [30]

There was no reason any longer for the McNeil brigade to remain in the southwestern corner of Missouri. It marched off across the state to Rolla, where it arrived on November 15. There, with the regiments formed in column of battalions, McNeil made them a short speech, thanking officers and men for their "prompt obedience of orders," and formally dissolved the brigade. [31] The Seventh went into camp in Rolla without tents or other shelter, to await orders to proceed to St. Louis. But no one complained about the lack of shelter, for food was plentiful, and what was just as important, the regiment received its first mail in three months. The men "received about six letters each and . . . for a time forgot camp life." [32] There was opportunity too to catch up on the war news, and all of it was good. It made the Jayhawkers "think that the war is now of short duration Gen Sherman will soon be heard from Gen Hoods army will proberly be *used up* and the end of the Rebellion draws nigh." [33]

After another inspection of horses which left the regiment with but seventy-five barely serviceable animals, the Seventh traveled by train to St. Louis on November 22. After a brief stay in camp near Jefferson Barracks, it moved to Benton Barracks on the twenty-seventh and for a few days enjoyed the luxury of living under a roof. The regiment had participated in the Price campaign for fifty-eight days, during which time it marched nearly one thousand miles and was in several skirmishes and fights, but had the good fortune not to lose a single man killed or wounded. Nevertheless, deaths and discharges because of illness, and the departure of time-expired men, left the Seventh greatly depleted in numbers. Companies averaged not much over thirty officers and men each, and the total strength of the regiment was well under four hundred.

A few days' rest in barracks helped to revive the bodies and spirits of the men. The arrival of mail from home and the ability to send letters

30. *Ibid.*, Pt. 1, 518.
31. Pomeroy, "War Diary," entry for November 15, 1864.
32. Webster Moses to Nancy Mowry, November 20, 1864, in Moses Letters.
33. *Ibid.*

were both a great help; it helped too when the ladies of St. Louis sent the regiment several barrels of apples to brighten its Thanksgiving dinner. On the twenty-eighth came the announcement of Major Malone's promotion to lieutenant colonel.[34] Three days later the men were issued new clothing to replace the rags in which they had returned from the Price campaign, and they exchanged their guns for the finest cavalry weapon of the Civil War, the seven-shot, breech-loading Spencer carbine.

The new clothing and the Spencers were an indication that the rest the regiment had enjoyed since its return to St. Louis was about to end, and on December 2 eight companies left the city for garrison duty at various points in east-central Missouri. Companies B and F were sent to DeSoto to guard the Iron Mountain Railroad; Companies C, D, and E went to Franklin to guard the Pacific Railroad; Company G went to Sulphur Springs; and Companies I and K were sent due west to Hermann, on the Missouri River.[35] Companies A and H were retained on garrison duty in St. Louis. Two weeks later, Companies C, E, A, and H were ordered to join the two companies already at DeSoto, and at the same time, Company G was moved from Sulphur Springs to Pilot Knob.[36] Individual companies were shifted about from time to time as flareups of guerilla activity in various areas required the attention of troops who knew how to deal with them. It was, of course, understood that in addition to maintaining a passive guard over the stretches of track and the bridges entrusted to their care, the Jayhawkers would also go on the hunt for guerillas whenever possible. This policy of an active campaign against the guerillas wherever they showed their heads was ordered by Major General Grenville M. Dodge, who assumed command of the Department of the Missouri December 9, Rosecrans having been relieved at Grant's specific request. At the end of his period of command some months later, Dodge reported that when he arrived in St. Louis, "The greater part of the State was in a state of confusion approaching anarchy, continually fermented by marauders, guerilla bands, and roving Confederates who were murdering, robbing, and committing all the outrages

34. Malone's commission as lieutenant colonel was dated November 19, 1864. See *Report of the Adjutant General of the State of Kansas*, I, 524. His promotion was announced to the regiment on November 28. See Pomeroy, "War Diary," entry for November 28, 1864.

35. Pomeroy, "War Diary," entry for December 1, 1864.

36. *Official Records*, XLI, Pt. 4, 830, 831, 906, and 979.

known to crime. . . . The troops . . . in the department were . . . taken away from the towns, and placed in the field, with orders to go into the brush and hunt down and exterminate all bands of guerillas and marauders . . . and before spring most of the guerillas and marauders were either killed, captured or driven beyond the State."[37]

The scattered companies of the Seventh did their share in the killing, capturing, and driving of guerillas spoken of by General Dodge. In early March they killed "Capt. Howard" and eight of his men; a few days later they killed two of "Bolin's gang" and wounded several more, and in April Lieutenant William W. Crane of Company K surprised another gang of fifteen guerillas in camp and killed four of them.[38] There were, of course, futile chases also, and occasionally an incident spiced with humor, as when a guerilla chieftain with a formidable reputation, named Jeff Thompson, was reported headed north toward Mineral Point with four hundred men behind him. Thompson's approach inspired a flurry of telegrams and despatches which take up several pages of the *Official Records*, including the following sprightly epistle sent by a Captain William T. Leeper to Colonel Malone: "There is not a man here who feels the least uneasiness, but we all think that we are sufficient to the day and hour thereof, and if Jeff, Thompson comes let him come and be d——d to him. Our wish is not to be ordered away until we see him or some other elephant. In short, I think it all a very great humbug."[39] And Captain Leeper proved to be correct, for Lieutenant John H. Wildey of Company C, who was sent out to look for the redoubtable Thompson and his four hundred guerillas, came back with a report of success; he killed "one-third of Jeff's command and captured all his horses. Number killed, 1; number of command, 3; aggregate, 3. This is all the rebel force there was."[40]

By and large, the Jayhawkers had a delightful winter of it, especially welcome after the exertions and hardships of September, October, and November. From Moselle Bridge on the Meramec River (which he usually spelled "Merrimac") Webster Moses wrote the following paean about it:

37. *Ibid.*, XLVIII, Pt. 1, 329–30.   38. *Ibid.*, 129, 183.
39. *Ibid.*, 209. Other despatches dealing with the Jeff Thompson scare are *ibid.*, 208, 209, 210, 211, and 226.
40. *Ibid.*, 226.

I wish you could come and see how comfortably we are situated. We have good new cabbins and good stables for our horses then the scenery is so beautifull the Merrimac is one of the prettyest streams of water I have ever seen and runs a few rods from our door . . . we have good kind neighbors this is the best place we have had since we have been in the service. . . . We have various ways of spending our leisure time during the day we hunt wild Turkeys and Deer or go fishing or visiting the neighbors Evenings we build a bright fire in our huge chimneys and pass the time either in reading telling long stories or talking often of those at home. . . . The weather is . . . very disagreeable but we stay in our quarters more closely build our fires brighter and think of the many poor soldiers who are exposed to all kinds of hardships without any shelter.[41]

This letter was written on December 16, which was also the second day of the battle of Nashville, in which General George Thomas, using the dismounted cavalry of General James H. Wilson as a scythe, nearly destroyed General Hood's army, an event prophesied by Moses three weeks before. And before Moses wrote his next letter to Nancy Mowry, Sherman, having completed the march from Atlanta to the sea, had presented to President Lincoln, "as a Christmas gift, the city of Savannah."

Indeed, the second half of Webster Moses' prophecy, that "the end of the Rebellion draws nigh," was also coming to pass. But while Sherman's troops were taking Savannah and Wilson's were pursuing Hood's defeated army, nothing but an occasional guerilla scare disturbed the Jayhawkers' enjoyment of an idyllic existence. Duties were negligible, and the citizens in the neighborhood either were, or pretended to be, friendly to the strangers the chances of war had deposited in their midst. It must be said, however, that Missouri hospitality exposed the boys from Kansas and Illinois to a considerable strain on their moral sensibilities. At Christmastime, Moses and the men of his detachment were "of course" invited to a neighborhood social gathering. They accepted with some apprehension, and it was an obviously shocked trooper who later reported to Nancy Mowry:

In my life I have seen a great many public gatherings of all descriptions but none equal to this . . . after dancing several sets supper was announced the supper was very good then *ladies* and *gentlemen* all had a smoke either cigars or pipe then dancing most of the time until 12 midnight when the Whisky was

41. Webster Moses to Nancy Mowry, December 16, 1864, in Moses Letters.

passed round when most of the *Ladies* and *Gentlemen* took a drink then another smoke indeed some were smoking most of the time which in decent society would be most disagreeable. I returned to camp completely disgusted with Mo society—if that is a specimen.[42]

Notwithstanding the horror produced by exposure to the strange and deplorable customs of what Moses called the *"Lager Beer Dutch"* of Missouri, it is doubtful if the Jayhawkers would have favored changing places with any other regiment in the service. Parents and friends took advantage of the proximity of the regiment and came visiting from Kansas and Illinois. On at least one occasion, a parental visit nearly led to an embarrassing situation. When Mrs. Eatinger arrived from Providence, Illinois, to visit her two sons, members of Company D, one of them, Richard, was absent from camp. He was, in fact, languishing in Myrtle Street prison in St. Louis as punishment for some military misdemeanor. The story, however, had a happy ending. Colonel Malone arranged to have Richard released from prison so that his mother could enjoy the company of both her sons. And now, too, the more serious members of the regiment began to make plans for the day, which could not be too far distant, when the war would be over. Fletcher Pomeroy, who was one of these, bought 160 acres of good Kansas farmland from Joel J. Crook, the assistant surgeon of the regiment. Another Jayhawker, on the other hand, Private William T. Johns, was relieved of the necessity of planning a peacetime career. He was convicted of stealing two trunks and their contents, worth three hundred dollars, from two ladies of Farmington, Missouri, and was sentenced to a dishonorable discharge and imprisonment for three years in the Missouri State Penitentiary.[43]

In January, 1865, horses were issued to those of the Jayhawkers who had been dismounted ever since their return from the pursuit of Price, and the regiment was gradually relieved of the duty of guarding bridges and tracks. As spring came on, it was used more and more in company-size detachments to hunt down roving bands of guerillas who, contrary to General Dodge's boast, had not all been killed, captured, or driven from Missouri.[44] One Jayhawker, however, was absent from these gue-

---

42. Same to same, December 29, 1864, *ibid.*
43. General Orders No. 15, February 10, 1865, in Seventh Kansas, Company Order Books.
44. *Official Records*, XLVIII, Pt. 1, 535 and 607; *ibid.*, Pt. 2, 496.

rilla hunts; this was Webster Moses, who was given a furlough to go back to Illinois to marry Nancy Mowry. Another absentee was William Cody. Contrary to his own later "recollections," the official records of the regiment indicate that his career as a Jayhawker was of an almost excessively prosaic and peaceful variety and left no scope for the heroics with which he later embellished it. On January 20 he was detailed for duty as hospital orderly, and four weeks later he was ordered to report for duty in St. Louis "as messenger at the office of the Freedmen's Relief Society."[45]

Great events were taking place while Webster Moses was on his way back to his regiment after his honeymoon. At nine in the evening of April 3, a despatch arrived at regimental headquarters at Pilot Knob announcing the evacuation of Richmond by General Lee and its occupation by the Army of the Potomac. Pomeroy, in characteristically restrained fashion, noted in his diary before he turned in for the night that there was "great rejoicing and enthusiasm in camp over the news."[46] Three days later, at noon sharp, a salute of one hundred guns was fired by order of the War Department in honor of Grant's victory. And hardly had the sound of this impressive salute died away when even more momentous news arrived: on April 9 General Lee surrendered the Army of Northern Virginia to General Grant. The next day, a two hundred gun salute was fired to signalize what everyone realized was nearly the end of the rebellion; and to make the salute as spectacular as possible, it was fired from the largest siege guns in camp. It was just two days short of four years from the moment when General Beauregard's artillerymen fired on Fort Sumter in Charleston Harbor, and the jubilation at Pilot Knob on April 10 was a reflection of the length and dreadful strains of a desperate, bloody, four-year war. Nowhere had the war been attended with greater horrors, nowhere had it been fought with a more uncompromising grimness, nowhere had it been more of a *civil* war, than in Missouri. There was, therefore, a good reason for the jubilation at Pilot Knob. On the evening of the tenth, a huge bonfire was lighted on top of the mountain which gave the town its name, and rockets were sent up, visible in sixteen counties, in honor of the glad tidings.

45. Orders dated January 20 [*sic*, January 2?], 1865, signed by Captain Edward Thornton; Special Orders No. 40, February 9, 1865, in Seventh Kansas, Company Order Books.
46. Pomeroy, "War Diary," entry for April 9, 1865.

But the rejoicing came to a shocked halt at Pilot Knob on April 15. Word came that day that President Lincoln had been assassinated. And Sergeant Fletcher Pomeroy set down in his diary words that the dead president would have been proud to have as his epitaph; "I feel," Pomeroy wrote, "as though I had lost a dear personal friend." And he added, "The nation has lost one whose place cannot be filled."[47]

The death of President Lincoln had a sequel in Pilot Knob that must also be told in Fletcher Pomeroy's words: "A rebel prisoner in the stockade here expressed his delight on learning of the death of President Lincoln. Our officers held a council to debate the propriety and justice of shooting him. When the final vote was taken there were 25 ayes and 5 nays. As the vote was not unanimous the case was referred to Department headquarters in St. Louis."[48] The reply from St. Louis arrived ten days later. It was in the negative:

This did not satisfy our boys, so he and another who had expressed like sentiments were shot today. . . . Our men knew it would not do to have a public execution after having received orders from department headquarters to the contrary. We had been using the prisoners occasionally for fatigue duty. . . . I needed a detail of men today to go out several miles for wood. They sent the prisoners. When they returned the two prisoners were not among them. The guard reported that those two men attempted to escape, and they had to shoot them to prevent their escape.

Feeling no doubt that the incident called for the expression of a moral judgment, Pomeroy added: "This act is not justifiable by all rules of war and justice, but it is certainly no more than could be expected under the intense excitement following so tragic an event as the assassination of our honored and beloved president by the hand of the rebel foe."[49]

JENNISON PAYS THE PIPER

The Fifteenth Kansas returned from the pursuit of Price to receive the plaudits of all Kansas. Jennison was "received by a salute" tendered him by his fellow townsmen of Leavenworth, "and a general joy seemed consequent upon his return."[50] George Hoyt also was "saluted upon his

47. *Ibid.*, entry for April 15, 1865.   48. *Ibid.*, entry for April 16, 1865.
49. *Ibid.*, entry for April 25, 1865.
50. This and the quotation which follows are from an unidentified clipping, Jennison Scrapbook.

arrival, and welcomed by his many friends," and it was noted with approval that he wore "the honors he won at Newtonia, with becoming grace." At the conclusion of the campaign, before starting north from the Arkansas River, General Blunt had issued a congratulatory order to his division. He recapitulated the events of the long campaign and singled out Jennison's brigade for special commendation, authorizing the regiments composing it "to inscribe upon their banners" the names of the five battles in which the brigade had distinguished itself, namely, Lexington, Little Blue, Big Blue, Westport, and Newtonia.[51]

But within a matter of days after the arrival of the Fifteenth in its home state, strange reports about its doings on the march south through Missouri and on the return march from the Arkansas River began to make the rounds. One story had it that in retaliation for the killing of a number of their wounded comrades after they had been taken prisoner, the Fifteenth had hanged a "couple of wounded rebels found in a house a few miles from Carthage."[52] It was said, further, that the Fifteenth had run amok on its way home; detailed and circumstantial stories were told of their misdeeds on their passage through Benton and Washington counties in Arkansas, of the plundering of "citizens indiscriminately of the last vestiges of moveable property that had been spared by all previous gangs of thieves," and of the burning of the houses of "peaceful citizens, whom they . . . made outcasts and beggars in their own country."[53] And in fact, Jennison's men appeared to glory in these squalid exploits; to make certain that all Kansas would know about them, they sent letters on ahead to the Leavenworth newspapers, boasting of what they had done. One such letter announced:

Bushwhackers . . . in life and property, have felt the pangs of retaliatory measures as justly and properly inaugurated and fully carried out by Col. Jennison. Arkansas guerilla mothers and sisters use the name of the latter already to frighten unruly children, and by the light of burning houses and beside the blackening timbers of their homes, wish perhaps that "dad hadn't been and gone off with Price or into the brush." . . . The country from

51. Blunt's congratulatory order (General Field Orders No. 6, Camp on the Arkansas River, November 8, 1864) is quoted in full in an unidentified clipping, *ibid.*
52. [Hinton], *Rebel Invasion*, 262
53. *Ibid.*, 310, quoting an article in the June 7, 1865, issue of the Arkansas *Journal*, which Hinton calls a "radical and loyal" paper.

Fayetteville to the line of the Cherokee nation will date from Jennison's campaign, and many a bushwhacker will find his corncrib empty and the crib itself invisible.[54]

And of course the responsibility for these "retaliatory measures" lay with the people of Arkansas, for, as the writer went on to explain, "every family in and around Cane Hill and below, has from one to four of its male members in the rebel army or among the licensed banditti of the CSA. . . . They hang like cossacks upon our rear, and better were a man with a millstone about his neck in the middle of the Missouri than almost anywhere in the *brush* after the command has passed. . . . We have gone through the pond, and the ducks won't settle again this winter."

But—and this must be set down on the credit side of the ledger when the responsibility of the people of Kansas for the horrors of the Civil War in Missouri is assessed—the winter of 1864–1865 was not the winter of 1861–1862, and conduct that was condoned and even applauded in the first winter of the war evoked a reaction of shock and disapproval three years later. Many of the officers of Jennison's brigade were horrified by what they had witnessed and made it their business to protest to General Blunt when they got back to Kansas.

On December 8 Blunt sent a despatch to Brigadier General J. M. Thayer, commanding the District of the Frontier, Department of Arkansas, to ask him to "ascertain all the facts" about the conduct of the Fifteenth Kansas on its passage through Washington and Benton counties; the information Blunt wanted was to be in the form of sworn affidavits, to be taken only from witnesses of unquestioned loyalty. Blunt explained that he had "learned unofficially that the command under C. R. Jennison . . . commited many acts of vandalism. . . . This outrageous conduct of Col Jennison and a portion of his Command . . . was wholly unauthorized by Superior officers and is very much deprecated. . . . I am causing an investigation into the conduct of Col. Jennison . . . with the [object] of meting out just punishment to the guilty parties."[55] Thayer had been ordered to evacuate the District of the Frontier before he received Blunt's despatch, and he was unable to procure the affidavits;

54. Letter datelined Newtonia, Missouri, November 18, 1864, unidentified clipping, Jennison Scrapbook.
55. Blunt to Brigadier General John M. Thayer, December 8, 1864, copy in Kansas State Historical Society, Topeka.

but Blunt collected enough information in other ways to satisfy him that the reports he had received were accurate.

Before Blunt was ready to act, Jennison went out of his way to make the general's task easier. On November 23, on reaching Fort Scott, Jennison issued orders formally dissolving his brigade, and on the same day he resumed command of the First Sub-District of South Kansas. On December 6 Blunt sent him orders cutting down the limits of his command to a five-county area.[56] This brought forth one of Jennison's characteristic outbursts; he sent the following protest to Blunt's adjutant general:

General Order No. 32 is received which leaves under my command part of 5 Cos. of the Fifteenth KVC. . . . My entire command now consists of less than . . . two hundred and fifty men for duty. I have been notified that unless I would run all military matters for J. H. Lane, my regiment would be broken up and would be crushed. I enlisted as a soldier, and not a politician, not thinking that national interests were to be sacrificed to personal ambition. Five Cos. of my regiment are given to a commander who is in the Dept. for . . . five months and during which time they never had a drill or dress parade nor military discipline whatever. . . . If I exhibited disqualifications for that command due my rank, I respectfully request to be informed of that fact. I do not forget I am ranking Col. of this Dept. . . . After a severe campaign my Regt. is scattered and placed under officers of other Regts., unprovided for and in great need of personal attention . . . which . . . I take pride in bestowing myself. Believing I know my right and what is due my Regt., I must decline the command of this Sub-District . . . rather than subvert both my own self-respect and my duty to the Govt and the people of Kansas to the selfish will of political shysters.[57]

Having gotten this fiery message off his chest, Jennison for good measure added a second offense by protesting to General Curtis directly, and not through channels, and further increased the gravity of this breach of military propriety by explaining that he did not go through channels because he did not want his protest "to fail in delivery, many important communications having failed to reach Dept. Hd. Qrs. as far as I have been able to learn." [58]

56. Records of the Adjutant General's Office.

57. *Ibid.* Jennison's despatch to Captain Hampton, datelined Mound City, December 10, 1864, is quoted in full in General Dodge's General Orders No. 92, St. Louis, April 4, 1865.

58. *Ibid.* Jennison's despatch to Major C. S. Charlot, General Curtis' AAAG, is also quoted in full in General Dodge's General Orders No. 92, St. Louis, April 4, 1865.

Blunt could not, of course, ignore the insulting language of Jennison's message to his adjutant general. He at once ordered his rebellious subordinate to turn over command of his regiment to Hoyt and to report under arrest forthwith to district headquarters at Paola.[59] But, mindful of Jennison's political power in the state, Blunt also took the trouble to reply to his insubordinate and disrespectful despatch. No doubt the reply was written mainly for the record and with an eye to publication when Jennison's journalistic friends raised the inevitable clamor over his new quarrel with his old enemies, the military authorities. It must not be forgotten that Blunt himself was a volunteer officer and a Kansas politician; keeping his fences mended was no new art to him. Whatever may be said of his diction and spelling, his reply to Jennison did not lack force:

> Your remarks about "politicians," "Jas H. Lane," "political shysters," etc., although evincing gross insubordination and disrespect . . . I shall pass over; as I am not sufficiently advised of the political combinations you have made and attempted to make with Jas. H. Lane and others to discuss the matter. . . . It is certainly a great virtue in a military man, while on duty with his command, to eschew partizen politics, and if you have maintained that virtue so far as to hold yourself entirely aloof from local or partizen politics while you have been in the military service, as your telegram would seem to claim for you, it will be a matter of history connected with your career that will be very much to your credit as a soldier. In subdividing my district . . . I have endeavored to do justice to all according to their merit, and . . . I thought I was quite well prepared to judge the qualifications of each to discharge the duties assigned to him.[60]

If Jennison was chastened by Blunt's rebuke, or even recognized it as such, he gave no sign of it. He reported in arrest at Blunt's headquarters, as ordered, and for the next three weeks allowed few days to pass without applying for an extension of the limits of the area to which the terms of his military arrest confined him. On the fourteenth of December he requested permission to go hunting in Miami County; on the sixteenth, to go to Mound City on family business; on the twenty-seventh, to go to Leavenworth on "private business;" and so on.[61] General Blunt was invariably accomodating and approved these requests, but on the twenty-third, when Jennison made bold to ask to be released from arrest entirely,

59. Blunt to Jennison, December 11, 1865, *ibid.*   60. *Ibid.*
61. For example, his requests of December 14, 16, and 27, all addressed to Captain G. S. Hampton, Blunt's AAAG, *ibid.*

he received a peppery reply, drafted by Blunt himself, the point of which no one could misunderstand: "In reply to note of this date requesting release from arrest I am directed by the general commanding to say that when he sees proper to release you from arrest he will do so without any suggestion from yourself or anyone else."[62]

Any quarrel between Jennison and his military superiors was bound to be promoted into a public and political issue by the colonel's friends, aided and abetted by the colonel himself. Jennison had hardly been relieved of his command when articles denouncing "military tyranny" began to appear in the pro-Jennison newspapers. "Blunt's arresting machine has commenced moving . . . again," wrote one editor, who then went on to "state the belief that the arrest is the result of political premeditation. We know that Lane wants Jennison's influence for his re-election, and by these means he hopes to get it or render him powerless."[63] Lane was, in fact, in the midst of a bitter fight, in which he was eventually successful, for reelection to the United States Senate.[64] Newspapers favorable to him had circulated reports that Jennison and Hoyt were supporting him; these reports had been denied as a "base libel" by the anti-Lane press, and shortly after his return to Kansas from Arkansas Jennison himself did the same in a vitriolic letter to the newspapers:

On my return from the pursuit of Price I found, to my chagrin and mortification, that I had been published . . . as a supporter of Jas. H. Lane, a man whom I have for many years despised. . . . [Lane] was the publisher of this falsehood, and such he well knew it to be at the time he uttered it. I never gave him any reason to believe that I should ever in any way advocate his claims to *any* position—much less that of United States Senator, a trust that he has most shamefully disgraced. . . . I believe now more fully than ever . . . that he is a villain of a darker hue, and more capable of treachery, deceit and corruption, than I had at that time imagined. . . . I further say that Jas. H. Lane, if he could

62. *Ibid.*

63. Unidentified clipping, Jennison Scrapbook.

64. In an unscrupulous manoeuver worthy of Lane himself, his enemies took advantage of their control of the Kansas legislature to elect Governor Carney to succeed him as U.S. senator. The election was held on February 9, 1864, a year earlier than it should have been. The subsequent national and state elections in November, 1864, resulted in the election of a pro-Lane legislature, and on January 10, 1865, by a four to one vote, the new legislature elected Lane to a second term as United States senator. Lane, however, was not destined to serve out his second term. He committed suicide in July, 1866.

subserve his own interests thereby, would as soon betray his country, or his Savior . . . as would Jeff Davis or Judas Iscariot.[65]

It is evident that Kansas politics in 1864 were not for the tender-skinned.

Two days after placing on record his poor opinion of Senator Lane, Jennison announced in a letter to the Leavenworth *Times* that there were but two reasons for his arrest: "First, that I am not the tool of J. H. Lane. Second, that I have publicly denounced the public stealing that is being carried on at . . . [Paola] by government officials under and with the knowledge of the present administration. *Do you want the proof?* Ask and ye shall receive."[66] The reference to "public stealing" in this communication is to a despatch Jennison had sent to Captain Hampton, Blunt's adjutant general, a week before his removal from command:

I wrote privately a day since to the general commanding, relative to a combination which from the best obtainable information has been formed . . . to raise the price of forage to an unprecedented degree by holding supplies on hand until the necessities of the services compel acquiescence in the demands of reckless and unprincipled speculators. . . . It has been strongly intimated that unless I comply with the desires of certain parties, a combined effort will be made to so abridge this sub-district that [those] portions in which said parties are interested will be included within those of other and less scrupulous commanders. . . . I am determined as long as I remain in command here—no matter how brief the period—to control affairs as far as I am able in the interest of the Government, notwithstanding the open and determined opposition of persons whose loyalty is at best impeachable. . . . Assuring you of my earnest desire to see all things work together for the good of the government and the welfare of the state, irrespective of the demands of ambition, of demagogues, and without being influenced by fear of opposition or hope of favor, I remain . . .[67]

Any reasonably literate letter bearing Jennison's signature is open to question as to its actual authorship, and it is quite apparent that the foregoing epistle, overflowing with the sender's prodigious integrity and devotion to the public weal, was either written for Jennison, or had

---

65. The newspaper articles denying that Jennison and Hoyt were supporting Lane are unidentified clippings, Jennison Scrapbook. Jennison's own letter, comparing Lane with Jefferson Davis and Judas, is datelined Mound City, December 19, 1864, and is in an undated clipping from the *Border Sentinel*, Jennison Scrapbook.
66. Leavenworth *Times*, December 21, 1864, clipping *ibid*.
67. Letter datelined Mound City, December 5, 1864, unidentified clipping, *ibid*.

benefited from extensive editing. But why was it written? Was there an actual conspiracy of profiteers to raise the price of forage the government had to buy? Such conspiracies were certainly common during the Civil War and not wholly unknown in more recent times. But why should Jennison, of all people, express such righteous indignation and horror over conduct that by the standards of the time—to say nothing of Jennison's own standards—was not too reprehensible? The parade of rectitude and the high-flown rhetoric of patriotism have a distinctly hollow ring. This eloquent humbug was written before Blunt cut down the size of Jennison's subdistrict, and it is neither surprising nor without significance that it found its way to the newspapers. It may be taken for granted that the virtuous colonel himself saw to it that the letter was published. It is as certain as such things can be that the letter was written after Jennison had somehow gotten wind of Blunt's intention to cut down the size of his command, and with the hope that it might frighten the latter into leaving him alone. If it had that effect, so much the better; if Blunt went ahead anyway, the letter would at least place in the worst possible light his motives for doing so. In the atmosphere of politics as practiced in Kansas in 1864, and for anyone with Jennison's code of political morality, this would have been nothing more than legitimate self-defense.

Blunt had not been frightened out of his intention to reduce the size of Jennison's command, nor was he afraid to bring Jennison before a military court to be tried for the way he had reacted to Blunt's General Orders No. 32. A general court-martial, with Major General George Sykes presiding, was appointed by General Curtis to meet at Fort Leavenworth on January 30, 1865, to sit in judgment over the unruly colonel.[68] The charges against him were disobedience of orders, insubordination, and conduct unbecoming an officer and gentleman. The court acquitted Jennison on the first two charges, but found him guilty of "conduct prejudicial to good order and military discipline" and sentenced him to be "reprimanded in orders by the General commanding the Department."[69] General Dodge, who had the duty of reviewing the verdict and sentence of the court in his capacity as department commander,

68. Special Orders No. 22, January 26, 1865, in Records of the Adjutant General's Office.
69. General Orders No. 92, Headquarters, December of the Missouri, St. Louis, April 4, 1865, *ibid.*

confirmed both, but quite properly criticized the court for excessive leniency; in his opinion, Jennison had been guilty "without just cause or excuse" of disobedience of orders, and, General Dodge added, "for such insubordination the sentence of the court is not an adequate rebuke."[70]

Jennison was now out of the woods, at the cost of a mild tap on the wrist, on the lesser of the two transgressions he had committed. But he still had to face the far more serious charges arising from his own and his men's conduct on the return march from the Arkansas River. By mid-December, Blunt had enough evidence in his possession to give him, in his opinion, adequate grounds for issuing orders to suspend "all payments . . . due the Fifteenth Regiment, Kansas Cavalry . . . until further orders . . . with a view to ascertain by proper investigation, who are the parties responsible for the depredations committed upon loyal citizens."[71] It is to be noted that these orders applied only to the Fifteenth Kansas, notwithstanding that Jennison had also had in his brigade and under his command the Sixteenth Kansas, a Colorado and a Wisconsin battery, and detachments of two other Kansas regiments and one Colorado regiment. Jennison was prompt to contend, in an inordinately long, fourteen-page letter to General Curtis, that since Blunt had no jurisdiction over the army paymasters, he could not legally issue orders to them, and that in any case, stoppage of pay prior to conviction by court-martial was illegal. But Jennison did not rest his case on these legal, or legalistic, arguments, which had no doubt been drafted for him by Hoyt; he contended also that Blunt's order was merely another example of the general's "spirit of vindictiveness" toward himself and his regiment.[72] In another long letter, written a few days later, he protested against the injustice of singling out the Fifteenth and declaring it "to be guilty of all these indefinite and questionable charges" and punishing it "while all others go free."[73] And his friends chimed in with letters to the newspapers. One such letter asserted:

That depredations were committed upon loyal people, with a knowledge that

70. *Ibid.*
71. General Orders No. 78, Paola, Kansas, December 18, 1864, reprinted in unidentified clipping, Jennison Scrapbook.
72. Jennison to Major C. S. Charlot, "for the information of the Major General commanding Department [of] Kansas," December 25, 1864, in Records of the Adjutant General's Office.
73. Jennison to Major General Curtis, December 30, 1864, *ibid.*

they were such, is a gross libel, not only upon the commanding officers, but upon the regiment itself, as brave and efficient an organization as ever was mustered in Kansas. . . . Soldiers are not unlike, and it can be nothing but ridiculous to suppose that all outrages . . . were committed by the 177 men forming the sum total of the Fifteenth Regiment in Arkansas . . . [and] that less than two hundred men by themselves in a brigade committed such outrages as are implied is simply preposterous.[74]

On January 5, while the Lawrence *State Journal* editorialized that the charges against Jennison would be "hushed up" and that Blunt "and those in command would not dare to push [Jennison] to the wall while he possessed information that would crush them," Blunt wrote General Curtis that "the matter of Col. Jennison's arrest . . . is progressing as fast as possible, but as every day brings to light some new and astounding facts in regard to him and other officers of his regiment it requires considerable time to have the charges all properly prepared. . . . Col. Jennison's countercharges against me . . . for the purpose as he claims of making a 'stand-off' to use his own language . . . will not avail him so far as I am concerned."[75]

And in fact Blunt was not to be intimidated. In due course, Jennison was brought to trial before a general court-martial again presided over by General Sykes. The highly technical and repetitious language of the four charges and fourteen specifications on which he was tried may be summarized as follows:[76]

1. That near Cane Hill, Arkansas, on December 12, without any provocation, he caused "a certain dwelling house, occupied only by defenceless women and children" to be burned and "the inmates thereof turned out of doors without food or clothing and shelterless from the inclemency of the season."

2. That on the march from the Arkansas River to Fort Scott he frequently left his command "and in company with officers of inferior rank and enlisted men, did roam at large about the country . . . entering

74. Undated clipping, Leavenworth *Times*, signed "A Soldier", in Jennison Scrapbook.
75. The Lawrence *State Journal* editorial is *ibid*. Blunt's letter of the same date to General Curtis is in Records of the Adjutant General's Office.
76. The full charges and specifications are in General Orders No. 153, Headquarters, Department of the Missouri, St. Louis, June 23, 1865, in Records of the Adjutant General's Office.

private houses . . . permitting officers and enlisted men to despoil the occupants . . . of their household effects and other personal property."

3. That "having in his custody" three prisoners of war, "two of whom, at least, claimed to be citizens loyal to the government of the United States," he permitted Captain Oren A. Curtis of the Fifteenth Kansas to hang them.

4. That by indifference, and sometimes by open encouragement, he allowed his men to commit "acts of unprovoked and wanton violence against the persons and property of unoffending men, and defenceless and unprotected women and children" in Arkansas as well as at Newtonia, Granby, Sarcoxie, Carthage, and other places in Missouri.

5. That he permitted his command "to engage in an indiscriminate system of destruction and pillaging of property from loyal as well as disloyal citizens."

6. That after seizing "a large amount of forage and a number of horses for his brigade," he permitted the acting brigade quartermaster to prepare vouchers as if the forage and horses had been purchased, and that he approved the vouchers "knowing the same to be false and fraudulent."

7. That having captured about 140 head of cattle "from alleged enemies of the United States," he permitted his acting brigade quartermaster to turn the cattle over "to unauthorized parties . . . with the intention of converting the proceeds of such cattle to private use." Part of the herd was turned over in this way to one James Bell, who swore to an affidavit that Jennison himself sold him the cattle at thirty dollars a head; part of the herd was turned over to Alonzo Jennison, the colonel's brother, who had accompanied the expedition and had certainly not gone "with the regiment for any good purpose."[77] One Jeff Anthony, who may or may not have been a relative of Daniel Anthony, was also sold 56 head of cattle by Jennison "with the intention of defrauding the Government."

To all the charges and specifications, Jennison pleaded not guilty. The trial began at 10 A.M., May 3, 1865, and ended on May 20. Jennison was

---

77. James Bell's affidavit, subscribed and sworn to February 13, 1865, is *ibid.* The reference to "Lon" Jennison's presence with the Fifteenth, in Par. 7, is in an undated clipping from the Leavenworth *Bulletin*, Jennison Scrapbook.

represented by Allen Blacker and T. M. O'Brien as counsel.[78] After hearing the evidence, the court found Jennison guilty of "Conduct to the prejudice of good order and military discipline"; "Gross and wilful neglect of duty, to the prejudice of good order and military discipline"; and "Defrauding the Government of the United States." While the court ruled him not guilty on the majority of the specific charges against him, including that of permitting Captain Curtis to hang the three prisoners, conviction on three of the principal charges was serious enough and justified the sentence that he be "dishonorably dismissed from the service of the United States."[79] The sentence of the court was confirmed by General Dodge on June 23; and on that day, Jennison ceased for the second and last time to be an officer in the service of the United States.[80]

Jennison subsequently protested, both by petition to the secretary of war and, as was his custom, by letters to the newspapers, that he had been illegally and improperly convicted, that there had been "gross misconduct upon the part of the presiding officer of the Court," and that he was the victim of "politicians and military thieves now barking under the cover of the kennel of the St. Louis commander," to wit, General Dodge.[81] But his protests and protestations were fruitless. With the war ended, the slave power destroyed, and the Union restored, neither the military authorities nor the people of Kansas were disposed any longer to

78. A transcript of the testimony given at Jennison's trial is in "Court Martial Records, Charles R. Jennison," National Archives, Washington. A dispassionate reading of the testimony, giving due weight to the probable bias of each of the witnesses for or against Jennison, leads to the inescapable conclusion that the verdict of the court was fully justified by the evidence and that the sentence was, if anything, too mild.

79. General Orders No. 153, Headquarters, Department of the Missouri, St. Louis, June 23, 1865, in Records of the Adjutant General's Office. Palmer asserts, "Black Flag Character," 460, that Jennison was sentenced to death by the court, and that the sentence was first commuted to imprisonment for life, and was then commuted again to a dishonorable discharge. Not only does the official transcript of the trial fail to substantiate Palmer's statement, but in addition, it is impossible that Jennison should have been sentenced to death or even to life imprisonment on the charges on which he was found guilty. Castel, on the other hand, Frontier State, 229, has confused Jennison's two trials. For his own and his regiment's actions on the return march from Arkansas, Jennison did not escape with a "mere reprimand." He was sentenced to a dishonorable discharge and, therefore, contrary to Castel's statement, did not resign his commission.

80. General Orders No. 153, Headquarters, Department of the Missouri, St. Louis, June 23, 1865, in Records of the Adjutant General's Office.

81. Undated petition to the secretary of war, ibid. Cf. undated clipping from the Leavenworth Conservative, Jennison Scrapbook.

view Jennison's trespasses with the complacency of 1861 and 1862. The Little Jayhawker failed to realize it, but his sun too had set at Appomattox.[82]

---

82. Following Jennison's court-martial, several of his officers were also tried on charges similar to those preferred against him. Some of them were sentenced to be dismissed from the service. Captain Swaine of the Fifteenth Kansas was sentenced to be hanged (the sentence was not carried out), and Captain Oren A. Curtis, who actually hanged the three "bushwhackers" mentioned in the charges against Jennison, was sentenced to one year at hard labor in the Missouri penitentiary.

CHAPTER XVII

The Way
Home

WHEN THE end of April came, General Joseph Johnston had already surrendered to Sherman at Greensboro, North Carolina; and with the surrender of General Richard Taylor near Mobile a few days later, the Civil War came to an end east of the Mississippi. It was nearly over in Missouri also. The Seventh Kansas at this time was widely scattered to the southwest of St. Louis. After many moves, Companies A, B, G, and H and regimental headquarters were at Pilot Knob; Companies C, E, and K were at Patterson, Company D at Centerville, Company F at Bloomfield, and Company I at St. Louis. In command of Company I was Captain Jacob M. Anthony, Daniel Anthony's younger brother, who had entered the regiment in April, 1862, as second lieutenant of Company A and was promoted to the captaincy of Company I in May, 1863, after the resignation of Captain John L. Merrick.[1] Captain Edward Thornton of Company G had just returned from Kansas with thirty-five recruits for the regiment; but with the fighting virtually ended, there was little enough to keep even the veterans occupied.[2] Military duties were at a minimum, and the erstwhile warriors of the Seventh found time hanging heavy on their hands. There was much sleeping in the midday heat of a warm spring, and much reading, letter writing, and cardplaying. But

1. *Report of the Adjutant General of the State of Kansas*, I, 528, 626.
2. *Official Records*, XLVIII, Pt. 2, 268.

mostly there was reminiscing and talk, and much of the talk was speculation concerning the future of the regiment, now that the war was over.

On May 10 the men learned through the regimental grapevine that Lieutenant Colonel Malone, Majors Charles H. Gregory and Levi H. Utt, and several of the captains had joined in petitioning General Dodge to have the Seventh retained in the service until the expiration of its veterans' second three-year term of enlistment in January, 1867, and that General Dodge had forwarded the petition to Washington for a decision by the War Department.[3] The news of the officers' action occasioned "considerable excitement" in the regiment. The enlisted men were up in arms, and no one was more indignant than the recently married Webster Moses. He wrote his wife: "If the officers succeed as they hope to they cannot remain with the Regiment as they would soon be shot down like dogs and not even get a decent burial. Our officers are a very *low set* of fellows who do not like the prospect of going to work for a living. We are getting up a petition to be discharged among the first as we were among the first that enlisted."[4]

Notwithstanding the desire of the Jayhawkers to be out of the service, there was still an occasional bit of work for them to do, for peace did not come to Missouri overnight. Bushwhackers were still active in the southeastern counties of the state. In the middle of May, one company of Jayhawkers was sent out to round up "Hildebrand's gang" in Saint Francis County; another company, divided into detachments, scoured Madison County, east of Pilot Knob, to "rid it of those thieves."[5] As late as the middle of June, a ten-man patrol of the Seventh, led by Sergeant Marion Cross of Company D, killed the "notorious" bushwhacker Dick Bowles and captured and brought back to camp five of his followers, who, Webster Moses opined, were going to "stretch Hemp."[6] Governor Crawford of Kansas, believing, or pretending to believe, that the eastern counties of his state were threatened by bushwhackers, asked to have the Seventh

---

3. Charles H. Gregory and Levi H. Utt had been promoted from captain to major on April 18, 1864, and December 27, 1864, respectively. See *Report of the Adjutant General of the State of Kansas*, I, 524.

4. Webster Moses to his wife, May 10, 1865, in Moses Letters.

5. *Official Records*, XLVIII, Pt. 2, 496, 510.

6. Webster Moses to his wife, June 10 and June 18, 1865, in Moses Letters. *Cf. Official Records*, XLVIII, Pt. 2, 937.

sent home to protect the border; and there was a move afoot at the same time to send the regiment to Fort Gibson, in Indian Territory, to be consolidated with other regiments and sent on an expedition to Red River.[7] Nothing came of these suggestions and proposals, and until nearly the end of June the Jayhawkers remained where they were.

On June 24 the four companies and regimental headquarters stationed at Pilot Knob were ordered to Cape Girardeau on the Mississippi River "to recuperate," although the men would have been hard put to explain what fatigues they had undergone in recent months to make necessary a period of recuperation. The move, at any rate, gave the four companies the opportunity to celebrate Independence Day at Cape Girardeau. There was a parade of cavalry, infantry, and citizens in the morning, headed by the regimental band of the Seventh; there was much oratory on the theme of the reunited country, and a patriotic salute fired by cannon. In the evening, Quartermaster Lieutenant James Smith and Fletcher Pomeroy rode into town, to "Frank's Garden," for refreshments; "there were many persons there, mostly foreigners, of all ages. The older persons were enjoying their beer and pipes, while the youngsters were having a lively dance. A few minutes there satisfied . . . [us] and we returned, considering that a demoralizing manner of celebrating our national birthday."[8]

The future of the regiment was still in doubt, to the increasing impatience and dissatisfaction of the men. On July 13 a petition signed by every Jayhawker except the officers was sent to General Dodge to counteract the petition that had been sent him by the officers two months before. The statement the officers had made that the regiment wanted to remain in the service until the end of its second term of enlistment was emphatically denied, and the petition declared that since the veterans had reenlisted for "three years or during the war," now that the war was manifestly over they were entitled to be discharged, and that the War Department could not hold them in the service for another year and a half without committing a gross breach of contract.[9]

Within a few days after this petition was forwarded to St. Louis, the long period of uncertainty ended, and ended unhappily, with the arrival

7. *Official Records*, XLVIII, Pt. 2, 293, 419.
8. Pomeroy, "War Diary," entry for July 4, 1865.
9. *Ibid.*, entry for July 13, 1865.

of orders directing the Jayhawkers to proceed by steamer up the Mississippi and Missouri rivers to Omaha, Nebraska Territory, and then overland to Fort Kearny, 170 miles to the southwest, on the Platte River. There they were to join in a campaign against the Plains Indians. With the orders came General Dodge's assurance that the regiment would be mustered out in the autumn or at the end of the campaign, whichever came first. These assurances did not allay the discontent caused by the orders with which they were coupled. The men had manifestly persuaded themselves that their petition to be discharged from the service would operate as a magic wand and would at once release them from an army that in their minds had lost its reason for existence. A war against Indians was not the war they had contracted to fight. They decided, to their own satisfaction, that the troubles with the Indians were a mere pretense and that the orders postponing their muster out were the result of "a deep game of the officers to keep up the excitement and keep us in the service so they can remain in and draw their big pay." [10] And Webster Moses, who "never disliked any thing so much as . . . going to Omaha," added that if the officers "keep it up long, they will awake some morning and find themselves missing." [11]

Nevertheless, orders were orders; the companies not yet at Cape Girardeau were promptly called in, and on July 18 the Jayhawkers boarded the three steamers that were to take them to Omaha. The men marched aboard the boats peaceably enough, notwithstanding their bitterness, but many of them proclaimed their intention to desert before the regiment reached Omaha. This was not an idle threat, for two days later, when the boats stopped at St. Louis, nearly a hundred men disappeared, their departure facilitated by the visit of the paymaster with four months' wages for each man. And many of those who did not desert at St. Louis let it be known that they intended to do so nearer their homes when the boats reached Leavenworth and St. Joseph. To add to the discontent of the men and to make desertion seem more attractive, there were no cooking facilities on the boats; for the fourteen days needed to make the upstream trip from Cape Girardeau to Omaha, the men lived on hardtack and raw bacon and made their coffee with hot water from

10. Webster Moses to his wife, July 18, 1865, and July 22, 1865, in Moses Letters.
11. Same to same, July 22, 1865, *ibid.*

the boilers, which, as Webster Moses wrote, "was not very *nice*."[12]
There was no longer any stigma attached to desertion, and the troopers,
believing that they had discharged their obligations to the government
and were kept in the army only by reason of the "tyrany of a few Officers," were leaving openly, singly, in groups, and in squads.[13] When the
boats docked at Omaha on July 31, most of the companies were down to
barely a dozen men each, and another thirty men, including five from
Company D alone, deserted on the night before the skeleton regiment
set off on its overland march to Fort Kearny on August 9.

Except for a plague of mosquitoes, the march west along the military
road from Omaha to Fort Kearny was rather pleasant. It was made in
leisurely fashion, averaging a mere ten miles a day. Prairie dog towns
along the road were visited, and wild grapes, growing on the islands that
dotted the Platte River, were picked to form the main ingredient of a
stew consisting of grapes, sugar, and hardtack that the men called "Platte
River Pudding." The mules that had been issued to the regiment at
Omaha to draw the supply wagons were wild and untrained, and the
teamsters had their hands full breaking them to harness. The officers had
more work than usual; the men had "lost all interest in trying to be 'good
Soldiers' "; there were more desertions, and the officers had to shoulder
carbines and stand guard over the horse lines at night to prevent the
"Boys" from making off with the animals.[14] Altogether, it was a sad tale
of the disintegration of a once proud regiment.

The Seventh, or what was left of it, reached Fort Kearny on August
26.[15] Two days later, just as the men were eating dinner, Lieutenant
Colonel Malone was handed orders to march the regiment back to Fort
Leavenworth immediately for muster-out. As soon as he read the orders,
Malone announced the happy news to the men, who reacted with a wild
outburst of joy. "Hats, dinner plates, camp kettles of coffee or soup were
waved or thrown into the air."[16] There were no slackers during the

---

12. Same to same, July 31, 1865, *ibid.*   13. Same to same, August 11, 1865, *ibid.*
14. *Ibid.*

15. General Dodge's report on the "Powder River Expedition," in which the Seventh was
to have taken part, states that the regiment arrived at Fort Kearny on August 20 and was ordered
on August 25 to return to Fort Leavenworth for muster-out. See *Official Records*, XLVIII, Pt. 1,
346. The dates given in the text are based on the daily entries in Pomeroy, "War Diary."

16. Pomeroy, "War Diary," entry for August 28, 1865.

next twenty-four hours while the regimental wagons were loaded with supplies for the return march; and in record time the Seventh was ready to set off on its march east. The mules and horses were "nearly worn out" by the outbound march, and the return journey was therefore slow, interrupted by frequent halts to rest the animals; but it is not without significance that the eastbound trip was accomplished in the same number of days as the journey west, notwithstanding that the distance from Fort Kearny to Fort Leavenworth is much greater than the distance from Omaha to Fort Kearny. Nevertheless, the eastward march seemed unbearably slow to the men, with the smell of freedom and home in their nostrils. There were, however, diversions on the way; Moses and a few of his friends, for example, made a five-day detour to hunt "Buffalow"; but even (or especially) to him, "one day seem[ed] allmost a week."[17] At last, after a final day's march of eighteen miles over rough, hilly country, the Seventh arrived at Fort Leavenworth on the evening of September 14 and went into camp on the same bluegrass pasture on which it had made its first camp when the Seventh Kansas Volunteer Cavalry began soldiering four years before.

The muster-out of a regiment, even one so reduced in numbers as the Seventh now was, was a lengthy process encumbered with army red tape; and when the Seventh arrived at Fort Leavenworth, there were already twenty regiments there, awaiting their turn to be mustered out of the service. Four days were required for the Jayhawkers to turn in to the quartermasters their horses and arms and other "public property." Those of the men who wished to do so were allowed to purchase their horses from the government after having them appraised by the quartermaster, and the men were also permitted to purchase their Spencer carbines at a price of ten dollars. Meanwhile, the company officers, pressing into service everyone with a legible handwriting, were making out discharge papers for their men and the required number of copies of the muster-out rolls and payrolls of their respective companies. These were at last completed on the twenty-sixth and delivered to the mustering officers to be checked and corrected, a process which required two more days. On Friday, September 29, the work was done and the

17. Webster Moses to his wife, September 7, 1865, in Moses Letters.

regiment was formally mustered out of the United States service. The next day, it was mustered out of the service of the state of Kansas also. And now the Jayhawkers were civilians once again, "free men" in Fletcher Pomeroy's words.[18]

The great majority of the men who had deserted on the way from Cape Girardeau to Fort Kearny evidently learned that their regiment was about to be mustered out. They rejoined the regiment at Fort Leavenworth and, with the connivance of the officers, got their names on the muster-out rolls, thereby becoming eligible for an honorable discharge, pay to the muster-out date, and more important, their four hundred dollar reenlisted veterans' bonus as well. As a result of the return of these short-term deserters, the strength of the regiment at muster-out was 501 officers and men.

There were a few final formalities still to be attended to before the regiment disbanded. On Sunday evening, October 1, Chaplain Lovejoy assembled the Seventh for its last religious service as a regiment. He preached in the open air, with the Jayhawkers standing and sitting on the grass around him. Lovejoy's last sermon was "pointed and impressive, and drew the attention of the men."[19] Some of them perhaps remembered, as they listened to the chaplain's words, the strange, quasi-religious, abolitionist rites that Company K had held four years before. The following evening brought a less solemn, more mundane occasion. Daniel Anthony gave a dinner for his comrades of the Seventh at Leavenworth, to which he invited all the officers and men. No doubt the dinner was the occasion for reminiscences of the stormy days of the first winter of the war, of Captain Cleveland's departure from the regiment, the fight at Columbus in January, 1862, jayhawking in Missouri, Colonel Jennison's strange headgear and abrupt resignation, the journey to Kentucky and Tennessee in the summer of 1862, the resignation of the host himself, the campaigns in the summer heat and winter cold in Tennessee and Mississippi, the long chase after Price. Perhaps there was talk, too, of some of those who were not present to enjoy Colonel Anthony's hospitality, talk of Captain Fred Swoyer, killed by one of his own men, of Captain Hodgman and Sergeant Daniel Holmes, killed by

18. Pomeroy, "War Diary," entry for September 30, 1865.
19. *Ibid.*, entry for October 1, 1865.

the enemy, of Captains John Brown, Jr., and George Hoyt, and of the many more officers and men who had resigned, or died, or been discharged, or deserted.

Not until October 6 were the army paymasters ready to pay off the regiment. They began in the afternoon and completed the job the next morning. When the last Jayhawker had received his money and signed the pay voucher, the officers and men shook hands all around, bade each other goodbye, and went their separate ways. The Seventh Kansas Veteran Volunteer Cavalry, once known as Jennison's Jayhawkers, ceased to exist.

Fletcher Pomeroy was one of those who had bought his horse from the government. He had ridden the mare for more than a year and, in his matter-of-fact way, had become attached to the animal. It was on her back, and in company with his friend, Private John T. Reeves of Company C, that he started for home on October 7. "Home," in his case, was the good Kansas land he had foresightedly bought from Assistant Surgeon Joel J. Crook. On the first night out of Fort Leavenworth, Pomeroy and Reeves camped out on the prairie. The next morning, they rode on in the warm autumn sunshine until their roads diverged. And there, on the prairie, they parted with a few friendly words. That evening, still faithful to the diary that had helped him through four years of war, Fletcher Pomeroy wrote his final entry: "I confess to a feeling of sadness at this separation from a comrade whose friendship had been proven during the trying scenes of four years of war, and had never failed. Will I see his face again in this life?"[20] Fifty years later, in his old age, when he finished making a clean copy of his wartime diary, he added this comment: "At the time of this rewriting, April, 1915, I have not seen Comrade Reeves."

PEACE COMES TO THE COLONELS

No matter how serious the scrape in which Jennison found himself with his military superiors, he could always count on devoted support in Leavenworth. No doubt this support was motivated in part by political considerations, but it seems quite clear that much of it stemmed from

20. *Ibid.*, entry for October 8, 1865.

personal loyalty to, and admiration for, the incorrigibly flamboyant Little Jayhawker. The depth and extent of this support can no longer be assessed, but there is no question that it was both fervent and vocal. While he was awaiting his second court-martial, pro-Jennison articles abounded in the newspapers; one of these asserted that "in that crisis where stout arms are needed to save the nation or protect our homes, Jennison would be to the country or to the state a helper and a protector."[21] There were those even then who urged his promotion to brigadier general, and a resolution to that effect was actually introduced in the Kansas House of Representatives.[22] In February, just after he had been sentenced to be reprimanded in orders for "conduct prejudicial to good order and military discipline," he was tendered a testimonial dinner at which his admirers presented him with a superb pair of Colt pistols, "ivory handled, burnished with silver and gold," and costing $150. The presentation was made by Captain Oren A. Curtis, Fifteenth Kansas Cavalry, Jennison's "tried friend," the same Captain Curtis who was shortly to be sentenced to a dishonorable discharge and a year's imprisonment at hard labor for hanging the three "bushwhackers" at Cane Hill three months earlier. It may have been only the ebullience induced by the champagne served plentifully at the dinner ("Heidsieck was abundant"), but Jennison was there described as "that gallant heart, that tried, true and fearless soldier, that original champion of human freedom," and he was assured that he was "one of the people of Kansas, and *they* will sustain him."[23] In the following month, he found it necessary to publish a "card" refusing an invitation, "signed by a large number of laboring men and by the principal merchants," asking him to stand as a candidate for mayor of Leavenworth. In declining the invitation, he stated that "While sincerely thankful for the respect and esteem which the petition manifests, I cannot, under any circumstances, leave my position in the field to become a politician."[24] For Jennison to talk in March, 1865, following his first court-martial and shortly before his second, of his "position in the field" was a considerable embellishment

21. Unidentified clipping, Jennison Scrapbook.
22. Article in the Leavenworth *Bulletin*, datelined Topeka, January 31, 1865, undated clipping, *ibid.* The resolution was never brought to a vote.
23. Unidentified clipping, datelined Leavenworth, February 16, 1865, *ibid.*
24. Unidentified clipping, *ibid.* The "card" is dated March 18, 1865.

of the facts, but there is no indication that this florid manifesto aroused the ridicule it deserved.

Daniel Anthony, who had no position in the field to give up, and was probably still smarting from his electoral defeat of the year before, did not share Jennison's reluctance to become a politician and announced his candidacy for mayor. The 1865 mayoralty campaign was a relatively tame affair compared to the excitements of the year before. Anthony's opponent on this occasion was Thomas Carney, who had just completed a term as governor of Kansas. Jennison once again came out against Anthony, whom he characterized as being more interested in seeking controversies than in promoting the welfare and interests of the city. But George Hoyt, who had seconded Jennison's attacks on Anthony in 1864, changed his allegiance in 1865 and announced his conviction that the latter was "the most honest, capable, energetic man in the city" and "the great leader and go ahead man in every enterprise for the interests" of Leavenworth.[25] Notwithstanding Hoyt's endorsement, Anthony was again defeated, but this time by a narrow margin; the vote was 1,251 for Carney and 1,156 for Anthony.

There were those who, unlike Hoyt, did not look upon Anthony as the "most honest" citizen of Leavenworth, and so far as one may judge on the basis of very scanty records, they had good grounds for their scepticism. By the summer of 1864, the jayhawking of cattle from Missouri was no longer the profitable enterprise it had been in the first two years of the war; there were, in fact, not many cattle left in the western counties of Missouri to be jayhawked. But enterprising Kansans found a new source of supply in the Indian lands of southeastern Kansas. The cattle were stolen, herded to any nearby military post, and there sold to the army quartermasters as having been purchased from the Indians. No doubt the accommodating quartermasters shared in the proceeds. So widespread and vicious did this traffic become that even Jennison, when in command of the First Sub-District of South Kansas, had issued orders threatening to arrest the cattle thieves and to punish them with a spell of hard labor on government fortifications.[26] Daniel

25. Unidentified clipping, *ibid.*
26. Printed Order, captioned "General Orders No. 1, Headquarters First Sub-District, South Kansas, Mound City, August 8th, 1864," *ibid.*

Anthony was one of those openly accused of being deeply involved in this large scale larceny, with his brother-in-law, John P. Osborne, acting as his front.[27]

The airing of such accusations during the mayoralty campaign, coming on top of the hostilities built up over the years, led to one of the most dramatic incidents in the far from prosaic history of Leavenworth. On Saturday afternoon, May 13, 1865, Jennison, dressed in civilian clothes and with two revolvers in his belt, was sitting in his buggy on Shawnee Street in front of the Planters House, talking to a friend named A. J. Angell, when Anthony came walking along the street. Anthony too was armed, carrying a revolver in his pocket. He explained later that he did not make it a practice to carry a gun and that he was only doing so at this time because "several men" had threatened his life and were "daily on the streets armed for this purpose."[28] As Anthony drew abreast of the buggy, Jennison said to Angell, "Hold on a moment, I want to speak with Anthony." He sprang from the buggy and walked toward Anthony. The exact sequence of events in the next few moments is clouded by the conflicting evidence of eyewitnesses who were called to testify six weeks later in the recorder's court in Leavenworth in the case of *The State of Kansas vs. Col. C. R. Jennison,* on charges of "Breach of the Peace and Shooting with Intent to Kill." Apparently the two principals exchanged a few words; Jennison said, "I want to talk with you," and Anthony replied, "I don't want to talk." Then, according to Anthony's testimony, Jennison drew his gun. Angell, on the other hand, swore that Anthony was the first to draw and that, in fact, Jennison did not draw his gun until after Anthony had already fired the first shot. Angell's testimony was supported by the evidence of Captain Tough, the erstwhile Red Leg chieftain.[29] Anthony's first shot struck Jennison in the leg; Jennison's shot missed. As Anthony retreated into the Planters House, he and Jennison exchanged several more shots, but the only

27. Leavenworth *Times,* February 28, 1865, clipping *ibid.*
28. Unidentified clipping, *ibid.*
29. Unidentified clippings, *ibid.* One of these reports appears to be from Mayor Carney's paper, the Leavenworth *Times.* An undated clipping from Anthony's paper, the Leavenworth *Bulletin,* also *ibid.,* comments: "It may be unnecessary for us to state that the pretended report of the testimony in Carney's paper . . . given in Jennison's case is grossly perverted, much of the testimony left out entirely, and some of the witnesses made to say exactly the opposite of their testimony."

casualty of the fusillade was an innocent bystander named Woods, whose neck was grazed by a bullet. Strangely enough, only Jennison was brought to trial as a result of this affray. Anthony suffered only the inconvenience of being arrested by the city marshal for the trivial offense of carrying concealed weapons. But neither did Jennison suffer any serious consequences, aside from his painful wound. The hearing before the recorder resulted in his acquittal, but he was ordered to post bond in the sum of five thousand dollars to keep the peace.

Anthony became a power in the public life of Kansas in the postwar years. Shortly after his marriage to Anne E. Osborne of Edgarton, Massachusetts, on January 21, 1864, he bought the Leavenworth *Bulletin*. In the spring of 1866 the postmastership of Leavenworth was taken away from him because his newspaper supported the Radical Republicans in Congress against the reconstruction policies of Andrew Johnson. In 1868 he was chosen to preside over the Kansas State Republican Convention, and four years later he was elected mayor of Leavenworth for the second time. Since the previous year, he had been the proprietor of a second newspaper, the Leavenworth *Times*. In 1874 he was reappointed postmaster of Leavenworth by President Grant. On the evening of May 10 of the following year, as he walked up the steps of the Leavenworth Opera House, a former employe with a grievance fired three shots at him. One of the shots severed an artery near the heart, and Anthony's recovery from this wound was considered a medical miracle, as well as an evidence of his iron constitution and his resolute will to live. After his convalescence, he resumed the direction of his newspapers as well as his extensive political activities. His blunt, forthright editorials and his equally blunt and forceful speeches kept alive old enmities and created new ones to the end of his life. He died in Leavenworth in his eighty-first year, on November 12, 1904. A short time before his death, he suggested that the following epitaph be carved on his tombstone:

> He helped to make Kansas a free state.
> He fought to save the Union.
> He published the Daily Times for nearly
> forty years in the interests of
> Leavenworth.
> He was no hypocrite.[30]

30. Blackmar (ed.), *Kansas*, I, 80.

It would have been completely out of character if Jennison's life in the postwar years had flowed along smoothly, in peaceable contrast with the storms that marked his wartime career. Whether in peace or in war, where Jennison was, tempers ran high and controversy flourished; and whatever his activities, they were sure to be conducted in an atmosphere of strife. From all indications, Jennison enjoyed a considerable measure of prosperity after the war. It would be excessively naive to trace the foundations of his material well-being to the medical practice he had given up well before 1861 or to the salary and perquisites he had enjoyed as colonel of cavalry in the war years. After the war, in partnership with his brother "Lon," he owned and operated a three hundred acre stock farm on the Lawrence road, some two miles south of Leavenworth.[31] The farm, located "in the midst of the most beautiful pastoral scenery," was the showplace of the neighborhood. It had "an abundance of good grass and clover, with an inexhaustible supply of water," varied with "a broad panoramic sweep . . . [of] teeming grain fields and densely wooded heights." The colonel's peach orchard was famous throughout the state, and so were his predigreed Durham cattle, his Chester White, Cheshire, and Berkshire hogs, and his large flock of "all the choice breeds of game chickens, viz., Heathwoods, Irish Grays, Jersey Blues and Deserters."[32] But the chief pride of the establishment was Jennison's stud of thoroughbred racehorses and standard-bred trotters, looked after by a trainer and a half-dozen stable hands and exercise boys. One newspaper noted the appropriateness of Jennison's connection with the breeding of racehorses in that "for some five or six years the Colonel enjoyed unusual facilities for selecting fast horses from numerous stables."[33] When he held a sale of his surplus yearlings, it was expected that the event would "most likely attract a large delegation of horsemen from all parts of the country and possibly General Grant, who claims to understand horses, however great an idiot he manifests himself in other respects."[34] As a breeder, Jennison also felt obliged to support the sport by racing his horses, which he did with varying success, and he gained

31. Unidentified clippings, Jennison Scrapbook. One clipping describes the Jennison farm as consisting of 160 acres and as located "two miles out of town." Another increases its size to "nearly three hundred acres" and places it "three miles south" of Leavenworth.
32. Unidentified clipping, *ibid.*   33. Unidentified clipping, *ibid.*
34. Unidentified clipping, *ibid.*

recognition for his contributions to racing by election to the boards of directors of the St. Louis Racetrack Association and of the Leavenworth Race Course.

But farming and the raising of blooded stock were not the only sources of Jennison's prosperity.[35] He also owned a palatial saloon in Leavenworth. In due time, in his capacity of saloonkeeper, he collided with the rapidly growing temperance movement. In March, 1874, the year in which the WCTU was organized, Jennison had the privilege of addressing the Temperance Alliance of Leavenworth, and the members thereof heard a collection of sophistries seldom if ever equalled on a public platform:

I have a parting word for the fair good women of Leavenworth. . . . Many of them I know to be pious, good women who have suffered grievous wrongs at the hands of drunken and brutal husbands. . . . My heart is with them in their conflict but my judgment is against the efficacy of their remedy. . . . It is not the licensed saloon that makes the drunkard. Saloonkeepers as a rule despise drunkards. . . . They would prefer that none such should ever enter their doors. . . . Let us therefore not vainly strike at the inexorable law of God and attempt to remove the temptations that enable him to try us. . . . Let the roll [of drunkards] be made and a copy deposited in every saloon in the city. Saloonkeepers to a man will cooperate . . . to keep the intoxicating draught from the lips of every drunkard. . . . I tender my aid in the good work. . . . No drunkard "need apply" is written boldly in every department of my establishment. He must go hence for the hidden jug of the prohibitionist or the hypocrite. . . . If in spite of this tender of loyal service in a good cause, my fair townswomen choose to make war upon me and my lawful rights, rather than accept my aid in glorious warfare against drunkenness, I respectfully assure them that I shall receive their assaults with firmness, fortitude and courage and successfully resist them with such gallantry and courtesy as no gentleman forgets in the presence of a modest and worthy womanhood.[36]

The demands upon his time imposed by his farm and saloon did not

35. A visitor from Vermont, Charles Monroe Chase, wrote in 1873 that Jennison ran a faro bank in Leavenworth and was "a sort of recognized leader of the gambling element and bar-room roughs of the city." See letter dated November 24, 1873, in C. M. Chase Letters, Kansas State Historical Society, Topeka. Chase's report may well be correct, notwithstanding that it appears to be based on common gossip, not always an infallible source of accurate information. His credibility, however, is greatly weakened by his description of Anthony in the same letter as "Another character of a like [*i.e.,* like Jennison] ilk." By 1873, Anthony was safely married, was a prosperous newspaper proprietor, and had become a pillar of respectability.

36. Pamphlet in Jennison Scrapbook.

prevent Jennison from playing an active part in Kansas politics. In the fall of 1864, while still colonel of the Fifteenth Cavalry, he had been elected to the Leavenworth City Council and was later chosen by that body as its presiding officer. In 1865 he was elected to represent the Third Ward of Leavenworth in the Kansas House of Representatives. His platform combined support for the policies of President Johnson with opposition to the granting of the suffrage to Negroes, and, somewhat surprisingly, a powerful denunciation of "Republican corruption." Of course he was accused, both during the campaign and after he had taken his seat in the legislature, of a desire to wreck the Republican party in Kansas, a wish ascribed to his hatred of Governor Samuel J. Crawford, whom he held responsible for behind the scenes manoeuvers to have him dismissed from the army. His opposition to Negro suffrage, an odd stance for the erstwhile practical abolitionist, was derided by his critics with the observation that many Negroes had a better education than he had. But it was his denunciations of Republicans as the party of corruption that gave hostile editors a field day. One of them wrote: "Great God! Just think of it . . . Jennison . . . [denouncing] corruption and dishonesty! Satan rebuking sin! Judas preaching fidelity! . . . For Jennison who has earned and unopposed worn the name of the greatest thief of modern times to denounce corruption is positively the most luscious joke of the season."[37] Jennison's supporters among the voters of Leavenworth also came in for a share of editorial abuse and commiseration. The *Kansas State Record* of Topeka wrote:

We say the Third Ward of Leavenworth may justly claim sympathy and commiseration for being obliged to rest under the ignominy of having C. R. Jennison represent it in the legislature. We speak of course of the respectable citizens of that ward; for nothing is clearer than that the blood tubs, the blacklegs, the shoulder-hitters and the pimps to whom Jennison is mainly indebted for his election are properly represented. Our pity and the pity of the masses of the people is reserved for those citizens who were powerless to prevent the disgrace which was forced upon them by the combination of all that is obnoxious in politics with all that is despicable in society.[38]

Notwithstanding these political valentines, Jennison was reelected to

37. Leavenworth *Bulletin*, November 25, 1867, clipping *ibid.*
38. Undated clipping, *ibid.* The report is datelined February 28, 1868.

the legislature in 1867. But now someone pointed out that under the terms of an amendment of the Kansas constitution adopted in the same year, Jennison was ineligible to hold office or even to vote in the state. He had been dishonorably discharged from the service of the United States, and amended Section 2, Article 5 of the state constitution explicitly provided that "no person who has been dishonorably discharged from the service of the United States . . . shall be qualified to vote or hold office in this state, until such disability shall be removed by a law passed by a vote of two-thirds of all the members of both branches of the legislature." There is, of course, no record of the political manoeuvers or horsetrades that followed this discovery, but on January 31, 1868, the two houses of the legislature, by a vote of seventy to twelve, passed an "Act relative to Charles R. Jennison" removing the constitutional disability. Subsequently, in 1871, he was elected to the state senate from the Third Senatorial District.

In 1884, Jennison, not yet fifty, was on the threshhold of middle age, but he was already in failing health. He had suffered for some years from "a severe pain in his side and a cough."[39] In search of a mild climate, he spent the early months of the year in the Southwest, but it was too late. A medical examination disclosed that "his left lung was nearly gone and his heart was affected."[40] He returned to Leavenworth on June 14, ten days after his fiftieth birthday, with all hope of recovery gone. A week later, on Saturday afternoon, June 21, he died. His wife and daughter were at his bedside at the end. He was buried in Greenwood Cemetery the next day. Dr. W. H. Thomas of the Congregational Church conducted the services at the graveside, in the presence of a large crowd of Jennison's friends.

The newspapers which had so often and so bitterly denounced the Little Jayhawker joined those which had supported him through thick and thin in bidding him farewell. The most dispassionate, most just, obituary was that of the Leavenworth *Daily Standard*, which wrote:

Thus peacefully ended the career of a man whose violent death has been many times predicted. . . . Charles R. Jennison was no saint. He never professed to be. It was his lot to play a stirring part in troublous times. He loved excitement,

39. Unidentified clipping, *ibid.*   40. *Ibid.*

disliked restraint and had little reverence of any kind; but in all his turbulent career, he retained qualities which made him popular with men who were his direct opposites in character. . . . He was a man with many faults, but true to a great cause when it needed every helping hand, and now that he is dead, the voice of his friends will be heard and the good he did will be remembered.[41]

41. June 23, 1884, clipping *ibid.*

Bibliography

UNPUBLISHED MATERIALS

Chicago Historical Society
    Daniel B. Holmes Collection.
Kansas State Historical Society, Topeka
    Daniel R. Anthony Papers.
    Samuel Ayres Collection
    C. M. Chase Letters.
    Simeon M. Fox Papers.
    John Ingalls Papers.
    Charles R. Jennison Scrapbook.
    Lyman, William A. "Reminiscences." Typescript.
    James L. McDowell Collection.
    Military History (Civil War) Collection.
    Webster W. Moses Letters.
    Pomeroy, Fletcher. "War Diary." Typescript.
    Charles and Sara T. Robinson Papers.
    Utt, John H. "History of the Seventh Kansas Regiment." Manuscript.
National Archives
    "Court Martial Records, Charles R. Jennison."
    Records of the Adjutant General's Office. Record Group 94. Compiled Service
        Records of: Daniel R. Anthony; Thomas P. Herrick; Charles R. Jennison;
        Albert L. Lee.
    Seventh Kansas Volunteer Cavalry. Company Order Books.
    Seventh Kansas Volunteer Cavalry. Regimental Letter and Order Book.
    Seventh Kansas Volunteer Cavalry. Regimental Order Book.
State Historical Society of Wisconsin, Madison
    Dutton, Ira C. Civil War Diary. Manuscript CX, Box 2.

Hulbert, David. Civil War Diary. Manuscript 83s.

Samuel G. Swain Letters. Manuscript 69s.

Waldo, Charles D. Civil War Diary. Manuscript 110s.

PUBLISHED RECORDS

Adjutant General's Office, Kansas. *Official Military History of Kansas Regiments.* Leavenworth, 1870.

The Congressional Globe: Containing the Debates and Proceedings of the Second Session of the Thirty-Seventh Congress. Washington, 1862.

Report of the Adjutant General of the State of Kansas. Leavenworth, 1867.

Report of the Adjutant General of the State of Kansas, 1861–'65: Military History of Kansas Regiments. Topeka, 1896.

Report of the Adjutant General of the State of Kansas for the Year 1864. Leavenworth, 1865.

U.S. War Department. *The War of the Rebellion: A Compilation of the Official Records of the Union and Confederate Armies.* Washington, 1880–1901.

NEWSPAPERS

Cincinnati *Gazette.*

Leavenworth *Bulletin.*

Leavenworth *Conservative.*

Leavenworth *Times.*

BOOKS

Andrews, J. Cutler. *The North Reports the Civil War.* Pittsburg, 1955.

Avery, P. O. *History of the Fourth Illinois Cavalry Regiment.* Humboldt, 1903.

Berry, Thomas F. *Four Years with Morgan and Forrest.* Oklahoma City, 1914.

Blackmar, Frank W., ed. *Kansas: A Cyclopedia of State History.* Chicago, 1912.

Blackmar, Frank W. *The Life of Charles Robinson.* Topeka, 1902.

Britton, Wiley. *The Civil War on the Border.* New York, 1890–99.

Brownlee, Richard S. *Gray Ghosts of the Confederacy: Guerilla Warfare in the West, 1861–1865.* Baton Rouge, 1958.

Carr, Lucien. *Missouri: A Bone of Contention.* Boston, 1888.

Catton, Bruce. *Grant Moves South.* Boston, 1960.

Castel, Albert. *A Frontier State at War: Kansas, 1861–1865.* Ithaca, 1958.

———. *General Sterling Price and the Civil War in the West.* Baton Rouge, 1968.

Channing, Edward. *A History of the United States.* New York, 1925.

Cody, William F. *An Autobiography of Buffalo Bill Cody.* New York, 1920.

Connelley, William E. *James Henry Lane: The "Grim Chieftain" of Kansas.* Topeka, 1899.

———. *Quantrill and the Border Wars.* Cedar Rapids, 1910.

Crawford, Samuel J. *Kansas in the Sixties.* Chicago, 1911.

DeVoto, Bernard. *The Year of Decision, 1846.* Boston, 1943.

Dorr, Rheta Childe. *Susan B. Anthony.* New York, 1928.

Edwards, John N. *Shelby and His Men: Or, the War in the West.* Cincinnati, 1867.

Fox, William F. *Regimental Losses in the American Civil War, 1861–1865.* Albany, 1889.

Garwood, Darrel. *Crossroads of America: The Story of Kansas City.* New York, 1948.

Granger, J. T. *A Brief Biographical Sketch of the Life of Major-General Grenville M. Dodge.* New York, 1893.

Hartpence, William R. *History of the Fifty-First Indiana Veteran Volunteer Infantry.* Cincinnati, 1894.

Hendrick, Burton J. *Lincoln's War Cabinet.* Boston, 1946.

Henry, R. S. *"First With the Most" Forrest.* Indianapolis, 1944.

Hickman, W. Z. *History of Jackson County, Missouri.* Topeka, 1920.

[Hinton, Richard.] *Rebel Invasion of Missouri and Kansas and the Campaign of the Army of the Border Against General Sterling Price.* Chicago, 1865.

Howe, Henry. *Historical Collections of Ohio.* Cincinnati, 1908.

Hunt, Elvid, and Walter E. Lorence. *History of Fort Leavenworth, 1827–1937.* Fort Leavenworth, 1937.

Jenkins, Paul B. *The Battle of Westport.* Kansas City, 1906.

Johnson, Robert U., and Clarence C. Buel, eds. *Battles and Leaders of the Civil War.* New York, 1884–87.

Larkin, Lew. *Bingham: Fighting Artist.* St. Louis, 1955.

Logan, John A. *The Great Conspiracy: Its Origin and History.* New York, 1886.

McElroy, John. *The Struggle for Missouri.* Washington, 1913.

Malin, James C. *John Brown and the Legend of Fifty-Six.* Philadelphia, 1942.

Miller, George. *Missouri's Memorable Decade, 1860–1870.* Columbia, 1898.

Mitchell, William A. *Linn County, Kansas: A History.* Kansas City, 1928.

Monaghan, Jay. *Civil War on the Western Border.* Boston, 1955.

Monnett, Howard N. *Action Before Westport.* Westport, 1964.

Moore, Henry M. *Early History of Leavenworth: City and County.* Leavenworth, 1906.

Myers, William Starr. *General George Brinton McClellan.* New York, 1934.

Nevins, Allan. *Ordeal of the Union.* New York, 1947.

———. *The War for the Union: The Improvised War, 1861–1862.* New York, 1959.

Nichols, Alice. *Bleeding Kansas.* New York, 1954.

Oates, Stephen B. *To Purge This Land With Blood: A Biography of John Brown.* New York, 1970.

Pierce, Lyman B. *History of the Second Iowa Cavalry.* Burlington, 1865.

Prentis, Noble L. *History of Kansas.* Kansas City, 1899.

Robinson, Charles. *The Kansas Conflict.* New York, 1892.

Russell, Don. *The Lives and Legends of Buffalo Bill.* Norman, 1960.

Schofield, John M. *Forty-Six Years in the Army.* New York, 1897.

Scott, William Forse. *The Story of a Cavalry Regiment: The Career of the Fourth Iowa Veteran Volunteers.* New York, 1893.

Sensing, Thurman. *Champ Ferguson: Confederate Guerilla.* Nashville, 1902.

Sherman, William T. *Memoirs.* Bloomington, 1957.

Smith, William E. and Ophia D., eds. *Colonel A. W. Gilbert: Citizen-Soldier of Cincinnati.* Cincinnati, 1934.

Speer, John. *Life of Gen. James H. Lane.* Garden City, 1896.

Spring, Leverett W. *Kansas: The Prelude to the War for the Union.* Boston, 1899.

The United States Biographical Dictionary: Kansas Volume. Chicago, 1879.

Waring, George E., Jr. *Whip and Spur.* Philadelphia, 1875.

Wilder, Daniel W. *The Annals of Kansas.* Topeka, 1886.

Wilson, James H. *Under the Old Flag.* New York, 1912.

Wyeth, John Allan. *That Devil Forrest: Life of General Nathan Bedford Forrest.* New York, 1959.

Zornow, William F. *Kansas: A History of the Jayhawk State.* Oklahoma City, 1957.

ARTICLES

Admire, W. W. "An Early Kansas Pioneer." *Magazine of Western History,* X, 688–702.

Blunt, James G. "General Blunt's Account of His Civil War Experiences." *Kansas Historical Quarterly,* I, 211–65.

Botkin, Theodosius. "Among the Sovereign Squats." *Transactions of the Kansas State Historical Society, 1901–1902,* VII, 418–41.

Castel, Albert. "Kansas Jayhawking Raids into Western Missouri in 1861." *Missouri Historical Review,* LIV, 1–11.

Connelley, William E. "The Lane Family." *Collections of the Kansas State Historical Society, 1923–1925,* XVI, 29–32.

———, ed. "Some Ingalls Letters." *Collections of the Kansas State Historical Society, 1915–1918,* XIV, 94–122.

Cornish, Dudley T. "Kansas Negro Regiments in the Civil War." *Kansas Historical Quarterly,* XX, 417–29.

Doerschuk, Albert N., ed. "Extracts from War-Time Letters, 1861–1864." *Missouri Historical Review,* XXIII, 99–110.

Fox, Simeon M. "The Early History of the Seventh Kansas Cavalry." *Collections of the Kansas State Historical Society, 1909–1910,* XI, 238–53.

———. "The Story of the Seventh Kansas." *Transactions of the Kansas State Historical Society, 1903–1904,* VIII, 13–49.

Greene, Albert R. "What I Saw of the Quantrill Raid." *Collections of the Kansas State Historical Society, 1913–1914,* XIII, 430–51.

———. "Campaigning in the Army of the Frontier." *Collections of the Kansas State Historical Society, 1915–1918,* XIV, 283–310.

Grover, George S. "Civil War in Missouri." *Missouri Historical Review,* VIII, 1–28.

———. "The Price Campaign of 1864." *Missouri Historical Review*, VI, 167–81.

Hannahs, Harrison. "General Thomas Ewing, Jr." *Collections of the Kansas State Historical Society, 1911–1912*, XII, 276–82.

Herklotz, Hildegarde Rose. "Jayhawkers in Missouri, 1858–1863." *Missouri Historical Review*, XVII, 266–84; XVIII, 64–101.

Hutchinson, William. "Sketches of Kansas Pioneer Experience." *Transactions of the Kansas State Historical Society, 1901–1902*, VII, 390–410.

Ingalls, John J. "Kansas, 1541–1891." *Harper's Magazine*, LXXXVI, 697–713.

———. "The Last of the Jayhawkers." *Kansas Magazine*, I, 356–62.

Johnson, W. A. "The Early Life of Quantrill in Kansas." *Transactions of the Kansas State Historical Society, 1901–1902*, VII, 212–29.

Langsdorf, Edgar. "Jim Lane and the Frontier Guard." *Kansas Historical Quarterly*, IX, 243–78.

Langsdorf, Edgar, and R. W. Richmond, eds. "Letters of Daniel R. Anthony, 1857–1862." *Kansas Historical Quarterly*, XXIV, 6–30, 198–226, 351–70, 458–75.

Lewis, Lloyd. "Propaganda and the Kansas-Missouri War." *Missouri Historical Review*, XXXIV, 3–17.

"Letters of Julia Lovejoy, 1856–1864." *Kansas Historical Quarterly*, XVI, 40–75, 175–211.

Lyman, William A. "Origin of the Name 'Jayhawker'." *Collections of the Kansas State Historical Society, 1915–1918*, XIV, 203–207.

Martin, John A. "Kansas in the War." *War Talks . . . Kansas Commandery of the MOLLUS*. Kansas City, 1906. Pp. 10–23.

Mitchell, William A. "Historic Linn." *Collections of the Kansas State Historical Society, 1923–1925*, XVI, 607–57.

Palmer, Henry E. "The Black Flag Character of the War on the Border." *Transactions of the Kansas State Historical Society, 1905–1906*, IX, 455–66.

———. "The Lawrence Raid." *Transactions of the Kansas State Historical Society, 1897–1900*, VI, 317–25.

Rollins, C. B., ed. "Letters of George Caleb Bingham to James S. Rollins." *Missouri Historical Review*, XXXIII, 45–78.

Speer, John. "The Burning of Osceola, Mo. and the Quantrill Massacre Contrasted." *Transactions of the Kansas State Historical Society, 1897–1900*, VI, 306–12.

Spring, Leverett W. "The Career of a Kansas Politician." *American Historical Review*, IV, 80–104.

Stephenson, Wendell H. "The Political Career of General James H. Lane." *Publications of the Kansas State Historical Society*, III, 11–172.

———. "The Transitional Period in the Career of General James H. Lane." *Indiana Magazine of History*, XXV, 75–91.

Woodhull, Alfred A. "Kansas in 1861." *War Talks . . . Kansas Commandery of the MOLLUS*. Kansas City, 1906. Pp. 10–23.

Index

Names marked with an asterisk are those of members of the Seventh Kansas Volunteer Cavalry; the abbreviation SKVC stands for Seventh Kansas Volunteer (later Seventh Kansas Veteran Volunteer) Cavalry.

*Allen, Perry, 261
*Allison, Henry, 315
Angell, A. J., 381
*Anthony, Daniel Read: in pioneer emigrant party, 6; as abolitionist and speculator, 6; in confrontation with Cleveland, 23; as recruiting agent, SKVC, 52; and background, 52–57; and R. C. Satterlee, 57; in Kansas City, 1861, pp. 64–81; in Parkville expedition, 81; protests poor weapons, 83; in fight with Upton Hays, 91–92; in Independence raid, 94–95; attitude of, toward jayhawking, 97–98; and German recruit, 105–106; prefers charges against W. A. Pease, 107; on killing livestock, 111; equips liberated slaves, 113; in Dayton and Columbus campaigns, 114, 116–17; stringent anti-jayhawking orders of, 126–27; and roundup of deserters, 127; and mutiny of Co. A, 128–29; corresponds with Gen. Hunter and Gov. Robinson, 130; suggests sending SKVC to Arkansas and Indian Territory, 131; reacts to Jennison's resignation speech, 141–42; efforts of, to become colonel of SKVC, 150–51, 155–57; efforts of, to restore discipline, 152–53; on journey to Tenn., 162–63; and mysterious court-martial, 163; gives reason for resignation, 170; involved in fugitive slave issue, 173–76, 178; his attitude toward A. L. Lee, 179; charges and specifications against, 180; efforts of, to have charges dropped, 181–82; resignation of and departure of, from SKVC, 183–85, 202; advocates tough war, 185–86; breaks up Peace Democrat meeting, 246; in conflict with Leavenworth *Inquirer*, 247–48; as mayor of Leavenworth, 252–53; gives speech following Lawrence Massacre, 256–57; is not allowed to welcome SKVC, 288–89; supports radical Lane faction, 317; involvement of, in reelection campaign, 318–24; gives

dinner for SKVC, 376–77; again tries for mayoralty, 379; is accused of dealing in stolen cattle, 380; in shooting affray with Jennison, 380–81; marriage, postwar career, and death of, 381

*Anthony, Jacob M., 370

Atchison, David: champions slavery in Kansas, 5; Lane suggests battle with, 13

*Ayres, Samuel: attitude of, toward secessionists, 86; reports few prisoners taken, 110; signs pro-Lee round robin, 157; resigns as chaplain, 268

*Bate, George D., 296–97

Benteen, Frederick W., 347

Bingham, George Caleb: description of, 38–39; on Jennison, 39; is captured, 47; describes Independence Corral, 62–63; sees company of armed Negroes, 92–94; recites SKVC atrocities, 106; charges of, against Jennison, 158–59

Blair, Charles W., 156

Blunt, James G.: is promoted to brigadier general, 138; orders Anthony to take command of SKVC, 157; organizes Red Legs, 215; commands District of Kansas, 325; commands Army of the Border, 333; fights Price, 334; leaves pursuit of Price, 342; victory of, at Newtonia, 348; issues congratulatory order, 358; asks investigation of Fifteenth Kansas atrocities, 359; in controversy with Jennison, 360–61; orders Fifteenth Kansas pay suspended, 365; on second Jennison court-martial, 366

*Bolton, John, 76, 329

*Bostwick, Burr H., 78

Bouton, Edward: commands Negro troops at Brice's Crossroads, 303; assists SKVC in march to Tupelo, 308–309

Brown, John: sons of emigrate to Kansas, 6; history and character of, 7; sons' stock of weapons, 9; in Ashtabula County, 16; Co. K, SKVC, swears to avenge, 18; compared with Jennison, 27

*Brown, John, Jr.: organizes militia company, 9; connection of, with Pottawatomie Massacre, 15; makes home in Ohio, 16; asked to testify about Harper's Ferry Raid, 16–17; organizes cavalry company, 17; poor health of, 18–19; resignation of, 19, 78, 161

Buford, Abraham, 307–308

Cameron, Simon: asked to authorize formation of Kansas Home Guard, 36; asks "Frontier Guard" to protect the president, 43; authorizes Lane to raise troops, 44; connection of, with Lane's "southern expedition," 124

*Campbell, Bayless S., 208

Carney, Thomas: promotes T. P. Herrick as colonel of SKVC, 239, 273; requests Jennison to raise force to protect Kansas, 255; offers Jennison colonelcy of Fifteenth Kansas, 255; antagonism of, to Lane, 317, 319; refuses to allow Kansas militia to cross border, 334; defeats Anthony for mayor, 379

Chalmers, James R.: raids Memphis and Charleston RR, 277; in fight at Wyatt, Miss., 278–79; delays advance of A. J. Smith, 307–308; in Smith's second campaign against Forrest, 315

Chenoweth, B. P., 177

*Cleveland, Marshall: appearance of, 19; commands Co. H, SKVC, 20; involved in raids into Missouri, 21–22, 42; and the results of confrontation with Anthony, 23; career of, after resignation, 23–26, claims Leavenworth as residence, 75

*Cline, Henry S., 296–97

*Cody, William H. ("Buffalo Bill"): enlists in SKVC, 76, 294; claims membership in Red Legs, 214, 294; works for Wild Bill Hickock, 294; in the campaign against Forrest, 305–306; on capture of Gen. Marmaduke, 341; as hospital orderly, 356

*Colbert, Edward, 203, 224

*Cole, Ira B., 76–77

Coon, Datus E., 195

Cornyn, Florence M.: in fight with Roddey's cavalry, 261–63; in raid through Mississippi, 265–66; involved in Tupelo campaign, 269–273

Crawford, Samuel J., 371–72

*Cross, Marion, 371

*Crook, Joel J., 355

Curtis, Oren A.: hangs prisoners, 367; makes presentation to Jennison, 378

Curtis, Samuel R.: wishes to send Jennison to southwest Missouri, 218; asks to retain SKVC in Kansas, 294–95; orders Jennison to release cabmen, 325; in campaign against Price, 333–37, 340–51; takes command of Pleasonton's division, 347–48; orders Jennison court-martial, 363

*Daley, John, 280

"Deed of Forfeiture" policy, 88–89

Deitzler, George W.: gives his opinion of Jennison's resignation, 138; in conflict with Jennison, 141–42; orders SKVC to bury dead horses, 153; reports SKVC "outrages," 167

Denver, J. W.: asks for report of march to West Point, 109; recommends SKVC be moved to Fort Riley, 153

Dickey, T. Lyle: describes fight at Coffeeville, Miss., 224–25; on raid against Mobile & Ohio Railroad, 227

*Dixon (or Dickson), Alonzo, 314–15

Dodge, Grenville M.: and role in Streight's raid, 242; and Streight campaign, 261; returns to Corinth, 265; gives opinion of cavalry performance, 266; given command of the Dept. of the Missouri, 352; reviews both Jennison courts-martial, 364–65, 368; petitioned by officers to have SKVC retained in service, 371; orders SKVC to Fort Kearny, 373

*Donaldson, Samuel, 240

Douglas, Stephen A.: and the Kansas-Nebraska bill, 3–4; opposes Lecompton Constitution, 11

*Downing, Andrew ("Curley Q, Esq."): as poet, 70; goes jayhawking, 113

*Driscoll, Alexander, 76, 128

*Eatinger, Richard, 355

Eighth Kansas Volunteer Infantry, 187

Elliott, Col., 114

*Ellsworth, Daniel, 69

Ewing, Thomas, Jr.: organizes Red Legs, 214; imposes martial law in Leavenworth, 253

Fagan, J. F.: commands division, 327; driven out of Independence, 333

Farrar, B. G.: and custody of Jennison, 143–44, 149, 152

Faulkner, W. W.: in fight against SKVC, 220; attacked at Tennessee River, 276–77

Fifteenth Kansas Volunteer Cavalry: Gov. Carney authorized to raise, 255; Jennison offered colonelcy of, 255; recruitment and muster in of, 257–58; and the shortage of horses, 259; becomes inactive, 260; welcomes SKVC to Leavenworth, 288; scattered in Missouri and Kansas, 324; in battle of Westport, 336; and killing of prisoners, 344; atrocities of reported in Arkansas and Missouri, 358; pay of ordered held up, 365

Fifth Ohio Volunteer Cavalry: in conflict with SKVC, 236–37; meets Cornyn's brigade, 273; in First Cavalry Brigade, XVI Army Corps, 273

First Alabama Volunteer Cavalry (U.S.A.): in First Cavalry Brigade, XVI Army Corps, 273; in attempt to block Stephen D. Lee, 280

First Kansas Volunteer Cavalry. See Seventh Kansas Veteran Volunteer Cavalry

Fisher, Hugh, 48

Fisk, S. B., 329–30

*Ford, Christopher A., 66, 224

Forrest, Nathan Bedford: raids Jackson, Tenn., 225–26; in western Tenn., 279–81; in battle at Okolona, 302; protests killing of prisoners, 304; A. J. Smith's campaigns against, 307–309, 312–15; in raid to Memphis, 315

Fourth Illinois Volunteer Cavalry: in Lee's brigade, 222; on Somerville, Tenn., expedition, 230

Fourth Iowa Volunteer Cavalry: description of trooper of, 84–86; sufferings of, in pursuit of Price, 349–50
*Fox, Simeon: describes Co. K abolitionist rites, 17–18; on Cleveland, 19; reaction of, to Jennison's recruiting poster, 58; on SKVC involvement in Independence Corral and Kansas City parade, 63; describes Co. A, 66; enlists in Co. C, SKVC, 67–68; on Co. H, 75; reports on commander of regiment, 97; on SKVC jayhawking, 100; on houseburning expedition, 105; reports Jennison's sale of jayhawked livestock, 112; on Jennison's resignation, 137–38; describes encounter with Gen. John A. Logan, 189–90; describes fight with Funderberger's guerillas, 197; at battle of Corinth, 208; on Coffeeville, Miss., fight, 224; and accusation of Col. Dickey, 227; comments on Leavenworth reception of SKVC, 290; on Capt. Thornton's buckskin breeches, 313–14; explains burning of Oxford, Miss., 314
Fremont, John C.: authorizes Jennison to raise cavalry regiment, 22, 50–52; asked by Robinson to remove Lane Brigade from Kansas, 47; in operations against Price, 58; on freeing of slaves of rebels, 121–22
"Frontier Guard," 43

Gamble, Hamilton R., 123
*Gannett, Isaac, 67
Gholson, S. J., 270–71
*Gilbert, John H., 68
*Gillen, John A., 276
Granger, Gordon: has SKVC moved to Rienzi, Miss., 193; transferred to Kentucky, 202
Grant, Ulysses S.: attempts to cure SKVC of jayhawking, 187, 189; takes over from Halleck, 191; issues orders on treatment of guerillas, 198; halts pursuit after battle of Corinth, 210; involved in Vicksburg campaign, 212, 219–220, 225–226; receives complaint of SKVC plundering at New Albany, Miss., 228; refers report of Somerville mutiny to Gen.

Hamilton, 232; begins Wilderness Campaign, 300; requests relief of Rosecrans, 352
*Gregory, Charles H.: becomes captain of Co. E, 73; qualities of, 73–74; attacks Jackson's cavalry, 219–20; recovers cattle from Confederates, 307; breaks through Confederate cavalry, 310; petitions to have SKVC retained in the service, 371
Grierson, Benjamin: commands pursuit of Van Dorn, 228; in raid to Baton Rouge, 265; commands cavalry of XVI Army Corps, 273; complains of absence of veteran cavalry, 297; replaced by Gen. Sturgis, 302; given command of cavalry division, 306–307; commands cavalry in A. J. Smith's second campaign against Forrest, 313
*Gross, Peter, 129

Halleck, Henry W.: reports SKVC misdeeds, 96–97, 100, 123; attempts to remove SKVC, 132–33; orders SKVC to Columbus, Ky., 162; reports on SKVC atrocities in Tenn., 168; gives orders concerning fugitive slaves, 172; leaves for Washington, 191; on treatment of active rebels, 198; on SKVC request to remain in Kansas, 295; orders SKVC moved to the Dept. of the Gulf, 300–301; rules on transfer of SKVC horses to Missouri, 329
Hamilton, Charles S.: in battle of Corinth, 208; in first Vicksburg campaign, 212; ordered to arrest A. L. Lee, 233; on Somerville mutiny, 233–34
Hatch, Edward: after battle of Corinth, 209; in battle against Chalmers, 277; praises SKVC for conduct at Wyatt, 279; commands First Cavalry Division, XVI Army Corps, 312
Hays, Upton, 91–92
Hedden, W. H., 223
*Henry, William, 221
*Herrick, Thomas P.: recruits Co. A, 65; complains of poor arms, 83; commands expedition against Col. Elliott, 114–16; in controversy over Jennison

testimonial, 139–40; in command of SKVC, 154–55; at Moscow, Ky., 164; in Vicksburg campaign, 212, 219; at Somerville, Tenn., 230, 232; on wearing civilian clothing, 235; is promoted, 239, 278; gives orders on horseracing, 242–43; sends Co. G to raid rebel dance, 280–81; responds to welcoming speech at Leavenworth, 289; promises to sign temperance pledge, 299; ordered to prepare SKVC to return South, 301; in A. J. Smith's second campaign against Forrest, 313; orders men to build durable camp, 316

Hinds, Russell, 33

*Hinsdale, Nathan B., 223

Hinton, Richard J.: describes desolation on Kansas-Missouri border, 343

*Hodgman, Amos: is promoted, 75; improves discipline of Co. H, 76; ordered to round up deserters, 142; fatally wounded at Wyatt, 279

*Hollarn, Patrick, 276

*Holmes, Daniel B.: enlists, 68; and "military library," 70; on Negro camp followers, 93; explains "jay-hawking," 111; is killed, 116

*Houston, David W.: captures prisoners, 209–10; on vigilance of pickets, 275

*Hoyt, George H.: elected captain of Co. K, 78; character of, 78; complains of poor weapons, 82; and "Deed of Forfeiture" policy, 89; and testimonial to Jennison, 138–40; arrested and released, 143, 149; on "slave hunting," 178; resigns commission, 200–202; involvement of, with Red Legs and recruitment of Negro regiment, 216–17; at Peace Democrat meeting, 246; in conflict with Anthony, 253; as lieutenant-colonel of Fifteenth Kansas, 255, 257; gives speech in St. Joseph, Mo., 326; commands Fifteenth Kansas, 333; in battle of Westport, 336; is saluted on return from pursuit of Price, 357–58; on Anthony for mayor of Leavenworth, 379

*Hughes, Isaac J.: shoots James C. Murphy, Co. B, 104; in Indepen-

dence, 113; in fight at Coffeeville, 223

Hunter, David: declares martial law in Kansas, 25; and Jennison's promotion, 90, 125; on Anthony's report on burning of Dayton and Columbus, Mo., 116–17; burns Virginia Military Institute, 314

Hurlbut, Stephen A.: in conflict with Gen. Hamilton, 233; on SKVC, 238; orders of, to SKVC, 242; in campaign against Forrest, 281, 297; is replaced, 302

Jackson, W. H., 219–20

*Jenkins, William S.: and Co. C, 67; and petition to have A. L. Lee appointed colonel of SKVC, 157; in Wolf River incident, 240; orders buglers to practice, 276; in A. J. Smith's second campaign against Forrest, 313

*Jennison, Charles Rainsford: and Lane, 14; in jayhawking raids, 21–22; and raising cavalry regiment, 22, 50, 51–52; description of, by friends and enemies, 27; compared with John Brown and J. H. Lane, 27; birth of and education of, 28; in Mound City, Kan., 29; as Free-State leader, 31; and "self-sustaining" war against Missourians, 31–32; leadership qualities of, 32; in execution of Russell Hinds, 33; in killing of Scott and Moore, 34; escapes arrest, 34–35; as captain of militia, 36; proposed for second-in-command, Southern Division, Kansas militia, 36; proposed for command of Kansas Home Guard, 36; and jayhawking, April-June, 1861, p. 37; abolitionist beliefs of, 38; Bingham's hatred for, 39; "ordered out of Kansas City," 39; on scout to Independence, 40; ordered back to Kansas by Gov. Robinson, 40; on July, 1861 raid into Missouri, 40; and Myers "train," 41; at Morristown, Mo., 42; suggested for secretary of war, 42; associated with Lane Brigade, 45; in operations against Price, 1861, pp. 46–47; in fight at Drywood Creek, 47; and marauding by his men in Missouri, 48; and recruiting poster for SKVC, 57; as colonel of SKVC, 59; on how to fight Civil War, 60; in the Independence Corral, 60–62; and the Kansas City parade, 62; persuades Chicago and Wyanet companies to join SKVC, 72–73; is not with SKVC at Kansas City, 81; complains of weaponry, 82–83; at muster-in of SKVC, 84; and proclamation to Missourians, 87; and "Deed of Forfeiture" policy, 88–90; promotion of, to brigadier general urged, 90; welcomes Co. K, 92; accused of arming company of Negroes, 93; and absence from regiment, 97; and attitude toward jayhawking, 98; and Halleck's complaint of his jayhawking, 100; and Washington's Birthday speech to SKVC, 100–101; and visits to the regiment, 108; and loot from jayhawking, 111–12; affected by political problems in Missouri, 120; on emancipation, 122; appointed acting brigadier general, 124–25; and mutiny of Co. A, 129; in conflict with Anthony, 129–30; resignation of, 133–34; resignation speech of, 134–37, 140–41; attacks Generals Denver, Sturgis, Halleck, 135–36; arrest of, 142; and abolitionist press, 145–46; and formal charges against him, 147; and hostile press comment, 147–48; and conditions of imprisonment, 148; release of, 148–49; and "grand military ball," 149; preference of, for colonel of SKVC, 151; and St. Louis Germans, 152; in Washington, 152; "restoration" of, to command of SKVC, 157–61; absence of, from army, 213; and firm of Losee and Jennison, 213; with Red Legs, 215; and Negro regiment, 216–18; on wearing non-regulation clothing, 235; at Peace Democrat meeting, 245–46; in conflict with Leavenworth *Inquirer,* 248; in Kansas Republican politics, 249; oratory of, 249; political ideas of, 249–50; "nominated" for president, 250; at National Ship Canal Convention, 250–51; speech of, in Chicago,

251–52; in conflict with Anthony, 253; asked by Gov. Carney to raise force to protect Kansas, 255; and colonelcy of Fifteenth Kansas, 255–56; speeches of, following Lawrence Massacre, 256–57; and applications for chaplaincy of Fifteenth Kansas, 259; in SKVC homecoming parade, 288; and welcoming speech to SKVC, 290; and anti-Lane faction, 317; supports J. L. McDowell for mayor of Leavenworth, 319–20; and election day disorders, 321–23; as post commandant, Fort Leavenworth, 324; and cabmen, 325; as commander of First Sub-District of South Kansas, 325; speech of, at St. Joseph, Mo., 326; under Gen. Blunt, 333; in fight at Byram's Ford, 334; in battle of Westport, 335–36; on return from pursuit of Price, 357; in controversy with Blunt, 360–64; protests to Gen. Curtis, 360; arrest of, 361–62; denies supporting Lane, 362–63; claims conspiracy to raise price of forage, 363–64; court-martialed, 364; protests holding up of pay of Fifteenth Kansas, 365; second court-martial charges against, 366–67; conviction and sentence of, 368; and "illegal" conviction, 368–69; in Kansas politics, 377–79, 383–85; at testimonial dinner, 378; opposes Anthony for mayor of Leavenworth, 379; in shooting affray with Anthony, 380–81; in farming and stock raising, 382–83; in controversy with Temperance Alliance, 383; in Kansas legislature, 384–85; death of, 385–86

*Johns, William T., 355

Kelton, J. C., 148–49
*Kendall, John, 75
Ketchum, W. Scott: ordered to restore Jennison to command of SKVC, 159
*Key, Richard, 162
*Kinnick, Joseph, 117–18
*Krause, Theodore, 280

Lane Brigade: organized, 45; in operations against Price, 47; in Osceola,

Mo., 47; marauding of, 48; Halleck's complaints against, 100

Lane, James H.: influence of, on Kansas history, 11; personal and political background of, 12–14; compared to Jennison, 27; radicalism of opposed, 36; and the "Frontier Guard," 43–44; raises regiments, 44–45; in conflict with Gov. Robinson, 45; commission of, 45; in operations against Price and McCulloch, 46–49; in sacking of Osceola, Mo., 47; asks three companies of SKVC to be sent to Kansas City, 63; Halleck complains against, 100; on "southern expedition," 124; as master of diatribe, 134; and restoration of Jennison to command of SKVC, 158–59; and Anthony's arrest, 181–82; is authorized to raise Negro regiment, 216; on Lawrence Massacre, 256–57; antagonism of, to Gov. Carney, 317

*Laverentz, Henry A., 66

*Lavery, Jackson T., 280

Lawrence, W. W. H., 173

*Lee, Albert L.: and Co. I, 77; sent to learn future of SKVC, 131; biography of, 156; appointed colonel of SKVC, 156, 179; Anthony's rivalry with, 170; approves Anthony's resignation, 184; and issue of theft of sugar and tobacco at Trenton, Tenn., 186–89; and camp routine, 192; on scouting expeditions, 194–95; on Kossuth ambush, 196; protests discrimination against SKVC, 199; collects corn and fruit, 200; comments on Hoyt's resignation, 201; takes over command of Sheridan's brigade, 202; complains of shortage of officers, 203; scouts the advance of Price and Van Dorn, 205; after battle of Corinth, 209; commands cavalry brigade, 212, 219; in Holy Springs, Miss., 220–21; in fight at Coffeeville, 225; and the Somerville mutiny, 232–34; requests authority to capture and chain Confederate officers, 237; promoted to brigadier general, 238; bids farewell to SKVC, 243

Lee, Stephen D.: in raid on Memphis & Charleston Railroad, 279–80; in battle of Tupelo, 309

*Leiber, William, 276

Lincoln, Abraham: Lane's influence on, 44–45; political problems of, in Missouri, 119–20; and Lane's "southern expedition," 124; and restoration of Jennison to command of SKVC, 158–59; death of, 357

Logan, John A., 189–90

*Lohnes, Thomas H., 66

Losee and Jennison: in Pike's Peak trade, 213; and Red Legs, 215–16; Jennison sells his interest in, 256

*Lovejoy, Charles H.: as chaplain of SKVC, 268; on morals and religious revival in SKVC, 299; preaches last sermon to SKVC, 376

Lovejoy, Julia: and C. H. Lovejoy, 269; devotion of, to SKVC, 269; describes fire on Mississippi River packet, 285; describes return of SKVC to Leavenworth, 288

Lovell, Mansfield: in battle of Corinth, 209; in fight with SKVC, 223–24

*Lyman, W. A.: on resignation of Jennison, 138; reports Rosecrans' anger re pursuit of Price and Van Dorn, 210; has pneumonia, 228–29

Lyon, Nathaniel: in the arrest of Jennison, 34–35; in control of St. Louis, 44; is killed, 46

McArthur, John, 195–96

McClellan, George B.: receives complaints of SKVC misdeeds, 123; on the slave issue, 137

*McCrum, James P., 276

McDowell, James L.: in mayoralty election in Leavenworth, 319–23

*McNamara, James, 68

McNeil, John: wants reinforcements, 330; in campaign against Price, 332, 337–39, 345–47, 349–50; career of, 344–45; dissolves his brigade, 351

McPherson, James B.: praises Utt and Co. A, 209; in first Vicksburg campaign, 212

*McSparren, Aaron, 276

*Malone, Francis M.: on scout to Hatchie River, 195; on wearing civilian clothing, 235; commands SKVC, 332; in campaign against Price, 338; releases Richard Eatinger, 355; petitions to have SKVC retained in the service, 371; ordered to march SKVC to Forth Leavenworth for muster-out, 374

Marmaduke, John S.: in Price's invasion of Missouri, 327; taken prisoner, 340

Martin, John E., 143

Medary, Samuel, 34

*Merrick, John L.: and Co. I, 77; resignation of, 153; signs round robin in favor of A. L. Lee as colonel of SKVC, 157; resigns commision, 370

*Merriman, Clark S.: and Co. D, 68; drills company, 72; preference of, for infantry, 73; on jayhawking expeditions, 113, 117; on scout to Columbus, Mo., 114–16; signs round robin in favor of A. L. Lee as colonel of SKVC, 157; in search of SKVC train for fugitive slaves, 177; involved in regimental court-martial after Somerville mutiny, 232

*Miller, John, 276

*Mitchell, John, 276

Mitchell, Robert B.: in Army of the Mississippi, 165; at Dresden, Tenn., picnic, 169; goes on leave, 174; in confrontation with Anthony over General Orders No. 26, pp. 175–76; relieves Hoyt as provost marshal of Humboldt, Tenn., 178; charges Anthony with disobedience of orders, 180

Mizner, John K.: in Army of the Mississippi, 202; shadows Price's movements, 203; praises role of cavalry, 204; in pursuit of Price and Van Dorn, 209; in First Cavalry Brigade, XVI Army Corps, 273; in fight against Stephen D. Lee, 280

Montgomery, James: history and jayhawking activities of, 30–31; on hanging of Hinds, 33–34; avoids arrest, 35; proposed as commander, Southern Division, Kansas Militia, 36; as colonel in Third Kansas Infantry, 45; in operations against Price, 46; reports guerillas in Kansas,

107; protests Jennison's appointment as colonel of Negro regiment, 217; commands Kansas militia regiment, 333

*Moorhouse, William S.: in controversy over Jennison testimonial, 139–40; sent to hunt guerilas, 300; ordered to rejoin SKVC, 301

*Morrill, E. N., 105

*Moses, Webster W.: enlists, 68; morality and jayhawking of, 71–72; loyalty of, to SKVC, 79; reports shooting of prisoner, 106; on jayhawking, 113, 117–18, 127; on doubtful future of SKVC, 131; on scenery at Fort Riley, 154; on the effects of slavery, 164; on excursion with F. E. Newton, 169; claims rebels afraid of SKVC, 195; becomes ill, 211; returns from hospital, 236; on leaving Germantown, 243; describes arrival of mail at Town Creek, 265; describes destruction on march to Corinth, 266; on end of war, 267; complains of campaigning on Christmas Day, 281; explains decision to "veteranize," 282–83; becomes engaged, 293; on noisy barracks, 295; refers to Bate-Cline-Ratliff "mutiny," 296; on boredom in camp, 298; reports anti-tobacco pledge, 299; would like SKVC sent South, 300; on Gen. Sturgis, 303; reports killing of prisoners, 304; lacks writing paper, 313; horse of, 349; describes winter quarters on Meramec River, 353–54; describes Missouri social, 354–55; marries Nancy Mowry, 356; on petition of officers to have SKVC retained in the service, 371; ordered to Fort Kearny, 373; on buffalo hunt, 374

Mound City Sharp's Rifle Guards: on raids into Missouri, 22; in formation of SKVC, 22; formation of, 36; and pail of whiskey, 37–38; associated with Lane Brigade, 45; in Independence Corral, 60–62, 64

*Mouriquand, J. P. D., 276

*Mowry, George, Jr.: enlists, 68; on Sheridan, 193; on Col. Lee, 210; reports Somerville mutiny, 232

*Mullen, Timothy, 231, 234
*Murphy, James C., 104

*Nessel, Joseph H., 75
*Newton, F. E.: and Daniel Holmes, 116; on Jennison's resignation, 138; on excursion with W. Moses, 169
Ninth Illinois Volunteer Cavalry, 304

Odlin, J. H., 183
Osborne, John P., 381

Palmer, H. E.: and Kansas City parade, 62
*Pardee, Horace: on expedition against Quantrill, 117; ordered to round up deserters, 127; resignation of, 153
Parrott, Marcus J.: on SKVC foraging party, 167; at Dresden, Tenn., picnic, 169; welcomes SKVC to Leavenworth, 289
*Pease, William A., 107–108
Pleasonton, Alfred: in Price campaign, 332, 337–39, 342, 347; on McNeil's disobedience of orders, 345; at Fort Scott, 347–48
*Pomeroy, Emerson, 275, 298
*Pomeroy, Webster: enlists, 68; morality of, 71; reports house-burning, 95; on Jennison's resignation, 138; on appointment of C. W. Blair as colonel of SKVC, 156; on thefts and SKVC, 199; captures prisoners, 222; describes fight at Coffeeville, 224; on Somerville mutiny, 234; views of, on spring, 238; on Streight raid, 242; fatalism of, 244; boasts of victory at Tupelo, 272; is promoted, 275; gathers materials for winter quarters, 280; returns from veterans' furlough, 292–93; describes SKVC journey to St. Louis, 295–96; on self-improvement, 298; reports SKVC temperance movement, 299–300; draws weapons for regiment, 300; buys Kansas land, 355; describes rejoicing at news of capture of Richmond, 356; on President Lincoln's death, 357; describes July 4 at Cape Girardeau, 372; on the muster-out, 376; on journey home, 377

Pomeroy, Samuel C.: elected U.S. senator, 14; praises Jennison, 90; in restoration of Jennison to command of SKVC, 158; in freeing Anthony, 181
Pope, John, 96
*Porter, Oscar G., 261
Price, Sterling: invades Missouri, 1861, pp. 46–47; and rumored invasion of Missouri, 107; in Iuka, 203–204; and attack on Corinth, 204; and 1864 invasion of Missouri, 326–27; marches toward Independence and Kansas City, 331, 334–35; in retreat, 340–51
Prince, W. E.: and Jennison, 39–41; asks Lane to stop looting by his troops, 48; ordered to assemble reinforcements for E. R. S. Canby, 132

Quantrill, William C.: chased by SKVC, 117; in Lawrence Massacre, 254–55
Quinby, Isaac: on harboring fugitive slaves, 172; threatens to have SKVC mustered out, 173–74; and the search for fugitive slaves, 177
*Quirk, Thomas, 315

*Rafety, James L.: and SKVC, 75; arrested for resisting search for fugitive slaves, 177; leaves SKVC, 202
*Ratliff, John, 296
*Ray, Francis M., 105
*Raymond, Joseph, 104–105
Red Legs: in operation, 201; organized, 214
*Reed, William W., 237
*Reeves, John T., 377
*Rice, Nelson, 315
Richardson, R. V.: at Somerville, Tenn., 230; in Chalmers raid on Memphis & Charleston Railroad, 277–78
Robinson, Charles: and organization of cavalry regiment, 22, 50; on Missouri, 36; in opposition to Lane, 36, 45, 47; and organization of Kansas Home Guard, 36; on resumption of jayhawking, 37; orders Jennison back to Kansas, 40; on recommending Jennison to raise regiment, 51;

recommends brigadier general's commission for Jennison, 51, 90; appoints A. L. Lee colonel of SKVC, 156

Roddey, P. D.: in fight at Leighton, Ala., 262–63; paroles Utt, 264

Rollins, James S., 39

Root, Joseph P., 156

Rosecrans, William S.: and revolving rifles for SKVC, 83, 210–11; on Capt. Odlin's letter regarding Anthony, 184; and pay of SKVC, 187; recommends Sheridan for promotion to brigadier general, 193; in battle with Price, 204–10; given command of the Army of the Ohio, 212–13; wants part of SKVC to enforce draft, 300; orders SKVC to Department of the Gulf, 301; and Gen. Washburn's appeal to keep SKVC, 316; prepares for Price's invasion of Missouri, 327–30; orders of, to Sanborn's and McNeil's brigades, 349; is relieved of command of Department of the Missouri, 352

Rowett, Richard, 276–77

Ruggles, Daniel, 270

Sanborn, John B., 349–50

*Sanders, Bazil C., 271

*Sanders, Edward, 208

Satterlee, R. C., 57

Scott, Winfield, 43

Second Illinois Volunteer Cavalry: with SKVC at Trenton, Tenn., 186; at Holly Springs, 225

Second Iowa Volunteer Cavalry: blames own jayhawking on SKVC, 167, 199; on scout with SKVC, 195; in battle of Booneville, 193; in pursuit after battle of Corinth, 209; in Lee's cavalry brigade, 212; in Grierson's raid, 265; "bobtails" of SKVC assigned to, 284

Second Michigan Volunteer Cavalry: in battle of Booneville, 193; blames own thefts on SKVC, 199

Second Tennessee Cavalry, C.S.A.: in fight at Tupelo, 270–71; opposes A. J. Smith's second campaign against Forrest, 307

*Service, John H., 76, 329

Seventh Illinois Volunteer Cavalry: in pursuit after battle of Corinth, 209; in Grierson's raid, 265; in fight at Byhalia, Miss., 218; in First Cavalry Division, XVI Army Corps, 312

Seventh Kansas Volunteer (later Veteran Volunteer) Cavalry: marauding tradition of, 50; participation of, in Independence Corral and Kansas City parade denied, 63–64; in Kansas City, 64, 80–81; nationality statistics of, 69–70; size of, 78–79; officers of, 79, 203, 311–12; loyalty of men to, 79; equipment and weapons of, 80–83, 352; ordered to Fort Leavenworth, 82; mustered in, 84; returns to Kansas City, 84; in first raid to Independence, 94–95; involved in jayhawking, 96–103; on expedition to Pleasant Hill, 104; atrocities of, in Missouri, 106–107; in West Point-Morristown area, 108–109; involved in plundering and arson, 110; in expedition against Col. Elliott, 114–16; effect of, on Missouri politics, 120; good name of, defended, 121; ordered to Humboldt, Kan., 123; celebrates Washington's Birthday, 127–28; future of, in doubt, 131; affected by Jennison's speech, 141; officers of give "grand military ball," 149; at Fort Riley, 154; on appointment of C. W. Blair as colonel, 156; ordered to Corinth, 161; on journey to Tennessee, 162; in and near Union City and Dresden, Tenn., 165–69; on fugitive slave issue, 175, 178, 200; and stoppage of pay, 188; and encounter with Gen. Logan, 189–90; in Army of the Mississippi, 191–92; on Sheridan, 193; in Rienzi, Miss., 193–94; camp of, attacked by Confederates, 196–97; in Lee's brigade, 212; leaves Corinth, 219; in fight with W. W. Faulkner's regiment, 220–21; in fight at Coffeeville, 223–24; in pursuit of Van Dorn, 227–28; in winter camp at Germantown, Tenn., 229; on expedition to Somerville, Tenn., 230–32; horses of, stolen by Fifth Ohio Cavalry,

236–37; depleted in numbers, 238;
considered most efficient regiment,
238; starts for Corinth, 243–44; in
First Cavalry Brigade, XVI Army
Corps, 273; in operations against
Chalmers, 277–79; in effort to block
Stephen D. Lee, 280; in winter quarters at Corinth, 280; on "Cold New
Year's Day," 281–82; and "veteran-
ization," 282–84; on journey to Kansas, 284–87; and reception at Leavenworth, 387–91; on journey to St.
Louis, 295–97; in camp on Bloody
Island, 297–301; in St. Louis,
298–99; returns to Memphis, Tenn.,
301; scouting in Moscow, Tenn.,
area, 304; accused of killing prison-
ers, 304–305; in A. J. Smith's first
campaign against Forrest, 306–10;
in First Brigade, First Cavalry Division, XVI Army Corps, 312; in A. J.
Smith's second campaign against
Forrest, 312–15; ordered to return
to Missouri, 316; delay of, in leaving
Memphis, 328; ordered to Rolla,
Mo., 330; in A. J. Smith's Army
Corps, 331; in St. Clair, Mo., "Indian Expedition," 332; in Gen. Mc-
Neil's brigade, 332; in pursuit of
Price, 332–33; at Little Santa Fe,
338; in attack at Little Osage and
Marmiton rivers, 346–47; and straw
vote for president, 350; on return
to Rolla, St. Louis, 351–52; on guard
duty in Missouri, 352; in winter
quarters in Missouri, 354–55; and
prisoners, 357; on garrison duty in
Missouri, 371; and petition to be
mustered out, 372; ordered to Fort
Kearny, 373; desertions of, 373; on
march to Fort Kearny, 374; ordered
to Fort Leavenworth for muster-out,
374; mustered out, 375–77
—Company A: mustered in, 65; description of, 65–67; equipment of,
82; in fight with Upton Hays, 91–92;
in fight at Columbus, Mo., 115; in
mutiny at Humboldt, Kan., 128–29;
and theft of sugar and tobacco at
Trenton, Tenn., 186–87; in battle
of Corinth, 209; and designation as
saber company, 211; in Oxford,

Miss., 222; on scout to Coffeeville,
227; in fight at Tupelo, 271; in attack against Faulkner's cavalry, 277;
reported to have shot prisoners, 304;
recovers cattle from Confederates,
307
—Company B: organized, 67; equipment of, 82; in fight with Upton
Hays, 91; and designation as saber
company, 211; at Oxford, Miss., 222;
in mutiny at Somerville, Tenn.,
231–32; reported to have shot prisoner, 304
—Company C: organized, 67; in Kansas City, 104; in fight at Tupelo,
271; in attack against Faulkner's
cavalry, 277
—Company D: organized, 68; statistics
of, 69–71; on journey to Kansas, 72;
votes to join SKVC, 73; on picket
duty in Moscow, Ky., 164; 23 men
of, present for duty, 238
—Company E: on journey to Kansas,
72; votes to join SKVC, 73; vital
statistics of, 73; desertions of, 74;
and theft of sugar and tobacco at
Trenton, Tenn., 186–87; equipment
of, 205; in attack against Jackson's
cavalry, 219–20
—Company F: organization and statistics of, 69, 74
—Company G: statistics of, 69; organization of, 74; and German recruit,
105; equipment of, 205; in raid on
rebel dance, 280–81
—Company H: statistics of, 18, 74–75;
elects a captain, 22; under Capt.
Hodgman, 76; equipment of, 82; in
fight with Upton Hays, 91; on march
to Independence, 95; in Kansas City,
104; in fight at Columbus, Mo., 115;
in battle of Corinth, 209; and designation as saber company, 211; and
herd of cattle, 307
—Company I: recruitment of, 77; and
herd of cattle, 307
—Company K: and abolition, 17–18,
74, 77–78; and attitude toward
rebels, 18; desertions of, 18; and
John Brown, Jr., 19, 161; in Kansas
City, 92; in first raid to Inde-

pendence, 94; in fight at Columbus, Mo., 115; on picket duty at Moscow, Ky., 164; and theft of sugar and tobacco at Trenton, Tenn., 186–87; on strike, 188

Seventh Missouri Volunteer Infantry: and SKVC, 162

*Shaiffer, Jacob, 276

Shelby, Joseph O.: in Price's invasion of Missouri, 327; at Byram's Ford, 335

Sheridan, Philip B.: in command of cavalry brigade, 192–93; on guerilla prisoners, 197; in conflict with SKVC, 199; transferred to Kentucky, 202

Sherman, William T.: in Vicksburg campaign, 226; in conflict with SKVC, 283–84; and Atlanta campaign, 300; in campaign against Forrest, 302–303, 305, 312

Sigel, Francis, 148

Sims, A. G.: and fugitive slaves, 173, 177–78

Smith, Andrew J.: on killing of prisoners by Federal cavalry, 304; in first campaign against Forrest, 305–10; in second campaign against Forrest, 312–15; in Missouri, 331

*Smith, James: 67, 372

*Snoddy, John T.: on Jennison's "Editorial Committee," 34; as recruiting agent for SKVC, 52; in battle of Corinth, 208

"Southern Kansas Jay-Hawkers." See Mound City Sharp's Rifle Guards

*Springer, George H. T., 69

Squires, A. B., 112

Stanton, Edwin M.: and loyal Missourians, 123; and reinforcements to E. R. S. Canby, 132; with the president at Fortress Monroe, 158

Steele, William, 41

Streight, Abel D., 241–42, 265

Sturgis, Samuel D.: and Capt. Steele, 41; appoints Anthony provost marshal of Kansas City, 81; and Jennison and Hoyt's arrest, 143, 146–47; relieved of command, 157; in campaign against Forrest, 303

*Swoyer, Fred: recruits men for SKVC, 67; character of, 67; in pursuit of

Price, 204; in mounted charge at Oxford, Miss., 222; killed, 67, 231, 234

Sykes, George: and Jennison courtsmartial, 364, 366

*Taylor, DeWitt C., 287

*Taylor, William, 280

*Tefft, James M., 237

Tenth Missouri Volunteer Cavalry: in Col. Cornyn's brigade, 261; in fight at Tupelo, 271; in First Cavalry Brigade, XVI Army Corps, 273; and troopers killed, 274

Thayer, J. M., 359

Third Alabama Cavalry, C.S.A., 194

Third Michigan Volunteer Cavalry: commander of, 202; in pursuit after battle of Corinth, 209; in Lee's brigade, 212; in advance to Oxford, Miss., 222; in First Cavalry Brigade, XVI Army Corps, 273; in effort to block Stephen D. Lee, 280

Thirteenth Alabama Battalion of Partisan Rangers, C.S.A., 270–71

Thomas, Lorenzo, 159

*Thornton, Edward: commands Co. G, 75; signs round robin for A. L. Lee as colonel of SKVC, 157; in raid on rebel dance, 280–81; and his buckskin breeches, 313–14; brings recruits to SKVC, 370

Tilghman, Lloyd: on Federal tactics at Coffeeville, 224; and SKVC prisoners, 237

Tough, William S.: and Red Legs, 214; and Anthony-Jennison shooting affray, 381

Twelfth Wisconsin Volunteer Infantry: ordered to New Mexico, 132; at Fort Riley, 154; in Tennessee, 165

*Underwood, Marcus L., 237

*Utt, Levi: raises Co. A, 65; description of, 65–66; in fight at Columbus, Mo., 115–16; praised by Gen. McPherson, 209; captures 11 guerillas, 240–41; in fight at Leighton, Ala., 262–63; wounded, 263; paroled, 264; petitions to have SKVC retained in the service, 371

Van Dorn, Earl: transferred east of
Mississippi, 203; in attack on
Corinth, 204–205; in Holly Springs
raid, 225–28
Van Horn, R. T., 41–42
*Vaughn, E. M., 128–29

Walker, Anson J., 25–26
Waring, George, 150–51
Washburn, Cadwallader C.: replaces
Gen. Hurlbut, 302; in campaign
against Forrest, 305, 315; wants to

keep SKVC, 316; and horses of
SKVC, 328–29
*Weston, William, 203
*Wever, Joseph L., 154
*Whitney, O. C., 264
*Wildey, John H.: explores Confed-
erate position, 221; and Jeff Thomp-
son guerillas, 353
*Wilson, William, 71
*Woodburn, Thomas J., 224
*Wright, James G., 276, 280

*Yeager, George I., 73